FLASHPOINTS IN THE WAR ON TERRORISM

Also by Derek S. Reveron
Promoting Democracy in the Post-Soviet Region
America's Viceroys: The Military and U.S. Foreign Policy

FLASHPOINTS IN THE WAR ON TERRORISM

EDITED BY

DEREK S. REVERON AND
JEFFREY STEVENSON MURER

Routledge
Taylor & Francis Group
New York   London

Routledge is an imprint of the
Taylor & Francis Group, an informa business

Routledge
Taylor & Francis Group
270 Madison Avenue
New York, NY 10016

Routledge
Taylor & Francis Group
2 Park Square
Milton Park, Abingdon
Oxon OX14 4RN

Library of Congress Cataloging-in-Publication Data

Flashpoints in the war on terrorism / edited by Derek S. Reveron and Jeffrey Stevenson Murer.
   p. cm.
   Includes index.
   ISBN 0-415-95490-8 (hardback : alk. paper) -- ISBN 0-415-95491-6 (pbk. : alk. paper)
   1. Insurgency--Case studies. 2. Political violence--Case studies. 3. War on Terrorism, 2001---Causes. 4. Jihad. 5. Islam and politics. 6. Terrorism. 7. United States--Foreign relations--2001- I. Reveron, Derek S. II. Murer, Jeffrey Stevenson.

JC328.5.F53 2006
363.325'161--dc22   2006008011

Visit the Taylor & Francis Web site at
http://www.taylorandfrancis.com

and the Routledge Web site at
http://www.routledge-ny.com

CONTENTS

Preface   vii

Acknowledgments   ix

Introduction: Flashpoints in the War on Terrorism   xi
DEREK S. REVERON AND JEFFREY STEVENSON MURER

SECTION I: THE NEAR EAST

Chapter 1   Israel–Palestine   3
             STEPHEN VAN EVERA

Chapter 2   Iraq   23
             JAMES S. ROBBINS

Chapter 3   Kurdistan   43
             KERRIE UROSEVICH

SECTION II: EUROPE AND THE POST-SOVIET REGION

Chapter 4   Kosovo   65
             SUSAN FINK YOSHIHARA

Chapter 5   Caucasus   87
             JEFFREY STEVENSON MURER

Chapter 6   The Fergana Valley of Central Asia   117
             CHRISTOPHER J. FETTWEIS

SECTION III: ASIA

Chapter 7   Thailand   137
             ROHAN GUNARATNA AND ARABINDA ACHARYA

Chapter 8   Indonesia   159
             ARABINDA ACHARYA AND ROHAIZA AHMAD ASI

Chapter 9   Kashmir   179
             SAMINA RAJA

Chapter 10   Philippines   201
             TOSHI YOSHIHARA

Chapter 11   Xinjiang   225
             DRU C. GLADNEY

SECTION IV: AFRICA

Chapter 12   The Trans-Saharan Arc   249
             STEPHEN A. EMERSON

Chapter 13   Sudan   267
             STEPHEN A. EMERSON

Chapter 14   Nigeria   287
             MICHAEL F. MORRIS AND CHARLES EDEL

Chapter 15   Conclusion: Resolving Political Conflicts   305
             JEFFREY STEVENSON MURER AND DEREK S. REVERON

Contributors   331

Index   337

PREFACE

For the last 15 years, there has been a debate within political science between those who largely see war as the world has known it coming to an end and others who see renewed great power competitions, culture clashes, or state failures unleashing an unstable period in world affairs. The debate is not simply an academic one; the governments and peoples of the world have a vote, too. While we are bombarded with media images from war zones, conflict has largely diminished during the past 15 years. In contrast to those that see a coming "clash of civilizations" or a "global war," the last 15 years have illustrated the opposite—global integration. Study after study shows that ethnic conflict is on the wane, new great power competitions among the United States, Japan, Russia, Europe, China, or India are not emerging, and violent conflict has been declining. Relations between potential military competitors have never been better and good governance has proven to channel grievances into peaceful resolution.

In spite of all the good news, occasional terrorist attacks dominate strategic thinking and foreign policy making. At the same time there are concerns about global jihadists waging a "cosmic war"; there are also many legitimate movements that resist patterns of global integration. While anti-Americanism is prevalent around the world, it has not readily translated into terrorism. In the period since the September 11, 2001 attack, the number of global attacks has been few. While any terrorist attack claiming one life is a tragedy, policymakers have tended to overestimate the scale of the attack, its relationship among the groups responsible for these attacks and those doomsayers calling for a global jihad. U.S. policymakers have uncritically accepted calls for global jihad and responded in kind by declaring a "global war on terrorism" on a militant form of Islam.

Characterized as the "green menace," we are told the enemies of freedom want to create an Islamic empire that stretches from Morocco to Indonesia. While there are a few terrorists who profess such a goal, they have neither the capabilities nor the opportunities to build such an empire. The people in Morocco to Indonesia have a vote, too; and they have overwhelmingly embraced their own national identities, unique forms of Islamic worship, and democracy. At the end of 2005, Freedom House notes that core countries of the Middle East in the last four years have seen steady progress toward creating freer societies. And there are many Muslim-majority countries that are now considered democratic—Indonesia, Turkey, Mali, Senegal, and Mauritania.

The succeeding chapters call into question the myth of the green menace and a global jihad by critically examining political conflicts around the world that have served as breeding grounds, ideological inspiration, or real battlefields for violent political Islamists. Had we approached this problem 25 years ago, we would have started with countries that sponsor terrorism. Yet today, the biggest threat comes from groups that claim no nationalist affiliation; however, attacks still occupy particular geographic space and terrorist groups draw strength from long-standing political conflicts. It is through these political conflicts that we examine the roles of Islam, culture, and economic transformation.

Derek S. Reveron   Jeffrey Stevenson Murer
Jamestown, Rhode Island   Swarthmore, Pennsylvania
June 1, 2006

ACKNOWLEDGMENTS

The idea to explore flashpoints began with Mark Croatti, who has tirelessly explored conflict zones in various parts of the world and has shared those insights with students in the Washington, D.C. area. I thank Mark for including me in his Flashpoints Lecture Series and for encouraging me to dig deeper into political conflict.

Like all intellectual projects, this one benefited deeply from friends and colleagues who unselfishly gave their time to review various chapters, discuss my ideas, and share insights on conflict. Steve Wrage of the U.S. Naval Academy was as always extremely helpful to me as the project developed. I miss our chats in Annapolis and hope we can soon discuss national security over a pint at Galway Bay. The National Security Decision Making Department at the Naval War College proved itself to be fertile ground for me to develop ideas on conflict, consider the direction of U.S. foreign policy, and discuss the strategy for the global war on terrorism. In particular, I appreciate the support of Tim Castle, Tom Fedyszyn, and Joan Johnson-Freese. Discussions with Chris Fettweis, Andrew Stigler, Larry Thompson, Mike Morris, Mac Owens, Jeff Norwitz, Ron Ratcliff, Steve Emerson, and John Garafano proved very stimulating during the writing process. Jonathon Stevenson was especially generous with his time and provided fantastic feedback on the introductory chapter. I hope to return the favor soon on one of his projects.

The editorial staff at Routledge were extremely professional. I thank Rob Tempio, Brendan O'Neill, and Takisha Jackson for making these words into a book.

Finally, none of my work would be possible without Kirie. She contributes to everything I write, listens to my ideas, and keeps me true to this labor of love I chose.

Derek

I would like to thank Derek for sharing this project with me. I have long wanted to write many things on this subject but had not yet found the right format or venue. This book has been a pleasure to produce and was just the format I was looking for.

I greatly appreciate the support of the Swarthmore College Political Science Department, which provided a very stimulating environment in which to work and create. Carol Nackenoff has been a true friend and mentor. I have greatly enjoyed the late night changing of the guard with Ken Sharpe and working the weekend shift with Keith Reeves. I must thank Ben Berger for many things, including great conversations and wonderful exchanges of ideas. Most of all I must thank Ben for introducing me to Rob Tempio, who helped to realize this project. Cynthia Halpern has been a great colleague and friend, and I greatly appreciate being able to bounce ideas off my office neighbors Jim Kurth and Ray Hopkins. Their advice has been extremely valuable. Carol and Tyrene White have been great chairs to work under. My Chechnya chapter would not have been possible without my research assistants Elizabeth Beirut and Yulia Savitskaya. Both were a great joy to work with, and Yulia's translations were invaluable. Finally, I must thank my partner, wife, and editor Trenholme Junghans. I cannot write a word without having her look it over. I share my work with her as I share my life.

Jeffrey

INTRODUCTION
*Flashpoints in the War on Terrorism**

Derek S. Reveron and Jeffrey Stevenson Murer

To fight an enemy who is near is more important than to fight an enemy who is far.[1]

**Muhammad Abd al-Salam Faraj,
executed for his connection to the
1981 assassination of Anwar al-Sadat**

We declared jihad against the U.S. government, because the U.S. government is unjust, criminal, and tyrannical. It has committed acts that are extremely unjust, hideous, and criminal, whether directly or through its support of the Israeli occupation of the Prophet's Night Travel Land [Palestine]. And we believe the U.S. is directly responsible for those who were killed in Palestine, Lebanon, and Iraq.[2]

Osama bin Laden

---

* Parts of the introduction appeared in Jeffrey S. Murer, "The Clash Within: Intrapsychically Created Enemies and Their Roles in Ethnonationalist Conflict," in *Violence and Politics: Globalization's Paradox,* edited by Kenton Worcester, Sally Avery Bermanzohn, and Mark Ungar, (New York: Routledge, 2002).

Terrorist operatives conduct their campaign of murder with a set of declared and specific goals: to demoralize free nations, to drive us out of the Middle East, to spread an empire of fear across that region, and to wage a perpetual war against America and our friends. These *terrorists view the world as a giant battlefield*—and they seek to attack us wherever they can.[3]

President George W. Bush

[The United States is at war with those whose] aim is to undermine Western influence, redefine the global balance of power, and establish a global pan-Islamist caliphate. Rather than simply seeking to overthrow a particular government in the traditional sense of insurgency, these extremists aim to fundamentally change the nature of the world order.[4]

The United States' National Military Strategic Plan for the War on Terrorism

"We have already made the mistake of declaring war on one of [political instability's] dangerous symptoms—terrorism ... and called it officially the 'Global War on Terrorism.'"*

General Tony Zinni

In spite of the overall decline in conventional war among developed countries, some scholars have cast the future security environment in terms of nation-state clashes over natural resources, modernization, and culture.[5] Yet America's security interests are more directly affected by the tension between Muslims and non-Muslims in political conflicts around the world.[6] These clashes have led to extreme violence and fueled terrorism not only within those regions, but globally. The U.S. government's National Intelligence Council forecasts that within the next 15 years "weak governments, lagging economies, religious extremism, and youth bulges will align to create a perfect storm for internal conflict in certain regions."[7] *Flashpoints in the War on Terrorism* explores the role of Islam, culture, and economic transformation within specific political conflicts in the eye of the storm.

As the opening quotations reveal, there is debate about the motivations of those seen as terrorists and there is a danger in over-interpreting

---

* Tony Zinni and Tony Koltz, *The Battle for Peace: A Frontline Vision of America's Power and Purpose* (New York: Palgrave Macmillan, 2006), p. 114.

grandiose claims made by al Qaeda. We argue that U.S. policymakers must move beyond a one-dimensional, bin Laden–centered worldview that treats the interface between religion and politics as seamless while minimizing the importance of identity politics. Such a worldview treats "terrorism" as a single, undifferentiated phenomenon. The contributors to this book all suggest that it is necessary for those who make and implement policy to understand the political, economic, and cultural causes of collective political violence. The authors echo General Tony Zinni, who led U.S. military forces in the Near East from 1997–2000: "The *real* threats do not come from military forces or violent attacks; they do not come from a nation-state or hostile non-state entity; they do not derive from an ideology (not even from a radical, West-hating, violent brand of Islam). The *real* new threats come from instability. Instability and the chaos it generates can spark large and dangerous changes anywhere they land."*

Policymakers must also understand the role Islam plays within that violence, both as a feature of identity and an idiom for political expression. Although the National Military Strategic Plan for the War on Terrorism makes clear that "it is not a religious or cultural clash between Islam and the West,"[8] both terrorists and policymakers alike continue to frame political conflict in religious terms.[9]

This is a comparative work that references Najib Ghadbian's analysis of four types of political Islam,[10] including its use as an idiom of resistance against authoritarian rule, political liberalization, or secularization. The cases selected all involve tensions between political Islam and influences seen as secular, Christian, Western or post-Soviet. Most of this book's contributors challenge the conventional assertion that terrorism is directly linked with political Islam. The one exception is the Sudan case, where the regime in power claims an affiliation with political Islam.

This book's organizing theme is in many ways a critique of current U.S. foreign policy and its focus on waging a "global war on terrorism."[11] This volume does not call into question the validity or legal foundations of the war, but acknowledges that war is a prime determinant of contemporary American national security decision making. This work does explore the extent to and manner by which local conflicts, principally related to territorial disputes, national liberation or internal repression, are linked in any systematic, global way. To be sure, al Qaeda can tap into insurgency networks for recruits and its logistics

---

* Tony Zinni and Tony Koltz, *The Battle for Peace: A Frontline Vision of America's Power and Purpose* (New York: Palgrave Macmillan, 2006), p. 214.

network, but many of these conflicts are driven by "opportunistic predation waged by packs, often remarkably small ones, of criminals, bandits, and thugs."[12] As John Esposito cautioned more than a decade ago, "Islamic movements have been lumped together; conclusions have been drawn, based more on stereotyping or preconceived expectations than empirical research."[13] This book attempts to help remedy the shortfall in empirical research.

Above all, the contributors, as social scientists, military analysts, and policy strategists, seek to dispel the simplicity of the notion of a "global jihad" and empirically assess Samuel Huntington's "clash of civilizations" hypothesis. Granted, Osama bin Laden, Ayman al-Zawahiri, and other figures have been very effective in using the idea of such a jihad of resistance against the West to obtain support and to recruit fighters into their cause. The global media have highlighted what were once remote conflicts in places like Aceh, Darfur, and Chechnya. Policymakers erroneously connected these conflicts in a global jihad and lost all sight of their origins, modes of expression, and nature of political conflicts. As evidence, about half of the groups listed by the U.S. Department of State as Foreign Terrorist Organizations can be classified as nationalist insurgencies.[14]

Visions of an emerging "green menace" are too readily accepted and supported by bin Ladenites' Internet pronouncements of a global strategy to create an Islamic empire from Morocco to Indonesia, a "restoration" of a grand caliphate that never existed. However, bin Laden's rallying cry is just that: a rhetorical device used for fundraising and recruitment. The conflicts often linked do not represent any global struggle against the West and their connections to one another are spurious at best. There are real economic and political reasons for the conflicts explored in this book. Solving them would do much to take the ideological wind out of the sails of those who call for a global jihad.

Foreign policy choices matter and affect conflicts that provide real reasons to fuel international terrorism. Continued American acquiescence to state repression in Chechnya, Palestine, or Xianjing; missteps made by ordinary soldiers at the Iraqi Abu Ghraib prison; and the indefinite detention of prisoners at Guantanamo Bay provide the justification for revenge that bin Laden hopes to inspire. Terrorist morale is sustained by foreign policy choices made by previous and current administrations; changing policy would go a long way to undercut terrorist motivations to continue attacking targets in the West. The longevity of al Qaeda and like-minded movements is sustained by ongoing instances of conflicts presented as "Muslim humiliations."

"Islamic Resistance" is also highly differentiated and takes on many forms. In Uzbekistan and Tajikistan, "Islamic Traditionalism" became the idiom of resistance to continued forms of political domination. Western capitalism is seen as yet another form of alien colonization and domination that began with Russian Imperial expansion and was solidified in the programs of the Soviet Union. In many ways, political Islam is a reaction to these forms of political domination, and violent actions are motivated by different events, circumstances, and goals. "Islamic" suicide bombers in Tashkent are not trying to achieve the same goals as bombers in Baghdad or Tel Aviv. Islam does not have the same political resonance and meaning in the hills above Sarajevo as in the hills above Kasht in Xinjiang. While the conflicts analyzed here are related through similar violent tactics, they are unique and in many cases predate the concept of global jihad. They are locally controlled and often have a nationalist orientation. As Daniel Byman points out, "None of these insurgencies are 'caused' by al Qaeda, and in almost all the cases the insurgents have their own agendas that are in many ways distinct from al Qaeda."[15] But al Qaeda takes advantage of these insurgencies, incorporating ongoing conflicts like the one in Chechnya, disputed territories like Kashmir, or unresolved self-determination movements like Palestine in its overall information campaign to illustrate that Islam is under attack and all Muslims should rally to attack the enemies defined by bin Ladenites. This message resonates strongly outside of the Middle East as well. Likewise, "The majority of separatist leaders, however, are reluctant to join the radicals. The radicals are *too* extreme; the radical approach threatens to destroy their own intent and their own identity; and a radical association that put their own organizations on the terrorist list has a grim downside. At the same time, they don't want to cut the radicals off absolutely. They are, after all, brother Muslims; and they sympathize with some of their Islamist visions. So they try to keep the radicals at a distance without totally disconnecting from them."*

Due to a lack of cultural awareness and political expedience, American policymakers too readily accept the bin Ladenites' assertions. As the riots across France in late 2005 or the attacks incited by the European publication of distasteful Muhammed cartoons in early 2006 suggest, it is all too easy to see Islam as the source of political tension and violence. The France crisis took on a different significance when viewed through lenses that highlighted issues of class or explored problems of racism. Shrinking educational opportunities, unemployment, economic dislocations, the restructuring of the welfare state, demographic

---

* Tony Zinni and Tony Koltz, *The Battle for Peace: A Frontline Vision of America's Power and Purpose* (New York: Palgrave Macmillan, 2006), p. 190.

shifts, and the historical legacies of imperialism, colonialism, and institutional deprivation play roles in all of the conflicts presented here. In short, these events can be explained as misplaced rage originating from struggling minority communities.

IDENTIFYING FLASHPOINTS, PIVOT POINTS, AND HOT SPOTS

Previous volumes, such as *The Pivotal States* by Robert Chase, Emily Hill, and Paul M. Kennedy, identified important crises as those with geostrategic significance (Mexico), at a "tipping point" in the process of modernization (Turkey), subject to failure that would result in regional disasters (Indonesia), and with particular significance to transnational issues like the environment (Brazil).[16] If unattended, pivotal states could cause regional instability. Thomas Barnett underscored the importance of assisting "seam states" such as South Africa and Pakistan that are used by terrorists to access the "functioning core" or the West to commit their attacks. Barnett asserted that by supporting the seam states, an effective buffer zone from international terrorists would be created.[17] Likewise, Max Singer and Aaron Wildavsky identified "zones of turmoil" where the West may have to intervene to promote democracy both to stabilize such regions and to assure the security of the developed states.[18]

Myron Nordquist and John Moore identified security flashpoints based on a range of controversial issues with the potential for provoking military confrontation in the world's salt water areas such as in the Persian Gulf or in the Spratly Islands because of natural-resource claims.[19] The World Conflict Report identified "hot spots" as those with high levels of political, social, economic, and military disruptions.[20] When one-party rule in Central and Eastern European countries collapsed, Robin Wright and Doyle McManus saw the source of new conflict through ethnopolitics later illustrated by conflicts in Yugoslavia and the post-Soviet Region.[21] Ethnopolitical rebellion was further explored by Ted Robert Gurr in *People Versus States*. Gurr's research suggests the United States should prioritize assistance to failing states to deny terrorists sanctuary. He also suggests that the key to channeling identity conflicts into nonviolent forms of expression is to recognize and accommodate difference.[22] This priority was reflected at least on paper in the 2002 National Security Strategy that states, "America is now threatened less by conquering states than ... by failing ones."[23] The policy paper went on to suggest that the promotion of civic and political pluralism serves as a solution to violent movements.

These previous volumes attempted to identify flashpoints, pivot points, or hot spots where the United States would or should intervene militarily. *Flashpoints in the War on Terrorism* departs from previous work in its selection of regions—namely those that have served as breeding grounds, ideological inspiration, or battlefields for political Islam-inspired violence. As Metz and Millen observed, "The United States is more likely to assist regimes threatened by insurgents linked to al Qaeda or its affiliates."[24] Thus, if one wants to understand where U.S. foreign policy is headed, a more nuanced comprehension of conflicts defined by violent extremists as assaults on Islam or by authoritarian governments' resistance to political Islamist terrorism is necessary. By isolating these conflicts, understanding their causes and exploring their links to the war on terrorism, *Flashpoints in the War on Terrorism* prioritizes the international crises that require resolution. An important goal of this work is to highlight the real causes of political conflict and test the "clash of civilizations" ideas that have dominated the debate thus far.

BEYOND A CLASH OF CIVILIZATIONS

As the dominant Cold War paradigm of international relations broke down in the late 1980s, two divergent streams of thought emerged to explain future sources of conflict.[25] The first, exemplified by Francis Fukuyama's "End of History" hypothesis, predicted the end of great ideological debates such as the one between the United States and the Soviet Union and argued "that liberal democracy may constitute the end point of mankind's ideological evolution and the final form of human government."[26] While history would not literally "end," as there would still be social development, international crises, wars, and defining moments, human societies would no longer fight over *types* of political systems and would instead focus on fully realizing what Fukuyama sees as the highest form of social development: liberal democracy. This line of thinking is reflected in renewed research of Kant's "democratic peace" thesis and manifested in an active American democracy promotion foreign policy in the 1990s.[27]

The second idea about future sources of conflict, a clash of civilizations, was taken from the final section in Bernard Lewis's 1990 article, "The Roots of Muslim Rage." Painting a bleak picture of Islamic reactions to Western culture, Lewis wrote: "It should by now be clear that we are facing a mood and a movement far transcending the level of issues and policies and the governments that pursue them. This is no less than a *clash of civilizations*—the perhaps irrational but surely historic reaction of an ancient rival against our Judeo-Christian heritage, our secular present, and the worldwide expansion of both."[28] Samuel Huntington advanced the hypothesis in his famous 1993 *Foreign Affairs* article, writing "that the fundamental source of conflict in this new world will not be primarily ideological or primarily economic. The great divisions among humankind and the dominating source of conflict will be cultural."[29] At bottom, this type of thinking leads to the notion of "the West against the rest."

Huntington's central claim equates culture with civilization, and when different civilizations encounter one another the inevitable result is conflict.[30] He states that "people divide themselves in terms of ancestry, religion, language, history, values, and customs" and that, in turn, the most important distinction is cultural.[31] For Huntington, these cultural differences represent the cleavages between civilizations, and conflict is born from the depths of these fault lines. He makes grand claims that contemporary conflicts are the result of the inability of civilizations to reconcile themselves and live in a peaceful coexistence. Huntington goes on to construct six archetypical civilizations: the Western, the Orthodox Christian, the Islamic, the Indian, the Sinic/Chinese/Japanese, and the African. Yet there are many problems with Huntington's construction. First, he mixes his definitions of culture. In his archetypes, he has two religious dimensions (Orthodoxy versus Islam), two ethnic distinctions (Indian versus Sinic), and two geographic constructions (Western versus African). That Africa appears as a residual category, and that Huntington obviously ignores Islam's significance in sub-Saharan Africa and within India itself is one conspicuous problem with this typology. His construction is also laden with classic realist balance-of-power competitions; the United States versus Russia is recast as the "Western" versus the "Orthodoxy"; India versus China is recast as the "Indian" versus the "Sinic"; and Europe versus Japan is recast as the "Western" versus the "Japanese." He makes no compelling argument of why the world should be so organized.

As the debate about "clash of civilizations" ensued, however, real political conflicts in the 1990s seemed to validate Huntington's claims. From numerous international media reports, one could easily imagine that the wars in Croatia, Bosnia-Herzegovina, and Kosovo-Metohija were inevitable. Often depicting these conflicts as a continuation of the wars against the Ottoman invasion dating back to the fourteenth century, the Western news media in particular readily accepted the myth that the factions involved in the fighting represented primordial groups that are constantly at war in the Balkans. Rather than evaluating mixed marriages between Croats, Bosnians, and Serbs (one-fourth of Sarajevo residents were "intermarried" prior to the Yugoslav wars and only 3 percent of Muslims in Bosnia attended mosque regularly)[32] or decades of peaceful coexistence, the narrative transmitted by various media implied that such commingling was the exception rather than the norm. Further reinforcing the divisive nature of relations among the various groups in Yugoslavia was the myth of the strong man. That is, Yugoslav President Josip Broz Tito's "unify by force" strategy explains relative calm from World War II until his death in 1980.[33] The same argument was used in Iraq after the United States' 2003 invasion toppled Saddam Hussein's government and plunged the country into turmoil. But as James Robbins notes in Chapter 2, it was Saddam Hussein's method of privileging certain tribes and repressing others that explains much of the chaos. After Tito's death, Yugoslav President Slobodan Milosevic pursued a similar strategy, which exploited ethnic differences for political gains. Both these cases reveal a deeper understanding of the political conflicts that emerged in Yugoslavia and Iraq. But, by seeing ethnic conflict exclusively through the "clash lens," policymakers ignore the importance of domestic politics on internal conflicts.

For example, Huntington explains conflict in Nigeria as a tripartite split between Christianity, Islam, and traditional religions. In Sudan it is Islam versus Christianity, and in India it is Islam versus Hinduism.[34] These examples all support Huntington's claims that "religion is the central defining characteristic of civilization."[35] He states that "races" may be divided by civilization, while religion can unite races into a single civilization. Yet in Nigeria, Michael Morris and Charles Edel observe in Chapter 14 that conflict there is driven by political competition over controlling natural resources, not religion.

The Sudanese war further illustrates how slippery Huntington's hypothesis can be. The conflict, which has claimed millions of lives, has been explained at various times as an ideological struggle between Muslims and Christians, a cultural conflict between modernizing forces and advocates of traditionalism, and an economic tussle between the geographic distinctions of the arid lowlands in the north and the savannas and rainforests of the south. In Chapter 13, Stephen Emerson explains the conflict in terms of the country's historical legacy, the inability of the political system to accommodate the aspirations of its southern minority, and the failure to develop a shared national identity.

In the context of Western civilization, Huntington ignores the significant national distinctions within the West, such as the United Kingdom and France, significant religious pluralism within Protestantism (nearly 33,000 denominations),[36] and social differences between the United States and Sweden. To miss the larger complexities of "Western societies" or contemporary conflicts is to deny the potential for any type of multiethnic or multireligious society. Further, it denies the very society that exists in the United States.

Huntington also points to the breakup of the former Soviet Union as providing numerous examples of these "fault-line" conflicts. Yet, many of these conflicts do not square with Huntington's archetypes. Should the territorial conflict between Azerbaijan and Armenia really be reframed as Islam versus Orthodoxy? If so, how should we understand the civil conflict in South Ossetia, as an internal struggle within Orthodoxy: Georgian Orthodoxy versus Russian Orthodoxy? Or, for that matter, how should we understand the conflict in Iraq? If religion were truly primary, the conflict would not be ordered as one fought by Sunni Kurds, Sunni Arabs, or Arab Shiites. We should speak of the conflict in terms of Sunni versus Shia or Kurd versus Arab—not the lexicon most readily used. Such reductions miss the complexities and motivations of different elements within conflicts. Just as there is no homogeneous group of Shi'a Arabs, the Kurds are likewise far from monolithic. Kurds are united by culture and language, not religion; for while the vast majority of Kurds are Sunni Muslims, there are also Christian and Shi'a Kurds. Similarly, Kurds have historically been divided in regional subgroups, stretching from present-day Iran to Turkey.

Furthermore, Huntington characterizes the civil strife in the Ukraine as a clash between the Orthodox and Western civilizations.[37] Yet, this would appear to either cast the Western civilization as a religious construction of Catholicism or ignore the historical legacies of Russian/Post-Soviet pressure in Eastern Ukraine as something other than Orthodoxy. Similarly, he suggests that the conflicts in the former Yugoslavia are a direct result of the intersection of the Western, the Orthodox, and the Islamic civilizations, again casting the Western exclusively as Catholicism. While this may be the understanding that many violent participants in conflicts would like the world to believe, it would be dangerous to accept this proposition without questioning it.

If the conflicts in Yugoslavia were caused by an "intersection" of civilizations, as Huntington would have us believe, then there never could have been a "Yugoslav" identity. Yet, Yugoslav military officers like Agim Ceku illustrate the contrary.[38] Additionally, many Yugoslav émigrés to the United States said that they felt uncomfortable during the various Yugoslav wars because they could not relate to the sectarianism that structured the fighting. Although they expressed a regional identity of a Croat, or Serb, and so on, they claimed they had a Yugoslav identity.[39] It was only after fighting broke out and nationalist leaders repudiated a Yugoslav identity that Balkan people defined themselves along nationalist lines. But this too is problematic; a powerful argument can be made that the "centuries-old" enemies of the Croats were not the Serbs but the Hungarians and Austrians (simply called Germans at the time).[40] This was not due to ethnic strife, but due to the political environment of occupation and domination.[41] Conflicts between Serbs and Croats do not appear until these groups, which saw one another as "brother southern Slavs," were joined in the United Kingdom of Serbs, Croats, and Slovenes.[42] In fact, these groups shared a common language until the brutal war of the 1990s provoked nationalist movements to differentiate these groups. It is only now that we can speak of separate Serbian, Croatian, and Bosnian languages. It is important to note that in spite of efforts to invent unique words within the three languages, the structure, syntax, and vocabulary are still Serbo-Croatian understood by all.

Rather than accepting the Huntington principle that groups of different religions or civilizations will inevitably fight, let us take up the proposition that Serbs and Croats, Azeris and Armenians, Georgians and Russians, and, for that matter, Hutus and Tutsis, do not engage in conflict because they are primordially different, but because they are very similar and have enjoyed at one time a unified collective narrative. It is not until conflict breaks out that national identity is heightened, which has more to do with political leaders projecting blame than any culture clash.[43] Political leaders in Serbia and Croatia are responsible for war that claimed hundreds of thousands of lives, not Orthodoxy, Catholicism, or Islam.[44]

Further undermining Huntington's claims are the responses to the Yugoslav wars by external forces. Huntington's hypothesis predicts that the leading Western states should have supported Croatia since it is predominately Catholic, Russia should have supported Serbia since it is predominately Orthodox, and leading Islamic states should have supported Bosnia-Herzegovina since it is predominately Muslim (though very secular). Yet, Russia did not use its veto on the UN Security Council to prevent U.S.-led military actions against Serbia. The United States, as a leading member of the West, did not unabashedly support the Croats against the Bosniacs or the Serbs, but rather brokered an alliance between Bosnian Croats and Bosnian Muslims, which contradicted expansion of the West through a greater Croatia. And there was general agreement among all major powers, regardless of "cultural distinction," that genocide was unacceptable by any party, that all individuals responsible for inciting violence will be held accountable, and that the final status of Bosnia-Herzegovina must be a multicultural, multireligious state, which persists to this day. If the start of the Bosnian war could be evidence of Huntington's clash of civilizations, certainly the Bosnian peace must refute Huntington's claims.

Although cultural distinctions can mark difference, culture is fluid.[45] Like other social phenomena of collective identity, such as class and gender, ethnicity and culture exhibit both constancy and flux. Thus, as some aspects of culture are stressed, others are attenuated. Traditions and customs can be assimilated just as they can become extinct. In light of the patterns of assimilation, growth, and extinction, it is difficult to argue that any given culture is exactly the same as it was centuries ago. Just as cultures change, so do conflicts; the dominant trend in the post–Cold War period is for states to break down into smaller units, not merge into larger cultural ones, as Huntington predicts.

Yet the clash of civilizations has given way to what Mahmood Mamdani has called *Culture Talk*, which "assumes that every culture has a tangible essence that defines it, and it then explains politics as a consequence of that essence."[46] Thus, it is unsurprising that after the 9/11 terrorist attacks, initial commentators, media exposes, and bestselling books focused on Islam.[47] But that is the wrong focus. No individual, including Osama bin Laden, can speak on behalf of the 1.2 billion Muslims in the world who are separated by different forms of worship, different languages, and important national identifications. Likewise, the face of Islam is not exclusively Arab; the largest Islamic countries (Indonesia, Bangladesh, and Pakistan) are not even in the Middle East. Glossing over these facts and failing to differentiate between the Middle East and Islam is what gives rise to arguments like Bernard Lewis's *What Went Wrong?*[48]

The study of a religion will not provide answers to the motivating forces within radical groups. Scholars like Olivier Roy explain that the role of Islam in shaping contemporary societies has been overemphasized. "The culturalist approach has been reinforced by recent tragic events, and more precisely by the way in which observers, politicians, and public opinion are trying to cast these events into an intelligible conceptual framework that might explain the incomprehensible."[49] We should no sooner think that Osama bin Laden represents Islam than the Ku Klux Klan represents Christianity. Likewise, we would no sooner associate Islam with terrorism than identify an Israeli air strike in Gaza as "Jewish boys dropping Christian bombs."[50] It is important to distinguish between those terrorists motivated by religious beliefs and political Islamist movements that developed in response to particular political, economic, and cultural contexts. While politicians have declared a "war" on such movements, defeating an insurgent movement is more of a political effort than a military one.

These are the most difficult problems for the essentialist-primordialists. The argument that cultural difference functions as a source of conflict appears to be a reactionary reading of the symptoms only after conflict has broken out.[51] As Paul Collier found in his study of 52 major civil wars, "conflicts in ethnically diverse countries may be ethnically patterned without being ethnically caused."[52] Even before the collapse of Realized Socialism, Brackette Williams suggested that ethnicity often masks class. She suggests that what may appear as ethnic conflict can be found, with a bit of deeper analysis, to be resource competition, with different "ethnic" groups standing for different class strata.[53] Likewise for Ted Gurr, "the politics of identity are based most fundamentally on persistent grievances about inequalities and past wrongs, conditions that are part of the heritage of most minorities in most countries."[54] Thus, it is unsurprising that some groups of oppressed Muslim minorities have resorted to violence. To be fair, religious frameworks or belief systems are an essential element in the psyche of terrorists, but religion is not the single defining characteristic.[55] This volume seeks to expose the underlying political and economic reasons for conflicts in regions that have been speciously linked to a global jihad.

In spite of this discussion, the clash-of-civilizations hypothesis has had a profound effect on thinking about conflict and has been a driving force in the global war on terrorism. A recent survey of international-relations scholars identified Samuel Huntington's "Clash of Civilizations" hypothesis as the third most productive debate in international relations and, ironically, the second least productive debate in the discipline.[56] These findings illustrate the controversial nature of Huntington's hypothesis and intimate how the idea of clashing civilizations has informed public discourse on international terrorism. It also illustrates that Huntington's hypothesis was never supported by real events. Yet, it is a lens that clouds understanding of the motivations of international terrorists, broad anti-Americanism, and U.S. foreign policy. As Stephen Walt noted, "by portraying the contemporary world as one of relentless competition, therefore, [Huntington] may be trying to provide us with the bogeyman we need to keep our house in order."[57] But the United States does not need a new bogeyman, but the fortitude to reconsider its policies that provide ideological fuel for international terrorists. While no policy change will ever rid the world of nihilists like bin Laden, changing some policies can go a long way to eliminating real sources of grievances, or to use the more fashionable term in U.S. Department of Defense parlance, "countering ideological support for terrorism."

And there is evidence to suggest such a change. A late 2005 poll conducted by the University of Maryland and Zogby International measured Arab attitudes toward political and social issues in six Arab countries. There was unsurprising support for the proposition that Arab attitudes toward the United States are overwhelmingly affected by U.S. foreign policy, not U.S. culture. Eighty percent of all respondents in all six countries base their view of the United States on its foreign policy, while only 11 percent base their view on American values.[58] Vice Admiral Lowell Jacoby, former director of the Defense Intelligence Agency, testified as much to Congress in 2005: "Our policies in the Middle East fuel Islamic resentment."[59] While such a statement would have provoked condemnation after 9/11, distance has allowed for more thoughtful examination of the underlying causes of terrorism, which is a symptom of a larger problem. With the exception of Sudan, political Islamist movements are in opposition to the ruling political regimes, many of which the United States supports financially, militarily, or politically, and some of which have a history of using repression to stifle political opposition.

Negative views of U.S. policies undoubtedly account for the United States being the second most feared country, after Israel, by people in Jordan, Lebanon, Morocco, Saudi Arabia, Egypt, and United Arab Emirates; 63 percent claim that the United States poses the biggest threat. When the Arab audience was asked about various reasons why they might sympathize with al Qaeda, a plurality of 36 percent acknowledged that the organization confronts the United States. In the same poll, only 6 percent said they sympathize with al Qaeda because it seeks to create an Islamic state. Thus, U.S. policies and bin Laden's willingness to stand up to the United States explain negative views of the United States. There is not widespread support for the creation of an Islamic empire or engaging in a "cosmic war" with the United States.[60]

CHAPTER OUTLINE

As a project, this book evaluates the appropriateness of U.S. foreign policy by examining the relevance of the "global war on terrorism" to specific conflicts on the ground. Each of the chapters seeks to find answers to the following questions:

- What is the role of political Islam in the conflict?
- What roles do external actors play within the conflict?
- What has been the progress or process of internationalizing or widening the conflict?
- What are the material considerations of the conflict?
- Can this conflict be recast in the frame of resource competition between classes or ethnic groups?

The answers to these questions are important and form the core of the succeeding chapters. Each author also provides the historical context of the political conflict, an understanding of how the conflict is linked to international terrorism, and the manner in which the conflict is linked to the U.S. global war on terrorism. The authors also consider each conflict's prospects for becoming a wider flashpoint. Although we organized the chapters by region, we prioritized the region and the individual conflict to reflect its intensity. Thus, we start in the Near East and conclude with sub-Saharan Africa.

Near East

In the popular imagination, the Near East more than any other region in the world is often associated with terrorism. To some degree this assessment is correct. From January 1, 2004, to January 1, 2006, the region was the site of nearly 61 percent of all terrorist incidents worldwide. These 4,017 terrorist events resulted in 8,419 deaths, slightly less than three-quarters of the total deaths worldwide for the same period. Yet, in another regard this is misleading, for it is the conflict in Iraq that is the site of most of the incidents and most of the deaths: 2,873 events resulting in 7,852 deaths, or 93 percent of the region's total, and 12,267 people wounded.[61] For the same 24-month period, there were only 73 events in Israel proper, only five of which were suicide bombings.[62] All told there were 90 deaths and 470 people wounded in Israel proper for the two-year period. To give greater insight into the region, three authors take up different aspects of the "War on Terrorism in the Near East." Analysis suggests that U.S. foreign policy in the region must take into account the variation of political struggles and the differing stakes within those contests if peace is to come to the Near East. Simplifying these conflicts may be appealing for politicians and the news media, but simplifications will only exacerbate tensions and prolong violence.

Steven Van Evera echoes some of these concerns about the Israeli-Palestinian conflict in Chapter 1. The Israeli-Palestinian conflict is a boon to al Qaeda. It feeds anti-Americanism in the Arab and Muslim worlds by fostering violence between a U.S. ally, Israel, and Palestinian Arabs who are largely Muslim. Arabs and non-Arab Muslims then blame the United States for Israel's belligerent actions, and U.S. standing among Arabs and Muslims suffers. The proliferation of global media has made what was once a local conflict an international one. The Israeli-Palestinian conflict gives al Qaeda a chance to pose as a defender of Arabs and Muslims against a predatory Israeli/American alliance. This enhances al Qaeda's image among Arabs and Muslims worldwide. Van Evera suggests that by looking to the past, one finds that this conflict is connected to assertions of land control and is far more associated with nationalism than religion.

In Chapter 2, James Robbins evaluates how the conflict in Iraq has affected the "global war on terrorism." No other single country has consumed more American attention, wealth, and political capital since 1990 than Iraq. That country is an important world energy producer and the focal point for American democracy promotion efforts in the Near East, and has become a battlefield and a rallying point for jihadists. Robbins argues that the aftermath of the 2003 Iraq war unleashed a flood of terrorism in the region and several scandals associated with the Coalition military intervention have provided new propaganda to fuel anti-Americanism around the world. While Iraq's role as a state sponsor of terrorism was not the strongest argument for war in 2003, it appears that terrorism is now the strongest reason the United States and its allies must succeed in its reconstruction efforts.

Like Van Evera's chapter on Israel/Palestine, Kerrie Urosevich's chapter on Kurdistan reminds us that terrorism has been utilized as a political tactic for quite some time. The Kurdish quest for independence throughout the twentieth century has been marked by betrayal, disappointment, and violence. Even as Kurds play an important part in the burgeoning democracy in Iraq, Kurdish nationalism and expressions of ethnic identity are problematic in other countries of the region, especially Turkey. Urosevich points out that much of the violence associated with Kurdish nationalism takes on yet another dimension: leftist politics. There are two major Kurdish forces active within Turkey, both of which have Marxist revolutionary roots. The first, the Kongra-Gel, is the latest incarnation of the Kurdish Workers' Party—PKK, renamed the Kurdish Free and Democratic Congress in 2002. The second, the People's Defense Force (HPG), grew out of the People's Liberation Army of Kurdistan (ARGK). The HPG claims that they are a "whole new Kurdish guerrilla army [that] has evolved itself to a modern and better 'Fourth Generation Warfare' (4GW) force," far beyond mere "terrorists, extremists, or thugs."[63] There were 164 terrorist events in Turkey between January 1, 2004, and January 1, 2006,[64] with as many incidences occurring in the southeast Kurdish areas as in Istanbul. Like the problems in Israel/Palestine, much of the violence associated with Kurdistan is secular and nationalist in nature.

Europe and the Post-Soviet Region

According to the National Counterterrorism Center (NCTC), far more terrorist events were associated with "secular-political" movements than with Islamic extremism for the period January 1, 2004, to March 31, 2005, the last date for this data set. The NCTC classified 1,474 events as secular-political, nearly double the number associated with "Islamic extremism," which was 772.[65] Of course, religious identity often contributes to a sense of national, collective identity. The combination of the two informs many of the conflicts in Europe.

The next three chapters examine political conflicts in Europe and Central Asia. In Chapter 4, Susan Fink Yoshihara examines the case of Kosovo, which was a hot flashpoint in the 1990s, and considers the origins of the conflict and the role the international community has played in preventing new flare-ups. Nationalism, not religion, is the main bone of contention in the Kosovo case. Yet religion acts as an intervening variable in the violence in an unexpected way. It is Orthodox Serbia that seeks to cast the conflict in religious terms and claim the territory of Kosovo as Serbia's spiritual homeland. Considering the Kosovar Albanian side of the conflict, she finds that Albanian identity has been a strong buffer against radical political Islam.

Jeffrey Murer examines conflict in the Caucasus region of Europe in Chapter 5, which has claimed 100,000 lives since 1994. The region has been the scene of intense and brutal fighting since the collapse of the Soviet Union. First, the Republic of Georgia suffered through a civil war in the early 1990s, resulting in two regions breaking away and declaring themselves separate from Georgia and associated with the Russian Federation. T'bilisi continues to consider Abkhazia and South Ossetia integral parts of Georgia, even at the risk of raising the ire of the Russian Federation. This tension makes it difficult for Georgia to play any buffer role in preventing Chechen rebels from escaping Russian security forces by moving south. Likewise, Russian forces have a hard time pursuing rebel forces into the mountains. Although foreign elements have tried to expand the war in Chechnya and radicalize the fighters, Murer finds that the conflict remains largely a nationalist one. Although violence has spread to neighboring Dagestan and North Ossetia, it appears that the perpetrators are Chechens looking to expand the theater of conflict. Even as Russian President Vladimir Putin has declared Chechnya to be a key theater for the Russia contribution to the "global war on terrorism," no end to the conflict or violence appears to be coming anytime soon.

In Chapter 6, Christopher Fettweis explores the complex relationship between the United States, authoritarian countries in Central Asia, and violent political Islamists in the Fergana Valley of Central Asia. Although few analysts were optimistic about the potential for stability in Central Asia when independence was thrust upon these peoples in 1991, the short history of the region has been surprisingly peaceful. Each state had a Soviet autocrat that was able to adopt nationalist trappings, assume power, and bring a measure of stability to his country. Even Tajikistan, where a civil war broke out immediately upon independence, has remained relatively calm since 1994. Just as significantly, violent political Islamist groups did not find willing audiences among the Central Asian people, most of whom seemed to be far more secular, or at least more moderate, than many other Muslim societies. Fettweis does caution, however, that "political Islam may be unpalatable to the majority of Central Asians at the beginning of the twenty-first century, but continued oppression may change minds as the century goes on."

Asia

While it is often the Near East that immediately comes to mind for most when thinking of the "war on terrorism," it would appear that South Asia is the most active site of international terrorism incidents. For the period between January 1, 2004, and March 31, 2005, South Asia experienced as many incidents of international terrorism as the Near East, including Iraq.[66] Further, the number of victims of terrorist acts in South Asia represented nearly half of all victims worldwide.[67] Within the region, India (3,313 victims), Thailand (715 victims), Philippines (709 victims), and Indonesia (399 victims) account for the vast majority of incidents.[68] Although so much attention is focused on Iraq, Asia may constitute the true focal point of the "global war on terrorism." However, on closer inspection of the various crises and conflicts in the region, it becomes apparent that while many groups claim an Islamic identity, the struggles are essentially nationalist ones, striving for either statehood or extensive regional autonomy.

In Chapter 7, Rohan Gunaratna and Arabinda Acharya examine the struggle between Islamic militants and agents of the central government in Southern Thailand. They document how this current conflict fits into a long-standing struggle for identity and conquest in the region. For centuries the Thai establishment has tried to forcibly convert the region to Buddhism and has engaged in a long program of "Thaification." However this conflict is not stuck in the past. Gunaratna and Acharya point out that there is much at stake in the conflict regarding the development of the Thai and Malaysian economies. The terrorism associated with their struggle can be seen as part of a conflict over regional political and economic autonomy.

In Chapter 8, Arabinda Acharya and Rohaiza Ahmad Asi explore similar conflicts between Christians and Muslims in Indonesia. They find that much of the violence on the archipelago is similarly connected to movements and struggles for national liberation or autonomy such as with the GAM—Free Aceh Movement—or to acts connected to economic grievances such as increased economic terrorism in East Kalimantan, especially attacks on oil facilities operated by Western multinationals like Unocal. Other targets across Indonesia have included Kentucky Fried Chicken and McDonald's. The authors find that even groups such as Jemaah Islamiyah (JI) have roots in indigenous anti-colonial movements such as Darul Islam. There are internationalist elements within Indonesia trying to expand conflicts, and some of the organizations based in Indonesia are involved in fundraising for other organizations in the region. Acharya and Asi also find that much of the political activity of these subversive groups is an outgrowth of the opening of Indonesian civil society. They suggest that some of these nationalist struggles are related to the growing pains of democracy after the authoritarian rule of General Haji Suharto. They also raise interesting questions regarding U.S. foreign policy in terms of who should be supported and who should be repressed in the name of "protecting" democracy.

Samina Raja explores the contentious and difficult politics of Kashmir in Chapter 9. While India is the site of the most terrorist incidents outside of Iraq with 3,313 victims during an 18-month period, most of the acts that occur outside of Kashmir are connected to communist or leftist revolutionary agitation.[69] Raja asserts that in actuality the conflict in Kashmir is likewise connected to development and economics. She finds that the astonishing lack of economic development within the region foments alienation and a culture of resistance toward Indian rule. She notes that this potentially nuclear flashpoint is often politically abstracted by all parties to the point where concrete steps toward conflict amelioration, such as ending governmental corruption, providing employment opportunities, and developing adequate infrastructure, are ignored at the expense of "high" politics. Raja's analysis of the conflict in Kashmir highlights the connection between material politics and acts of terrorism.

In Chapter 10, Toshi Yoshihara comes to similar conclusions in exploring the conflict in Mindanao, in the southern Philippines. He chronicles the evolution of the many groups leading the struggle for

Mindanao independence, from the Moro National Liberation Front to the Moro Islamic Liberation Front to Abu Sayyaf, which is often singled out by the United States as an important group in the network of global terrorism. Yet Yoshihara finds that the leadership of Abu Sayyaf is driven largely by greed. Many of the acts of terrorism are kidnapping for profit or other acts otherwise associated with transnational criminal organizations. He finds that by contrast the Moro Islamic Liberation Front struggles to establish a separate political space for southern Muslims who find themselves estranged within the larger Christian culture of the Philippines.

Dru Gladney in Chapter 11 explores tensions between the People's Republic of China and its Uyghur population. Located in the northwestern corner of China, Xinjiang Uyghur Autonomous Region is China's largest province and home to about 18 million people, half of whom are ethnically and culturally distinct from the Han Chinese. The Uyghur living in Xinjiang are predominately Muslim, and have long been the target of Beijing, which declares its authority is challenged by "religious extremist forces" and "violent terrorists." Since 9/11, the Chinese government charged that Uyghur groups had links with the Taliban in Afghanistan and is supported from abroad by radical Islamist organizations. However, Gladney finds that links to al Qaeda are tenuous at best and that the sources of discontent for Uyghur opposition groups remain the same: massive, unrestricted Han migration to the region. This has led to a dramatic increase in the gap between the wealthy and mainly Uyghur poor, a decrease in educational opportunities, higher mortality rates among Uyghur, unresolved health problems due to nuclear testing in the region, and increased restrictions on religious and cultural practices. Although Uyghur groups do not pose a serious threat to the People's Liberation Army, continued repression and a failure to solve broader social and economic problems can lead to future conflict.

Africa

The final section explores this volume's critical questions in Africa. In Chapter 12, Stephen Emerson examines why Africa's trans-Sahara region is becoming more integral to U.S. security. This vast expanse of almost three million square miles—about the size of the continental United States—sweeping across West Africa into Sudan contains some of the poorest, most vulnerable, and conflict-ridden countries in Africa. Many U.S. officials see the trans-Sahara as ripe for terrorist exploitation and increasingly view it as the next battlefield in the global war on terrorism. Heavy-handed American counterterrorism initiatives, however, risk militarizing the region and internationalizing local conflicts, further inflaming chronic political, social, and economic problems. Rather than focus on strengthening traditional security mechanisms, Emerson believes the emphasis should be on helping the countries of the region achieve successful political and economic transformations, thereby defusing conflict and strengthening security.

Emerson then examines in Chapter 13 the links between Sudanese conflict, instability, and terrorism in the context of Africa's longest-running civil war. Since it gained independence in 1956, Sudan has constantly struggled to cope with deep-seated political, social, and economic divisions amid efforts to build a shared national identity. The failure over the past 50 years of Sudanese leaders and institutions to meet this challenge has produced chronic instability and immense human suffering. It has also made the country vulnerable to outside interference, including terrorist exploitation. As a key country in the strategic, yet highly volatile, greater Horn of Africa, the future of regional and African security, Emerson believes, will be increasingly tied to progress on resolving the country's longstanding problems. While there is hope for optimism with the recent signing of the north–south peace agreement that ended the civil war, the ongoing crisis in Darfur demonstrates how fragile and fleeting peace and stability can be in this part of the world.

Finally, in Chapter 14, Michael Morris and Charles Edel examine Nigeria, which is one of the United States' most important strategic allies in Africa because of its size, large oil reserves, and central role in regional peacekeeping operations. Yet instability plagues Africa's most populous country. Because of Nigeria's growing internal instability, the country is both fertile ground for the radicalization of political Islam and a strategically attractive target for al Qaeda. Overall, Nigeria's global economic importance, its struggle with a democratic transformation, and its fight against radicalizing political Islam make Nigeria an important test case for U.S. policy and strategy in the early twenty-first century.

Each of these chapters raises significant questions about the ways in which the various conflicts are portrayed. By analyzing these regions in terms of material, religious, social, and economic cleavages, regional or national identities become clearer and their roles in stimulating and perpetuating conflict can be better appreciated. One conclusion resonates through all of the contributions: attention to economic grievances and inequalities may go a long way in ameliorating conflicts worldwide associated with the "war on terrorism."

NOTES

1. Muhammad Abd al-Salam Faraj, *The Neglected Duty*, trans. In Johannes J. G. Jansen, *The Neglected Duty: The Creed of Sadat's Assassins and Islamic Resurgence in the Middle East* (New York: Macmillan, 1986), p. 162. For a broader treatment of the philosophical underpinnings of violent political Islam, see Christopher Henzel, "The Origins of al Qaeda's Ideology: Implications for US Strategy," *Parameters* (Spring 2005), pp. 69-80; Gilles Kepel, *The War for Muslim Minds: Islam and the West* (Cambridge: Belknap, 2004); Olivier Roy, *Globalized Islam: The Search for a New Ummah*, (New York: Columbia University Press, 2004); Paul Berman, *Terror and Liberalism* (New York: W. W. Norton, 2003).

2. Osama bin Laden, "1997 Interview with Peter Arnett," Online. Available HTTP: <http://news.findlaw.com/hdocs/docs/binladen/binladenintvw-cnn.pdf>.

3. George W. Bush, "Address to the Nation," December 18, 2005. Emphasis is ours.

4. Chairman of the Joint Chiefs of Staff, *National Military Strategic Plan for the War on Terrorism* (Washington, DC: Department of Defense, 2006), p. 11.

5. Michael T. Klare, "The New Geography of Conlict," *Foreign Affairs* (May/June 2001), pp. 53-61; Thomas P. M. Barnett, *The Pentagon's New Map* (New York: Putnam, 2004); Samuel Huntington, *The Clash of Civilizations: Remaking World Order* (New York: Touchstone, 1996).

6. Martin E. Marty argues, "The collision of faith, or the collisions of peoples of faith, are among the most threatening conflicts around the world in the new millennium." *When Faiths Collide* (Oxford: Blackwell, 2005), p. 1.

7. National Intelligence Council, *Mapping the Global Future: Report of the National Intelligence Council's 2020 Project* (December 2004), p. 14. Online. Available HTTP: <http://www.cia.gov/nic/NIC_globaltrend2020_es.html>.

8. Chairman of the Joint Chiefs of Staff, *National Military Strategic Plan for the War on Terrorism* (Washington, DC: Department of Defense, 2006), p. 4.

9. For example, the *National Military Strategic Plan for the War on Terrorism* is primarily focused on al Qaeda and associated movements, which seek to exploit Islam for political ends. The strategy also defines the "extremist" as the enemy and the "moderate" as the ideal. See page 11.

10. Najib Ghadbian, "Political Islam: Inclusion or Violence" in *Violence and Politics: Globalization's Paradox*, Ungar, Mark, Sally Avery Bermanzohn, and Kenton Worcester, eds. (New York: Routledge, 2000).

11. "The GWOT is a war to preserve ordinary peoples' ability to live as they choose, and to protect the tolerance and moderation of free and open societies." See Chairman of the Joint Chiefs of Staff, *National Military Strategic Plan for the War on Terrorism* (Washington, DC: Department of Defense, 2006), p. 12.

12. John Mueller, *The Remnants of War* (Ithaca, NY: Cornell University Press, 2004), p. 1.

13. John Esposito, *The Islamic Threat: Myth or Reality?* (New York: Oxford University Press, 1992), p. 235.

14. Robert Pape posits that the global jihadist network is an array of essentially nationalist insurgencies of which religion is merely an accelerant. See *Dying to Win: The Strategic Logic of Suicide Terrorism* (New York: Random House, 2005).

15. Daniel Byman, *Going to War with the Allies You Have: Allies, Counterinsurgency, and the War on Terrorism* (Carlisle, PA: Strategic Studies Institute, 2005), p. 7.

16. Robert Chase, Emily Hill, and Paul M. Kennedy, eds., *The Pivotal States: A New Framework for U.S. Policy in the Developing World* (New York: W. W. Norton, 1998).

17. Thomas P.M. Barnett, *The Pentagon's New Map* (New York: Putnam, 2004).

18. Max Singer and Aaron Wildavsky, *The Real World Order: Zones of Peace/Zones of Turmoil* (Chatham, New Jersey: Chatham House Publishing, 1993).

19. Myron H. Nordquist and John Norton Moore, *Security Flashpoints—Oil, Islands, Sea Access, and Military Confrontation* (New York: Springer, 1998).
20. National Defense Council Foundation, *World Conflict Report*, 2002. Online. Available HTTP: <http://www.ndcf.org/Conflict_List/World2002/2002Conflictlist.htm>.
21. Robin Wright and Doyle McManus, *Flashpoints: Promise and Peril in a New World Order* (New York: Knopf, 1991).
22. Ted Robert Gurr, *Peoples Versus States: Minorities at Risk in the New Century* (Washington, DC: United States Institute of Peace Press, 2000).
23. George W. Bush, *National Security Strategy of the United States of America* (September 2002), p. 1.
24. Steven Metz and Raymond Millen, *Insurgency and Counterinsurgency in the 21st Century: Reconceptualizing Threat and Response* (Carlisle, PA: Strategic Studies Institute, 2004), p. 18.
25. Overall, conflict has been on the decline for the last decade. The Center for International Development and Conflict Management notes in its 2005 *Peace and Conflict* report: "The global trend in major armed conflict has continued to decrease markedly in the post-Cold War era both in numbers of states affected by major armed conflicts and in general magnitude. According to our calculations, the general magnitude of global warfare has decreased by over sixty percent, peaking in the mid-1980s, falling by the end of 2004 to its lowest level since the late 1950s." See Monty G. Marshall and Ted Robert Gurr, *Peace and Conflict 2005*, p. 11. < http://www.cidcm.umd.edu/inscr/pc05print.pdf>
26. Francis Fukuyama, "The End of History?" *National Interest* 16 (Summer 1989), p. 4.
27. Derek Reveron, *Promoting Democracy in the Post-Soviet Region* (Lewiston, NJ: Edwin Mellen Press, 2002).
28. Bernard Lewis, "The Roots of Muslim Rage," *The Atlantic* (September 1990), part II. Emphasis is ours.
29. Samuel Huntington, "The Clash of Civilizations," *Foreign Affairs* (Summer 1993), p. 22.
30. This section is partly based on Jeffrey S. Murer, "The Clash Within: Intrapsychially Created Enemies and Their Roles in Ethnonationalist Conflict," in *Violence and Politics: Globalization's Paradox*, edited by Kenton Worcester, Sally Avery Bermanzohn, and Mark Ungar, (New York: Routledge, 2002), pp. 210–212.
31. Samuel Huntington, *The Clash of Civilizations: Remaking World Order* (New York: Touchstone, 1996), p. 21.
32. E. Vulliamy, *Season in Hell: Understanding Bosnia's War* (New York: St. Martin's Press, 1994), p. 157.
33. Tito himself came from a multiethnic family; his father was a Croat and his mother was a Slovene.
34. Huntington, *The Clash of Civilizations*, pp. 45–47.
35. Huntington, *The Clash of Civilizations*, p. 47.
36. According to the *World Christian Encyclopedia* (2001) by David B. Barrett, *et al*, there are "over 33,000 denominations in 238 countries." Every year there is a net increase of around 270 to 300 denominations.
37. Huntington, *The Clash of Civilizations*, p. 37.
38. The Kosovar Albanian Ceku was a Belgrade-educated Yugoslav military officer who fought for Croatia in the early 1990s and then led Kosovar Albanian forces against Serbia in 1999. If Huntington were correct, Ceku should have fought on behalf of Muslim Bosniak forces, not Catholic Croatia. Though not indicted for war crimes, the Serb government requested that the International Criminal Tribunal for the former Yugoslavia investigate Ceku for his role in leading Croat forces against the Krajina Serbs during Operation Storm.
39. Derek S. Reveron, "Yugoslavians in Chicago: An Identity Crisis" (typescript, University of Illinois at Chicago, n.d.).

40. Djurdja Knezevic, "The Enemy Sides of National Ideologies: Croatia at the End of the 19th Century and in the First Half of the 20th Century," in *Pride and Prejudice: Central European University History Department Working Papers* (Budapest: CEU Press, 1995), p. 109.

41. A union of the crowns of Croatia and the Kingdom of Hungary was formed in 1102. Thus began an 800-year connection to Hungary and, subsequently, in 1699 the Hapsburg Empire.

42. Knezevic, "The Enemy Sides of National Ideologies," p. 110.

43. For example, it was Serbian leader Slobodan Milosevic who reignited his political career through nationalism. See Vamik Volkan, *Blood Lines: From Ethnic Pride to Ethnic Terrorism* (New York: Farrar, Straus, and Giroux), pp. 50–80.

44. For a list of those indicted or held accountable for war crimes, see the International Criminal Tribunal for the former Yugoslavia, < http://www.un.org/icty/glance/index.htm>.

45. Anthony D. Smith, *National Identity: Ethnonationalism in Perspective* (Reno, Nevada: University of Nevada Press, 1991); Jeffrey Stevenson Murer, "The Clash Within: Intrapsychically Created Enemies and Their Roles in Ethno-Nationalist Conflict" in *Violence and Politics: Globalization's Paradox*, edited by Kenton Worcester, Sally Avery Bermanzohn, and Mark Ungar (New York: Routledge, 2002), pp. 209–225; Jeffrey Stevenson Murer, "Historical Contingency and the Political Economy of Nations," *International Politics*, Volume 39, Number 2, June 2002, pp. 235–244.

46. Mahmood Mamdani, *Good Muslim, Bad Muslim: America, the Cold War, and the Roots of Terror* (New York: Pantheon Books, 2004), p 17.

47. For example, Karen Armstrong's *Islam;* Peter Bergen's *Holy War, Inc.;* Bernard Lewis's *What Went Wrong?*

48. Juan Cole wrote: "Lewis never defines his terms, and he paints with a brush so broad that he may as well have brought a broom to the easel. He begins by speaking of the 'Islamic world' and of 'what went wrong' with it. He contrasts this culture region to 'the West,' and implies that things went right with the latter. But what does he mean by the 'Islamic world?' He seldom speaks of the Muslims of the Indian subcontinent, who form a very substantial proportion of the whole. Malaysia and Indonesia are never instanced." See "Review of Bernard Lewis' 'What Went Wrong: Western Impact and Middle Easter Response,'" *Global Dialogue*, 4, 4 (2002). Online. Available HTTP: <http://www.juancole.com/essays/revlew.htm>.

49. Olivier Roy, *Globalized Islam: The Search for a New Ummah* (New York: Columbia University Press, 2004), p. 16.

50. Quoted in John Esposito, *The Islamic Threat: Myth or Reality?* (New York: Oxford University Press, 1992), p. 196.

51. Collective identity can be radically altered in the face of dramatic social dislocation, and in the process of restructuring the boundaries of ethnic identity, conflicts can develop. See Murer, "The Clash Within: Intrapsychially Created Enemies and Their Roles in Ethnonationalist Conflict," in *Violence and Politics: Globalization's Paradox*.

52. Paul Collier, "The Market for Civil War," *Foreign Policy* (May/June 2003), p. 40.

53. Brackette F. Williams, "A Class Act: Anthropology and the Race to Nation Across Ethnic Terrain," *Annual Review of Anthropology*, Vol. 18 (1989).

54. Gurr, p. xiv.

55. Bruce Hoffman, "'Holy Terror': The Implications of Terrorism Motivated by a Religious Imperative," *Studies in Conflict and Terrorism* 18, no. 4 (1995); David C. Rapoport, "Fear and Trembling: Terrorism in Three Religious Traditions," *American Political Science Review* 78 (1984); David C. Rapoport, "Sacred Terror: A Contemporary Example from Islam," in Walter Reich, ed., *Origins of Terrorism: Psychologies, Ideologies, Theologies, States of Mind* (Cambridge: Cambridge University Press, 1990).

56. When scholars were asked, "What do you consider the most productive contro-versies/research programs in international relations in recent years?" 25 percent answered clash of civilizations. When asked, "What do you consider the least pro-ductive controversies/research programs in international relations in recent years?" 29 percent responded with clash of civilizations. See Susan Peterson, Michael J. Tierney, and Daniel Maliniak, *Teaching and Research Practices, Views on the Dis-cipline, and Policy Attitudes of International Relations Faculty at U.S. Colleges and Universities*, College of William and Mary, August 2005. Online. Available HTTP: <http://mjtier.people.wm.edu/intlpolitics/teaching/surveyreport.pdf>.

57. Stephen Walt, "Building up new bogeyman," *Foreign Policy* (Spring 1997).

58. Shibley Telhami, "Arab Attitudes Towards Political and Social Issues, Foreign Policy, and the Media," A Public Opinion Poll conducted jointly by Professor Shibley Telhami, Anwar Sadat Chair for Peace and Development at the Univer-sity of Maryland, and Zogby International, October 2005. Online. Available HTTP: <http://www.bsos.umd.edu/sadat/TelhamiArabSurvey-2005.htm>.

59. Vice Admiral Lowell E. Jacoby (USN), Director, Defense Intelligence Agency, "Tes-timony before the Committee on Senate Select Intelligence," February 16, 2005.

60. Mark Juergensmeyer characterizes the conflict as a "cosmic war" in *Terror in the Mind of God: The Global Rise of Religious Violence* (Berkeley, CA: University of Cali-fornia Press, 2003).

61. All of the related statistics are from the National Counterterrorism Center's World-wide Incidents Tracking System (WITS). See also The National Counterterrorism Center, "Chronology of Significant International Terror for 2004." April 27, 2005. <www.tkb.org/NCTC/Home.jsp>. The NCTC Web site is part of the Terrorism Knowledge Base, created by the National Memorial Institute for the Prevention of Terrorism (MIPT) and the Office for Domestic Preparedness, U.S. Department of Homeland Security.

62. The NCTC tracks events in the West Bank and the Gaza Strip separately. From Janu-ary 1, 2004, to March 31, 2005, there were 390 events in the Gaza Strip, resulting in 34 deaths and 154 people wounded; there were 60 events in the West Bank, resulting in 11 deaths and 52 people wounded. For the period between January 1, 2004, and January 1, 2006, MIPT reported 824 incidents in the "Occupied Territories," result-ing in 134 deaths and 437 persons wounded. MIPT does not break out separate sta-tistics for the Gaza Strip and the West Bank. Online. Available HTTP: <http://www. tkb.org/NCTC/RegionReportModule.jsp>.

63. "Emergence of a better Kurdish 4GW frightens Turkey," August 10, 2005. Online. Available HTTP: <www.dozame.org>.

64. The National Counterterrorism Center's Worldwide Incidents Tracking System (WITS). See also The National Counterterrorism Center, "Chronology of Sig-nificant International Terror for 2004." April 27, 2005. Online. Available HTTP: <www.tkb.org/NCTC/Home.jsp>.

65. NCTC counted 699 events as "Islamic Extremist (Sunni)"; 12 as "Islamic Extremist (Shi'a)"; and 61 were "Islamic Extremist (unknown affiliation)." The National Coun-terterrorism Center's Worldwide Incidents Tracking System (WITS). See also The National Counterterrorism Center, "Chronology of Significant International Terror for 2004." April 27, 2005. Online. Available HTTP: <www.tkb.org/NCTC/Home.jsp>.

66. The NCTC recorded 1,906 incidents in South Asia, including India, Kashmir, and Pakistan; the same WITS report recorded 2,026 incidents in the Middle East, includ-ing Israel, the Gaza Strip, the West Bank, and Iraq. The National Counterterror-ism Center's Worldwide Incidents Tracking System (WITS). See also The National Counterterrorism Center, "Chronology of Significant International Terror for 2004." April 27, 2005. Online. Available HTTP: <www.tkb.org/NCTC/Home.jsp>.

67. There were 22,927 victims of terrorism, according to the NCTC, including 15,239 hostages from kidnapping incidents. The total number of victims worldwide from January 1, 2004, to March 31, 2005, numbered 45,629. The National Counterterrorism Center's Worldwide Incidents Tracking System (WITS). See also The National Counterterrorism Center, "Chronology of Significant International Terror for 2004." April 27, 2005. Online. Available HTTP: <www.tkb.org/NCTC/Home.jsp>.
68. The National Counterterrorism Center's Worldwide Incidents Tracking System (WITS).
69. The National Counterterrorism Center's Worldwide Incidents Tracking System (WITS). See also The National Counterterrorism Center, "Chronology of Significant International Terror for 2004." April 27, 2005. Online. Available HTTP: <www.tkb.org/NCTC/Home.jsp>.

I
The Near East

Israel–Palestine

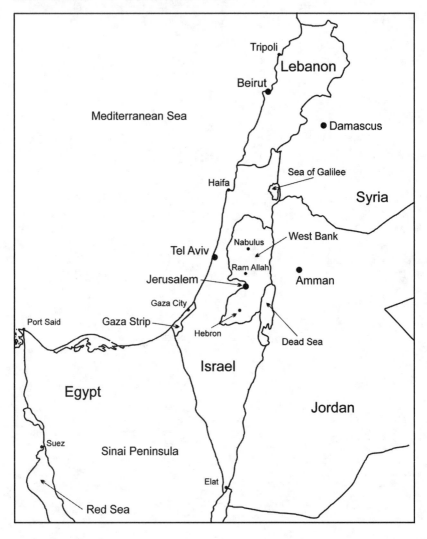

1

ISRAEL–PALESTINE[1]

Stephen Van Evera

NATURE OF THE FLASHPOINT

The Israeli-Palestinian conflict is a boon to al Qaeda. It feeds anti-Americanism in the Arab and Muslim worlds by causing violence between a U.S. ally, Israel, and Palestinian Arabs who are largely Muslim. Arabs and non-Arab Muslims then blame the United States for Israel's belligerent acts. U.S. standing among Arabs and Muslims suffers accordingly. The Israeli-Palestinian conflict also gives al Qaeda a chance to pose in its propaganda as a defender of Arabs and Muslims against a predatory Israeli/American juggernaut.

Al Qaeda exploits the widespread anti-Americanism generated by the Israeli-Palestinian conflict with an enhanced organizational image to win new recruits, to persuade Arab and non-Arab Muslim societies to shelter its leaders and operatives, and to dissuade these societies from cooperating with American efforts against al Qaeda. As a result, al Qaeda is strengthened while U.S. efforts to destroy it are hampered. The terrorist threat to the United States is increased and hardened against American countermeasures.

Therefore, the United States should treat the Israeli-Palestinian conflict as a major menace to U.S. national security and move firmly to end it. Moreover, a strong U.S. push for peace could well succeed, as many pieces needed for a settlement are now in place. The Israeli-Palestinian conflict poses a large threat but it is also ripe for solution.

HISTORICAL CONTEXT[2]

The Israeli-Palestinian conflict stems from the effort of the Jewish people to recover their ancient homeland against the resistance of its modern Arab Palestinian inhabitants. The conflict has religious overtones, as both sides have sometimes mobilized their followers around religious themes. These religious overtones have grown louder in recent years. But at the conflict's root is a clash of secular, national movements that both claim Israel/Palestine as their national homeland. The parties fight less over religious faith than over a land that they have not been able to share.

How Did the Matter Begin?

In ancient times the Jews were a major presence in the territory between the Jordan River and the Mediterranean Sea—today's Israel/Palestine—for more than 1,300 years, from around 1200 B.C.E. until approximately 135 C.E. The Jews lived mainly in the highlands of Israel/Palestine. This is today's West Bank area and is now inhabited mainly by Palestinian Arabs. The Philistines, a non-Jewish nation, settled the coastal plains, where most Israeli Jews now live. Thus, ironically, Israeli Jews now live mainly where the ancient Philistines lived, and the Palestinian Arabs now live mainly where the ancient Jews lived. The Jews are near their ancient homeland but not squarely on it.

Twice the ancient Jews established independent kingdoms. The first endured for nearly 500 years, from about 1000 B.C.E. to 528 B.C.E. The second survived some 83 years, from 140 B.C.E. to 63 B.C.E., when the Roman Empire conquered and annexed it.[3]

Rome then ruled the Jews harshly. In response, the Jews launched vast but disastrous rebellions against Roman rule in 66–73 C.E. (the Great Revolt) and in 132–135 B.C.E. (the Bar Kokhba Rebellion).[4] When Rome smashed the Bar Kokhba revolt it slaughtered nearly half the Jewish population of the area[5] and dispersed most of the rest to the four winds. To erase any trace of the Jews, Rome renamed the rebelling province after the Philistines as "Syria Palestina"—hence, the modern name Palestine.

Modern Origins: Christian Oppression of European Jewry

The dispersed Jews settled heavily in Europe but found little welcome there. Instead, Christian Europeans relentlessly oppressed their Jewish neighbors, especially in the centuries since 1000 C.E. For example, during the Crusades (1096-1291) marauding Christians massacred thousands of Jews in many parts of Europe and the Middle East. Jews

then were expelled en masse from Britain, parts of France (four times), Spain, Portugal, and other places during the period 1290–1497.[6] Later the Jews were hunted and killed by the Spanish Inquisition and were caged in ghettos throughout Europe. They were massacred again in Eastern Europe in 1648 (more than 100,000 Jews were killed), subjected to pogroms in Russia in the nineteenth and early-twentieth centuries, and mass-murdered during the Russian Civil War of 1917–1921 (more than 100,000 Jews were killed), mostly by White Russian forces.[7] The oppression culminated with the Nazi German holocaust of 1941–1945 that killed 5.6 million more. Soviet dictator Josef Stalin was planning another great killing of Jews when he died in 1953. Jews fleeing these horrors were sometimes refused refuge by nearby states. Even after the Holocaust, Polish Christians drove thousands of Jews from Poland.[8]

Europe's Jews tried many stratagems to tame or appease the rage of the Christians. Some made their religious practice less visible to give less offense to Christians. Some supported greater rights for the poor on the theory that class injustice fed anti-Semitism. Some even supported Jewish assimilation into Christianity. Nothing worked. Jews made stellar contributions to European culture, science, commerce, and public life, but they won little gratitude from the Christians. Instead Christian abuse continued without reprieve, excepting only a brief period of Jewish emancipation in the early-to-mid nineteenth century.[9]

The Jews Seek a Haven

This relentless Christian abuse, and the despair it engendered among many Jews doubting that it could ever be subdued, finally drove Leo Pinsker, Theodore Herzl, and others to launch the Zionist movement in the late-nineteenth century.[10] They believed that the Jews could find safety only in a secure Jewish state, and they set about to create one.

These early Zionists were secular Jews who sought to free the Jews from oppression, not to realize Jewish religious or historic claims to the land of Israel.[11] But they used Jewish religious and historical claims to mobilize other Jews to support Zionism. They chose the ancient Jewish home in Israel/Palestine as the site for their Jewish state, mainly to allow the use of religious and historical appeals to mobilize broader Jewish support for their project.

The early Zionists foresaw that Palestinian Arabs would resist Zionism by force if they pressed ahead. But they saw no other solution to their predicament and so continued forward.[12] To them the clash with the Arabs came not as a surprise, but rather as a tragic trial that the Zionist movement could not escape.

Jewish efforts to settle in Israel/Palestine began in 1881, at a time when only 4 percent of the population of Israel/Palestine was Jewish.[13] The movement floundered for two decades, but gained real momentum with the publication of Herzl's *The Jewish State* in 1896 and the 1897 Zionist congress at Basel.[14] Zionism gained still more momentum in 1917 when the British government issued the Balfour Declaration, announcing that Britain would look with favor on the creation of a Jewish home in Palestine. This British endorsement proved important when Britain took control of Israel/Palestine after World War I and allowed further Jewish immigration.

The 1948 War

The Jewish community grew to 30 percent of the population of Israel/Palestine by 1944 and 32 percent by late 1946.[15] During this period the Zionist leadership decided that the time had come to reach for statehood. They launched a violent revolt against British rule, beginning in earnest in 1945.[16] Pressed by this revolt Britain decided to withdraw from Israel/Palestine in 1947 and threw the problem into the lap of the new United Nations. The U.N. devised a partition plan that divided Israel/Palestine (then called Palestine) into two states and one international zone: a Jewish state on 55 percent of the territory, an Arab state on 40 percent, and an international zone including Jerusalem and Bethlehem on the remaining 5 percent.[17] But the partition plan of the territories were so entangled that both states lacked defensible borders. This helped prime the region for war by leaving both sides dissatisfied with their boundaries.

The Zionist leaders formally accepted the partition plan, although privately they did not regard the borders presented as final. They aimed to somehow gain more territory later, in part to gain greater security and in part to acquire more land for settlement.[18] The neighboring Arab states rejected the plan because they did not accept the Jews' right to any state in Israel/Palestine. They also disputed the fairness of a partition that awarded 55 percent of Israel/Palestine's territory to a Jewish community comprising only 32 percent of the population.[19]

Fighting between Jews and Palestinians in Israel/Palestine erupted soon after the U.N. partition plan was approved on November 29, 1947, and continued through the winter and spring. When Israel declared its statehood on May 15, 1948, five nearby Arab states—Egypt, Jordan, Syria, Iraq, and Lebanon—joined the fight and attacked Israel. The Arab states' motives were mixed. For example, Jordan sought only to

annex the Palestinian state, not to destroy Israel, while Egypt sought to destroy Israel and forestall Jordan's move.

Israel won a decisive military victory by early 1949 at the heavy cost of some 6,000 Jewish lives. It conquered large new territories in the war, expanding its domain from 55 percent to 78 percent of Israel/Palestine. It also cleansed Israel of most of its Palestinian Arab population. Some 700,000–750,000 Palestinians fled from Israel during the war, while only 92,000 remained.[20] For decades, Israelis claimed that the Palestinians left voluntarily but it now seems the Israelis expelled most of them, often by violence or threat of violence. The former director of the Israeli Army Archives, historian Aryeh Yitzhaki, estimated that during the 1948 war Israeli forces conducted about 10 large massacres of Palestinians (more than 50 victims killed) and about 100 smaller massacres (one or a handful killed).[21] In one massacre, at Lydda, some 250–400 Palestinians were killed and perhaps another 350 died in a later forced march.[22] This violence was small compared to the violence of other expulsions in modern times, such as those conducted by Hitler and Stalin, but it proved enough to trigger a larger exodus, which remains a sticking point on negotiations of the "right of return." The 700,000–750,000 Palestinians refugees of 1948 plus their descendants now total about 4,000,000 people—the largest refugee population in the world. Their demand to return to Israel or to be compensated for their losses remains a major issue between Israel and the Palestinians.

Who Is Morally Responsible for This Tragedy?

Israelis and Palestinians each hold the other responsible. Yet, these verdicts seem unfair, as both communities did only what most people would do if standing in their shoes. Responsibility lies instead with Western Christian societies, which for centuries treated their Jewish citizens with unprovoked cruelty. Their crimes against the Jews set the whole Mideast calamity in motion.[23] They had no shred of justification for their deeds, which they committed without reason or excuse. Accordingly, they carry prime culpability. And with this culpability comes a duty to help in all possible ways to bring the Israeli-Palestinian conflict to a just and peaceful conclusion.

The Conflict Since 1948

A series of Arab-Israeli interstate wars followed in 1956, 1967, 1969–1970, 1973, and 1982. A violent Palestinian uprising, or intifada, against Israel from 2000–2005, capped these wars. Most important was the 1967 war, which was inadvertently sparked by the reckless belligerence

of Egypt's President Gamal Abdel Nasser. In that war, Israel conquered East Jerusalem and the West Bank from Jordan, the Gaza Strip from Egypt, and the Golan Heights from Syria. This gave Israel control over all of Israel/Palestine and more. It also gave Israel control over a vast and unhappy Palestinian population—a population that Israel could not assimilate or enfranchise without the state losing its Jewish character. Yet this population also could not be easily dominated. Since 1967, all serious proposals for resolving the Israel-Palestinian conflict have been variants of a simple formula: Israel withdraws from nearly all the lands it seized in 1967 in exchange for a full and final peace that includes effective measures to ensure Israel's security. However, from 1967–1988 both sides pursued extreme aims that precluded such a settlement. Israel insisted on retaining much or all of the Palestinian territories it occupied in 1967, and it sent Jewish settlers into these territories to consolidate its control over them. Meanwhile the Palestinian leadership clung to the goal of erasing Israel from the map and expelling most Jews from Israel/Palestine.

Motion toward a withdrawal-for-peace solution began in late 1988 when Palestinian leader Yasser Arafat finally recognized the state of Israel, thereby de facto accepting Israel's existence within its 1949 borders. This led to the Oslo Accords process of 1993–2001, which saw Israel and the Palestinians negotiate a possible settlement based on a land-for-peace trade. At a climactic meeting hosted by U.S. President Bill Clinton in July and August 2000 at Camp David, Maryland, Israeli Prime Minister Ehud Barak's government offered the Palestinians the Gaza Strip and 86–91 percent of the West Bank (76–81 percent up front with more to come later), a small piece of Israeli territory equivalent in size to 1 percent of the West Bank, and part, but not all, of Arab East Jerusalem.[24] The West Bank would be divided into two or three noncontiguous pieces. The Palestinians rejected the plan while failing to make a comprehensive counteroffer.

Both Israel and the Palestinians were more forthcoming on peace terms at a later conference in Taba, Egypt, in January 2001. Before that conference, in December 2000, President Clinton proposed parameters for a peace settlement that envisioned Israeli cession of the Gaza strip, 94–96 percent of the West Bank, and Israeli territory equivalent in size to 1–3 percent of the West Bank, plus all of Arab East Jerusalem, to the Palestinians in exchange for a full and final peace.[25] Both sides accepted the Clinton plan, albeit with reservations, and used its parameters as a basis for the Taba negotiations. These negotiations made progress but had not reached a settlement when Israel ended negotiations to conduct a national election, held on February 7, 2001.

During the interval between the Camp David meeting and the Taba talks, the Palestinians launched a campaign of violence and terror against Israel, starting on September 29, 2000. This Palestinian violence backfired, provoking a popular backlash among Israelis that helped hardliner Ariel Sharon to defeat the more moderate Barak in the February 7, 2001, Israeli election. Sharon then opted not to renew negotiations on taking office as prime minister. In the U.S., the newly inaugurated George W. Bush administration likewise chose not to push for renewing negotiations, which then ended despite Palestinian objections.

The breakdown of the Taba talks was a significant lost opportunity, as the two sides were not far apart when the talks ended. Most experts believe that with more time, and without an Israeli election for prime minister, the two sides could have compromised on the remaining issues and end the conflict.[26]

After Sharon's election, the Palestinian intifada continued for four years until a truce was arranged in early 2005. About 1,000 Israelis and more than 3,000 Palestinians died in the violence. During these years, Sharon refused Palestinian pleas to renew negotiations, arguing that the Palestinians were not serious about making peace and so were unfit negotiating partners. Instead, he pursued a policy of unilaterally withdrawing Israeli control over population centers while retaining substantial Palestinian territory. Most important, he withdrew Israeli forces and settlers from the Gaza strip in the summer of 2005. Sharon seemed poised for further unilateral withdrawals, this time from the West Bank, when he suffered an incapacitating stroke in early January 2006.

Two upheavals in Palestinian politics also occurred during this period. Longtime Palestinian leader Yasser Arafat died in November 2004. His death brought the more moderate Abu Mazen to the fore as president of the Palestinian Authority and as leader of Fatah, historically the strongest Palestinian political party. Abu Mazen opposed violence and seemed willing to make peace with Israel on reasonable terms. On the other hand, the radical Islamist group Hamas won control of the Palestinian parliament in a surprise election victory in late January 2006. In its public statements, Hamas had always rejected a two-state solution to the Israeli-Palestinian conflict, instead seeking Israel's destruction. Hamas also used violence, including many terrorist attacks on Israeli civilians within Israel. The rise of Abu Mazen was a step toward Palestinian moderation, while the election of Hamas was a step back toward extremism. At this writing, it is unclear how the two sides will move forward.

LINKS TO INTERNATIONAL TERRORISM

How does al Qaeda endure against U.S. efforts to destroy it? How does it still find recruits and support? An important reason lies in the poison spread through the Mideast region by the Israeli-Palestinian conflict. Opinion polls show that the conflict is highly salient in the Arab and Islamic world. These surveys also show that U.S. policy toward Israel/Palestine is deeply unpopular among Arabs and Muslims, and that the U.S. itself is also deeply unpopular in these quarters. Further, polls show that the first and second phenomena cause the third: Arabs and Muslims resent the U.S. largely because they care about the Israeli-Palestinian conflict and disapprove of U.S. policies toward that conflict.

A March 2001 poll commissioned by the University of Maryland asked respondents in five Arab states—Egypt, Jordan, Kuwait, the United Arab Emirates (UAE), and Lebanon—to identify the "single most important issue" for themselves, including local political and social issues. In Egypt, a whopping 79 percent named the Palestinian-Israeli conflict; 60 percent said the same in Jordan, Kuwait, the UAE, and Lebanon. An additional 20 percent in these last four countries identified the Palestinian-Israeli conflict as among their top three issues.[27] Similarly, a spring 2002 Zogby International survey of five Arab states—Egypt, the UAE, Kuwait, Lebanon, and Saudi Arabia—found that about two-thirds of respondents viewed the Palestinian issue as "very important" or "the most important" issue facing the Arab world today.[28]

These poll numbers may be somewhat inflated because some respondents may have feared declaring a prime concern about local governance—taking issue with the government can be unsafe in Egypt and elsewhere in the Arab world. Thus, some whose main concern is local malgovernance perhaps stifled that thought and spoke of Israel/Palestine instead. But even discounting heavily for this possibility, these polls indicate broad and intense public concern over the Israel/Palestine question.

There are three reasons: the intifada that flared in the Palestinian territories after September 29, 2000; the new Arab satellite TV, including Al Jazeera, Al Arabiya, and other channels; and the strength of supranational Arab and Muslim identities in the region. The intifada gave the conflict a dramatic and cruel face, ripe for inflaming television coverage. Satellite TV, which appeared only in the 1990s, provided a new medium for piping this cruel face into the homes of Arabs and Muslims far from Israel/Palestine. Their Arab/Muslim identities were aroused by these images, stirring anger even among non-Palestinians.

Arabs widely disapprove of the expansionist policies pursued by Israel under former Prime Minister Ariel Sharon's government (2001–2006) and fault the United States for giving him almost unconditional support. The spring 2002 Zogby survey found minuscule support in five Arab states for U.S. policy toward the Palestinians: only 2–6 percent of respondents in Egypt, Saudi Arabia, Kuwait, and Lebanon voiced approval, and only 10 percent in the UAE. By contrast, 89–94 percent of respondents in Egypt, Saudi Arabia, Kuwait, and Lebanon and 83 percent in the UAE voiced disapproval of U.S. policy toward the Palestinians. In the world of opinion surveys such huge majorities are equivalent to unanimity. A similar picture emerged in the three non-Arab Muslim states that Zogby surveyed. Approval of U.S. policy stood at 10 percent in Pakistan, 5 percent in Indonesia, and 3 percent in Iran; disapproval registered at 79 percent, 75 percent, and 95 percent, respectively.[29] This highlights that the Israeli-Palestinian conflict is not merely an Arab concern but also animates the wider Islamic world.

Arab/Islamic hostility toward American policy translates into enmity for the U.S. as a whole. A March 2004 Pew Research Center poll of four Muslim countries found unfavorable views of the U.S. outnumbering favorable views by 61 to 21 percent in Pakistan, 63 percent to 30 percent in Turkey, 68 percent to 27 percent in Morocco, and a remarkable 93 percent to 5 percent in Jordan.[30] A Zogby International study taken three months later found even deeper hostility toward the United States in six Arab states. Those with unfavorable views of the United States outnumbered those with favorable views by 69 percent to 20 percent in Lebanon, 73 percent to 14 percent in the UAE, 88 percent to 11 percent in Morocco, 78 percent to 15 percent in Jordan, 94 percent to 4 percent in Saudi Arabia, and 98 percent to 2 percent in Egypt.[31] The hostility these polls reveal is especially ominous as it extends even to traditional U.S. allies like Egypt, Jordan, Saudi Arabia, Turkey, and Pakistan.

Finally, Arabs and Muslims explain their enmity toward the United States as stemming largely from U.S. policies toward the Israeli-Palestinian conflict. Despite President Bush's interpretation, they do not hate the United States for its freedoms, but rather for its policies. In a May 2004 Zogby poll, 76 percent in Jordan, 78 percent in the UAE, 79 percent in Lebanon, 81 percent in Saudi Arabia, 84 percent in Morocco, and 95 percent in Egypt declared that American policy toward the Arab-Israeli dispute was "quite important" or "extremely important" in shaping their attitude toward the United States.[32] Similar majorities indicated that their views of the United States are shaped more by American policy than American values, by majorities ranging from 76:16 in Jordan up to 90:1 in Egypt.[33]

Anti-Americanism in the Arab/Islamic world matters because it fosters a friendly environment where al Qaeda can flourish, raising new recruits and money while evading the American dragnet. An Arab/Muslim public friendly to the U.S. would act as its eyes and ears, helping it glean the intelligence that is vital to successful counterterror. But a population hostile to the United States sits on its hands, letting the terrorists hide in its midst while the United States searches blindly. Osama bin Laden, Ayman al-Zawahiri, and other al Qaeda leaders run free in northwest Pakistan today because the people of that region are militantly anti-America and pro-al Qaeda. These dangerous fish could swim no more in Mao's metaphorical sea if the public willed otherwise—as it would if it viewed the United States with more approval.

The Israeli-Palestinian conflict is not the sole cause of Arab/Muslim popular hostility toward the United States. The war in Iraq and anti-American propaganda from al Qaeda and other Islamist movements that raise other grievances against the United States also stoke the fire. Winding down the Iraqi occupation would help, as might stronger public diplomacy to counter al Qaeda's propaganda. But U.S.-Mideast relations will not heal fully while irritation from the Israeli-Palestinian conflict persists. In the meantime, al Qaeda will benefit accordingly.

Al Qaeda's leaders will not be weaned from their campaign of terror by an Israeli-Palestinian peace settlement. Terror is their way of life, their reason for being. They cannot be conciliated; they must be destroyed. To achieve this destruction, al Qaeda's support base must be stripped away, and that can only come by engineering a large improvement in Arab/Muslim public attitudes toward the United States. This will leave the extremists friendless and exposed, soon to face capture or death. The Israeli-Palestinian conflict should be ended not to appease their anger but to bring their demise.

Links to the Global War on Terrorism

The Israeli-Palestinian conflict fuels friction between the United States and other governments as well as local populations. Often the United States needs the help of these governments against al Qaeda and other foes, and U.S. national security suffers accordingly. America's NATO allies are essential to defeating al Qaeda, but disputes over the Israeli-Palestinian conflict have frayed U.S. relations with these allies. Disagreements stemming from Arab-Israeli strife have also disrupted important U.S.-Syrian cooperation against al Qaeda. For a time after the 9/11 attacks, Syria gave the United States valuable assistance against al Qaeda, including intelligence information that helped thwart an al

Qaeda attack on the U.S. Fifth Fleet headquarters in Bahrain and an attack on an American target in Ottawa. Many American lives were perhaps saved. By 2002, Syria was also an important source of intelligence on al Qaeda and an important ally against it.[34] Syria's secular regime has long been targeted by Islamist radicals, including al Qaeda, so the regime has worked to develop intelligence against these movements, often surpassing U.S. intelligence. It has hundreds of files on al Qaeda and has penetrated al Qaeda cells throughout the Middle East and Europe.[35] But Syrian cooperation later ended, foundering on frictions with the U.S. that stem largely from Syria's conflict with Israel, which is aggravated in turn by the Israeli-Palestinian conflict.

So the bad news is that the Israeli-Palestinian conflict is damaging U.S. national security. The good news is that many pieces are now in place for a peace settlement. Six components in particular bear mention.

First, years of negotiation have made clear to both sides the peace terms that each can and cannot accept. If they want peace they know what its parameters must be. Long months of fumbling in the dark for a mutually acceptable formula will not be necessary. That formula is well known.

Next, most Israelis and Palestinians now agree on the same peace terms. Specifically, polls taken in December 2004 and January 2005 show that 54 percent of Palestinians and 64 percent of Israelis endorse the parameters for settlement proposed by President Clinton in December 2000.[36] Despite the public agreeing on terms, their leaders cannot do likewise.

The radical Hamas group did take control of the Palestinian parliament after winning free and fair elections in early 2006. Hamas has long opposed a compromise peace settlement with Israel. However, its opposition to compromise puts it at odds with the pro-compromise Palestinian majority. Many of those who voted for Hamas did so only to protest corruption in the ruling Fatah party. They still dislike Hamas's rejection of peace with Israel. In the end, Hamas will have to align itself with the moderate Palestinian majority on policy toward Israel or be swept from power in the next election.

Third, the Palestinian intifada that began in September 2000 has made major Arab states more predisposed to foster peace. They fear that passions stirred by watching the intifada could cause their citizens to mobilize in ways that threaten their regimes. Crowds chanting "down with Israel" at noon could switch to "down with Mubarak" or "down with Abdullah" 10 minutes later. A truce dampened the intifada in early 2005, but if peace is not agreed on the intifada will likely reignite, so these regimes now favor peace. Their new mood was signaled by the Abdullah peace plan, offered by the Arab League at its March 2002 summit and relaunched at its March 2005 summit, which envisions a settlement that involves acceptance by the Arabs of Israel's 1967 borders, no demand for large return of the 1948 refugees to Israel, and full integration of Israel into the larger Arab world.[37] If the Palestinians and Israelis want to make peace they will now find many other Arabs willing to help it happen.

Fourth, Israelis are increasingly worried that Israel will lose its Jewish character unless it makes a land-for-peace trade. This worry extends even to some elements of the Israeli political right, who see the West Bank as Israeli territory but now accept that demographic realities require Israeli withdrawal.

Next, Israel no longer faces a credible threat of conventional attack from its east. Israeli hardliners have long claimed that a land-for-peace trade was unwise because Israel needed to hold the West Bank as a buffer against possible invasion from the east by Iraq and Syria. But over the past 20 years, the threat of eastern invasion has largely disappeared as the economies of Syria and Iraq have stagnated, their Soviet sponsor and arms supplier has collapsed, Israel developed its nuclear arsenal, and the United States has smashed Saddam's regime and put Iraq under occupation. The size of the eastern threat was always debatable, but Saddam's demise makes clear that it exists no more, as Syria poses no serious threat by itself. Hence, Israel can now be more forthcoming about trading land for peace.

Finally, Israel now faces a dangerous new threat from al Qaeda that gives it more interest in reaching peace with the Palestinians. Before 2001, al Qaeda focused its violence on the United States while leaving Israel unmolested. But since 9/11, al Qaeda has targeted Israel as well, as dramatized by al Qaeda's 2002 attack on Israelis at Mombassa, Kenya. Therefore, the Israeli-Palestinian conflict threatens Israeli security (along with U.S. security) by helping al Qaeda to find recruits and sanctuary, and by hampering U.S. efforts against al Qaeda. This gives Israel a cogent new reason to seek peace with the Palestinians.

So if the United States pushes for peace, it pushes on an open door. But peace is not possible on any terms. The range acceptable to both sides is very narrow. The terms come from four major peace plans that have been widely discussed in recent years: the Clinton parameters of December 2000, the Abdullah Plan of March 2002, the Geneva Accord of December 2003, and the Ayalon-Nusseibeh (or "People's Voice") initiative, also of December 2003. These proposals distill to four key elements:

1. Israel would withdraw from all the territories it occupied in the 1967 war, except for minor border adjustments involving equivalent gains and losses for both sides, in exchange for a full and final peace.
2. Control of the city of Jerusalem would be shared along ethnic lines. Control of its holy places, including the Temple Mount/Noble Sanctuary area, would also be shared.
3. The West Bank and Gaza would form a Palestinian state that accepted sharp limits on its military forces in order to ensure Israel's security.
4. The Palestinians would not insist on a large return of Palestinian refugees to Israel, instead seeing their right of return recognized mainly by generous compensation to the refugees.

Neither side will accept terms outside these parameters. Israel will never agree to a large return of refugees to Israel; Palestinian insistence on a large return would torpedo peace. And the Palestinians will accept no deal that they cannot credibly claim involves full Israeli withdrawal from the occupied territories. Egypt's Anwar Sadat and Jordan's King Hussein both gained full Israeli withdrawal from Egyptian and Jordanian territory in exchange for full peace in their earlier peace deals with Israel. Today's Palestinian leaders need to claim that they won the same terms to quiet their own radicals, who will otherwise accuse them of surrendering the national cause by accepting second-best treatment: "Not even what Sadat got! Not even what Hussein got!" Accordingly, Israel will torpedo peace if it offers less than full withdrawal—as it did at the failed talks at Camp David II in the summer of 2000, where it unwisely insisted on retaining 9 percent of the West Bank and parts of Palestinian East Jerusalem.[38]

PROGRESS AND PROSPECTS

What U.S. action does peace require? The two sides cannot make peace on their own; the U.S. must lead them to it. Specifically, Washington must frame its own final-status peace plan and use carrots and sticks to persuade both sides to agree. Enough with Oslo-style, open-ended peace plans: The two sides will move forward more willingly if they know their destination. And enough with passive mediation: Strong U.S. persuasion is necessary. When either side needs incentives to move it forward, inducements—both positive and negative—should be starkly framed and firmly applied.

The U.S. final-status plan should involve a full Israeli withdrawal in exchange for full and final peace, in line with the four previous peace plans. The United States should use the first phase of the 2003 Quartet Roadmap as its work plan to start the parties toward its final-status agreement; then it should omit the Roadmap's second phase (which would create a Palestinian state with provisional borders) and move directly to its third phase: final-status negotiations. The United States should closely oversee forward progress on the Roadmap, framing a schedule for the fulfillment of both sides' Roadmap obligations and enforcing compliance with that timeline.

The Palestinian leadership needs American persuasion in three areas. First, the leadership of Hamas must declare that it accepts Israel's existence and favors a two-state solution to the conflict. Its stated aim of destroying Israel must go. Second, the whole Palestinian political elite—of both Hamas and Fatah—must accept the duty to disarm their own party's militias and other terrorist groups that operate in the Palestinian territories, to establish firm government control of all instruments of force, and to end violence against Israel. And third, the Palestinian leadership must accept that any peace settlement will recognize the Palestinian right of return by awarding compensation for losses, not by physical return to Israel. Some Palestinians choke on the notion that Palestinians who were driven from Israel in 1948 cannot return there. Yet the necessities of peacemaking require that the Palestinians accept this. Fatah may quickly accept these positions, but Hamas will likely require greater pressure. Washington should apply whatever weight is needed.

Israel's government also needs strong American persuasion. Most Israeli leaders see the need for some further Israeli pullbacks from the Palestinian territories. But the near-total Israeli pullback that peace requires will meet fierce opposition from the Israeli settler movement and others on the Israeli far right. Without strong U.S. pressure these expansionist elements in Israel will likely persuade the Israeli government to keep enough occupied territory to preclude a peace settlement.[39]

Accordingly, the United States must actively press the Israeli government to offer near-total withdrawal in exchange for peace. Carrots should include the prospect of large economic aid to cover the cost of adjusting Israeli defenses to new borders and the prospect of a full formal alliance with the United States, to even include NATO membership, if Arab-Israeli peace is achieved. As a stick, the United States should explain that no U.S. government can remain allied to another government that pursues policies that injure U.S. national security. The United States should elaborate that an Israeli policy of retaining large chunks of the West Bank precludes an Israeli-Palestinian peace settlement; that the Israeli-Palestinian conflict injures U.S. national security;

that any Israeli policy of expansion therefore injures U.S. national security; and that the U.S. therefore insists, as a firm condition for continuing the U.S.-Israel strategic relationship, that Israel discard any policy of expansion. Instead, Israel must agree to make peace within the terms of the four peace plans mentioned above.

The United States should also insist that Israel take the first steps toward such a peace. Most importantly, Israel must halt settlement expansion and dismantle newer settlement outposts, in line with its obligations under the 2003 Quartet Roadmap. Such a U.S. policy, pursued with vigor, will likely bring the Palestinians and Israelis to a settlement. The public on both sides already favor moderate policies that align with peace, and they will not support leaders whose policies threaten rupture with the United States. Hence, leaders on both sides will find themselves impelled toward peace if the United States forcefully applies its carrots and sticks to get them there.

Of course, the current climate in Washington precludes a policy of active U.S. pressure on both sides. Instead, the Bush team now plans only coercion of Hamas plus some passive mediation unlinked to a strong U.S. policy. This will not be nearly enough to bring peace. Even the current ceasefire will likely collapse unless it is reinforced by strong U.S. pressure for peace aimed at all parties. The present Mideast calm is refreshing, but without a far more forceful U.S. policy it is only the calm before another storm.

Americans who care about U.S. national security should therefore work to change the Washington climate. U.S. security requires al Qaeda's defeat, and that demands a Palestinian-Israeli peace. The U.S. government is derelict if it does not pursue such a settlement—soon and with full force.

NOTES

1. Parts of this chapter have appeared as "Vital Interest: Winning the War on Terror Requires a Mideast Peace Settlement," *The American Conservative*, Vol. 4, No. 5 (14 March 2005): pp. 7–10; and as *Why U.S. National Security Requires Mideast Peace* (MIT Center for International Studies, Audit 05-5, May 2005). Online. Available HTTP: <web.mit.edu/cis/pdf/Audit_5_05_VanEvera.pdf>.
2. Valuable surveys of the Israeli-Palestinian conflict include Benny Morris, *Righteous Victims: A History of the Zionist-Arab Conflict, 1881–2001* (NY: Vintage, 2001); Avi Shlaim, *The Iron Wall: Israel and the Arab World* (NY: W. W. Norton, 2000); Mark Tessler, *A History of the Israeli-Palestinian Conflict* (Bloomington, IN: Indiana University Press, 1994); and Charles D. Smith, *Palestine and the Arab-Israeli Conflict: A History with Documents*, 5th ed. (New York: St. Martin's, 2004).
3. Smith, *Palestine and the Arab-Israeli Conflict*, pp. 1–3.
4. On this rebellion see Yehoshafat Harkabi, *The Bar Kokhba Syndrome: Risk and Realism in International Politics* (Chappaqua, NY: Rossel, 1983).

5. Harkabi, *Bar Kokhba*, p. 46.

6. Martin Gilbert, *Jewish History Atlas* (London: Weidenfeld and Nicolson, 1973), pp. 43–44.

7. Gilbert, *Jewish History Atlas*, pp. 53, 82.

8. Histories of anti-Semitism include James Carroll, *Constantine's Sword: The Church and the Jews: A History* (Houghton Mifflin, 2001); Marvin Perry and Frederick Schweitzer, *Anti-Semitism: Myth and Hate from Antiquity to the Present* (NY: Palgrave, 2002); Edward H. Flannery, *The Anguish of the Jews: Twenty-Three Centuries of Antisemitism*, rev. ed. (New York: Paulist Press, 1999); and Israel Pocket Library, *Anti-Semitism* (Jerusalem: Keter, 1974).

9. In the Arab and Muslim world, Jews were also oppressed but less severely. Smith, *Palestine and the Arab-Israeli Conflict*, pp. 8, 10–11.

10. A good account is Walter Laqueur, *A History of Zionism* (New York: Schocken, 2003), pp. 40–135.

11. Laqueur, *History of Zionism*, pp. 40–96, *passim*; and Smith, *Palestine and the Arab-Israeli Conflict*, p. 34.

12. Vladimir Jabotinsky, leader of the Revisionist Zionist movement, wrote in 1923 that "Every indigenous people will resist alien settlers as long as they see any hope of ridding themselves of the danger of foreign settlement. This is how the Arabs will behave and will go on behaving so long as they possess a gleam of hope that they can prevent 'Palestine' from becoming the Land of Israel." Shlaim, *Iron Wall*, p. 13. Ben Gurion thought in similar terms. See ibid., pp. 17–19.

13. Specifically, the population of Israel/Palestine then comprised some 24,000 Jews and 565,000 Arabs, of whom about 90 percent were Muslim, with Christians comprising most of the rest. Tessler, *A History of the Israeli-Palestinian Conflict*, pp. 43, 124.

14. On Herzl see Laqueur, *History of Zionism*, pp. 84–135.

15. Tessler, *History of the Israeli-Palestinian Conflict*, p. 266; and Smith, *Palestine and the Arab-Israeli Conflict*, p. 185.

16. Smith, *Palestine and the Arab-Israeli Conflict*, pp. 170–71, 180; Tessler, *A History of the Israeli-Palestinian Conflict*, p. 256.

17. Morris, *Righteous Victims*, p. 186.

18. Shlaim, *Iron Wall*, pp. 28–29, speaking of Ben Gurion. See also ibid, p. 21, quoting Ben Gurion.

19. Morris, *Righteous Victims*, p. 186.

20. Shlaim, *Iron Wall*, p. 54.

21. Guy Erlich, "Zionist Massacres in 1948: New Evidence," *Ha'ir*, May 6, 1992. Online Available HTTP: <www.deiryassin.org/op0010.html>. Yitzhaki said: "In almost every conquered [Arab] village in the War of Independence, acts were committed [by Israeli forces] which are defined as war crimes, such as indiscriminate killings, massacres, and rapes." Ibid. Israeli military historian Uri Milstein likewise said that in the 1947–48 War, "Each battle ended with a massacre" and "the concept of taking prisoners was unknown" to both Israelis and Palestinians. Ibid.

22. Norman G. Finkelstein, *Image and Reality of the Israel-Palestine Conflict* (London: Verso, 1995), p. 55. Other valuable studies of the 1948 expulsion include Benny Morris, "Revisiting the Palestinian Exodus of 1948," in Eugene L. Rogan and Avi Shlaim, eds., *The War for Palestine: Rewriting the History of 1948* (Cambridge, UK: Cambridge University Press, 2001), pp. 37–59; and Morris, *Birth of the Palestinian Refugee Problem Revisited*.

23. Some Palestinians refer to the creation of Israel and the ensuing chaos as "al nakba" or the cataclysm. See http://www.alnakba.org.

24. The best account of events at Camp David II and Taba is Jeremy Pressman, "Visions in Collision: What Happened at Camp David and Taba?" *International Security*, Vol. 28, No. 2 (Fall 2003), pp. 5–43. For Israel's offer at Camp David II see ibid., p. 16–18. The 91 percent figure uses Israel's method for measuring the West Bank, the 86 percent measure uses the Palestinian method. Ibid., p. 17. Israel proposed to delay the transfer of another 10 percent of the West Bank for 6 to 21 years, so by Israeli accounting the Palestinian state offered at Camp David II would have initially comprised only 81 percent of the West Bank; by Palestinian accounting the Palestinian state would have initially comprised only 76 percent. Ibid, pp. 17-18.

25. Pressman, "Visions in Collision," p. 21.

26. Pressman, "Visions in Collision," p. 22.

27. Shibley Telhami, *The Stakes: America and the Middle East* (Boulder, CO: Westview, 2002), p. 98.

28. John Zogby, "Why Do They Hate Us?" *The Link,* Vol. 36, No. 4 (October-November 2003), p. 3–13. Online. Available HTTP: <www.ameu.org/uploads/vol36_issue4_2003.pdf>. Specifically, respondents who considered the Palestinian issue "the most" or "a very important" issue facing the Arab world were 80 percent in Egypt, 64 percent in Saudi Arabia, 76 percent in Kuwait, 78 percent in Lebanon, and 64 percent in the UAE. Ibid.

29. Zogby, "Why Do They Hate Us?" p. 8.

30. *A Year After Iraq War: Mistrust of America in Europe Ever Higher, Muslim Anger Persists* (Pew Research Center for the People and the Press, March 16, 2004). Online. Available HTTP: <www.people-press.org/reports>.

31. Zogby International, *Impressions of America 2004: How Arabs View America: How Arabs Learn About America* Zogby International. Online. Available HTTP: <www.aaiusa.org/pdf/Impressions_of_America04.pdf>, p. 3, table 1.

32. *Arab Attitudes Towards Political and Social Issues, Foreign Policy, and the Media* (Anwar Sadat Chair for Peace and Development and Zogby International, May 2004). Online. Available HTTP: <www.bsos.umd.edu/SADAT/>, pp. 8–9.

33. *Arab Attitudes Towards Political and Social Issues,* p. 8. Respondents to the June 2004 Zogby poll likewise said that U.S. policy was important in shaping their attitude toward the United States, by important/unimportant percentage ratios of 89:7 in Morocco, 81:3 in Saudi Arabia, 71:20 in Jordan, 89:5 in Lebanon, and 72:16 in the UAE. Zogby International, *Impressions of America 2004*, p. 4, table 2b.

34. Seymour Hersh, "The Syrian Bet," *The New Yorker*, July 28, 2003; and William James Martin, "Clean Break with the Road Map," *Counterpunch*, February 14–15, 2004, pp. 12-14.

35. Hersh, "Syrian Bet."

36. *In the Post-Arafat Era, Palestinians and Israelis Are More Willing to Compromise: For the First Time Majority Support for Clinton's Permanent Status Settlement Package.* Palestinian Center for Policy and Survey Research. Online. Available HTTP: <www.pcpsr.org/welcome.html>.; and reported in Akiva Eldar, "Poll: Majority of Palestinians Now Support Two-State Solution," Haaretz, January 18, 2005. Confirming a continuing trend toward moderation on peace terms among Palestinians is Khalil Shikaki, "Willing to Compromise: Palestinian Public Opinion and the Peace Process," *United States Institute of Peace Special Report* No. 158, January 2006. Online. Available HTTP: <www.usip.org/pubs/specialreports/sr158.html>, pp. 9–11.

37. Suleiman al-Khalidi, "Arab Leaders Relaunch Peace Offer," Washingtonpost.com, March 23, 2005.

38. Pressman, "Visions in Collision," pp. 16, 18. This 9 percent figure uses Israel's method for measuring the West Bank. The Palestinian method for measuring indicates that Israel insisted on retaining 14 percent. Ibid., p. 17.

39. Some observers think that without U.S. pressure, Israel may even be willing to pull back as far as the security barrier that Israel is now building to prevent Palestinian terrorists from entering Israel. Some 92 percent of the West Bank is outside the security barrier, so such a move would leave 92 percent of the West Bank for the Palestinians. However, this would still involve annexing to Israel 8 percent of the West Bank and all of Palestinian East Jerusalem, including the Muslim holy places. Some 195,000 Palestinian East Jerusalemites and 10,000 Palestinian West Bankers would be unwillingly annexed as well. Steven Erlanger, "Israel, on Its Own, Reshaping West Bank Borders," *New York Times*, April 19, 2005. No Palestinian leader would accept such terms.

Iraq

2

IRAQ

James S. Robbins

NATURE OF THE FLASHPOINT

Iraq has been at the center of U.S. national security policy since the end of the Cold War. No other single country has consumed more American attention, wealth, and political capital since 1990. Furthermore, given the magnitude of the U.S. investment in Iraq, coupled with its strategic location, the country is likely to remain one of the most significant U.S. policy interests for years to come.

Iraq's location at the center of the energy-producing Near East is one factor making it essential to U.S. interests. Iraq has the world's fourth greatest proven oil reserves, and borders on three other countries in the top five (Saudi Arabia, Iran, and Kuwait). As long as the global economy remains dependent on fossil fuels, Iraq and the Near East generally will be vital for the United States.

Iraq is also important to the United States because it has become a test bed for the spread of democracy in the region. The Near East, with the exception of Israel, has not been fruitful ground for democratic development. Twentieth-century democratic experiments in many Middle Eastern countries (including Iraq in the period 1932–1958) fell victim to either traditionalist or socialist forms of authoritarianism. Or institutional democracy gave way to civil war, as in the case of Lebanon. Political development in the region is currently being threatened by several strains of radicalized political Islam, which is generally hostile to Western conceptions of democracy and claims to seek the establishment of a transnational Caliphate based on Sharia law. The United States has committed itself to seeing that the democratic experiment succeeds in Iraq and hopes that other countries in the region may follow suit. This critical ideological conflict will also keep Iraq at the center of American policy for many years; the failure to support democracy in Iraq would be a lost opportunity of historical proportions.

Iraq is also related to several regional and global issues of concern to the United States, such as preventing the proliferation of advanced weapons such as weapons of mass destruction (WMDs) and long-range missiles; the protection of U.S. allies in the region, particularly Israel; and the desire to check the power of states such as Iran that might seek regional hegemony and thus obtain disproportionate influence over the global petroleum-dependent economy. A stable, prosperous, and democratic Iraq would be an important U.S. ally in the region for all of these reasons. Finally, the aftermath of the 2003 Iraq War unleashed a flood of terrorism in the region, and several scandals associated with the Coalition military intervention have provided new propaganda to fuel anti-Americanism. While Iraq's role as a state sponsor of terrorism was not the strongest argument for war in 2003, it appears that terrorism is now the strongest reason why the United States and its allies must succeed in its reconstruction efforts.

HISTORICAL CONTEXT: THE U.S. AND IRAQ

U.S. policy toward Iraq has evolved significantly in the past several decades, and can be broken down into four distinct phases: dual containment, conflict and containment, regime change, and democratization and insurgency.

Dual Containment

The roots of the conflict between the United States and Iraq date to two important events in 1979: the Iranian revolution and Saddam Hussein's power consolidation. The former event fomented an international crisis based on fear of the spread of militant Islam as openly espoused by Iran's Ayatollah Khomeini. Saddam's consolidation of power gave him the means to exploit the chaos in Iran to extend his international power and influence by force. Furthermore, because of regional and international concerns about Khomeini's revolution, Saddam could count on little if any serious international opposition to his aggressive actions. The two events merged when Iraq invaded Iran on September 22, 1980.

The principle issues at stake during the Iran-Iraq War were control over the Shatt al Arab waterway (an important and disputed oil shipment route on the border between the two countries) and Iraq's territorial claims on the Iranian province of Khuzestan. Saddam expected a quick victory in a limited war against a weakened opponent. Instead, the invasion gave the Iranian revolutionary government a cause around which to rally the nation, and initial Iraqi gains were met with fierce and effective counterattacks. The result was a grueling military stalemate that lasted eight years and resulted in millions of casualties.[1]

The United States did not have an interest in seeing either party emerge victorious. The U.S. had broken relations with Iraq after the 1967 Six-Day War with Israel, and had recently seen the overthrow of its chief ally in the region, Shah Mohammad Reza Pahlavi of Iran. That led to the humiliating hostage crisis with Khomeini's government. In September 1980, the United States gave support to the UN Security Council Resolution 479 calling for a peaceful resolution of the dispute. However, Iranian battlefield successes in 1982 spurred the United States to begin supplying Baghdad with dual-use assistance to help prop up Iraqi forces on the battlefield. This was seen as a lesser-of-two-evils approach; the alternative was allowing Iran to win the war and potentially spread its radical Islamist revolution throughout the region. The expression "dual containment" was devised to describe a situation in which the United States sought to keep a balance of power between the combatants, and thus contain both Iraq's Baathist totalitarianism and Khomeini's Shiite fundamentalism. According to a study by the U.S. Arms Control and Disarmament Agency (ACDA) the United States provided $24 billion in supplies to Iraq between 1981 and 1985.[2] Other countries in the region, particularly Saudi Arabia and Kuwait, fearing Iranian expansionism, also loaned Baghdad billions of dollars.

Iran and Iraq expanded their conflict to the Arabian Gulf by attacking each other's oil tankers and, in the case of Iran, tankers from countries supporting Iraq. The United States intervened in the so-called "Tanker War" in 1987 with Operation Earnest Will, in which Kuwaiti oil tankers were reflagged as American vessels and escorted through the Arabian Gulf to protect them from attacks by Iranian or Iraqi forces. In the related Operation Prime Chance (1987–1989), U.S. forces took direct action primarily against Iranian gunboats and also against oil platforms being used to harass tankers and U.S. warships. During this period, an Iraqi warplane accidentally attacked the frigate USS Stark, killing 37 members of its crew and wounding 21. Though at the time it was one of the worst accidents of its kind in peacetime U.S. naval history, a crisis with Iraq was averted because Iran was considered the principal threat.

The Iran-Iraq war lasted until August 20, 1988, when a ceasefire was declared. Both countries suffered casualties estimated in the millions.[3] But from the point of view of the United States and the front-line regional states, the conflict had successfully blunted Iran's revolutionary fervor. However, the war had allowed Saddam Hussein to further militarize Iraq, and at the conflict's end, his country had, on paper, the fourth largest army in the world.

Conflict and Containment

The next phase of U.S.-Iraqi relations began in the summer of 1990. On August 2, Iraqi forces invaded the Emirate of Kuwait and quickly overwhelmed the country's small defensive force. Iraq had never recognized Kuwaiti sovereignty, and instead accepted the 1913 Anglo-Ottoman Convention, which defined Kuwait as an autonomous region inside Iraq—the "nineteenth province," according to Baghdad.[4] Kuwait had been an important supporter of Iraq during the Iran-Iraq War, and had loaned Baghdad $14 billion, a debt for which Iraq asked to be forgiven for successfully defending the Arabian Peninsula from Iranian expansionism. In July 1990, Kuwait refused to cancel the debt and Iraq accused the Emirate of hiking oil production to drive down prices and make it even more difficult for Iraq to repay its loans.[5] Iraq and Kuwait also had a long-standing border dispute (ironic, since Iraq did not recognize Kuwait's sovereignty), which was exacerbated when Iraq accused the Kuwaitis of "slant drilling" into their oil reserves.

As with the war with Iran, Saddam sought to use military power to expand his rule and influence, and to settle his outstanding territorial and financial issues with Kuwait. The initial stage of the invasion was a complete success, and Kuwait City was quickly occupied. However, the United States feared that this move was only the first step in a projected takeover of the entire peninsula, which was seen as an unacceptable consolidation of power in this sensitive region.[6]

The invasion prompted intervention by the United States and 30 Coalition countries under Operations Desert Shield and Desert Storm. The intervention was justified under United Nations Security Council Resolutions 660 (condemning the invasion of Kuwait) and 678 (authorizing UN Member States "to use all necessary means to uphold and implement resolution 660 and all subsequent relevant resolutions and to restore international peace and security in the area"). These events had far-reaching consequences. UNSCR 660 and 678 and other similar resolutions formed the legal basis not only for the expulsion of Iraq from Kuwait in 1991, but for all subsequent actions and resolutions passed by the Security Council with regard to Iraq over the next 13 years. The Coalition deployment to Saudi Arabia was also significant in that six years later, Osama bin Laden cited the permanent presence of American forces in "Muslim holy lands" that began in 1990 as being the impetus behind al Qaeda's declaration of war on the United States.[7]

In the brief war that followed—called the "Mother of All Battles" by Saddam's regime—Iraqi forces were defeated decisively. Kuwait was liberated after 100 hours of ground combat on February 24–27, 1991.[8] Given its limited mandate, the Coalition did not attempt to drive on to Baghdad in order to overthrow Saddam's regime, but rather called for a ceasefire, which left a substantial portion of the Iraqi defense forces intact. The United States encouraged groups to take action against the regime; some organized resistance, particularly in the Shia areas in southern Iraq and the Kurdish area in the north. However, when it was clear that international assistance was not forthcoming to aid these rebellions, they were quickly and brutally put down by Saddam's security forces. (This is explored later by Kerrie Urosevich in Chapter 3.)

While Saddam's brutal human rights record was abhorred, the main international concern was based on Iraq's ambitions to be a regional power. As part of the ceasefire agreement, the international community sought to limit future threats from Saddam's regime. Under UNSCR 687 (April 1991), Iraq was instructed to "unconditionally accept" the destruction, removal, or rendering harmless "under international supervision" of all "chemical and biological weapons and all stocks of agents and all related subsystems and components and all research, development, support, and manufacturing facilities." It was also required to "unconditionally agree not to acquire or develop nuclear weapons or nuclear-weapons-usable material" or any research, development, or manufacturing facilities, and "unconditionally accept" the destruction, removal, or rendering harmless "under international supervision" of all "ballistic missiles with a range greater than 150 km and related major parts and repair and production facilities."[9] Furthermore, Iraq was instructed not to "use, develop, construct, or acquire" any weapons of mass destruction. The United Nations Special Commission (UNSCOM) was created to inspect and verify that Iraq's chemical and biological weapons programs were fully dismantled, and the International Atomic Energy Agency (IAEA) was charged with verifying the elimination of Iraq's nuclear weapons program. Iraq was also instructed not to "commit or support terrorism, or allow terrorist organizations to operate in Iraq." In 1991 and 1992, "no-fly zones" were established in northern and southern Iraq, respectively. These were intended to prevent the regime from using air assets against Kurds and Shi'ites. This had the effect of extending the war against Iraq throughout the 1990s, resulting in frequent air strikes from the more than 200,000 missions flown to maintain the no-fly zones.

UNSCR 687 established the framework for a contentious relationship between Iraq and the international community that lasted more than a decade. In May 1991, Iraq agreed to allow inspectors "unrestricted freedom of entry and exit without delay or hindrance of its personnel, property, supplies, [and] equipment." Nevertheless, within months Iraq had begun to resist the inspection process, by verbal intimidation, refusing to grant access and information, and, in some cases, physical threats. Iraqi resistance to the inspection regime became more vigorous over the next five years.[10] Matters came to a head on October 31, 1998, when Iraq announced it would end all forms of cooperation with UNSCOM, and the inspectors were expelled. The United States and Britain responded with Operation Desert Fox from December 16–19, 1998. At the same time, UNSCOM was replaced by the UN Monitoring, Verification, and Inspection Commission (UNMOVIC), but Iraq did not allow inspectors back into the country again until the eve of war in 2003.

In addition to dismantling Iraq's advanced weapons programs and maintaining the no-fly zones, the international community also sought to contain Iraq through economic sanctions. A strict sanctions program was established by UNSCR 661 in August 1990 and later was explicitly linked to fulfillment of the disarmament requirements adopted after the war. Sanctions—in particular, limits on oil exports—were seen as an effective way to deny Hussein's regime the capital to rebuild its military strength. However, the program was criticized by those who argued that the privations were not being felt by the regime and its support apparatus, but by innocent Iraqis. In an attempt to mitigate these effects, UNSCR 986 established the Oil for Food Program in April 1995.[11] The program allowed the partial resumption of Iraq's oil exports specifically to buy food and medicine. However, the program was plagued by cheating and corruption.[12]

A final means whereby Saddam tried to escape containment was by strengthening ties to international terrorism. Saddam had long been involved with terrorists and had been a major supporter of the Palestinian Liberation Organization. Iraq was also tied to Hamas and the Palestinians' Islamic Jihad. In the run-up to the 2003 war, the Bush Administration cited Saddam's program of providing financial awards to the families of suicide bombers who hit Israeli targets as a cause of concern.

A final, controversial issue was the extent to which Iraq maintained ties to Osama bin Laden. Before 9/11, U.S. analysts took it as a given that bin Laden, an Islamic fanatic reactionary, and Saddam Hussein, a secular Baathist modernizer, could never align or cooperate. However, there was sufficient ambiguity that led a majority of Americans to believe there was a connection between Iraq and the 9/11 attacks, in spite of the 9/11 Commission's findings that reiterated the government's position that "found no 'compelling case' that Iraq had either planned or perpetrated the attacks."[13]

Regime Change

The Coalition opted not to overthrow Saddam's rule during Operation Desert Storm, though some hoped that the damage to the regime would be sufficient to destabilize it to the point where either ethnically based insurgent forces or Baathist competitors for power within the regime would remove Saddam from power. However, the failure of Coalition troops to advance to Baghdad allowed Saddam to portray the war as a victory, the hoped-for coup did not materialize, and the few uprisings inside Iraq were quickly crushed.

Regime change did not become the explicit policy of the United States until 1998. The Iraq Liberation Act, which was signed into law by President Clinton on October 31 of that year (coincidentally, the same day international weapons inspectors were expelled), stated that "it should be the policy of the United States to seek to remove the Saddam Hussein regime from power in Iraq and to replace it with a democratic government." The law provided for assistance to Iraqi opposition groups, and in subsequent years, around $8 million was funneled annually to the Iraqi National Congress, an umbrella organization under the leadership of Iraqi exile Ahmed Chalabi. However, these efforts had little impact, and the INC in particular was criticized for being unable to account for the millions in assistance it was receiving.

After the 9/11 terrorist attacks, the Bush Administration moved Iraq to near center stage of its foreign policy. The 2002 National Security Strategy noted, "we must be prepared to stop rogue states and their terrorist clients before they are able to threaten or use weapons of mass destruction against the United States and our allies and friends."[14] The case for implementing by force the standing regime change policy grew steadily over the next 18 months, and centered on four issues: weapons of mass destruction, terrorism, international aggression, and human rights.[15] Some policymakers, such as Deputy Secretary of Defense Paul Wolfowitz, saw regime change as an opportunity for a geopolitical reordering of the Middle East, placing a free, democratic pro-Western state in the middle of this critical region.

Other decision makers in the White House and the Pentagon began to focus on a threat they referred to as "the Nexus."[16] The Nexus was the intersection of three component parts: international terrorism, rouge states, and weapons of mass destruction. It was thought that a WMD-armed country might strike at the United States through a global terrorist network. And because the act would not be traceable back to the country of origin, the rogue state could not be deterred by the certainty of a counterattack. After 9/11, potential threats of this nature were no longer acceptable. Because of its refusal to allow arms inspections, historic ties to international terrorist groups, and ongoing conflict with the United States, Iraq was seen as the most threatening potential Nexus state.

Although there were many stated reasons for going to war with Iraq, a decision was made to make the WMD issue the central rationale. This was done in order to have the firmest legal basis on which to act, based on prior Security Council resolutions, and also to find common ground within the U.S. bureaucracy.[17] It was also believed that this would be the best way to assemble both a domestic and international coalition against Saddam Hussein and in favor of regime change.

Iraq was warned that "it will face serious consequences as a result of its continued violations," language that many interpreted as a threat of war. From the American point of view, military operations in Iraq were already authorized under existing Council resolutions, including resolution 678 (1990) and resolution 687 (1991) and were already being carried out through the no-fly zones. The United States noted, "Iraq repeatedly has refused, over a protracted period of time, to respond to diplomatic overtures, economic sanctions, and other peaceful means designed to help bring about Iraqi compliance with its obligations to disarm Iraq and permit full inspection of its WMD and related pro-grams."[18] On October 2, 2002, the U.S. Congress passed Joint Resolution 114 authorizing the use of the United States Armed Forces to "defend the national security of the United States against the continuing threat posed by Iraq and enforce all relevant United Nations Security Council resolutions regarding Iraq."

Saddam Hussein did not help his case during this period. While denying that he possessed WMDs, his denials were always couched in terms that left the matter in some doubt.[19] Inspectors had not been per-mitted in the country since 1998, and the fact that the earlier round of inspections had found Iraq's programs more advanced than first sus-pected led to some concern that Saddam was attempting to rebuild.

Meanwhile, the United States and other Western intelligence sources were being given intelligence (later shown to be groundless) that Saddam was in fact rebuilding his program, and continued regime intransigence and bewildering behavior did nothing to dispel that belief.

IAEA and UNMOVIC inspectors began arriving back in Iraq on November 27, 2002, though they found the regime "on the whole cooperated rather well" compared to its behavior prior to 1998. On December 7, Iraq submitted a 12,000-page report claiming it had no weapons of mass destruction or other types of weapons banned by the United Nations. But over the next several months, inspectors discovered some discrepancies. The January 27, 2003, report from chief UNMOVIC inspector Hans Blix concluded that "Iraq appears not to have come to a genuine acceptance—not even today—of the disarmament, which was demanded of it and which it needs to carry out to win the confidence of the world and to live in peace."[20] The following day, President Bush announced in his State of the Union message that Saddam's regime "has shown utter contempt for the United Nations and the opinion of the world," and that the Coalition is prepared to take action even without a UN mandate. An UNMOVIC interim report in February 2003 was ambiguous, though Mohamed El Baradei, reporting for the IAEA (as its chief), said his agency had found no evidence of prohibited nuclear programs. In March, the United States and Britain attempted to push a UN ultimatum, which was blocked by a veto threat from France and Russia. Nevertheless, on March 17, President Bush announced, "Saddam Hussein and his sons must leave Iraq within 48 hours. Their refusal to do so will result in military conflict commenced at a time of our choosing."

Operation Iraqi Freedom began two days later on March 19 with an attempted decapitation strike on Iraqi command posts that failed to kill Saddam Hussein but did temporarily disrupt the Iraqi leadership. The ground offensive followed early the next morning, with heavy aerial attacks beginning on March 21. The campaign was fought well ahead of the planned timetable, and in three weeks, on April 9, Coalition troops advanced into central Baghdad, signaling the end of Saddam's regime for all practical purposes. Major combat operations were declared over on May 1.

Operation Iraqi Freedom resolved the four outstanding issues that had led to war. Although stockpiles of weapons of mass destruction were not found, evidence was discovered that the regime intended to reconstitute these programs once the sanctions had been lifted. In any case, Saddam's downfall guaranteed that WMDs in Iraq would no longer be an issue. Likewise, the regime would no longer be able to give support to international terrorist groups. The threat of further aggression against Iraq's neighbors was lifted, and human rights groups inside Iraq began the dismal task of unearthing mass graves and cataloging the atrocities committed during Saddam's quarter century of rule.

Democratization and Insurgency

While regime change settled the outstanding issues that led to war, it introduced new challenges for Iraq on the road to democracy. The initial enthusiasm of the Iraqi people for their liberation soon gave way to chaos and violence. Pre-war assumptions about the post-regime environment were highly unrealistic.[21] The Pentagon had failed to adequately plan for Phase IV (post-conflict) operations, and the plans that did exist focused mainly on coping with expected humanitarian crises in a permissive environment. The assumption that oil revenue could be used to fund Iraqi reconstruction proved unfounded. Added to this were conflicting lines of authority inside the country, and general acceptance (if not encouragement) by the Coalition of the initial looting and disorder, which set a tone of insecurity. Retired Army Lieutenant General Jay Garner was appointed as the first Director of Reconstruction and Humanitarian Assistance for Iraq, but his inability to bring the situation quickly under control coupled with internal politics in the Administration led to his replacement on May 11 by Ambassador L. Paul Bremer III as head of the newly formed Coalition Provisional Authority. Within two weeks, Bremer had disbanded the Iraqi Army and begun a radical de-Baathification of the Iraqi government and bureaucracy, moves that were expedient ideologically, but more than any others set the stage for the resulting insurgency.[22]

The term "insurgency" is problematic when used to describe the situation in Iraq. In 2005, there were scores of armed groups committing violent acts, ranging from attacks on the Iraqi infrastructure to kidnapping, sniping, setting improvised explosive devices (IEDs), suicide bombings, and in some cases massed attacks on fixed positions. The groups were driven by a variety of motives, from apolitical criminal activity to cross-cutting issues of competition for political and economic power among traditional ethnic, religious, and tribal groups. There was also the notable influence of outside non-state actors, such as al Qaeda, and state actors, predominately Iran and Syria.[23]

Ethnic conflict plays an important role in Iraq, though as with many such conflicts ethnic and political divisions are closely related. The tripartite breakdown between Shia Arab, Sunni Kurd, and Sunni Arab obscures many diverse interests that crosscut these groups, particularly tribal interests on which Saddam Hussein based his power.

During Saddam Hussein's reign, tribal and ethnic politics were a critical undercurrent in Baathist politics and the regime's method of rule. The group of al-Takriti tribes, especially Hussein's own tribe the Albu Nasir, were an important bulwark of his rule, and were rewarded with status, position, and wealth.[24] Other tribes throughout the country were courted in similar traditional ways in order to maintain a balance of power, with terror and reprisal awaiting those who showed disloyalty. Because these were the most favored groups in the Saddam period, they lost the most in the regime change and therefore have the biggest issue with the Coalition.

The Sunni Arab Insurgents   The various Sunni Arab insurgent groups are motivated by four basic issues. Most important is the loss of the political power and influence that they enjoyed under Saddam Hussein's regime. The Sunnis generally represent around 20 percent of the population, and fear that their minority status will hurt them in a new government based on majority rule. Second, they are concerned about the loss of economic influence and wealth that has accompanied their loss of political power. Oil is the main source of wealth in the country, and the Sunni tribes are not concentrated in either of the main oil regions in the north or south. This has caused fears of impoverishment. It is important to note that one of the main Sunni political demands during the debate over the Iraqi Constitution in 2005 was that oil be considered a national resource, not a provincial one. A third issue is the fear of reprisal. Both Kurdish and Shia groups suffered atrocities under Saddam's regime, and those Sunni groups most closely associated with Saddam are mindful of vengeance. In the chaotic period after the liberation of Iraq, retribution squads hunted down some of the more egregious offenders of Saddam's regime, and there have been periodic conflicts between ethnic and tribally based militias.

A fourth issue is simple anger at the Coalition forces and fear that they may become a permanent occupation force. Groups opposed to the new government have encouraged the belief that Iraq will become a puppet state of the United States, and the slow moves towards establishing sovereignty in Iraq seemed to validate this concern. The Interim Governing Council, comprising 25 Iraqi ministers appointed by the Coalition in July 2003, under the guidance of the CPA, was viewed as an illegitimate, neocolonial body. Not until the Coalition moved aggressively in 2005 to transfer full authority to a sovereign Iraqi government did these fears begin to allay, though they are likely to persist for as long as Coalition forces are present in Iraq.

The predominately Sunni Arab-based insurgent groups, both Baathist die-hards and tribal rejectionists (sometimes overlapping) number in the scores, and have varying motives and objectives. These can include driving out the Coalition, destabilizing and discrediting the Iraqi government, placing their groups in favorable bargaining positions vis-à-vis the government in Baghdad or Provincial or local governments, and perhaps to place themselves in a position to bring back Baathist rule.

Unlike the foreign insurgents in Iraq, these groups are generally not ideologically opposed to democracy, but see it as a system in which they are placed at a disadvantage. They also object to the Coalition's role in establishing it (or imposing it, in their view). Most Sunni political groups boycotted the January 2005 elections as a symbolic protest, though after the success and international acclaim of the elections they viewed this as an error. Sunni groups bargained effectively for positions in the new government, with the threat of increased violence should they not be accommodated in some way. They took part in the October 2005 Constitutional referendum, and also participated widely in the December 2005 parliamentary elections, even threatening foreign insurgents with reprisals should they seek to disrupt the proceedings. This did not mean that the Sunni groups had renounced the use of force—far from it. Their attacks continued on Coalition targets and groups like police that they see as collaborating directly with the Coalition. These Sunni groups see no contradiction between "legitimate resistance to foreign occupation" and simultaneous political participation within the government, and it is a mistake to believe that participation by itself implies that those who participate also see the system as legitimate.[25]

The insurgency is clearly not a nationwide phenomenon. Eighty-five percent of the insurgent attacks in Iraq occur in areas where 40 percent of the population lives. Al Anbar Province accounts for a third of all attacks, with only 5 percent of the population. A map of violent incidents demonstrates a prevalence of insurgent activity in areas mostly populated by Arab Sunnis, and in particular those areas previously most supportive of the regime. In the last week of October 2005, for example, which was a typical period, there were no attacks in the predominately Kurdish provinces of Dahuk, Arbil, and As Sulaymaniyah. On average, there was less than one per day in the majority Shia provinces of Al Basrah, Maysan, Dhi Qar, Al Muthanna', An Najaf, Al Qadisiyah, Wasit, and Karbala. However, there were high per-day averages in areas with proportionately greater Sunni presence, such as Babil (25 percent Arab Sunni, with an average of 2 attacks per day), Diyala (65 percent, 6 attacks), Ninawa (91 percent, 10 attacks), former Baathist stronghold Salah ad Din (99 percent, 16 attacks), and al Anbar (99 percent, 28 attacks). The most active insurgent area, Baghdad, which is 61 percent Arab Sunni and averaged 23 attacks per day in this period, is more difficult to analyze in a strictly ethnic context. Given its symbolic value, insurgents travel there to commit attacks.

The Foreign Insurgents   The foreign fighters in Iraq are the smallest of the insurgent groups in terms of numbers, but they are the most determined, most ruthless, and best financed of any of the groups.[26] They are predominately non-Iraqis and come from many countries in the Middle East, North Africa, Asia, and Europe. Most of them are organized under the banner of the *Tanzim al-Qa'ida fi Bilad al-Rafidayn*, or al Qaeda Organization in the Land of the Two Rivers, led by Jordanian terrorist Abu Musab al Zarqawi. Zarqawi, a longtime associate of Osama bin Laden, had previously founded a group called the *Jama'at al-Tawhid wal-Jihad*, or Unification and Holy War Group, but formally merged with al Qaeda and swore fealty to bin Laden in October 2004. In December 2004, bin Laden declared Zarqawi "the prince of al Qaeda in Iraq" and asked "all our organization brethren to listen to him and obey him in his good deeds."[27] The foreign fighters are much less numerous than the domestic insurgents, but they receive tacit support from anti-Coalition elements inside the country that see them as useful for attacking Coalition targets even if they do not agree with the al Qaeda program. Al Qaeda and other groups in Iraq also receive financial and material support from a variety of state and non-state sources, chiefly in Saudi Arabia, Syria, and Iran, countries in which there are interests that want to see the Iraq experiment fail. Other supporters see the conflict as an opportunity to attack the United States by proxy.

Al Qaeda's objectives are similar to the domestic insurgents in that they also seek to drive out the Coalition and destabilize and discredit the Iraqi government. However, its political agenda is more radical. Al Qaeda seeks to erect a Sharia-based theocracy and to make Iraq the seat of a renewed Caliphate, harkening back to the Baghdad-based Abbasid Caliphate of the ninth to thirteenth centuries. It is a more ideologically driven struggle, part of the wider jihadist opposition to the West and its influence in the region. As such, al Qaeda has taken a harder line on the democratization issue. Democracy is viewed as a Western-inspired attempt by flawed humanity to usurp God's law.[28] In January 2005, Zarqawi decreed that "in accordance with the religion of God Almighty, democracy is unrestrained atheism that is clear to everyone except for those who are blind in sight or mental vision. Everyone who believes in democracy, calls for it, endorses it, or embellishes it will be viewed as an infidel and apostate even though he calls himself Muslim."[29]

Thus, where Sunni rejectionists have tried to use the democratic political system to their benefit when possible, the foreign fighters have viewed this as a foolish compromise with conviction. To al Qaeda, violence was not only a sanctified but also a mandatory form of resistance. Al Qaeda mounted attacks against political candidates, elected officials, polling places, and voters alike, though they did not disrupt the political process.

The foreign fighters are too few to directly achieve their goals in Iraq, so al Qaeda has adopted a revolutionary strategy to exploit the cleavages in Iraqi society to foment chaos, and through these means to destabilize the government and create opportunities for seizing power. They seek to provoke a civil war between the Sunnis, Shia, and Kurds.[30] In some respects, by 2004, a civil war had broken out. Private militias from the various groups were active, and groups sought to achieve political goals through force by occupying cities, for example. However, large-scale ethnic civil conflict in Iraq has not materialized. Most Iraqis, while opposed to the presence of Coalition forces, are satisfied with the course of political development and do not see that level of internecine violence as a useful alternative.

Al Qaeda has also pursued a strategy of internationalizing the conflict when possible. It has conducted attacks against international targets inside Iraq, such as the August 19, 2003, bombing of the United Nations headquarters in Baghdad, which precipitated the UN's pullout from Iraq. The kidnapping of foreign nationals inside Iraq is commonplace, with the frequent demand being that the country in question end its support for the Iraqi government. But the internationalization strategy has not proven otherwise fruitful for al Qaeda. For example, the November 9, 2005, bombing of three hotels in Amman, Jordan, which killed 60 and wounded more than 100, only earned Zarqawi formal expulsion from the al-Khalayleh tribe and turned the Jordanian people from supporters of the al Qaeda effort in Iraq to bitter enemies.

Coalition Strategy

As noted above, the early steps by the Coalition to build democracy in Iraq were maladroit. The failure to transfer power expeditiously to Iraqis created a belief that the Coalition was establishing a puppet regime, and this among other things helped fuel the insurgency. The Coalition has since pursued a three-track strategy in Iraq, with overlapping elements of maintaining and extending security, pursuing political reforms, and promoting economic development.[31]

The Coalition has faced the traditional challenges of dealing with an insurgency, primarily trying to find an elusive enemy in an environment in which the local population is at best noncommittal and frequently supports the insurgents' aims.[32] Military power can maintain control of areas when present, but insurgents will seek to assert authority in gaps. Sometimes this has led to punishing urban combat to liberate areas from insurgent control, such as Operation Phantom Fury, the battle for Fallujah in November 2004.[33] Coalition military force has been useful in preventing long-term insurgent takeovers of urban areas. But while this has prevented insurgents from expanding their zone of control, it has not ended their activities; they simply relocate elsewhere. Six months after the battle in Fallujah, General John Abizaid stated that the insurgency in general was as strong as it had been before the attack.[34]

PROGRESS AND PROSPECTS

Iraq will remain an important U.S. interest in the foreseeable future, because of the centrality of energy to U.S. and global economic security, and because of the substantial investments in Iraq made by the United States over the past decade and a half. If the U.S.-led project in Iraq succeeds, a democratic Iraq will not seek to possess weapons of mass destruction, will not support state terrorism, and will not threaten its neighbors. This may take some time as the Iraqi democratic political culture develops; Iraq will have to contend with corruption in government, political deadlock, occasional constitutional crises, assassinations, and other sporadic political violence. Therefore, it is important for the United States and other countries not to expect the new Iraqi government immediately to meet the highest standards of transparency and good governance, while at the same time maintaining a judicious, persistent pressure for Iraq to develop along the path of democratic best practices.

Some long-standing issues will remain. It is conceivable, and in fact likely, that Iraq's Kurdish minority will seek greater degrees of political autonomy, with the ultimate goal of creating an independent Kurdish state. Iran will seek to extend its influence over Iraq, working through the Shia community, although it is unlikely that Iraq will become an Iranian client state, even with strong Shia parties in the government. Iraqi Arab Shia will be unwilling simply to hand over their hard-won power to their Iranian Persian coreligionists. The radical political Islamist tendency will also be present, whether manifested through violence or electoral politics, and the challenge will remain of Iraq turning from democracy to theocracy either by the sword or though the ballot box. Neither would be satisfactory developments from the U.S. perspective.

It is highly unlikely that the foreign terrorists represented by al Qaeda would succeed in their goal of taking over Iraq and erecting a Caliphate. Once Coalition forces withdraw from Iraq, the rationale among Sunni oppositionists for sustaining the foreign fighters will evaporate, and they will be likely be driven out by their previous supporters. However, even in the unlikely event of an al Qaeda-backed coup in Iraq and the declaration of a Caliphate, this would prompt another intervention by the Coalition, likely with more substantial international support than was evident in the 2003 intervention.

The more likely long-term impact of the conflict in Iraq on terrorism would be manifested in other countries, as foreign fighters who had trained in Iraq returned home to use their newly acquired skills against their native governments. The model for this development is the experience in Afghanistan in the 1980s, when U.S. and Saudi-backed foreign mercenaries (aka Mujahedin) fought with Afghan guerrillas against Soviet forces and their Afghan socialist allies. When the Soviets withdrew in 1989, the foreign fighters returned to their original countries. Throughout the 1990s, radical Islamist guerrilla movements cropped up across the Muslim world, led largely by Afghan war veterans—a phenomenon called "blowback."[35] The most famous of these leaders was Osama bin Laden.

The conflict in Iraq is a potent recruiting tool for the global terrorist network. Occasional Coalition missteps such as the Abu Ghraib prison scandal, the uses of excessive military force, or other cultural insensitivities provide images for terrorist propagandists.[36] It appeals to those who desire to fight the "infidels" who have "defiled Muslim lands." Those who survive the conflict will, like their Mujahedin predecessors, emerge with both the means and motives to further their terrorist careers elsewhere. A CIA analysis from the summer of 2005 noted that Iraq was "serving as a real-world laboratory for urban combat," and that "the war was likely to produce a dangerous legacy by dispersing to other countries Iraqi and foreign combatants more adept and better organized than they were before the conflict."[37] Methods learned in Iraq have already been transplanted to the guerrilla struggle in Afghanistan. Iraq veterans could breathe new life into failing insurgencies in other predominantly Muslim countries, or seek to organized armed groups in Europe or North America. This "Blowback 2" scenario is potentially the greatest future threat to U.S. national security that will emerge from Iraq in the near future. It is not strictly speaking an

Iraq issue, though the country will have played the role as midwife to a new and expanded international terrorist threat.

NOTES

1. An overview of the conflict can be found in Dilip Hiro, *The Longest War: The Iran-Iraq Military Conflict* (London: Grafton, 1989).
2. U.S. Arms Control and Disarmament Agency, World Military Expenditures and Arms Transfers (Washington, DC: U.S. Arms Control and Disarmament Agency, 1987).
3. Micah L. Sifry, ed., *The Iraq War Reader* (New York: Touchstone, 2003), p. 416.
4. Hiro, op. cit., p. 12.
5. Majid Khadduri and Edmund Ghareeb, *War in the Gulf, 1990-91: The Iraq-Kuwait Conflict and Its Implications* (Oxford: Oxford University Press, 1997), pp. 106–108.
6. Saddam's rationale for the war is explicated in detail in Jerry M. Long, *Saddam's War of Words: Politics, Religion, and the Iraqi Invasion of Kuwait* (Austin: University of Texas Press, 2004). U.S. decision making was compounded by the revelation that in a July 1990 meeting with U.S. Ambassador to Iraq April Glaspie, in which she said that the United States had "no opinion" about the border dispute. Saddam's troops were already massing on the Kuwait border, a fact that Glaspie knew. Thus, from Saddam's point of view, he may have believed he had a green light from the United States to invade Kuwait. Note that accounts of this meeting vary, but in none of them was Saddam explicitly told not to invade.
7. Osama bin Laden had famously offered to defend the kingdom with his Afghan-trained guerrillas, an offer that the crown graciously declined.
8. C.f. Rick Atkinson, *Crusade: The Untold Story of the Persian Gulf War* (New York: Houghton Mifflin Co., 1993).
9. UNSCR 687, April 3, 1991. This provision was in part a response to Iraq's use of SCUD missiles to attack targets in Saudi Arabia and Israel during Operation Desert Storm.
10. See, for example, the IAEA "Report on the Twelfth IAEA On-Site Inspection in Iraq Under Security Council Resolution 687 (1991)" May 26 to June 4, 1992. The report notes, "In the course of the twelfth mission there was a definite stiffening in the Iraqi attitude to working with the inspection team." A full account of the techniques used by Iraq can be found in Michael V Deaver, *Disarming Iraq: Monitoring Power and Resistance* (Westport, CT: Praeger Publishers, 2001).
11. First proposed in August 1991, UNSCR 706, which Iraq rejected. Baghdad did not accept the proposal until May 1996, and it was implemented the following December.
12. C.f. Independent Inquiry Committee into the United Nations Oil-for-Food Program, *Report on the Manipulation of the Oil-for-Food Programme* (October 27, 2005). Online. Available HTTP: <http://www.iic-offp.org/documents.htm>.
13. For poll results, see Steven Kull, "Misperceptions, the Media, and the Iraq War," Program on International Policy Attitudes. Online. Available HTTP: <http://www.pipa.org/OnlineReports/Iraq/IraqMedia_Oct03/IraqMedia_Oct03_rpt.pdf>; National Commission on Terrorist Attacks Upon the United States, *The 9/11 Commission Report* (Washington, DC: Government Printing Office, 2003), p. 334.
14. George W. Bush, *National Security Strategy of the United States of America* (17 September 2002), p. 14.
15. A prominent example of an atrocity that tied together human rights and the WMD issue was Saddam's use of chemical weapons against Kurdish civilians in Halabja in March 1988.

16. See in particular Under Secretary of Defense for Policy Douglas J. Feith's analysis, "U.S. Strategy for the War on Terrorism," Remarks to the Political Union University of Chicago, Chicago, Illinois, April 14, 2004.

17. See transcript, "Deputy Secretary Wolfowitz Interview with Sam Tannenhaus, Vanity Fair," May 9, 2003. Online. Available HTTP: <http://www.defenselink.mil/transcripts/2003/tr20030509-depsecdef0223.html >.

18. John D. Negroponte, U.S. Permanent Representative to the United Nations, Statement Before the UN Security Council, New York, New York, March 27, 2003.

19. The *Comprehensive Report of the Special Advisor to the DCI on Iraq's WMD* (October 6, 2004) concluded: "The Iran-Iraq war and the ongoing suppression of internal unrest taught Saddam the importance of WMD to the dominance and survival of the regime. Following the destruction of much of the Iraqi WMD infrastructure during Desert Storm, however, the threats to the Regime remained; especially his perception of the overarching danger from Iran. In order to counter these threats, Saddam continued with his public posture of retaining the WMD capability," pp. 40–41.

20. Dr. Hans Blix, "An Update on Inspection," remarks delivered to the United Nations Security Council in New York, January 27, 2003.

21. For information on some of the issues and challenges of prewar planning, see General Tommy Franks, *American Soldier* (New York: HarperCollins, 2004).

22. Larry Diamond argues decisions like these were a part of a "long chain of U.S. miscalculations." C.F. "What Went Wrong in Iraq," *Foreign Affairs* (September/October 2004), pp. 34–56.

23. Deputy Secretary of Defense Paul Wolfowitz, "Testimony to the Senate Armed Services Committee: Hearing on Military Operations in Iraq and Afghanistan," Washington, DC, February 3, 2005.

24. Note that even within these "loyal" tribes there were significant disputes with the regime, as is naturally the case when people compete for power at that level. C.f. Amatzia Baram, "The Iraqi Tribes and the Post-Saddam System," *Iraq Memo #18*, Brookings Institution, July 8, 2003.

25. The standard work explaining this dynamic of participating in democratic politics while attempting to undermine the system remains Lenin's 1920 essay, "Left Wing Communism, an Infantile Disorder."

26. For an assessment of the foreign fighters in Iraq, see Anthony Cordesman, "Iraq and Foreign Volunteers," CSIS Report, November 17, 2005. Analyses that seek to downplay the threat posed by the foreign fighters by looking only at numbers are flawed; the foreigners tend to be much more strongly motivated and deadlier than the Iraqis.

27. The bin Laden videotape was aired on al Jazeera on December 21, 2004. Zarqawi was killed in a U.S. airstrike on June 7, 2006. At this writing, it is unclear whether this will seriously impact operational activities carried out by his group.

28. C.f., James S. Robbins, "Al-Qaeda Versus Democracy," *Journal of International Security Affairs,* Fall 2005, pp. 53–59.

29. "Legal [Islamic] Judgment Regarding Democracy, its Proponents," Statement issued by the Legal Committee of Al-Zarqawi's al-Qaeda of Jihad in the Land of the Two Rivers. Online. Available HTTP: <http://www.almjlah.net/vb, January 27, 2005>.

30. See the July 9, 2005, letter from Ayman al-Zawahiri to Zarqawi, released by the Office of the Director of National Intelligence on October 11, 2005.

31. The Coalition Strategy is laid out in the *National Strategy for Victory in Iraq*, released November 30, 2005.

32. C.f. John A. Nagl, *Learning to Eat Soup with a Knife* (Chicago: University of Chicago Press, 2005).

33. C.f. Bing West, *No True Glory: A Frontline Account of the Battle for Fallujah* (New York: Bantam Dell, 2005).

34. "Abizaid: Insurgency Still Strong," *Christian Science Monitor*, June 24, 2005, p. 1.

35. C.f. Mary Ann Weaver, "Blowback," *The Atlantic Monthly*, May 1996.

36. C.f. Brigadier Nigel Aylwin-Foster, British Army, "Changing the Army for Counterinsurgency Operations," *Military Review* (November-December 2005). Online. Available HTTP: <http://usacac.leavenworth.army.mil/CAC/milreview/download/English/NovDec05/aylwin.pdf>.

37. See Douglas Jehl, "Iraq May Be Prime Place for Training of Militants, C.I.A. Report Concludes," *The New York Times*, June 22, 2005.

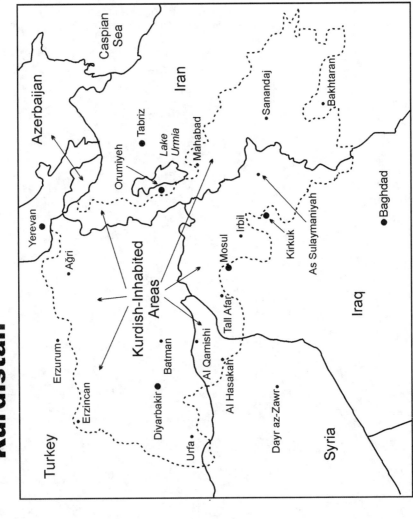

Kurdistan

3

KURDISTAN

Kerrie Urosevich

The Kurdish issue is going to be the next big problem in the Middle East. The more they taste freedom, the more conscious they become, and the more they will demand.[1]

Henri Barkey, former member of U.S. Department of State

INTRODUCTION[2]

In 1995, I had opportunities to share multiple conversations with members of the Kurdistan Worker's Party or *Partiya Karkeran Kurdistan* (PKK) over Turkish coffee in Antalya. One particular PKK member emphatically stated: "If it weren't for Ocalan and his fighters, my entire family would be dead right now. I owe it to my family and to other Kurds suffering in eastern Turkey to carry on the fight. The PKK provides hope for the youth." His personal accounts of family torture and suffering, his passion for survival, and his fear and devotion to the cause left an intense impression on me, one I have pondered for almost 10 years. Additionally, with the current occupation in Iraq, the issues of "Northern Iraq" or "Southern Kurdistan," depending through which lens you are viewing, have surfaced with the possibility of more autonomy and empowerment for Kurds throughout the region. In order to fully understand the various issues plaguing Kurdistan and how Kurds have become integral policy dilemmas for the United States and others, it is important to explore how Kurdistan has become a flashpoint for the

United States' war on terrorism, reveal Kurdistan's historical aspiration for autonomy, describe the intractability of the Kurdistan conflict, and provide policy recommendations for seeking resolution.

NATURE OF THE FLASHPOINT

The Kurds are a nation without a state and are estimated to number 25–30 million. Twelve to 15 million live in Turkey; 6–8 million live in Iran; 4–5 million live in Iraq; and approximately 1 million live in Syria. About 70,000–80,000 Kurds also live in Armenia and in Azerbaijan.[3] They are a mountainous tribal people who claim to be descendents of the Medes and of Indo-Aryan origin. Records suggest that the Kurds date back to at least 400 BCE.[4] The Kurdish nation covers an estimated 200,000 square miles and is endowed with many natural resources, primarily oil and water. The Kurds developed a modern sense of nationhood in opposition to the pressure imposed upon them by their host nation-states. The destruction and oppression that forced many Kurds to leave their homeland and retreat to the mountains has had the unintended effect of regenerating Kurdish culture and preserving Kurdish language, religion, and traditions. In spite of their population size, cultural richness, and resources, Kurdish moves toward an independent state for nearly a century have been caught up in regional and international politics.

In his 2001 documentary, *Good Kurds, Bad Kurds,* Kevin McKiernan reveals that the value of the Kurds to the American government essentially depends on which side of the border they live on and how much of a problem they present to U.S. allies. The majority of Kurds in Iraq are considered "good" Kurds because they opposed Saddam Hussein, while the Kurds in Turkey are considered "bad" because they oppose a U.S. ally. For McKiernan, "It doesn't seem to matter that there are four times as many Kurds in Turkey, or that both populations have suffered intense repression from their respective governments."[5] With this backdrop, the Kurdish question has become a flashpoint for U.S. foreign policy for several reasons. First, the Kurdish population is essential to the United States' efforts in the Near East to advance its foreign policy agenda. Second, Kurdistan independence movements place considerable strain on U.S.-Turkey relations. Finally, the internationally sanctioned no-fly zone over northern Iraq throughout the 1990s gave the Kurds a great deal of autonomy. Now that U.S. policy in Iraq is focused on creating a federal state there, Kurdish autonomy that developed during the last decade may be viewed as threatened by a broader Kurdish independence movement. What is certain, however, is that the Kurdish question is becoming more prominent and is a departure from the past where the Kurds have resided in the shadows of U.S. foreign policy.

Calls for an independent Kurdistan are not new and are in fact rooted in international law. Following World War I, the Kurds were promised an independent state by the Treaty of Sèvres, signed on August 10, 1920. Expectations of an independent state quickly dissipated when, in 1923, Britain and its allies supported the final Treaty of Lusanne and determined that the Kurds belonged to Turkey. This decision fatefully denied Kurds opportunities for self-determination and set the ball rolling for Kurdish resistance.

Since the 1920s, Kurds have been alternately deserted and supported by various U.S. administrations determined by the convenience of their political utility.[6] Examples for support of or allying with the Kurdish nation include NGO and academic support for the exploitation of Kurdish human rights within Turkey, militia support against Saddam Hussein for over 15 years within Iraq, protection of Kurdish communities in northern Iraq under the no-fly zone, political support for Kurdish leadership in the new Iraqi government, and financial and political support for Kurdish democratic movements within Syria and Iran. Paradoxically, the U.S. has squelched Kurdish independence movements in Turkey by politically and financially supporting the Turkish military, deserting Kurdish militia fighting against Saddam in 1991, suppressing notions of an independent Kurdistan in Iraq while advocating federalism, designating Kurdish groups such as the PKK in Turkey and Ansar al-Islam as terrorist groups under the similar banner of "Kurdish separatists," and rejecting bills directed at recognizing Saddam's acts of terrorism against Iraq's Kurdish minorities.

Since the United States' 2003 invasion of Iraq, the dilemma of supporting Iraqi Kurds without alienating Turkey, Syria, and Iran has been magnified with a much greater risk to international security. While much attention in Iraq is focused on the insurgency (see Chapter 2), Kurds in northern Iraq who resist democratization are often aligned with Ansar al-Islam, a U.S.-designated foreign terrorist organization.

Groups like Ansar and others that resist the creation of an Iraqi federal state jeopardize Iraqi stability. Without stability in the northern region, particularly in Kirkuk, which holds the second largest oil deposits in Iraq, the United States risks losing not only economic opportunities, but also credibility worldwide.

Pawns for Policy Advancement

The United States has historically used the Kurds to advance its military and political efforts throughout the region. Most notably in Iraq, Kurdish solidarity in the north has been critical for the United States to effectively use the Kurdish militia for a military alliance and to advance U.S. goals of democratization. Significant international mediation efforts occurred throughout the 1990s, prompted by the internal fighting between northern Iraqi Kurdish parties: the Kurdistan Democratic Party (KDP) and Patriotic Union of Kurdistan (PUK). Fighting that flared up in May 1994 lasted eight months and between 600 and 1,000 Kurds were killed, according to various sources.[7] The fighting was described as the worst in 30 years. Fractures along religious, tribal, feudal, and dialectal lines overlap and serve as the foundational conflict cleavages. Conferences, including a variety of mediations and negotiations in France, Ireland, Iran, Turkey, the United States, and the UN, have attempted to reestablish peaceful relations between the parties. International nonprofit groups, Kurdish human rights groups, and academic forums mobilized to address the conflicts between the KDP and PUK. These efforts led to a conclusion of the Kurdish Civil War in 1998, when a peace agreement was signed with the assistance of the United States.

The Kurdish peshmerga fighters (literally, those who face death) were essential to U.S. policy in Iraq during the Gulf War in 1991 against Saddam's regime. As I write, Kurdish fighters are aligned alongside U.S. troops in stabilizing Iraqi Kurdistan, and they played an essential role in the overthrow of Saddam's regime in 2003. Time will tell if success for the Kurds in Iraq will result in Kurdish support of the American "Global War on Terrorism." Not only does the United States depend on the Kurds for military support, but the Kurds also prove to be the only realistic, secular democratic ally in the region. In the near future, they could be an economic ally as well. If the Kurds are granted control of an important oil-producing region, they will gain the strategic importance they have always desired, consequently increasing their strategic intimacy with the United States.

In 2004, domestic pressure to send troops home encouraged the U.S. administration to invest heavily in backing conflict-resolution efforts. The most notable investment appeared to be from PeaceWatch, through the United States Institute for Peace, which is currently "working with Iraqis to prevent and reduce interethnic and inter-religious violence, speed up stabilization and democratization, and reduce the need for continuing presence in Iraq."[8] Some of PeaceWatch's leading programs involve training new Iraqi government personnel in conflict management; training Iraqi facilitators to conduct results-oriented dialogues among government and civil society leaders; conducting conflict management skills workshops in cities throughout Iraq; establishing an Iraqi Centre for Dialogue, Reconciliation, and Peace; establishing an Iraqi Special Tribunal to prosecute leaders from Hussein's regime; and providing seed money for a variety of initiatives focused initially on interethnic and women's issues. Naturally, U.S. conflict resolution efforts may benefit the various parties in Iraq, but, according to the United States Institute for Peace, efforts are meant to "speed up stabilization and democratization."

One final example illustrating the narrow use of the Kurds by U.S. foreign policy makers involves Iran. In the 1970s, the United States supported the Kurdistan Democratic Party (KDP) under Mustafa Barzani in Iraq to support opposition to Tehran through the Soviet-engineered Kurdistan Democratic Party of Iran (KDPI).[9] A CIA memo revealed the United States's true intentions: "Iran, like ourselves, has seen benefit in a stalemate situation, in which Iraq is intrinsically weakened by the Kurds' refusal to relinquish semi-autonomy. Neither Iran nor ourselves wishes to see the matter resolved one way or the other."[10] Smaller groups within Syria and Iran have benefited from U.S. support to resist authoritarian regimes and to push democratic agendas.

These examples highlight that U.S. political, military, and economic support for the Kurds. Although they can be perceived as altruistic, they are undeniably self-serving. The United States' relationship with the Kurds is confounded by other foreign policy goals in the region.

The Conundrum of Allying with Turkey

The ramifications of U.S. loyalty to Turkey as its NATO ally have affected Kurds around the region, most notably among Turkey's own Kurdish communities and Kurds residing in Iraq. At the behest of Turkey, the United States established a no-fly zone over Northern Iraq to protect Kurdish communities targeted during Saddam's 1988 Anfal Operation on the town of Haljaba. The attacks resulted in anywhere from 6,000–200,000 deaths.[11] The no-fly zone was established not only to protect Kurds from Saddam, but also to prevent a massive influx of refugees into Turkey. Turkey feared an exodus of refugees would ignite existing nationalist movements among its own Kurdish population. U.S. General Anthony Zinni captured the chaos in 1991:

Urged on by promises of U.S. military support (that subsequently was not provided), the Kurds had mounted a revolt against Saddam, which Saddam had brutally crushed. The Iraqi military had then pushed the panicked Kurds into the mountains along the Turkish border, slaughtering many in the process. Just about the entire Iraqi Kurdish population was involved in the exodus; hundreds of thousands of refugees were now pouring over the border, few carrying more than the clothes on their backs, all of them in dire straits. The Turks (who had had a previous experience with Kurdish refugees, and have a Kurdish problem of their own) refused to let the refugees down from the mountains; and the harsh winter conditions were threatening to devastate these traumatized masses.[12]

Although the no-fly zone pacified Turkish anxiety, it allowed Kurds a sense of autonomy and opportunity to reclaim their identity. Until the 2003 U.S.-led invasion of Iraq, Kurds in northern Iraq established their own operating government, Kurdish education system, militia, and local and international business enterprises. Three significant impediments to the realization of political, economic, and military success in northern Iraq have been the recent loyalty to U.S. efforts in Iraq, violence by Ansar al-Islam, and U.S. fidelity to Turkey as a NATO ally.

Congressman Bob Filner captured the instrumental nature of U.S.-Kurdish relations: "Without adequate resources, the Kurdish experience with democracy was doomed from the start."[13] During the first Gulf War, Turkish Prime Minister Necmettin Erbakan demanded that the United States (1) must not pursue policies to fragment the "unity" of Iraq, (2) should not support an "independent" Kurdish state in northern Iraq, (3) should stop supporting NGOs that pursue policies to establish an infrastructure for an independent Kurdish state, (4) must follow U.N. resolutions and not its own objectives (i.e., an independent state in northern Iraq), and (5) must support Turkey's war against the PKK both within Turkey and in northern Iraq.[14]

The roots of Turkish loyalty to the United States is exemplified most gravely by the United States' resistance to passing the 1988 Prevention of Genocide Act that was introduced by Peter Galbraith, senior advisor to the U.S. Senate Relations Committee (1979–1993). After witnessing first-hand the repercussions of Saddam's infamous Anfal Operation, Galbraith stated: "I imposed every sanction on Iraq that I could think of. The legislation banned oil sales, required the United States to oppose loans, cut off $700 million in agricultural and export credits, and banned any export requiring a license."[15] The bill won Senate approval in just 24 hours. Hopeful that the bill would pass, Galbraith found himself up against American capitalism. Bill Frenzel, then a Congressman from Minnesota, took a public stand against the bill:

It's very hard to be *for* genocide, or against people who are against genocide, but I couldn't see anything in that resolution that could prevent any single drop of blood being shed. All I could see was that it was doing harm to the United States, rather than to the perpetrators of the alleged genocide.[16]

Ultimately, President Reagan decided that the bill was "premature." Galbraith responded: "What would have made it ripe for action? The killing of all the Kurds? It was an absurd statement." Reagan insisted he would use presidential veto to kill the bill, thus preventing a vote in the House of Representatives. Consequently, the bill eventually died when Congress adjourned that session.

Essential Success in Iraq

The Kurds, with their own language, culture, and political ideologies, have been fighting for autonomy from the Iraqi government since the birth of the state in 1932. Kurdish resistance was a frequent target during Saddam's reign. "According to Human Rights Watch, the Iraqi government systematically destroyed 4,000 to 5,000 Kurdish villages from 1977 to 1987. Then, in a series of attacks in the late 1980s, Saddam's forces slaughtered more than 100,000 Kurds."[17] The most publicized attack was the 1988 Anfal Operation.

Having survived under a genocidal, dictatorial government in Baghdad, Kurds in northern Iraq do not want to endorse a strong federal government, but instead wish to preserve Kurdistan's government, territory, and laws. In March 2004, the Kurdistan Regional Government (KRG) contributed to the creation of the interim constitution, otherwise known as the Transitional Administrative Law (TAL). The KRG put forth the following proposals to secure Kurdistan's autonomy through Kurdistan's Constitutional Proposal:

(1) Legal supremacy within Kurdistan (Article 1).
(2) Kurdistan's National Guard was established from the retrained *peshmerga*, and to exclude the Iraqi armed forces from Kurdistan save when granted permission (Article 2).
(3) Exclusive ownership of natural resources within Kurdistan, confining federal control to petroleum reservoirs currently in commercial production (Article 3).
(4) Fiscal autonomy, including the right to raise taxes and discretion in expending federal block grants (Article 4).
(5) Kurdistan's assent to the ratification of the permanent constitution (Article 5).[18]

A handful of articles directly reflect the wishes of Kurds in the updated Constitution, which was approved in October 2005, but it is up to the Supreme Federal Court to decide the difficult questions about federalism, who owns the oil, and how democracy and Islam should be balanced.

Contrary to Kurdish wishes for a secure autonomous region, if not full independence, Arab parties and the American occupation propose a more "majoritarian, centralized, and mono-national federation."[19] Alternately, groups supporting the Islamic Movement of Kurdistan (IMK), such as Ansar al-Islam, resist any form of democratization and are seeking an independent Islamic State dictated by Shari'a Law. If Kurds are granted an autonomous northern region and substantial leadership in the Iraqi federal government, there is a greater chance that an Islamic democratic state will be realized. Such a realization could provide a launching pad for the United States to advance democratization efforts in the region. Autonomy would most likely result in an influx of Kurdish communities from Turkey, Iran, and Syria, thereby initiating a variety of nationalist movements within and surrounding Iraq. Destabilization could either jeopardize U.S.-Turkey relations or promulgate democratic and capitalistic movements throughout the region. The conundrum is proving to be an interesting balancing act for the United States.

HISTORICAL CONTEXT

With nearly 30 million Kurds spread across six countries, Kurdish identity is maintained through a common culture and shared sense of deprivation. The Kurdish language is related to Farsi and is thus an Indo-European language. While Kurdish nationalists rely on the fact that someone speaks Kurdish as evidence of a Kurdish identity, the language divides as well as unites. Kurdish has been written in at least three different alphabets: the Arabic/Persian alphabet in Iraq and Iran, the Latin alphabet in Turkey, and the Cyrillic alphabet in the former Soviet Union. Kurds primarily practice Islam, but their approach varies on geographic location. Sunni is the majority that resides in Turkey, Syria, and northern Iraq. Those that reside in the eastern part of northern Iraq and Iran are Shi'a.

The amount of Kurdish participation in civil society has depended on the various political regimes in Turkey, Iraq, Syria, and Iran. Generally speaking, since the early 1990s until the 2003 U.S. invasion, Iraqi Kurds have enjoyed the greatest autonomy through the protection of the U.S. and British no-fly zone. Under the current regimes in Turkey, Iran, and Syria, Kurds enjoy very little participation in civic affairs, particularly related to their own cultural traditions. For example, the majority of Kurds, including members of the Welfare Party living in Turkey, are denied citizenship, education, or broadcasting in their native language. To date, the Turkish government does everything it can to discourage the acknowledgment of a "Kurdish nation."

The Boundaries

Turkey It is estimated that 15 million Kurds reside in Turkey, the largest population of Kurds anywhere, which is approximately 20 percent of Turkey's population. The majority of Kurds resides in the east and southeast areas of the country and has greatly suffered under Turkish domination. Kurdish rights have ebbed and flowed, depending on the ruling presidential administration. Competition for natural resources has played a lucrative role in fighting within Turkey. The headwaters of the Euphrates and Tigris rivers are both in heavily populated Kurdish areas of Turkey. The two oil pipelines and rivers symbolize the confluence of two of the world's most prized commodities: oil for the West and Japan and water for Israel and the neighboring Arab states. For the past 20 years, the most well-known Kurdish group, with approximately 4,000 fighters, has been the PKK. It has resisted assimilation tactics by the Turkish government, defending its cultural, political, and economic rights. Despite current pressures by the European Union, Turkey has yet to legislate changes to its Constitution that provide for civil rights to its Kurdish minorities. It could be argued that U.S. denial of humanitarian support to Kurdish communities in Iraq and Turkey has aided the proliferation of PKK activities.

Iraq Although Turkey has probably taken more Kurdish lives than is suspected by outsiders, Turkey has not captured world attention like the Kurdish situation within Iraq. That country has been accused of the most brutal depredations against its Kurdish population. Ironically, Iraq has also gone furthest toward accepting, or in recent years tolerating (unwillingly) Kurdish autonomy.[20] In Iraq, Kurds represent about a quarter of the population, with 4–5 million inhabitants, who have played a highly visible role in Iraqi politics. The benefits of the Food for Oil Program, UNSCR 986, as well as the established no-fly zone have been significant for Iraqi Kurdistan. With a 13 percent share of the proceeds from the sale of Iraqi oil, Kurds have succeeded in rebuilding the north, and the Kurdish regional government has seen rapid development. The decade-long period of limited international protection through the no-fly zone did provide Iraqi Kurds an opportunity to develop institutions and autonomy, but Saddam Hussein prevented Iraqi Kurds from participating more broadly in Iraqi politics. Since the current U.S.-led war in Iraq, Iraqi Kurds have diligently worked to secure positions in the Iraqi interim government. During the first Parliamentary elections in January 2005, the Kurdish Alliance—a coalition of eight groups dominated by the two main parties, the Patriotic Union of Kurdistan (PUK), headed by Iraq's current president, Jalal Talabani, and the Kurdish Democratic Party (KDP), headed by Masoud Barzani—won 75 out of 275 seats in the National Assembly, while the Islamic Kurdish party won two seats. What the Kurds have accomplished in 12 years is extraordinary. They have not only been advancing politically, but territorially as well. Kurds have pushed into areas previously controlled by Iraqi authorities. South of Mosul and Kirkuk, Kurdish fighters have evicted thousands of Arabs from villages that the Kurds claim as their own. The Kurdish Alliance's top priority is to find a solution for who will govern Kirkuk and control its oil.

Iran   Approximately 8 million Kurds live in Iran (roughly 15 percent of its population) and are concentrated in the northwest areas. Yet the fact that 40 percent of Iranians still live below the poverty line suggests that the economy is weak. Given the lack of rights and self-determination for Kurds residing in Iran, they will likely fall much lower on the socioeconomic scale than the average Iranian. Although fighting and assassinations have occurred between Kurdish and Iranian parties, Kurds in Iran are more assimilated in their nation-state than in other Kurdish enclaves. This assimilation has been caused by two specific factors. First, Kurds have been a part of the Persian Empire since the sixteenth century and have naturally adapted over the centuries. Second, assimilation polices implemented by the Iranian government greatly limited Kurdish autonomy. But because they are non-Farsi speakers and the majority are Sunni rather than Shiite, the Kurds have maintained a somewhat separate identity. Since the early 1990s, the government has been more lenient towards the cultural demands of the ethnic groups in Iran. The schools in Kurdistan are allowed to teach Kurdish language, Kurdish history, and traditions. Politically, the main Kurdish party in Iran is the Soviet-engineered Kurdish Democratic Party (KDPI), which was formed in September 1945. Iranian Kurds have become susceptible to intra-Kurdish and inter-state coercion. As one Iranian expressed, "I think success for Kurdish autonomy, and even more so, the creation of a Kurdish nation, impossible."[21] Despite the perceived hopelessness, in 2005, Bahaeddin Adab founded the Kurdish United Front, which is committed to peacefully demanding democracy and equal rights for

Kurdish minorities in Iran. Based on a recent opinion poll, the movement is supported by the majority of Kurdish Iranians.

Syria Roughly 1–2 million Kurds (10–15 percent of the population) are concentrated along the Iraqi and Turkish borders. The Syrian Kurds have generally been less influential and have indulged in fewer separatist movements than Kurds in Turkey and Iran. In Syria, the Kurds have never constituted a very serious threat to the regime. According to Michael Collins Dunn, "The Baath of Syria, like the Baath of Iraq, are Arab nationalist in ideology and have little place for non-Arabs." [22] The main political voice for the Kurds has long been the Syrian Communist party, led by Syrian Kurd Khalid Bakdash. But the party has been marginalized, and Syrian Kurds are not a major political force. Syria was known to support Talabani and the PUK for many years as a means of undermining its rival Iraq.

LINKAGES TO TERRORISM

Two major Kurdish-backed groups have been designated by the U.S. State Department as "foreign terrorist organizations." [23] The PKK and its splinter groups are focused on achieving cultural rights self-determination and independence in Turkey. In deep ideological contrast, Ansar al-Islam has been accused of aligning with al Qaeda in Iraqi Kurdistan, fighting for the establishment of a Kurdish theocracy under Shari'a law, and resisting secular Kurdish groups like the KDP and the PUK.

Kurdish "Terrorist" Organizations

Abdullah Ocalan, a student leader with a Marxist orientation, founded the PKK in 1974. The political denial of Kurdish identity by Turkey through the banning of the use of the Kurdish language, denying citizenship, attacking Kurdish communities, and controlling natural resources in Kurdish areas of Southeast Asia has fueled PKK motivations. Estimated at 4,000 fighters, the PKK has waged a violent and persistent war against the Turkish authorities in southeastern Turkey, resulting in more than 30,000 casualties. The war with the PKK has also involved Turkey in broader international issues. The PKK made incursions into Iraq in 1990, 1991, 1992, 1995, and 2003. "While the majority of Turkey's Kurds do not *openly* support separatism from the Turkish state, many do support the PKK as the only force fighting for broader Kurdish cultural, economic, and political rights." [24] Kurds in Turkey are generally fearful of the PKK and its use of violence. Yet as David McDowall, a historian of the Kurdish separatist movement expressed:

"The only reason why the Kurds have supported the PKK was that the Turkish state forces were able to be equally terrifying to the Kurds. So they said, 'Blood is thicker than water. I'd stick with a devil that is a Kurdish devil, rather than with a Turkish devil.'"[25]

Abdullah Ocalan was arrested in 1999 and is still being held in Turkey, facing the death penalty on terrorism charges. Between 2002 and 2003, the PKK dedicated itself to nonviolent engagement with Turkey, but the cease-fire ended in 2004. The PKK has been involved with other Kurdish groups throughout the region, bolstering support for Kurdish rights and ultimately advocating for an independent Kurdistan.

In contrast to the nationalist roots of the PKK, Ansar al-Islam was originally formed and funded by al Qaeda in 2001 as the Jund al-Islam (Soldiers of Islam), according to The Terrorism Knowledge Base. Al Qaeda continues to provide some funding and training.[26] Led by Abu Abdallah al-Shafii, who took over for Mullah Krekar in 2003, Ansar advocates for an ultra-orthodox Islamic ideology reminiscent of Wahhabism, which was founded in Saudia Arabia. It is presumed that Iraqi Kurds affiliated with Ansar al-Islam spent time in Afghanistan, initially fighting against Soviet forces during the 1980s and alongside the Taliban.[27]

Ansar was originally situated along the Iranian border, receiving military and financial support from Iran. While Iran found the Taliban dangerous and opposed the Talibanization of the region, there are several possible reasons it supports Ansar. Having a democratic proto-state on its border threatens Iran's Islamic republic. Continued guerrilla activity and any movement designed to spread Islamism in Kurdistan benefits Tehran. By supporting implementation of an Islamic state in Iraqi Kurdistan, Tehran may gain influence among the various factions within the new Iraqi government. Finally, the realization of an autonomous northern Iraqi region in Iraq will undoubtedly serve as a haven for Iranian Kurds seeking democratic agendas.

Although Operation Iraqi Freedom took a serious toll on Ansar's infrastructure through repeated bombings of its sanctuary in Iraqi Kurdistan, "the U.S. occupation may have spurred a resurgence of the organization and an infusion of new members in the form of foreign jihadists."[28] Since the U.S. invasion, membership has increased to an estimated 2,000–4,000, with an influx of foreign fighters from countries such as Afghanistan, Iran, Syria, Jordan, Morocco, Palestine, and Saudi Arabia. Many of those fighters fought alongside Afghan forces resisting Soviet invasion.

Ansar al-Islam's original resistance during its inception in 2001 was primarily directed toward secular Kurdish groups. Since the U.S. invasion, its focus has become increasingly anti-American, strengthening its ability to recruit worldwide. Within Iraq, they have been able to appeal to Sunni groups. Dan Darling notes, "While most Baathists do not adhere to the radical brand of Islam favored by Ansar, the anti-American bent of the organization would certainly make it attractive for Iraqi Sunnis, who are concerned more with their hatred of the Coalition and fear over Shiite nationalists than anything else."[29] According to Michael Rubin, Ansar regards the United States as the principal enabler of its Kurdish enemies, as well as an imperialist power that has defiled Muslim holy land through the presence of U.S. troops in Baghdad, the one-time center of the Caliphate and the crown jewel of Arab culture."[30] It appears that Ansar al-Islam no longer works as a miniature organization that controls a specific area.

The designation of these two groups as "Kurdish separatist terrorist groups" becomes highly problematic, considering that the motivations and/or targets of the two groups differ exponentially. The PKK seeks separation from Turkey with the desire for a democratic state, while Ansar al-Islam rallies around the pursuit of an Islamic state in Iraq. The generic publication of their respective "acts of terrorism," numbers of members, and ethnic profiles creates an illusion that the groups are somehow similar, resulting in misguided strategies for resolution.

Advancing U.S. Policies through "Terrorist Groups"

The Kurdish issue in Turkey proves especially difficult for the United States. On the one hand, the United States supports the right of self-determination. The United States Institute for Peace has held a number of forums to address both Kurdish rights to self-expression as linguistic freedom and public usage, and to condemn the Turkish government for its treatment of the Kurdish ethnic minority. On the other hand, the United States also provides Ankara with CIA intelligence regarding the movements and activities of the PKK, and provides military aid and hardware to the Turkish military so that it can pursue PKK fighters. The fact that the PKK declares its aims to promote secular democracy and defend Kurdish ethnic rights does not seem to hold sway over the United States, given that the Turkish government declares the organization to be a terrorist movement. Such paradoxes seem to run through much of U.S. policy regarding the Kurds. Even in Iraqi Kurdistan, the United States both supports and condemns expressions of Kurdish nationalism. Ansar al-Islam, which promotes a Wahhabist interpretation of Sunni Islam and opposes many of the PUK policies, is also seen by the United States as a terrorist organization. Specifically, the group was labeled a Specially Designated Terrorist Group (SDTG) that permits the use of military force in order to neutralize the organization.[31] Although the group formed in the autumn of 2001, it did not receive much attention until the run-up to the U.S. invasion of Iraq.

Colin Powell, in his speech to the United Nations' Security Council in February 2003, mentioned the terrorist threat posed by Ansar al-Islam and presented intelligence reports suggesting Ansar had established chemical labs and had access to weapons of mass destruction. Powell also suggested that there was a relationship between Ansar al-Islam, Saddam Hussein, and al Qaeda. Although estimates put Ansar al-Islam's membership at around 600, Powell nevertheless suggested that the group posed a significant threat to the United States. Surely such a small organization could be neutralized with little effort from a military superpower. Thus, it could be argued that the U.S. government linking Ansar al-Islam to the issue of weapons of mass destruction in Iraq and suggesting that the group posed a significant threat to U.S. security were mere tactics to garner additional international support for an invasion of Iraq. Curiously these tactics have resulted in something of a paradox: Since the U.S. invasion, membership in Ansar al-Islam has increased fourfold.

U.S. foreign policy on the Kurdish question waffles, depending on the political and economic gains envisaged by the United States at the time. James Ciment comments, "Every regional power with a Kurdish minority—and even a few without—has tried to use the Kurds for its own ends, sometimes for the purposes of keeping rival states off balance and sometimes, much to the chagrin of pan-Kurdish idealists, for the purposes of pitting one Kurdish national group against another."[32]

Previously implemented techniques to (a) deny rights of the Kurds in Turkey to maintain Turkish support and (b) prematurely propagate an imminent threat of a radical Islamic group in Northern Iraq has arguably perpetuated the global war on the West, instead of resolving the global war on terrorism. This is particularly true in the case of Ansar al-Islam. Mohamed Gharib, a Kurdish militant and the Ansar media chief said, "You wouldn't believe if I told you we were happy [to be attacked]. They gave us the sense that we were so true, so right, that even America had to come fight us."[33] Destabilizing the region, rallying nationalist movements, and jeopardizing access to valuable natural resources have all been reasons used by the United States to continue the suppression of Kurdish empowerment. Rather than supporting a minority that appears committed to democratic ideals and processes, the United States continues to support states plagued by human rights abuses and corruption aimed at those very groups interested in democratizing. It is this dichotomy that has plagued the Kurds and surrounding nation-states for decades. What if the United States and its allies could step outside the nation-state "box" and imagine an environment where self-determination was considered a democratic criterion? Would destabilization be the automatic consequence? In light of the recent proliferation of terrorist groups worldwide, the United States does not have much to lose.

PROGRESS AND PROSPECTS

Substantive and procedural issues for nation-states that inherently shape the Kurdistan conflict include the loss of natural-resource control, an upsurge in violence with the realization of Kurdish autonomy, the loss of profit from intra-conflict revenue sharing, and the loss of opportunities for the establishment of Shari'a law. Conversely, Kurdish issues comprise legislated political representation; equitable economic opportunities and the right to defend themselves through legislation; the ability to preserve, protect, and perpetuate their culture; an equitable share of natural-resource profits; the expansion of the Kurdish region in Iraqi Kurdistan; citizenship for all Kurds within existing borders; and retribution for Arab assimilation techniques, genocidal attacks, and a century of marginalization. The aforementioned diverse interests shape the following conflict-resolution recommendations.

Conflict-Resolution Recommendations

The Kurds have experienced a long and violent history with their host nation-states, and their positions have consistently centered on the realization of human rights for their people. Considering that the Kurdistan conflict is an intractable rights-based conflict and the multitude of stakeholders come to the table with divergent interests, multifaceted prevention, intervention, and resolution approaches are needed. The utilization of Track Two (unofficial diplomacy), citizen-based diplomacy is essential. The restructuring of Iraq, minimal violence between Kurdish parties, and relative stability between Kurds and their host nations creates a ripe moment to attempt transforming the Kurdistan narrative. The following recommendations and strategies should not be taken in a linear fashion, but rather simultaneously.

First, UN-sponsored truth commissions should be established in each country to elicit conversations and appropriate restitutions to advance trust among Kurds and their nation-states. The reversal of Arabization techniques should be legislated along with restorative justice initiatives to demonstrate the nation-states' commitment to resolving their internal conflicts.

Next, constitutional amendments for allowing Kurdish self-determination, such as equitable participation in national politics, equitable access to education, the right to rule their own autonomous regions, educating and broadcasting in the Kurdish language, the right to practice religion and culture of choice, and the right to benefit from the profits of oil exports based on population within existing international borders is critical. Cease-fire agreements have been signed, but there is little incentive for Kurds to stop their fight.

Although the United States, France, and other Western powers have played influential roles in mediating cease-fires, they lack the credibility to encourage governmental reform. International organizations that have a mandate to mediate in the realm of Track One (official diplomacy) initiatives, such as the UN or Organization of Islamic Countries, should be appointed to mediate on Kurdish-related issues.

Third, the creation of a regional Committee for Democratic Solution in Iraq could institutionalize conflict-resolution efforts in the region and serve as an example for neighboring nation-states. The committee would consist of professionals from academia, lower-level government, NGOs, and businesses who are trained in mediation, negotiation, and facilitation. The Conference on Democratic Resolution, held July 5–6, 1998, where Ocalan submitted a paper, discussed the possibility of such a committee.[34]

Finally, forums and conferences dedicated to the Kurdish issues and interests have proven successful in the past. The Brookings Institution notes, "A new network such as a NGO clearinghouse, specifically devoted to early warnings, and linking local and international NGOs to a central facility, could in theory enhance the timely quality of those signals, legitimate them, and enable the outcries of NGOs to be heard in the headquarters of the UN and in Washington, London, Bonn, Paris, and Tokyo. Had a recognizable channel existed in 1994, the Rwandan genocide might have been forestalled."[35] The greatest impediment for a network like this is convincing the political leaders of parties to fully participate, rather than simply sending statements.

CONCLUSION

In 1923, Western powers determined through the Treaty of Lausanne that the Kurds belonged to Turkey. Turkish became the country's language and its culture, forcing Kurdish identity into the shadows. As the Near East is potentially in another state of transformation, the West now has the power to reverse its unkept promise and empower Kurdish communities throughout the region to resist authoritarian regimes and continue to build on democratic ideals.

An independent Kurdistan, with all its resources shared equitably based on population, would be the ultimate solution. The first step would be the establishment of an autonomous region for Kurds in Iraqi Kurdistan. Yet Dunn sees that "the West is not about to condone an independent Kurdistan that might undermine the security of NATO ally Turkey, even if it discomfits Iran and Iraq and would thus be a logical instrument of 'dual containment.' Geopolitics is not yet ready for Kurdistan."[36] But sometimes history plays tricks on geopolitics.

Autonomy in Iraq may set the course for an independent or quasi-independent Kurdistan. But while Iraq may face dissolution given its deep Arab-Kurdish and Sunni-Shiite divisions, Turkey, Iran, and Syria are not anywhere near fragmenting. At the Kurdish Conflict Resolution Forum in 1998, Graham Fuller said:

> First of all, as I look at this Kurdish problem, I think rather than describing it as either ethnic or terrorist or economic or symptomatic of a broader issue, it's a practical problem. There is a crisis of minorities worldwide. And my simple-minded philosophy for the future is that those countries that cannot satisfy their minorities, allowing them to live the kind of life they wish, those countries are doomed to eternal civil war or turning into pariahs or losing their democracy or other very unpleasant things. And we see this globally.[37]

The deeper interests and needs are not only relevant to Iraq, but to the larger Kurdistan question. They trigger and sustain resistance throughout the Arab world to U.S. policy. Until policymakers throughout the Arab and Western worlds invest the needed time and resources into implementing strategies for redress, ending support for regimes and organizations that conduct acts of terrorism, and researching and creating collaborative resolutions, the fight will remain under the guise of mutual security threats. Unless this happens, the Kurds will tragically continue to be utilized as pawns by nation-states vested in the Middle East.

NOTES

1. Quoted in John Hassell, "Kurds Offer a Model but Also Challenge for a Postwar Iraq," Newhouse News Service, May 1, 2003.

2. The research on which this chapter is based utilized conflict-resolution mapping techniques created by Paul Wehr, Professor Emeritus, Department of Sociology at the University of Colorado Boulder. The chapter is a revised version of my presentation at the International Studies Association Annual Convention held in Honolulu, Hawaii, in March 2005. The author gratefully acknowledges the assistance of Dr. Carolyn M. Stephenson, Professor of Political Science at the University of Hawaii–Manoa, and Dr. Louis Kriesberg, Maxwell Professor Emeritus of Social Conflict Studies at Syracuse University, for their invaluable reflections and recommendations.

3. Ibid.

4. James Ciment, *The Kurds: State and Minority in Turkey, Iraq, and Iran* (New York: Facts on File, 1996), p. 1.

5. Kevin McKiernan, a photojournalist, has visited Turkey and northern Iraq a dozen times since the Gulf War. His work has appeared in *Time*, *Newsweek*, and *The New York Times*, and on ABC, CBS, and NBC. Online. Available HTTP: <http://www.arabfilm.com/cat.html?deptID=6>.

6. Ofra Bengio contends that the Kurds are not considered a strategic asset by the United States. C.f. "Autonomy in Kurdistan in Historical Perspective," *The Future of Kurdistan in Iraq*, Brendan O'Leary, John McGarry, and Khaled Salih, eds. (Philadelphia: University of Pennsylvania Press, 2005), p. 181.

7. Ibid.

8. United States Institute for Peace. Online. Available HTTP: <http://www.usip.org/peacewatch/2004/6/iraq1.html>.

9. "Neither Kurdish group gained much in the long run from accepting support from their enemy's enemy." Michael Collins Dunn, "The Kurdish 'Question': Is There an Answer? A Historical Overview," *Middle East Policy* Vol. 4, no. 1 (1995): 83. Online. Available HTTP: <www.questia.com>.

10. Ibid.

11. The discrepancies in how many Kurds were actually killed by the chemical attacks in Halajaba are substantial. If statisticians include the total who died directly in the attack and who went missing, the numbers reached 200,000. However, those who went missing could also be accounted for in the refugee numbers.

12. Tom Clancy with Anthony Zinni and Tony Koltz, *Battle Ready* (New York: Putnam, 2004), p. 200.

13. Congressman Bob Filner (D-CA), Washington Kurdish Institute, *Kurdish Conflict Resolution Forum* (July 28–29, 1998). Online. Available HTTP: <http://www.kurd.org/kcrf/KCRF.html>.

14. Ami Ayalon, Edna Liftman, Bruce Maddy, eds., *The Middle East Contemporary Survey*: 1994, Vol. 18 (Boulder, CO: Westview Press, 1997), p. 638.

15. CBC News: The fifth Estate: The Forgotten People—One Man's Battle. Online. Available HTTP: <http://www.cbc.ca/fifth/kurds/battle.html>.

16. Ibid.

17. Quoted in John Hassell, "Kurds Offer a Model but Also Challenge for a Postwar Iraq," Newhouse News Service, May 1, 2003.

18. Brendan O'Leary, "Power Sharing, Pluralist Federation, and Federacy." The Future of Kurdistan in Iraq. Brendan O'Leary, John McGarry, and Khaled Salih, eds. (Philadelphia: University of Pennsylvania Press, 2005), p. 59.

19. Ibid.

20. Ibid.

21. Valadi Mansour, "The Kurds in Iran: From the Mahabad Republic Until Present," personal interview with father. (April 19, 1998). Online. Available HTTP: <http://www.valadi.com/Kurds.html>.

22. Michael Collins Dunn, "The Kurdish 'Question': Is There an Answer? A Historical Overview," *Middle East Policy* Vol. 4, no. 1 (1995), p. 86.
23. MIPT Terrorism Knowledge Base, http://www.tkb.org/Group.jsp?groupID=3501.
24. Washington Kurdish Institute, *Kurdish Conflict Resolution Forum* (July 28–29, 1998). Online. Available HTTP: <http://www.kurd.org/kcrf/KCRF.html>.
25. Jean-Christophe Peuch, "Turkey: Government Under Growing Pressure To Meet Kurdish Demands," *Radio Free Europe/RadioLiberty* (August 17, 2005). Online. Available HTTP: <http://www.rferl.org/>.
26. MIPT Terrorism Knowledge Base, http://www.tkb.org/Group.jsp?groupID=3501.
27. *The Christian Science Monitor,* "The Rise and Fall of Ansar al-Islam" (October 16, 2003). Online. Available HTTP: <http://www.csmonitor.com/2003/1016/p12s01-woiq.html>.
28. Washington Kurdish Institute, *Kurdish Conflict Resolution Forum* (July 28–29, 1998). Online. Available HTTP: <http://www.kurd.org/kcrf/KCRF.html>.
29. Dan Darling, ed. Rohan Gunaratna, *Ansar al-Islam Dossier, Center for Policing Terrorism* (July 30, 2004), p. 18.
30. Michael Rubin, "The Islamic Threat in Iraqi Kurdistan," *Middle East Intelligence Bulletin*, December 2001.
31. Treasury Department statement regarding the designation of Ansar al-Islam, Feb 20, 2003. Online. Available HTTP: <http://www.treas.gov/press/releases/js48.htm>.
32. James Ciment, found in Louis Proyect "Resistance: In the eye of the American Hegemon, The Kurdish Pawn." Online. Available HTTP: <http://www.swans.com/library/art10/iraq/proyect.html>.
33. *The Christian Science Monitor,* "The Rise and Fall of Ansar al-Islam" (October 16, 2003). Online. Available HTTP: <http://www.csmonitor.com/2003/1016/p12s01-woiq.html>.
34. *Kurdistan Observer,* "Ocalan: My historical mission for peace ceases," Ozgur Politica, (July 6, 2003). http://home.cogeco.ca/~konuche/8-7-03-apo-historic-mission.html.
35. The Brookings Institution, *Vigilance and Vengeance: NGOs Preventing Ethnic Conflict in Divided Societies* (Washington, DC, 1996): p. iii.
36. Michael Collins Dunn, "The Kurdish 'Question': Is There an Answer? A Historical Overview," *Middle East Policy* Vol. 4, no. 1 (1995), p. 86.
37. Graham Fuller *(RAND Corp),* July 28, 1998, Washington Kurdish Institute, *Kurdish Conflict Resolution Forum* (July 28–29, 1998). Online. Available HTTP: <http://www.kurd.org/kcrf/KCRF.html>.

II

Europe and the Post-Soviet Region

Kosovo

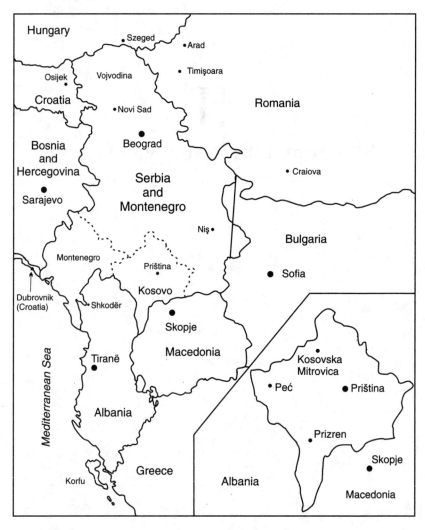

4

KOSOVO

Susan Fink Yoshihara

NATURE OF THE FLASHPOINT

In March 2004, NATO leaders prepared to gather in Kosovo to commemorate the fifth anniversary of their largest military campaign: a war to liberate the Muslim population of Kosovo from the repressive Serbian government. Suddenly, the small province broke out into its worst ethnic violence since the end of the 1999 war, leaving 20 dead, 800 injured, and 400 ethnic Serbs and Roma displaced.[1] This time it was Muslims burning Orthodox Christian churches, destroying neighborhoods, and killing and injuring hundreds. As NATO responded with increased military forces, it appeared that the UN vision of building a multiethnic state in the heart of the Balkans was about to vanish.

In the aftermath of this crisis, the international community was faced with deciding Kosovo's final status, and leaders remain deeply divided on the issue. Muslim Kosovar Albanians seek independence; Serbs want autonomy for their Orthodox Christian minorities. Extremists promote a "Greater Albania" or "Greater Kosovo" on one side; Serb nationalists clamor for "Greater Serbia" on the other. Meanwhile, economic and political progress has been slowed by continued ethnic animosity, which prevents quelling such extremist aspirations.

This chapter looks at the reason why getting the resolution to Kosovo's final status right is so critical to the broader war on terrorism. It shows how, no matter the final-status outcome, the pattern of corruption, ethnic division, uneven and stunted economic development, and problems with international administration threaten to make Kosovo a flashpoint for future violence. While incursion by international terrorist groups like al Qaeda is unlikely, continued hostilities or future atrocities could reignite calls for international intervention.

HISTORICAL CONTEXT

The Balkans, and Kosovo in particular, have a history of diverse religions and cultures coexisting throughout hundreds of years of political change.[2] The idea of Greater Albania and Kosovo's independence has been attributed to the fallout from the rapid decline of the Ottoman Empire and its deleterious effects on Albanians after a period of privilege under the Ottoman Turks.[3] Kosovar society has become increasingly divided between ethnic Muslim Albanians and Orthodox Serbs in the seven years of international occupation and administration. Calls by the Kosovo Liberation Army (KLA)[4] for an independent Kosovo and Greater Albania in the last decade inspired the 6 million Albanians living in the Balkan countries of Albania, Macedonia, Greece, and the former Yugoslavia to seek greater recognition or more autonomy.[5] With active NATO involvement beginning in 1998, open warfare defined along national lines was largely avoided, and national leaders in these countries condemn any notion of creating a Greater Albania. Today Kosovo, once the Balkan flashpoint, is a virtual international protectorate that with continued international attention can resist external forces attempting to reignite the conflict and create a Greater Albania at the expense of state sovereignty.

Albanian Nationalism

Albanian nationalism can be directly attributed to political decisions made by powers outside the province and by the violence and international attention that ensued from these decisions. Julie Mertus has explored the rise of Albanian nationalism between 1971 and 1981, during which time Yugoslavia "indulged" Albanian nationalism by giving Albanians in Kosovo the opportunities for a re-flowering of Albanian culture at a time when other nationalities had to keep expressions of nationalism under wraps.[6] The cultural leeway led to political dissent, and Kosovar Albanians comprised the largest percentage of political prisoners during the 1970s and 1980s. In addition, the government claimed to have uncovered scores of underground Kosovar Albanian separatist organizations during that time.[7]

The torture of Albanian prisoners added even more fuel to the flame of secession, created so-called "martyrs" for the cause, and drove the structure of the resistance into a small, loosely connected, underground "web" of cells. Not only did Belgrade's repression of Albanian nationalism strengthen the independence movement, but it gave the plight of the Kosovar Albanians' international attention throughout the decade, which was exemplified by National Geographic's cover story featuring the province in 1990.[8] It has been argued that it is international politicization and media coverage, more than machinations in Belgrade or Pristina, that drove the conflict to a head in 1999, resulting in NATO military intervention.[9]

Historical Patterns of Inequality

Arguments about ideological underpinnings and historical foundations of contemporary politics, while seemingly trivial to decision makers in the West, are of daily consequence to the people of Kosovo,[10] where, "history is war by other means."[11] The Albanians maintain that they are descendents of the ancient Illyian people and that their language is one of the seven original Indo-European tongues. Serb nationalists, on the other hand, maintain that the Albanians arrived only 300 years ago in the Balkans and that they are in fact Serbs.[12] Along with disputing their very origins and rights-of-claim to the province, contemporary nationalists find in the nineteenth century and World War II ample ammunition to illustrate genuine atrocities committed by individuals on both sides of the conflict. Taken with the violence that occurred during the past several decades, a sort of structural violence emerged.[13] Vengeance and retaliations, long part of clan codes of honor, were increasingly committed along ethnic and religious lines, producing cohesion of identity on both sides.[14]

Struggle for Liberation and Terrorism

Nationalism, not religion, is the main contention in the Kosovo case. Yet religion acts as an intervening variable in the violence, and in furthering the goal of independence on one hand or continued Serbian sovereignty over the region on the other. While the conflict is not religious in nature, the nature of religion and identity is a complex one, and comprehending the cultural dimension is vital in understanding the dynamics of cooperation and conflict.

Annexed by Serbia in 1912, Kosovo was a highly autonomous province of the Republic of Serbia until Serbian leader Slobodan Milosevic negated its autonomy in 1989. This act, followed by outright discrimination against ethnic Albanians and repression of political dissent in the province, provoked calls for Kosovo's liberation. The vanguard of this movement was a group of younger leaders who created the KLA in Macedonia in 1992 with the goal of uniting the ethnic Albanian populations of Kosovo, Albania, Greece, and Macedonia into Greater Albania.[15] Framed along the lines of local clans, it operated in dispersed cells and did not have a rigid, hierarchical structure. The KLA gained notoriety and popular support after the Dayton Accords in 1995, when negotiators decided against addressing the issue of Kosovo's status, undermining support for Kosovo's political moderates, and giving legitimacy to KLA's extremist views and tolerance for its terrorist attacks against Serbian Police outposts in Kosovo. The unfortunate result of leaving Kosovo off the table at the Dayton Accords was a seeming indifference to the moderates.[16] Having lost legitimacy at Dayton, the moderates' leader, Ibrahim Rugova, even expressed fears about returning to Serbia. It was not coincidental that the KLA's first attacks on Yugoslavia came shortly after the accords marginalized the moderates, neglected the question of Kosovo altogether, and seemed to give a green light to the extremes on both sides.[17]

Escalation of the violence throughout 1997 paralleled a shifting of the locus of legitimacy among Albanians from the moderates to the extremists led by the KLA. Legitimacy among Kosovar Albanians is largely determined by clan elders, rather than by popular support. The councils of elders among the clans agree on the best courses of action for the nation and disseminate their conclusions via an intricate communications network throughout the clans. This same cohesion is evident in the KLA insurgent attacks that seem extremely well-coordinated, with troops of various clans showing up to attack a common target, but without formal planning.

The organization's numbers swelled as Serbian crackdowns against it grew more brutal, especially because of Serb violence and "ethnic cleansing." Whereas the KLA was reported to have 500 members in 1998, by the beginning of 1999 it was 12,000 to 20,000 strong. It grew even stronger in popular support when the United States gave material support to the group in its common fight against regular Yugoslav military (VJ) forces. The Americans removed the KLA from its list of terrorist organizations in 1998, and began to cultivate KLA leaders as interlocutors for negotiations with the Serbs. The coordination of NATO airpower and KLA ground forces forced Serbian troop withdrawal in June 1999.[18] However, since the end of the conflict in 1999 and international occupation and administration of the province, the KLA was officially disbanded and its members entered the Kosovo Protection Corps (KPC). Its leaders entered a parallel government, the Provisional Institutions of Self-Government (PISG). Agim Ceku, who was made head of the KLA after fighting with the Croatian Army, was put in charge of transforming the KLA into the KPC in June 1999. Hashim Thaci, the KLA member often pointed to by NATO as the embodiment of the Kosovo "freedom fighters," served as prime minister of the provisional government and chairman of the Democratic Party of Kosovo (DPK).[19] These transitions notwithstanding, attacks attributed to the KLA continued in Macedonia into 2001 and led to the Ohrid Agreement that set minimum quotas for ethnic Albanians in the Macedonian government.[20]

Since the end of the 1999 NATO campaign and the 2000 elections, many of the Kosovar Albanians have felt a de facto independence with the presence of the UN administration. Continued Serb exclusion from Kosovo has become the fundamental demand of many Kosovar Albanians, but it is sharply at odds with the desires of the international community.[21] Kosovo's first democratically elected government put former KLA leader Ramush Haradinaj in office as prime minister. Haradinaj was seen as a reformer, but had to step down in 2005 after he was indicted for war crimes and voluntarily faced trial in The Hague. His replacement was seen as more moderate, but the tension between moderates and extremists remains in Kosovo. Hardliners in the PISG declare their intent to expel all Serbs and see national independence as the only way to guarantee security. The success of the extremists inside the government in rallying the population to its cause of a Greater Albania remains unclear.

The International Crisis Group (ICG) believes that Albanian Muslims may be preparing to turn their frustrations into violence that is increasingly aimed toward the international presence. The popular Serbian and Macedonian press has echoed this fear,[22] and tension between UNMIK and Kosovar Albanians remains high.[23] UN property was burned during the riots of March 2004. Some suggest that the anti-international sentiment is uneven. For example, whereas the American sector has been relatively peaceful, the French sector is troubled, and anti-French sentiment among Kosovar Albanians is strong.[24] The anti-Western sentiment is growing and may make the conflict more mutable into the broader goals of global terrorism.

LINKAGES TO TERRORISM

If there is a link between the KLA and al Qaeda or other international terrorist movements, it is not ideational. The KLA gets no perceivable credibility or legitimacy among the Kosovar Albanian people by linking itself to a broader fight either for Islam or against the United States. When such anti-Western rhetoric is used, it is localized, i.e., it is directed toward the "occupying" forces on the ground in Kosovo. The lack of explicit linkage to a broader movement of religious extremism persists even though there are several sources asserting that groups such as al Qaeda, and even Osama bin Laden himself, were on the ground in Kosovo in 1998. Bin Laden apparently set up terrorist training camps in neighboring Albania with the support of the leadership, but his attempts to recruit followers in Kosovo largely failed. No KLA members or former members are reported to be among the detainees in Guantanamo Bay, Cuba, for example.[25]

On the other hand, the influx of weapons and training in 1998 may have contributed to the material support for the KLA against the Serbs; this may have occurred even with the consent of the Clinton administration. At the time the Americans shifted their policy, questions were raised about the wisdom of allying with a group that not only used extremist tactics, but was also connected to international organized crime, drug trafficking, and other illegal behavior. Facing this legacy is problematic for American policymakers now waging a war on terror or struggle against the kind of violence that the KLA employed.

Although there may not be obvious ideational links between the KLA and international terrorists, there may be material ones. Some have claimed that the explosives used in the terrorist bombings in London on July 7, 2005, and the on the Madrid railway on March 11, 2004, were provided by a former KLA leader who maintains connections to Hashim Thaci and operates from Kosovo with links in Bosnia.[26] There is a perception among many international officials working inside Kosovo that the province is under the influence of mafia-like organizations.[27] Kosovo's porous borders make it a route and destination for international trafficking.[28] International attempts to combat drug and human trafficking, especially sexual slavery, have met the stone wall of corrupt judges and a weak criminal justice infrastructure. This is further complicated by a legacy of clan codes and vendettas that perpetuate violence and frustrate efforts to instill a modern system of justice.

The conflict in Kosovo does not appear to play a large role in the broader use of violent religious extremism. For example, a survey of Osama bin Laden's speeches from 1998–2005 reveals that he has ignored the conflict. This is conspicuous since bin Laden justifies terrorism against the United States as retribution for American intervention in other Muslim states such as Somalia, Bosnia, Iraq, and Afghanistan, as well as its lack of intervention in other Muslim territories such as Palestine. It is likely that America's war against Serbia and support to the Kosovar Albanian insurgency serve as contradictory evidence to bin Laden's message.

Analysts in the West remain puzzled about why Arab leaders do not give more credit to the United States and European nations for coming to the aid of Muslim nations four times in the 1990s, first in Kuwait, then in Somalia, and particularly in Bosnia and Kosovo.[29] Arab indifference toward Kosovo and bin Laden's exclusion of the case can be explained by the inherent weakness of their claim that there is a clash of civilizations between the Christian-Western and Muslim worlds. Some argue that the pattern of Western support for Albanian Muslims does not fit the "branding" of Islam as a religion of liberation from oppression.[30]

Their indifference also bolsters those who see global terrorism as a violent struggle within Islam. Extremists, and even some Arab leaders, may ignore the plight of Kosovar Albanians because the Albanian practice of Islam varies sharply with their own.

The Nature of Islam in Kosovo

As Noel Malcolm has noted, the Kosovo conflict is deceiving, because on the surface it looks very much like an ethnic and religious conflict,[31] but upon examination,

> The idea of ethnic or religious hatred welling up from popular psychology starts to seem less convincing. The Albanians of [the] Kosovo of today are in many ways politically mobilized people, but religion has played almost no role at all in that mobilization.[32]

Mobilization was based on the perception of irreconcilable differences between the Orthodox Serbs and Muslim Kosovar Albanians. This was not always so. According to Ger Duijzings:

> What predominates now in the minds of most Serbs and Albanians, as well as of most outside observers, is the image of a deeply rooted and unbridgeable rift between Serbs and Albanians ... If we adopt a long-term perspective, we do not need to go far back into history to see that *Kosovo was essentially a pluralistic society, where various ethnic groups coexisted, many languages were spoken, and all major religions of the Balkans were represented.*[33] [emphasis added]

Albanian nationalism is secular, and the Albanian practice of Islam is largely subsumed into cultural and national identity. When one refers to himself in Kosovo, he does not say "I am a Muslim" or "I am a Christian," but rather "I am Albanian," or "I am a Serb." And in the company of other Albanians, clan identity becomes more prevalent and divisive.[34] This is in contrast to Bosnian, Serbian, and Croatian nationalism, where advocates on several sides of the Yugoslav civil war spoke the same language and so painted their adversaries in religious terms. In Kosovo, it is the national and linguistic divide that trumps.

Attempts to inject a romantic or religious form of Albanian nationalism, similar to that in Bosnia, have failed in the past. Shiite-oriented Sufism, which is said to outnumber Sunni Muslims in some cities in Kosovo, is seen as an "abomination" to Wahhabis from Saudi Arabia and made it difficult for the Saudis to make inroads in 1999.[35] The Wahhabi preachers, armed with money and the promise of rebuilding destroyed towns and mosques, were offended by the presence of gravestones, which they called idolatrous. When they destroyed the priceless headstones without hindrance from UN security officials, Albanians protested.

It is indicative of the intent of the humanitarian groups such as the Saudi Joint Relief Committee for Kosovo (SJRCK) that most of their efforts were focused on mosque-building as opposed to other needs such as employment or health.[36] The focus on education was limited to Wahhabi instruction, and radio broadcasts were in Arabic and propagated fundamental Islam. All of these efforts met with condemnation by Kosovar Albanian leaders and were viewed as an attempt to wipe out Albanian culture through Wahhabi Islam. The KLA-backed news agency warned:

> For more than a century, civilized countries have separated religion from the state ... we now see attempts not only in Kosovo but everywhere Albanians live to introduce religion into public schools ... Supplemental courses for children have been set up by foreign Islamic organizations who hide behind assistance programs ... It is time for Albanian mosques to be separated from Arab connections and for Islam to be developed on the basis of Albanian culture.[37]

And yet, by 2004, children were increasingly seen wearing the short pants of Wahhabist schools and Albanian women walked the streets of Pristina fully covered in the garb common to Arab Muslim women.[38] While this may well be an indication of the rising popularity of fundamental Islam, it is also widely rumored that these women are paid $20,000 to wear the burqua.[39] In a nation as poor as Kosovo, this is strong incentive to worship, study, and clothe oneself in the "foreign" religion if it means providing basic needs for the family.

In April 2005 the Belgrade-based BKTV reported that Kosovo as well as Bosnia had become "springboard[s] for Islamic terrorists."[40] In particular, analysts warned of a terrorist "green line" for fake documents and arms that passed into Western Europe through Kosovo, Macedonia, southern Serbia, and Bosnia. Additionally, to the Serbian eye it appears that the increasing presence of religious instruction and separate classrooms for boys and girls in southern Serbia are indicators of the growing presence of political Islam inside the country.[41]

Serbian Radical Party chairman Tomislav Nikolic announced publicly that Serbians should prepare to defend itself from Kosovar Albanian "terrorists" organizing under the aegis of the Kosovo Protection Corps for attacks on southern Serbia. He claimed that the group was awaiting helicopters and other armaments from Croatia.[42] While other Serbian leaders downplay such reports, these warnings have left Serbs in northern Kosovo and southern Serbia in a heightened sense of fear and vulnerability.

Whether for lack of evidence or lack of Pristina's incentive to investigate, links to al Qaeda remain difficult to confirm. One former KLA fighter in the Kosovo and Macedonia wars, Samindin Xherairi (alias Hoxha), has been linked to al Qaeda but also to German and American intelligence, but he insists that these links are not provable. In one confidential 2002 report, Hoxha was said to have been in charge of setting up a branch of Hezbollah in Kosovo, and his phone number was among those taken from al Qaeda members.[43] Even so, he insisted that there are no Kosovar Albanian links to the group because,

> Albanians have realized who favors their issues and which are the decision-making circles. We expect the UN to accept Kosova's statehood; therefore, what kind of decision-making factor is Al-Qa'idah? All those who have worked for national issues, even before the 1960s, knew that the solution to the problem of Kosova is in the West.[44]

The U.S. KFOR commander of the multinational brigade (MNB Southwest) also maintained that while he could not rule out that there were individuals with links to al Qaeda in Kosovo, he ruled out the presence of active groups inside Kosovo.[45]

Serbian Religious Nationalism

Serbs do not share the secular-political approach to the conflict. In many ways, Kosovo occupies a sacred place not only in the soil but in the minds of Serbian Orthodox Christians. Some see the primary Serbian attachment to the province not as economic, but as "sentimental and religious":

This is where the Serbian nation found its ethnic identity and Christian soul, and where hundreds of historic churches and monasteries stood dating back a thousand years. The Patriarchate of Pec is to the Serbs as Rome is to the Catholics, and Mecca to Muslims.[46]

The Serbian Orthodox Church, with influential ties to the government in Belgrade, has asked that Kosovo and its monasteries be declared "sacred land" akin to Jerusalem for Muslims and Jews.[47] Yet, while the "lost heart of the Balkans" has religious significance for Orthodox Christians, there is little evidence that conflicts in Kosovo were religious in nature until the politicization of religion in the nineteenth century.[48] The destruction of a Serbian Orthodox church during the March 2004 riots gave credence to the extremists on the Serb side. Therefore, ensuring the safety of Christian sites is in the best interests of the international community.[49]

PROGRESS AND PROSPECTS

Several material conditions have persisted during the seven years of international presence that may contribute to further violence if unresolved, or could help immunize the province from extremism if sufficiently addressed. Slow repatriation and continued ethnic division, undermined credibility of the international presence, and stunted economic, social, and political development cause conflict and hamper cooperation.

Serbs Slow to Return

Building multiethnic, multiconfessional democracies is one of the means to fight the spread of international terrorists and the states that harbor them. Kosovo was to be a model for this plan, but is now in jeopardy of becoming a cautionary tale. Fewer than 10 percent of the 180,000–200,000 Serbs who fled Kosovo during the NATO campaign have returned, despite the efforts of international organizations.[50] They left when Serbian troops withdrew and around 800,000 Albanians, who had fled during the harsh Serb crackdowns, were repatriated. Barbed wire now protects those few Serbs who have come home. In Orahovac, only 500 of the 3,000 Serb residents remain, and these fear using their native tongue on the street, and do not leave their "ghetto" without an armed escort.[51]

In a typical case in the small town of Klina, a multiethnic village where 60 percent of the property belonged to Serbs before the NATO bombing, only a few Serb families have returned.[52] An American official working at the UN Office of Returns in Klina explains that the biggest obstacle to Serb repatriation is not Serb fear of return, but Albanian fear of Serbs: "Albanians were afraid that we weren't just going to bring Serbs back, but that we were going to bring Serbia back to Kosovo."[53] At the root of the fear, according to Albanians in Klina, are their missing relatives.[54] The ICRC lists nearly 2,700 missing persons from the Kosovo wars.[55] Missing family members is a constant reason cited for continued suspicion and fear on both sides.[56]

Extreme positions have hardened since the 1999 international intervention along with few avenues of mutual understanding and cooperation at the popular level. When Serbs boycotted entry into Kosovo's provisional institutions in June 2005, Serb leaders warned that they risked allowing the Albanian majority "to make their own moves against those on the Serbian side."[57] The fear for security and lack of avenues for communication in a common language makes the civil society vulnerable to manipulation from local leaders and outside actors.

The Dark Side of the International Presence

Since 1999, there have been five special representatives for the UN secretary-general for Kosovo. The ongoing uncertainty about final status and withdrawal of donor support and investment caused a reversal of post-conflict reconstruction and a subsequent recession in 2003. Unemployment rose to 60 percent, and the violence of early 2004 can be attributed in part to this economic reality. In a tacit admission that violence and the unresolved final status are linked,[58] UNMIK loosened the 2002 "standards before status" restrictions in 2004, calling for "standards and status" and status review beginning in mid-2005 led by former president of Finland, Maarti Ahtisaari.[59]

Yet, the resolution of final status is not the only driver of violence. Another complication is the continued feeling of victimhood on both sides. As the Macedonian Albanian leader Arben Xhaferi once aptly explained, "People don't want to be weak citizens but strong soldiers, because they know that in the Former Yugoslavia, to be a weak citizen was to be a potential victim."[60] From this perspective, it was the KLA's excitation of violence that mobilized the international community, and especially the Contact Group and NATO, into a war against Serbia. The prolonged four-pillar international government has kept Serbia from governing Kosovo and has thus made any return of Serb authority unthinkable to Albanians. The representatives of the disputing parties are asymmetric and distant, since one is in Belgrade, and the others are local and clan leaders in Kosovo. This asymmetry will make negotiation for and implementation of final status complex.

Meanwhile, international sympathies on the ground have shifted. Only two years into the KFOR mission, an American KFOR soldier captured the international mood swing noting, "I got used to thinking of Serbs as the oppressors, because of Bosnia. But here we're really protecting Serbs from the Albanians."[61] Major General Lewis MacKenzie, former UN commander in Bosnia, said:

> The Kosovar Albanians played us like a Stradivarius violin. We have subsidized and indirectly supported their violent campaign for an ethnically pure Kosovo. We have never blamed them for being the perpetrators of the violence in the early 1990s, and we continue to portray them as the designated victim today, in spite of evidence to the contrary.[62]

Unsurprisingly, at the same time international perceptions of the Albanians worsened, the relationship between the internationals and Belgrade grew closer.[63] While UNMIK agreed to work more aggressively for the safety of Serbs against Albanians in the divided city of Mitrovica, the situation has devolved such that UNMIK often looks the other way as an organized and emboldened Serb-backed security force and civilian groups enforce policies of hardline Serbians in North Mitrovica.[64]

It is Mitrovica that has been the scene of the successive incidents of mass violence in February 2000, April 2002, and March 2004. The ICG has criticized the UNMIK and the NATO-led KFOR for failing to enforce their mandates and acquiescing in policing the "makeshift" security arrangements that keep citizens of the municipality separated from their homes on the other side of the Ibar River.[65] Serbs and Kosovar Albanians live in enclaves in the city and rarely interact.

After the 1999 NATO operation, Vojislav Kostunica, Serb nationalist and later president, declared publicly, "KFOR enabled and in some way supported or was helping the terrorists."[66] Suspicion has persisted, and Serbs felt betrayed by UNMIK and KFOR after the March 2004 riots for failing to expose the Albanian causes of the violence.[67] This suspicion has given way to open attacks on KFOR troops over the years. One observer noted:

> There is an indelible sense that UNMIK has a vested interest in maintaining the status quo. On their fat-cat salaries, the internationals are widely perceived as self-serving profiteers, while among the locals only a small elite of translators and landlords are prospering.[68]

Further undermining international legitimacy between 2002 and 2005, UN personnel in Kosovo were implicated in the most egregious cases of human trafficking and prostitution in a scandal that was widespread among UN peacekeeping and police.[69] Internationals are said to account for 20 percent of the customers for illegal prostitution in Kosovo even though they account for 2 percent of the population.[70] Here the nexus of international presence and the history of Kosovo's links to organized crime are most apparent.

Poor Human Development and Economic Progress

Human development has suffered from the symptoms of conflict and sluggish repatriation.[71] Serbia and Montenegro remain among the highest-ranked nations in two of the twelve indicators for failing states: the rise of factionalized elites and uneven economic development along group lines. Despite international intervention, the province remains among the most divided nations and territories internationally.[72] A 2005 Freedom House listing of nations in transit found Kosovo has a high ranking of the provinces in the Balkans in all categories of political and civil society, but the democratic index in Kosovo shows a declining level of political freedom and religious tolerance, and has not yet established freedom of the press.[73]

More than half the Kosovar population of 2 million lives at or below the poverty line.[74] With Kosovo still officially a province of Serbia but run entirely by the parallel structures of the international community and fragile local government, its economy operates outside the limits of a sovereign state. This makes investors and insurance agencies reluctant to operate and has resulted in a shadow, even criminal, economy.[75] The attraction of foreign direct investment is considered the most important factor in raising the GDP of economies in transition. While other countries in the region have been able to attract FDI, Kosovo's many problems continue to keep investors at bay and negatively affect FDI in Serbia, Montenegro, and, to a lesser extent, Macedonia.[76] USAID cites problems of poor infrastructure, the lack of a trained workforce, and political uncertainty and corruption as causal factors in stymieing foreign investment.[77]

Three Emerging Vulnerabilities

In addition to these persistent problems, there are at least three more emerging issues that could push events either way to weaken or strengthen Kosovo's resistance to more violence and possible exploitation by global terrorists.

The first vulnerability for extremism is a new permissiveness in Kosovar society. An open society promoted by the international administration has undermined traditional authority and inspired experimental behavior. This dramatic cultural change has the potential to fuel a conservative backlash as traditional families reject the negative trappings of modernity.

The second vulnerability comes from external political trends. Europeans who put their trust in economic development to solve Kosovo's political and social problems advocate keeping the province inside Serbia to hasten its entry into the EU.[78] The recent "no" vote of France and the Netherlands for further expansion of the EU jeopardizes this prospect and the support that moderates in Kosovo and other former communist societies have enjoyed in the last decade.[79] While economic progress is essential, the people of Kosovo consistently choose policies that promote independence and the removal of Serbs over policies that improve their economic well-being.

Finally, demographic trends, comprising a high Albanian birth rate alongside the diminishing Serb population, will regionalize Kosovo's ethnic dynamics. In Macedonia, Muslim population is rapidly increasing as a percentage of the overall population, and unemployment remains high. This combination has rekindled anxieties among regional leaders about a *de facto* Greater Albania.[80] Likewise, Serbian minorities as well as Albanians in Macedonia, Montenegro, and Albania will remain wary of international prescriptions along these lines. International decision makers must accept this reality, make policies that anticipate its ramifications, and resist attempts to lower the Albanian birthrate that may spark fears of renewed ethnic cleansing.

FIVE LESSONS FOR THE U.S. GLOBAL WAR ON TERRORISM

The search for parsimony in policy may not give due credit to the complexities of local circumstances. Policy based on the most elegant counterterrorism strategy can be dangerous if not coherent with local circumstance. With a view to closing the gap between strategic perception and local circumstance, this chapter has looked at the relationship between religion, identity, and violence in a region in which security and not religious rivalries are the local frame of reference for conflict and cooperation. Five preliminary lessons emerge:

Don't conflate ends and means. The Kosovo case offers broader lessons for those shaping American counterterrorism strategy who often assume that secular Muslims, like moderate Muslims, are not the chief concern for policymakers. Albanian Muslims are secular in their outlook and yet continue to resort to violence, including terrorist tactics.

Watch out for international actors. The situation in Kosovo also forces the United States to examine the assumption that the violence there has been primarily the result of internal conflict. External actors have played a role in the violent nature of responses to local disputes. Reaction to external decisions, such as the Dayton Accords, should stand as reminders to Western policymakers in the years ahead that while Kosovar Albanians look to the West, it is mostly as guarantor of their independence from Serbia. What's more, the international presence must regain equilibrium in guaranteeing minority rights and maintain the highest standards of ethical behavior lest it become a lightening rod for extremist, anti-Western sentiment.

Sovereignty still counts. After seven years as a UN protectorate, often called a model for international administration and reconstruction, many conclude that it is Kosovar impatience for final settlement that ultimately fans the flames of violence. The most recent violence is just one of three incidents in two decades in which uncertainty about sovereignty has led to bloodshed in the region. Western decision makers increasingly refer to a "conditional sovereignty" for Kosovo. This term, while attractive to theorists and policymakers, has little relevance in the hearts and minds of the Kosovar and Serbian people. An overly optimistic attachment to the notion of conditional sovereignty without persistent international attention and investment in Kosovo risks putting American policy dangerously out of touch with facts on the ground.

Some contend that granting any kind of sovereignty will increase insecurity for Serbs in the province, as well as in Serbia and Montenegro, legitimizes a corrupt government in Pristina and creates a moral hazard since it will undermine the word of the UNSC. UNSCR 1244, under which NATO intervened in 1999, expressly ruled out independence. Some claim that if it is granted to Kosovar Albanians it will encourage other disgruntled minorities throughout the world to use violence leading to international intervention in order to gain independence. Prominent Americans have recently called publicly for independence.[81] Yet, the United States must walk the line between the short-term goal of averting Kosovar Albanian violence and the long-term prospects for creating an ethnically intolerant Muslim secular state in the heart of the Balkans that may be increasingly vulnerable to international crime and terrorism in the coming decades.

Support the moderates. The Kosovo case vindicates framers of the American counterterrorism strategy who claim that bolstering moderates is the key to fighting violent extremism. U.S. Senator Joseph Biden noted, "If we get Kosovo right, Muslims around the world will be reminded how the United States came to the aid of Kosovo's Muslim population and helped them build a strong, independent, multiethnic democracy."[82] Ironically, it was by U.S. and international failure to learn this lesson in 1995 that helped the KLA transform quickly into a popularly supported, burgeoning regional terrorist organization that was able to gain international legitimacy due to strategic circumstances. Decision makers must be even more careful that future policies bolster moderates in Pristina and Belgrade, as well as in Macedonia and Albania.

Culture matters. Finally, in the war on terrorism a debate has emerged about the root causes of violent religious extremism: Is it primarily a clash of ideas or a clash of culture? The Kosovo case shows that culture can be a strong buffer against radical ideas. As Kosovar society is increasingly exposed to outside forces, the very traditional culture that has immunized it from manipulation may be weakened with deleterious effects for Kosovars and for the war on terrorism. Policymakers can help Kosovars bolster the best of their traditional culture while modernizing their political system.

In the years ahead, Kosovo could provide a model for the way the United States can successfully suppress extremism during post-war nation building. On the other hand, it could prove a disastrous case of failed reconstruction, a reflash of ethnic and religious retrenchment, and a magnet for religious extremists. While the roots and conditions of the conflict are essentially material and political, the secular nature of Islam in Kosovo cannot be expected to immunize the province from the dynamics of religious extremism indefinitely so long as underlying socioeconomic problems remain unresolved. The failure of successive political regimes to resolve these issues have caused the Kosovar people to suffer unspeakably, especially in the last decade. There now opens a window of opportunity to reverse their fortune and make good on the promises of democracy.

NOTES

1. Tim Judah, "Kosovo sets out on Road to Independence," *Financial Times*, 24 October 2005.
2. Ivo Andric's famous novel, *The Bridge on the Drina*, is a classic explanation of how diverse populations lived together throughout a stormy history.
3. The idea of a separate Albania is a complex one. The state of Albania itself emerged in 1912 as a compromise of the great powers, with Italy desiring special rights over the state. But the Albanian desire for its own state stretches back to at least 1878, when the first Albanian resistance movement formed and promoted independence as its goal. The Albanians sent a representative to the Congress of Berlin, but were denied access by Bismarck, who did not recognize them. In their drive for a separate Albanian state, the sovereign state of Albania does not satisfy the nationalist Albanians, who see an independent Kosovo as central to greater Albania. There are important reasons for this. First, Kosovo is much more advanced economically than Albania due to its 70 years as part of the political, social and economic system of Yugoslavia.

Second, there is an influential Kosovar diaspora in Italy and Germany, among other states, that lobbies specifically for Kosovo independence.

4. Ushtria Çlirimtare e Kosovës (UÇK) is known in English as the Kosovo Liberation Army (KLA). Formed in 1992, the UCK advocated a campaign of armed insurgency against the Serbian authorities. In mid-1996, the UCK launched attacks on Yugoslav and Serbian police forces.

5. Albanian populations are estimated at 3,129,000 in Albania; 1,672,000 in Kosovo; 67,000 in Serbia (excluding Kosovo); 509,000 in Macedonia; and 650,000 in Greece. The largest Albanian population outside the Balkans is found in Germany, where there are an estimated 400,000.

6. Julie Mertus, *How Myths and Truths Started a War* (Berkeley: University of California Press, 1999), p. 22.

7. Ibid.

8. Alex Bellamy, *Kosovo and International* Society (New York: Palgrave, 2002), p. 16; Kenneth Danforth, "Yugoslavia: a House Much Divided," *National Geographic*, August 1990.

9. See, for example, Stacy Sullivan, *Be not Afraid for You Have Sons in America: How a Brooklyn Roofer Helped Lure the U.S. into the Kosovo War* (New York: St. Martin's Press, 2004); and Phillip Knightley, *The First Casualty: the War Correspondent as Hero and Myth-Maker from the Crimea to Kosovo* (Baltimore: The Johns Hopkins University Press, 2000).

10. For example, in October 2002, during the trial of Slobodan Milosevic in The Hague, a telling exchange took place in which the former president, conducting his own cross-examination, entered a heated debate with the president of Croatia. Specifically, the two argued about whether the Croatian's party (HDZ) based its program on the teachings of the same man who inspired the Croat Fascists, and whether contemporary Serb nationalism was informed by the same man who maintained that all Bosnian Muslims and most Croats were in fact Serbs. Dejan Djorkie, "Coming to Terms with the Past: Former Yugoslavia," *History Today*, June 2004, p. 17.

11. Tim Judah, *Kosovo: War and Revenge* (New Haven: Yale University Press, 2002), p. 1.

12. See, for example, William Dorich, *Kosovo* (Los Angeles: Graphics Management Press, 1992).

13. Norwegian scholar Johan Galtung founded the discipline of peace research and is credited with articulating the concept of structural violence, which is a combination of legacy political realities that caused daily patterns of exclusion and humiliation of certain groups: deliberate harassment and normalization of discrimination of Kosovar Albanians by Belgrade, and similar behavior toward Serbians in the province today. For an account of the normalization of extreme violence, see Andre Sibomana, *Hope for Rwanda: Conversations with Laure Guilbert & Herve Deguine* (London: Pluto Press, 1997), p. 49.

14. Ger Duijzings, *Religion and the Politics of Identity in Kosovo*, p. 26.

15. Memorial Institute for the Prevention of Terrorism (MIPT) Terrorism Knowledge Base, available at http://www.tkb.org/group.jsp?groupid+3517 [November 19, 2005].

16. The *Kosovo Report*, which is written findings of an independent commission on Kosovo headed by Richard Goldstone, found that leaving Kosovo off the agenda in Dayton had three escalating effects: It gave the FRY a free hand in Kosovo, demoralized and weakened the nonviolent movement in Kosovo, and led directly to a decisive surge of support among Kosovars for the path of violent resistance as the only politically realistic path to independence. Independent International Commission on Kosovo, *The Kosovo Report* (Oxford: Oxford University Press, 2000), p. 59.

17. There are some reports that KLA attacks occurred earlier than 1996, but the evidence points toward 1996 as the first organized violence by the entity calling itself KLA.

18. See Derek S. Reveron, "Coalition Warfare: The Commander's Role," *Defense & Security Analysis*, June 2002.
19. MIPT Terrorism Knowledge Base.
20. Elizabeth Pond, "Kosovo and Serbia after the French Non," *The Washington Quarterly*, Vol. 28, No. 4, Autumn 2005.
21. According to Undersecretary of State Nicholas Burns, the key indicator of progress is, "the commitment of Kosovo's Albanians to create a multiethnic Kosovo that fully includes Serbs, setting the conditions for those who fled to return and live in safety." The American chief of mission in Pristina, Phil Goldberg, pointed to the superficiality of material changes when he said: "The road signs will be in Serbian as well as Albanian. The question is whether they point the way for displaced Serbs to return to their homes, or direct them out of Kosovo."
22. "Security situation in Kosovo worsens due to 'terrorist attacks,'" Belgrade-based radio B92, November 17, 2005. The announcer reported, "UNMIK police commissioner Kai Vittrup said in Pristina that the security situation in Kosovo has worsened due to a range of terrorist attacks against UNMIK and Kosovo Police Service personnel and vehicles … [adding] that these terrorist attacks had been directed by those who want to impose their solution of the Kosovo final status, adding that security forces would decisively fight such terrorist activities."
23. Interview with university professor working in Pristina, September 2005.
24. This may be attributed to perceptions about the French-Serbian alliance, which resulted in its initial position against the 1999 NATO campaign. France maintained that KLA were terrorists until late in 1998, only changing its position after strong U.S. and British lobbying.
25. American interrogator of detainees, interview with the author, September 2005.
26. "Ignore at Peril: the Growing Cauldron of Kosovo and Bosnia," *Strategic Policy*, November/December 2005, p. 7.
27. American, Albanian, and European officials working for separate agencies in Kosovo, interviews with the author, August 2005.
28. Vesna Peric Zimonjic, "Balkans: Independence of Kosovo Put on Hold by the UN," *IPS-Inter Press Service*, March 1, 2005.
29. Stephen Schwartz, "The Arab Betrayal of Islam," *Middle East Quarterly*, Spring 2002. Available at http://www.meforum.org/pf.php?id=166 [August 5, 2005].
30. Tanveer Ahmed, "Brand Islam," *On Line Opinion*, August 3, 2005. Available at http://www.onlineopinion.com.au/view.asp?article=3735 [August 5, 2005].
31. See "Macedonian Commentary Warns Kosovo Becoming Base for Extremists, Organized Crime," *Makedonja Denes,* August 9, 2005; and, "Albanian 'terrorists' in Macedonia ready for 'action' over Kosovo-Serb party," *Makedonija Denes*, December 1, 2005.
32. Noel Malcolm, *Kosovo: a Short History* (New York: Harper Collins, 1999), p. xxviii.
33. Ger Duijzings, *Religion and the Politics of Identity in Kosovo* (New York: Columbia University Press, 2000), pp. 8–9.
34. Miranda Vickers, *Between Serb and Albanian: A History of Kosovo* (New York: Columbia University Press, 1998).
35. Stephen Schwartz, "The Arab Betrayal of Islam."
36. Whereas these humanitarian services are extensive in countries like Egypt and Pakistan, producing a virtual parallel government services structure, they are meager by comparison in Kosovo.
37. *Kosovapress News Agency,* December 29, 1999.
38. Kosovar Albanian woman working with the OSCE in Pristina, interview with the author.

39. Ambassador Christopher Hill, negotiator at the Rambouillet talks and former U.S. ambassador to Macedonia, interview with the author, December 2005.
40. Goran Radosavljevic Guri, former Serb gendarmerie commander and analyst for the Center of the Fight against Terrorism, quoted in *Financial Times*, "Islamic terrorists being recruited in Bosnia, Kosovo," April 28, 2005. Available at http://web-lexis-nexis.com [April 30, 2005].
41. Goran Radosavljevic Guri in "Islamic terrorists being recruited in Bosnia, Kosovo."
42. "Serbian Deputy says Kosovo Albanian 'terrorists' preparing to mobilize," *Financial Times*, December 7, 2005. Available at http//web.lexis-nexis.com [April 30, 2005].
43. "Former Kosovo Liberation Army member denies Al-Qa'idah, intelligence links," *Financial Times*, November 24, 2004 [April 30, 2005].
44. Ibid.
45. Richard Rossmanith, "KFOR Commander says 'no indications' of Al-Qa'idah Active in Kosovo," *Financial Times*, January 22, 2005.
46. Raju C. G. Thomas, "Impending Western Determination of Kosovo's Future."
47. Vesna Peric Zimonjic, "Balkans: Independence of Kosovo Put on Hold by the UN."
48. Noel Malclom, p. xxi.
49. On May 13, 2005, the United States pledged $1 million to a UNESCO effort to protect all of Kosovo's religious and historical sites, especially Serb sites.
50. Kosovo's population of 2 million is 90 percent Albanian. Serb exoduses in 1690 and 1739 ended the long-standing Serb majority, and Kosovo emerged in the twentieth century with an Albanian majority. Serb numbers were boosted by recolonization efforts in the 1920s, but an Albanian population boom and renewed Serb emigration from Kosovo since the 1960s saw Serb numbers shrink to 10–15 percent of the population by the late 1990s; perhaps 100,000 more left in 1999.
51. Jason Lee Steorts, "Ethnic Cleansing, Continued," *The National Review*, September 12, 2005, p. 30.
52. Daniel Williams, "Ethnic Rivalries Still Bitter in Balkans," *Washington Post Foreign Service*, November 6, 2004, A18.
53. David Hally, quoted in Eleanor Beardsley, "For Serbs, a slow road back to Kosovo," *The Christian Science Monitor*, June 22, 2005, p. 6.
54. One family that tried to return to its squatter-occupied property was driven away by an angry Albanian crowd and beseeching international troops, apparently fearing that massive violence would be touched off at any moment. Only Albanian is heard on the streets, and a large mural honoring the KLA adorns the community center where once life was "terribly good" for Serbs living alongside Albanians. Eleanor Beardsley, "For Serbs, a slow road back to Kosovo."
55. See ICRC Web site at http://www.familylinks.icrc.org/home.nsf/home/webfami-lylink [October 9, 2005].
56. Some critics argue that the number of missing persons, like the fear of Serb return, is overstated. Raju Thomas points out that, while Western sympathies for Albanians virtually rests on the fact that Serbian troops killed more than 100,000 Albanians and drove out 800,000 more, only 1,500 bodies have been found on all sides since 1999. He argues that given the higher Albanian birth rate—the highest in Europe—in 25 years the Albanian Muslims will outnumber the Serbs in Serbia, whose birthrate is among the lowest in Europe. Raju G. C. Thomas, "The Impending Western Determination of Kosovo's Future," available at http://www.politika.co.yu/cyr/tekst.asp-f=22178&r=20.htm [July 28, 2005].
57. Kosovo Federal Foreign Minister Vuc Draskovic quoted in Radio Free Europe/Radio Liberty, "Draskovic Urges Kosovo Serbs to Join Province's Institution," June 28, 2005.
58. See International Crisis Group report, *Bridging Kosovo's Mitrovica Divide*, September 13, 2005.

59. "Standards before status" was a means of heading off Albanian pressure for independence and required the Kosovar PISG to meet UN political and institutional standards before negotiations regarding final status could begin.

60. Steven Erlanger, "Use Words, Not Guns, Balkan Leader Tells Rebels," *The New York Times*. March 28, 2001, A4.

61. Ibid.

62. Quoted in John Pilger, column of December 13, 2004, *Newstatesman*, p. 15.

63. Early on in the international mission, Albanians made up the majority (65 out of 70) of detainees for local violence, and NATO troops began providing round-the-clock protection to Serb enclaves in fear of grenade attacks and the planting of Improvised Explosive Devices (IEDs). UN news online, available at http://www.un.org/peace/kosovo/news/kosovo2.htm#Anchor70.

64. International Crisis Group (ICG), "Bridging Kosovo's Mitrovica Divide," September 2005, p. 24.

65. Ibid, 1.

66. David Lynch, "Yugoslav Leader Assails NATO," *USA Today* 14 March 2001, p. 1.

67. NATO troop strength has remained fairly steady at 17,500. This was augmented in March 2004, but the reason given was not explicitly the riots. The U.S. contribution has remained at about 1,700, and these are primarily National Guard.

68. Helena Smith, "A bad model for Iraq," *Newstatesman*, March 19, 2004, p. 18. See also Zeljka Jevtic: "They expelled Serbs, now turning on Kfor," published by Serbian newspaper *Blic*, October 14, 2005.

69. Marie Vlachova and Lea Biason, eds. *Women in an Insecure World: Facts, Figures, and Analysis* (Geneva: Geneva Center for Democratic Control of Armed Forces (DCAF), 2005).

70. ISN Security Watch, "UN Kosovo Police Arrested for Sex Trafficking," September 1, 2005.

71. The IOM reports interviewing Kosovar refugees in Western Europe found that "political reasons," "ethnic conflict," and "poor living standards" were the primary reasons refugees did not return to the province. "Religious intolerance" was an intermediate causal factor, according to the survey.

72. Fund for Peace, The Twelve Indicators of State Failure, available at http://www.fundforpeace.org/programs/fsi/fsindicators.php [November 18, 2005].

73. Forum 18 News Service, "Kosovo: Religious Freedom Survey 2003," September 9, 2003. Available at http://www.forum18.org/Archive.php?article_id=137&printer=Y [May 7, 2005].

74. Helena Smith, "A bad model for Iraq," *Newstatesman*, March 29, 2004, p. 18.

75. Lindsey Hilsum, *The New Statesman*, February 21, 2005. Available at http://web.lexis-nexis.com [April 30, 2005].

76. Gabor Hunya, "Foreign Direct Investment in Southeast Europe 2003–2004" report commissioned by OECD, June 2004. Available at http://www.investmentcompact.org/pdf/Min2004FDIinSEE.pdf [September 30, 2005].

77. David Leong, Deputy USAID Mission Director, Kosovo. Speech of May 25, 2004. Available at http://www.usaid.gov/missions/kosovo/Press/Speeches/Foreign_investment_speech.htm [September 30, 2005].

78. International Commission on the Balkans, "The Balkan's in Europe's Future," Secretariat Centre for Liberal Strategies, Sofia, 2005.

79. Elizabeth Pond, "Kosovo and Serbia after the French Non," *The Washington Quarterly*, Vol. 28, No. 4, Autumn 2005.

80. Macedonian Prime Minister Vlado Buckovski claimed, "All Kosovo politicians, including President Ibrahim Rugova, should sign a declaration that would exclude any possible unification of territories with majority Albanian population in the region." Quoted in Jasmina Mironski, "Kosovo independence could harm Balkans: analysts," cited in *Agence France Presse*, November 18, 2005.
81. Among those who have publicly called for Kosovar independence are former Clinton administration officials Richard Holbrooke, General Wesley Clark, and Ambassador Christopher Hill.
82. Joseph Biden, quoted in "Independence only way forward for Kosovo: Holbrooke," *Agence France Presse*, November 8, 2005.

Caucasus

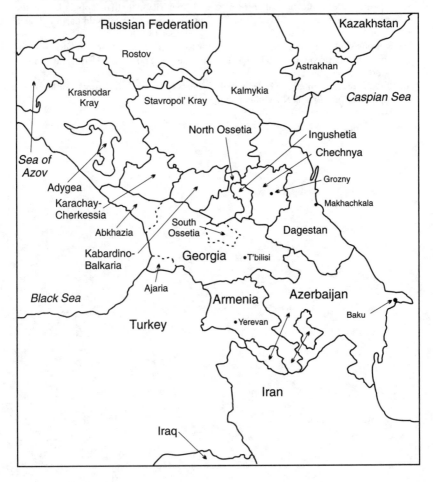

5

CAUCASUS

Jeffrey Stevenson Murer

NATURE OF THE FLASHPOINT

Before U.S. operations began in Afghanistan as a response to the 9/11 attacks, and long before the U.S. invasion of Iraq, an active theater in the global war on terrorism had been established for years in Chechnya. Running from the lowlands of the Nogay Steppe high into the northern slope of the greater Caucasus Mountains, Chechnya has been a conflict flashpoint since the mid-1990s. After the breakup of the Soviet Union, Chechnya declared its independence in 1991. To bring Chechnya back under Moscow's control, President Boris Yeltsin authorized a military intervention in the mountainous republic. Two years later, after nearly 50,000 deaths,[1] the Russian forces withdrew, only to return again three years later in September 1999. Combat has continued ever since.

While the conflict has changed little, guerrilla fighters hiding in the highlands coming down for hit-and-run actions against well-armed but apathetic Russian forces that control the cities and lowlands, the rhetoric justifying the conflict—from both sides—has changed. Previously justified as a necessary security action to maintain the territorial integrity of the Russian Federation, the Kremlin's Interior Ministry forces, military Special Forces, and counterinsurgency units now battle Islamist terrorists, representing Russia's commitment to the global war on terrorism. As for the Chechen rebel fighters who once limited operations to within the previously autonomous republic, they have struck targets in Moscow, Volgodonsk in Rostov, Buynaksk and Kaspiysk in Dagestan,

Nazran in Ingushetia, Nalchik in Kabardino-Balkaria, and Vladika-vkaz and Beslan in North Ossetia.[2] This chapter explores how this bid for independence became part of the frontline against a "global jihad."

Putin's Connection to 9/11

On September 12, 2001, Russian President Vladimir Putin called U.S. President George Bush to offer Russia's support. In comments made on Russian television, Putin blamed Osama bin Laden for the attacks on the World Trade Center and Pentagon and continued by saying, "We have reason to believe that bin Laden's people are connected with events currently taking place in our ... Chechnya."[3] He suggested that America's enemy was the same as Russia's enemy: "Our American partners cannot but be concerned with this circumstance. So we have a common foe, and that common foe being international terrorism."[4] The 9/11 attacks provided the Russian authorities with a new justification, and perhaps even a bit of legitimacy, for their campaign in Chechnya. In a communiqué issued on September 24, 2001, Putin added, "Russia's contribution to the American-led retaliation against the Taliban in Afghanistan would take the form of a massive attack against the rebellious Chechens."[5] By reframing the then two-year-old renewal of the conflict begun in 1994, Putin shrewdly called on the West to reevaluate its criticisms of Russian tactics in the Northern Caucasus in exchange for Moscow's cooperation in the U.S.-led coalition fighting the global war on terrorism. At the end of September, after Putin addressed the *Bundestag*, German Chancellor Gerhard Schröder commented that it was time for the West to recognize that Russia is also "battling terror" in the breakaway republic of Chechnya.[6] Putin had succeeded in a diplomatic coup linking international terrorism with the Chechen conflict.[7] The connection had not always been so clear or so accepted by the West.

The Kremlin justified its second intervention as an "antiterrorist operation."[8] During a December 1999 Russo-Sino summit, Russian President Boris Yeltsin and Chinese Premier Jiang Zemin issued a joint statement affirming, "No country [should] interfere in another sovereign country's attack on domestic terrorism." In a separate communiqué, China backed Russia's "attack against the Chechen terrorist and separatist activities."[9] But the West did not quite see it that way. Italian Foreign Minister Lamberto Dini stated that Moscow risked financial and economic assistance from the European Union if it continued its attacks on Chechnya. Following the November heavy bombing of Chechnya's capital Grozny, U.S. General Wesley Clark, NATO Supreme Allied Commander, condemned the attacks, suggesting that

Russian forces were "indiscriminately" killing civilians.[10] The Council of Europe threatened Russia with suspension. Chris Patten, European Union External Affairs Commissioner, said that Moscow "should not expect business as usual" as it pursued this aggression in the Caucasus, and suggested that the EU was considering revoking Russia's Most Favored Nation trading status.[11] Yet, Putin was able to shift discussions of Chechnya from one of human rights tragedy to a fight against bin Laden and "international terrorism."

HISTORICAL CONTEXT

There is an old tale in the Northern Caucasus that when God was sprinkling the peoples over the earth like salt, he clumsily spilled his shaker on the Caucasus Mountains. One can travel just a few kilometers and encounter an entirely different language that is mutually unintelligible to that from the last village. Even when large groups speak a common language, dialects may be distinct. For example, in the Russian Republic of Dagestan, the farthest east of the seven republics that constitute the Northern Caucasus, 1.8 million people speak 34 different languages.[12] The largest group, the Avars, who number 500,000–600,000, divide into 14 further linguistic branches, each of which has its own name and dialect.[13] Among the Caucasians are ethnic Russians who have been living in the region since colonial conquest in the middle of the nineteenth century. The farther west one moves along the mountains, the more ethnic Russians are to be found in each republic. At the western end of the region, Adygea has the highest proportion of ethnic Russians: 68 percent compared with 22 percent Adygey. The proportion of ethnic Russians in Chechnya and Ingushetia at the time of the last census in 1984 was nearly the inverse of Adygea: 23 percent Russian and 58 percent ethnic Chechen or Ingush.[14] Also, 98 percent of Chechens can speak one of six indigenous dialects. In contrast to Dagestan, where the Russian language is unifying, the unity of the Chechen language serves to identify the indigenous people in opposition to the Russians, who use language as another tool of colonization.

Early Russian Colonization

Christianity reached the Northern Caucasus through the Christianization of the Roman Empire in the fourth century CE, while Islam made quick inroads in the eighth century; the new religion took hold quickly in Dagestan in 733.[15] Even when the Ottomans moved into Transcaucasia in the mid-seventeenth century, the millet system allowed the Christian confession to continue in Armenia and Georgia. Ottoman advances into the northern Caucasus occurred at the same time the Russians were pushing out the remnants of the Golden Horde from the Don Steppe. Early Russian adventures into the region fared far less well than their Ottoman counterparts. In 1605, a combined Dagestani and Ottoman force massacred 10,000 Russian soldiers moving southward after capturing Astrakhan. This was merely a prelude to the struggle of the region's Russian colonization.

After Peter the Great began his southern colonization effort in earnest, his forces took the important port city of Derbert in Dagestan in 1722, moved on Baku in 1723, and built the strategically important fortress "The Holy Crucifix" (now Budyonnovsk) on the Sudak River in 1722, marking the beginning of Russian colonial expansion into the Caucasus. As Catherine the Great renewed southward expansion, she too built a powerful fortress. Vladikavkaz, or "Victor of the Caucasus," became a key part of a system of fortifications to hold new gains in the region. In 1799, construction began on the Georgia military highway connecting Vladikavkaz to Christian Georgia. In response, a Chechen cleric named Mansur[16] claimed to have had a vision from Mohammed calling on him to repulse the Russians and organize a resistance force. He declared a ghazawat or holy war against Catherine's encroaching forces.[17] Mansur took the fight eastward to Dagestan to thwart the Russian thrust down the Caspian coast, but failed when he could not overpower the Russian forces in the fortress of Kizylar. After regrouping, Mansur took the fight westward into Kabardino-Balkaria but was driven back again.[18] It is the struggles of Mansur that connect the wars of colonization resistance to contemporary Chechnya. Yet the great Mansur was not the most significant resister to Russian colonization.

Shortly after Mansur took up arms, a Dagestani Avar named Shamil was born in 1796. Throughout his adolescence the Northern Caucasus region was witness to great violence, as Tsar Nicholas I appointed a hero of Borodino to be responsible for military strategy in the Caucasus. Russian General Aleksey Yermelov ruled as if "atrocities were policy."[19] He said, "I desire that the terror of my name should guard our frontiers" and that he would "find no peace as long as a single Chechen remained alive."[20] Yermelov also built a significant fortress, which he named Groznaya, or terrible or formidable.[21] Shamil was educated in a Sufi order, and in 1828 traveled on a hajj to Mecca where he met Abdel Kader,[22] a North African from whom he learned guerrilla military tactics. Upon his return, he joined his childhood friend Ghazi Mollah, the first Imam of Dagestan, in a renewed resistance against the Russians. Becoming the third Imam of Dagestan in 1834 after Ghazi was killed by the Russians, Shamil became known as the Lion of Dagestan for his tenacious fight against Yermelov and other Russian generals. For nearly 30 years, this mountain warfare continued until 1859, when the Russians finally captured Shamil.[23]

In the rhetoric of the present conflicts in Chechnya, much is made about Shamil being an Imam and, like Mansur, issuing a ghazawat, as a call to resist. The term refers to armed-insurrection, particularly against infidels or non-Muslims. Yet the Caucasian Wars were not so much religious as they were bloody struggles against colonization and subjugation. Like American expansionism that subjugated native peoples, Russia viewed the Caucasus wars of colonization through a manifest destiny lens. From the subjugated or indigenous perspective, Shamil and Mansur evoked ghazawat or jihad to preserve independence and inspire Caucasian resistance, not to call for a global caliphate.

Much like the conflict today, the Russians made negotiations and signed treaties with certain Chechen leaders, even while Shamil's resistance army was still in the field. Tsar Alexander I executed an agreement titled "A Treaty Concluded with Chechens about Their Subjugation to Russia," which permitted local autonomy and use of Shari'a. It included the following passage:

> We commit ourselves and the entire Chechen nation to swear on the Holy Koran eternal allegiance to the All-Holy Russian Imperial Throne according to our custom. ... We commit ourselves ... to always remain loyal and not undertake any harmful acts against Russian nationals either through the use of weaponry or any other means. ...[24]

Unfortunately, Russian regional military commanders did not follow through with their charge to maintain peace in the region with a similar spirit. There was frequent violence between mountain people and the military garrisons assigned to watch over them. Nevertheless, Chechens and other Caucasians frequented the market cities of Kizlyar, Mozdok, and Vladikavkaz.[25] For all of the contention between Chechens and Russian authorities, there were also institutions of inclusion.

Even so, it is rare for Russians, especially regarding the Chechens, to look on the Caucasians as being part of Russian society.

Later Caucasian Independence Movements

When the Imperial Russian structures collapsed in 1917, the North Caucasus tried to create a single self-ruling state. Dagestan, Chechnya, Ingushetia, North Ossetia, and Kabardino formed the United Highlanders.[26] Following the Bolshevik Revolution, the eastern territories[27] (except for Kabardino) created the Republic of North Caucasus Mountains (RNCM), hoping to stay out of the civil war between the White monarchists and the Bolshevik Reds. In May 1919, Anton Denikin and his White army conquered much of the North Caucasus and banned the RNCM. Whites were seen as the embodiment of the ruthless Imperial State, and having escaped the colonial rule, if even for a short time, Caucasians were not going to submit easily. In the high mountains of southern Chechnya and Western Dagestan, Uzun Hadji created a resistance force and declared the North Caucasus Emirate (NCE) adopting the institution of Shari'a as law.[28] Hadji was approached by Bolshevik commanders and promised local autonomy if the Emirate would join the Reds against Denikin. In February 1920, the Bolsheviks expelled the Whites and were looked upon as liberators. But soon the Bolsheviks banned both the NCE and the RNCM, rounded up the leaders of both movements, and either exiled or executed them.[29] From 1921 until 1924, the Bolsheviks themselves tried to keep these eastern territories together in the Soviet Mountain Republic, which included Kabardino-Balkaria, Karachay-Cherkessia, Chechnya, Northern Ossetia, and Ingushetia. However, each was made an Autonomous Republic until Chechnya and Ingushetia were joined together in 1934.[30]

After the Germans invaded the Soviet Union in 1941, Chechen resistance elements began organizing in the mountains. In the summer of 1942, Operation Blue brought German spearhead units deep into the Northern Caucasus region, crossing the River Terek and stopping just beyond Grozny. The Nazis were so optimistic about conquering the oil-rich region they established a National Committee of the North Caucasus, which claimed to represent ethnic people who wanted to secede from the Soviet Union. The Committee distributed a newspaper titled *Gazavat* (Ghazawat, or Holy War), the motto of which was "Allah above us, and Adolf Hitler beside us."[31] Enough Caucasians went to the German side to form the Nordkaukasische Legion, or Northern Caucasus Legion, a Waffen SS unit.[32] In retaliation, Stalin deported some 500,000 Chechens and Ingush in 1944.

All told, Stalin moved more than 1.5 million people from their homes, transporting Volga Germans, Karachievtsi, Crimean Tatars, Kalmyks, Ingush, and Chechens en masse to Eastern Siberia, the Urals, Central Asia, and Kazakhstan.[33] Once the Caucasian people were moved, officers and soldiers from the NKVD[34] pillaged property. While in exile Chechens and other deportees were restricted in their movements, the types of occupations they could hold, and the amount of education they could access. "Any complaint to a higher administrative body was treated as a counter-revolutionary act."[35] After Stalin's death in 1953,

Chechens and Ingush began returning home on their own, unauthorized. In 1956, about 30,000 Chechens made the long trek back from Kazakhstan to the Caucasus. Toward the end of that year, authorities finally buckled and Khrushchev issued a resolution that restored the national autonomy to Kalmyks, Karachi, Balkars, Ingush, and Chechens.[36] The deportations had taken their toll, however. Many died while in exile or in transit in one or the other direction. Some 22 percent of the deported Chechens perished during 12 years of forced exile.[37] Once these displaced people returned home they often found their houses either ransacked or occupied by other people, namely Russians.

In 1958, a race riot broke out in Grozny. Heller and Nekrich suggest it was the most serious "racial" clash in the Soviet Union after World War II.[38] Although Khrushchev's resolution explicitly permitted autonomous rule to the Chechen and Ingush people, the Russian rioters called for the creation of an all-Russian local government, and many took to wearing ribbons so as not to be mistaken for a Chechen.[39] These tensions continued from 1958 through the 1970s.

Soviet Collapse and Claims of Independence

1991 seems a part of the distant past, yet it is important to remember some of the events of that disastrous and auspicious year. It began with an omen as Mikhail Gorbachev sent tanks into Vilnius to crush Lithuania's drive for independence. On January 12, 1991, Soviet tanks stormed barriers erected by unarmed civilians blocking the entrance to the media offices in the capital city. Interior Ministry soldiers fired on the crowd, killing 13 and injuring 140.[40] Two days later, other Interior Ministry troops stormed a police station in Latvia to suppress any independence movements. Armenian and Azeri militias faced off in Nagorno-Karabakh, and many Abkhazians were agitating for an independent Abkhazia, fearing that if Georgia withdrew from the Soviet Union they might be subject to "Georgianization." Outside of the Soviet Union, Slovenia and Croatia declared their independence from Yugoslavia by the end of 1990 only to face intervention from the Yugoslav People's Army. All that had stood as the status quo since the end of World War II appeared to be disintegrating. Former Ukrainian President Leonid Kravchuk recalled the atmosphere: "The whole country was falling apart before our very eyes and not because we were planning it. The Baltics had left the fold, the war in Armenia, Azerbaijan, the events in T'bilisi. The whole country was waiting in lines. The economy was plummeting, and we needed to find a way out."[41]

In Chechnya, just as elsewhere in the USSR, there was a push to displace the communist regime. Doku Zavgayev, the chair of the Chechen-Ingush ASSR, openly supported the August putsch; once it failed, he knew his days were numbered. Supporters of Dzhokhar Dudayev stormed the parliament building in Grozny, killing the city Communist Party chair Vitali Kutsenko and effectively dissolving the Soviet.

Dudayev was an interesting figure. Born in 1944, he grew up a deportee in Kazakhstan. Lying about his ethnicity to avoid anti-Chechen hostilities, he rose through the ranks of the Soviet Air Force, graduating from the Gagarin Air Force Academy in 1974. In 1987, as a major general, he commanded the air base in Tartu, Estonia, where he refused to shut down the Estonian parliament and television stations. In 1990, as his unit withdrew from Estonia, he resigned and returned to Chechnya to become engaged in politics. He married a Russian woman (he spoke Russian far better than Chechen), but an October 1991 referendum confirmed Dudayev as president. He declared the independence and sovereignty of the Chechnya Republic of Ichkeria,[42] as well as its succession from the Russian Federation.

Through many of the same processes, Yeltsin came to power, agitating for Russian independence from the Soviet Union. Yeltsin's appeal was so great that 80 percent of the voters in the Chechen-Ingush Autonomous Soviet Socialist Republic cast their ballot for him as the president of the Russian Federation in June 1991.[43] It was later that autumn that President Yeltsin tried to send troops to rein in Dudayev and the Chechens. However, Chechen security forces stood firm, and eventually Yeltsin backed down. On December 25, 1991, the Soviet Union was dissolved.

To establish formal hierarchies of power and to make clear the relationship between the Central State and regional administrations, Yeltsin signed the Federation Treaty in March 1992 along with the leaders of all the constituent parts of the Russian Federation, 21 ethnic enclaves with the status of an Oblast, 10 autonomous regions, 6 territories, and 49 oblasts or provinces. Only two republics did not sign: Chechnya and Tartarstan. The latter reached a separate agreement on February 15, 1994, leaving Chechnya isolated and vulnerable as the only non-signatory of the new Federation Treaty.[44] In 1994, Russian forces entered Chechnya to "restore the Constitutional order."

The First Chechen War

The initiation of hostilities at the end of 1994 is a bit puzzling given that the Kremlin had left Chechnya much to its own devices for three years. It seems more than possible that Yeltsin could have negotiated with Dudayev and worked out a deal like the one struck with Mintimer Shaymiev, president of Tartarstan, under which Moscow conferred particularly broad powers on the autonomous ethnic republic to the point where it was possible to refer to the relationship between Tartarstan and Russia as a "confederation."[45] The December 11, 1994, invasion is all the stranger when one considers that the November 26 Federal Counterintelligence Services (FSK)[46] coup plot was an utter disaster. The fighting was extremely one-sided, as Russian losses numbered around 300 with minimal Chechen losses. The failed coup was the harbinger of things yet to come.

The failures encountered by Russian soldiers in the first few days of the conflict seem to indicate that neither the Defense Ministry nor the FSK was consulted during the Russian Security Council's decision of November 28, 1994. Russian analysts Emil A. Payin and Akardy Popov wrote for a RAND Corporation report:

> The unusually sharp criticisms that were expressed shortly after the outbreak of hostilities by Deputy Defense Ministers Gromov and Kondratiev affirm this conclusion. This also indicates that this policy option most likely had not even been discussed at the Defense Ministry's Collegium. Many observers and military experts maintain that the campaign was hastily and poorly prepared, and that the only possible explanation for this is the fact that it had been planned behind the back of the "High Command" and was presented to them as a fait accompli.[47]

It would seem that Yeltsin's personal policy advisors formulated the decision. The approval of figures like Deputy Prime Minister Sergei Shakhari and Presidential Chief of Staff Sergei Filatov prevailed over those of dissenters such as Prime Minister Victor Chernomyrdin, Justice Minister Yuri Kalmykov, Foreign Minister Andrei Kozyrev, and Chief of Foreign Intelligence Service Yevgeny Primakov.[48] Eventually, the Defense and Interior Ministers, along with Sergei Stepashin, Director of FSK, decided to go along with the plan after raising initial doubts. It would seem the cabinet came around to the idea that a quick and decisive war would be good for the Yeltsin presidency, whose poll numbers before the 1996 election were abysmal.

Some 40,000 Russian forces deployed to Chechnya. The initial push was to Grozny, which was bombarded into ruin. As the Russians gained control of the urban areas and the lowlands, Shamil Baysaev led a June 14, 1995, rebel assault on the city of Budyonnovsk in Stavropol Krai, the oblast to the north of Chechnya. By attacking southern Russia, Basayev and his assault team hoped to show how the costs of the conflict would grow, and persuade the Russians to withdraw from Chechnya. The band first attacked the police station, then the town Hall in Budyonnovsk, and finally took the hospital, holding nearly 1,500 people hostage. The demand of the hostage-takers was simple: Russia quit Chechnya. On June 15, Basayev demanded journalists be allowed into the hospital so that he could tell them of the atrocities the Russians were committing in Grozny and elsewhere in Chechnya. These came mostly in the form of zachistka operations, or "mopping-up," as Russian soldiers went house-to-house looking for rebels, taking property and committing rapes as well.[49] After continued skirmishes and mounting hostage deaths, the Russians withdrew. On June 18, Prime Minister Chernomyrdin made a deal with Basayev, whereas a cease-fire would be declared in Chechnya, negotiations would begin to settle the status of the republic, and Basayev and his 120 or so men could leave under safe passage. All told, 125 civilians and 25 police or security forces were lost and 415 people were wounded. Basayev's audacious attack worked; it was a turning point in the war.

Although the cease-fire held only until August, it gave the rebels much-needed time to regroup. The 10,000 Russian soldiers that had taken Grozny were withdrawn, leaving a garrison of 3,000 who came under regular guerrilla attacks. By 1996, Dudayev named Basayev Commander of the Chechen Armed Forces. In January, the Russian-controlled zone held an election after which the former Communist head of the Chechen-Ingush ASSR, Doku Zavgayev, was declared the new President. Dudayev claimed that it was a rigged election and that Zavgayev was simply a puppet installed by Moscow.[50] This was just the first of many such competing Chechen governmental structures.

Shortly after the Russian-supported election, a rocket honed in on Dudayev's satellite phone signal and killed him. Zelimkhan Yandarbi-yev succeeded Dudayev and convinced Yeltsin to engage in cease-fire talks. In August, Basayev was ready to launch his massive counteroffensive against Russian forces in Grozny. His force of 5,000 trapped the smaller Russian garrison. With no possibility of a timely relief for the garrison, Yeltsin agreed to negotiate. He sent General Alexander Lebed, the much-beloved Afghan War veteran, to sign a cease-fire agreement with the rebel Chief of Staff Aslan Maskhadov. Signed at the end of August, the Khasavyurt Accords evolved into a peace settlement that called for a full Russian withdrawal and final-status talks on Chechen independence within five years. Under de facto independence, Basayev stepped down from his post as military commander to run in Chechnya's second presidential election in January 1997. He lost to

Maskhadov, having garnered only 23 percent of the vote. The OSCE certified the election as free and fair.[51]

If the conflict in Chechnya appeared to have ended in January 1997, it was as many things in the region: not what it would appear. Maskhadov, like Dudayev before him, found it extremely difficult to jump-start the Chechen economy. A new industry did spring forth and it was quite lucrative, although not necessarily good for long-term growth or economic stability: kidnapping for ransom. No one seemed safe. The contractors hired to rebuild Chechnya, the aid workers who provided food and comfort to Chechnya's displaced and homeless, the journalists who told Chechnya's story to the outside world, the businessmen, the missionaries, the academics, the researchers—they were all targets of kidnapping and torture, and some were rumored to have been sold into slavery.[52] Between 1997 and 1999, more than 1,000 hostages were taken for ransom.[53]

Although Chechnya may have been granted *de facto* independence, attacks against Russian targets did not end. Immediately following the Russian withdrawal from Chechnya in 1996, bombings began in Dagestan. In November 1996, a bomb in an apartment block in Kaspiysk killed 69 people, mostly the family members of the Russian military garrison there. Bombs began going off elsewhere in Russia. President Maskhadov condemned all such actions. In June 1998 events turned on Maskhadov when an explosive device detonated under his car. The president walked away but four others were killed.[54] In October 1998, the head of the anti-kidnapping squad within the Chechen Interior Ministry, Shadid Bargishev, was assassinated. The president's authority was not being recognized. In an attempt to rein in some of the competing powers, Maskhadov appointed Basayev Prime Minister in January 1998, although he held the appointment for only six months. Accused of being a puppet of Moscow himself, Maskhadov decreed in February 1999 the institution of Shari'a over the next three years, as proof of his and his government's commitment to Chechen independence. In an attempt to stave off a civil war, Maskhadov appeared to set in motion what so many Chechens believed was inevitable: a second war with the Russians. This was too much for Moscow.

LINKAGES TO INTERNATIONAL TERRORISM

The bombings continued into 1999. Explosions rocked Moscow on the mornings of September 8 and 13, when two powerful bombs were detonated in rented flats on the ground floor of two large apartment blocks.[55] The bombings were similar down to nearly every detail, and demonstrated a high level of sophistication and access to military-grade explosives. In the first apartment block bombing, the poorly pre-fabricated concrete building collapsed, crushing 94 people. The second blast killed 124. Russian authorities immediately pointed their fingers at Chechnya. Moscow Mayor Yuri Luzhkov said after the second bombing that he could easily follow a "Chechen trail." Then Prime Minister Putin addressed Parliament on September 14 and linked the attacks to Chechnya, but added that it was necessary to distinguish ordinary Chechens from terrorists.[56] The bombings continued on September 16 when a powerful car bomb exploded in the southern Russian city of Volgodonsk; 17 people died and more than 500 were wounded.[57] The police received calls stating that the "Dagestan Liberation Army" was responsible for the bombing, not the Chechens. Further, Basayev, who usually happily took credit for his actions, said in a newspaper interview, "The latest blast in Moscow is not our work, but the work of the Dagestanis. Russia has been openly terrorizing Dagestan. ..."[58] Russian journalist Anna Politkovskaya put it well when she wrote: "The Russians laid the blame on 'Chechen terrorists'—only to get a stout denial from Shamil Basayev that he was involved."[59] The Russian authorities went even further, claiming that they had evidence linking the bombings to "international terrorists." This implied the involvement of Osama bin Laden, who was wanted by the United States at that time for his role in the bombings of embassies in Kenya and Tanzania.

Another catalyst to the second war was a raid into Dagestan made by Shamil Basayev and his lieutenant, Amir Khattab. The latter, a native of Saudi Arabia and self-professed Wahhabi, went to Afghanistan at the age of 17 to fight with the mujahedin. He moved home when the Soviets withdrew in 1992, although he returned in 1994. Not satisfied assisting refugees, he moved to Chechnya in 1995 and quickly jumped into battle. With his Afghanistan experience, he became Basayev's Deputy Chief of Staff and the Chief of Military Training for the Central Front. A videotape of Khattab and his fighters destroying a tank column in 1996 can still be found for sale in the markets of the rebel-controlled areas. Georgi Derlugian called Basayev and Khattab "Che Guevaras in turbans." He wrote in the New Left Review that they "are more interested in overthrowing the pro-Russian corrupt order in Dagestan than creating an Islamic state."[60]

On August 7, 1999, Basayev, Khattab and an army of 2,000 took the villages of Tsumadin and Botlikh (as well as five others), held an Islamic shura or council, and declared Dagestan's secession from Russia. Two days later, Vladimir Putin, then the head of the FSB, was nominated by Boris Yeltsin to be Prime Minister and went down to Dagestan "to take charge" of the expulsion of Bsayev and his Islamic fighters himself. Basayev and Khattab retreated at the end of the month, sustaining heavy losses.

At the end of September, the Interior Ministry in conjunction with the Nationalities Ministry initiated "Operation Foreigner," which expelled 15,000 "undesirables" from Moscow and required nearly 70,000 to re-register with the police. Russian forces then reentered Chechnya on October 1, 1999. After Russian air forces bombarded Grozny, surface-to-surface missile strikes were launched against the capital city at the end of October, killing at least 250 people. Although the Russian forces were able to take Grozny by February 1, 2000, it came at a heavy price. The Committee of Soldiers' Mothers disputed official casualty reports and claimed that by the middle of January 2000, some 3,000 Russian soldiers had died and another 5,000 were wounded.[61] Yet many Russian government officials believed—as they had in 1994—that this would be a short and relatively easy campaign.

Taking the Fight to Russia

When the Chechen forces withdrew from Grozny in the face of the Russian advance in February 2000, Aslan Maskhadov also withdrew and joined them as a fighter. He became the second most wanted man in Chechnya by the Russian authorities, with a $10 million bounty on his head. While it is unclear what military role he served, he became the political leader of the Chechen resistance, and he was often photographed with Basayev. With even the government out of Grozny, Basayev's new strategy was to take the fight to Russia by hitting targets all over southern Russia as well as hitting high-profile targets in Moscow.

As the fighting became more ferocious throughout 2000, a number of shifts in the conflict began to make it apparent that this war was not going to be a replay of the first for either side. In April, Mary Robinson, the United Nations Human Rights High Commissioner, toured Chechnya and Dagestan and called on Russia to account for the growing number of human rights abuses. The Justice Minister Yuri Chaika responded by saying that actions in Chechnya were related to antiterrorist operations and were therefore covered by provisions in the law. When Robinson pointed out that no state of emergency had been called, the Justice Minister replied that this was all part of fighting terrorism.[62] In response, the Parliamentary Assembly of the Council of Europe suspended the voting rights of the Russian delegation and demanded that the Council of Ministers expel Russia. Human Rights Watch later issued a report that presented allegations of "indiscriminate and disproportional aerial bombardment, arbitrary detention, torture, and extortion."[63]

The bombing campaign that began in 1997 intensified throughout 2000. Car bombs began going off regularly in Dagestan.[64] Suicide bombings began occurring in urban areas in Chechnya, with five occurring over the first two days of July. Also during that summer, Metro stations in Moscow became targets. Bombings began to occur with greater frequency in the Stavropol region and in central Chechnya, especially in the cafes frequented by Russian soldiers in Grozny. Even so, Putin declared Chechnya sufficiently pacified that the antiterrorist operations could move from the Defense Ministry to the FSB.

After Putin's declaration, a number of high-profile attacks outside of Chechnya kept the conflict in the public spotlight and suggested that the entire North Caucasus region was becoming destabilized—it appeared that rebel fighters and their allies could move with impunity around southern Russia. In October 2002, the most audacious attack in the conflict to that point occurred in Moscow when 40 guerrillas attacked the Dubrovka Theatre, taking nearly 900 people hostage.[65] Russian security forces immediately surrounded the theater, and a siege began that lasted three days, during which time the rebels released as many as 200 hostages. At nearly five o'clock in the morning of the third day, Russian Special Forces stormed the theater, fearing that the rebels had begun to kill hostages. In an effort to subdue the hostage-takers, the Special Forces introduced a nerve-agent gas through the theater's ventilation system. In the ensuing battle, the Special Forces soldiers killed all of the rebels inside of the theater. However, 129 of the hostages also died, all except two from adverse effects related to exposure to the gas.[66]

2004 was an especially deadly year in Russia. In February, suicide bombers blew up a Moscow subway train, killing 41 and wounding more than 100. In August, a female suicide bomber killed 8 and wounded 50 after she detonated her device outside a Moscow subway station. Two female suicide bombers later destroyed two airliners bound for southern Russia, killing 88. In the Caucasus, yet another suicide bomber attempted to assassinate Ingush President Murat Zyazikov, who was only slightly injured.[67]

With Maskadov having fled into the mountains to join the resistance fighters, Moscow appointed a new president, Nikolai Koshman. Unhappy with his performance, Putin selected Ahmad-Hadji Kadyrov, who was the Mufti of Chechnya from 1995–1999, as the next administrative head.[68] During Victory Day[69] celebrations, President Kadyrov was killed in a Grozny stadium by a massive bomb placed beneath his reviewing podium. It would appear that the rebels could strike any-where. Events in September reinforced that sentiment.

Beslan School Number 1

The first day of the new school year is a celebration in Russia. On September 1, 2004, 32 fighters infiltrated the town of Beslan in North Ossetia, stormed School Number 1 as it was holding its festivities, and in short order took 1,300 (mostly children) hostage. Like the assault on the Dubrovka Theatre, the demand of the hostage-takers was for the Russians to quit Chechnya. The fighters rounded up all of the hostages and placed them in the school's gymnasium. Most disturbingly, the Chechen guerrillas strung explosives and detonating cable throughout the gym. The explosives placed high on the walls or strung overhead, the detonators were wired to pedals, on which the militants stood. As security forces surrounded the school it became clear that a sniper's bullet would actually trigger the destruction of the entire gym by knocking any one of the militants off his or her respective pedal.[70]

Three days after the siege began, and with conditions squalid inside the school, it was hoped that negotiations could lead to some hostages being freed. Aslan Maskhadov denied that any of his forces were involved and volunteered to come to Beslan to negotiate with the hostage-takers, an impressive offer considering the bounty on his head. With the school compound surrounded by Special Forces; local militia; FSB units; Interior Ministry forces; and hundreds of armed, anxious, and nervous parents, disaster was a small misstep away. Unfortunately it came in the middle of the third day when shots rang out, followed by a series of explosions, and then a running gun battle. It is not clear who fired the first shot, but when firing ceased it was not the outcome that the parents desired: 331 civilian hostages had died. Eleven soldiers died in the assault, including the leader of the elite FSB special operations unit.

While Basayev claimed responsibility for the raid, it is not immediately apparent that Chechens had carried out the attack or that it was the work of "foreign operatives," i.e., people from outside of the Russian Federation. Aslambek Aslakhanov, the Chechen State Duma Deputy who was present during the siege and offered to negotiate between the guerrillas and the Russian authorities, said that when he spoke to the militants, they did not speak Chechen. "They were not Chechens. When I started talking with them in Chechen, they had answered, 'We do not understand, speak Russian.'" Stanislav Kesaev, the North Ossetian Parliament's chief investigator, concluded that the "vast majority of the attackers were Ingush." Survivors of the attacks confirm this, stating that the leader of the attack, a figure referred to as "the Colonel" gave his orders in Ingush.[71] Immediately following the attacks on Beslan, the Russian and Western media reported that the leader of the attack was Ali Taziev, an ethnic Ingush and former member of the pro-Russian external security forces Ingush police. However, Russian state prosecutors announced on September 20, nearly three weeks after the raid, that it was in fact led by another Ingush, Ruslan Tagirovich Khuchbarov.[72]

When state prosecutors asked Nur-Pasha Kulaev, reportedly one of the attackers, what were the nationalities of the 32 guerrillas, he responded: "Ingush, one Arab, one Ossetian, one slant-eyed person, and the rest were Chechen and Ingush. Four or five Chechens and four persons spoke only Russian, the rest were Ingush."[73] Russian journalist Svetlana Meteleva reported that the identity of at least 17 attackers could be determined: one Ukrainian, six Chechens, and the rest were Ingush.[74] These identifications were in stark contrast to what State Prosecutor Nikolai Shepel announced in September 2005. He said the attack was the work of an Arab mercenary, Abu-Dzeyt, and that there was "circumstantial evidence [that] showed the terrorists entered Russia illegally."[75] The Beslan Mothers' Committee responded by stating that it was "outraged" by Shepel's words. Spokeswoman Ella Kessayeva said that the group of attackers included inhabitants of the neighboring republics, but not international terrorists. She said that Shepel's remarks were just the latest in a "string of lies."[76]

It would appear that Basayev had as much to gain as Putin by emphasizing the Chechen connection, but as with many aspects of the Chechen conflict, the connection to "international jihadists" seems to be overdrawn. A headline that ran in the *Christian Science Monitor* proclaimed "Al Qaeda among the Chechens" above a story reporting on the terrorist attacks at School Number 1 in Beslan.[77] President Putin makes frequent references to al Qaeda, blaming the organization for the two near-simultaneous airplane bombings in August 2004.[78] The North Ossetian Interior Minister at the time, Soslan Sikoyev, who himself had been kidnapped twice by separatist militants made a similar connection: "I think it's al Qaeda. I think it's Saudi Arabia, Arabs, and possibly Afghan terrorists—and terrorists who are here in Russia as well."[79] Yet in the very same piece, the academics and analysts interviewed all asserted that al Qaeda was not responsible for the raid. Michael Radu, a terrorism expert at the Foreign Policy Research Institute in Philadelphia, stated in the article: "This is not an al Qaeda operation: These are autonomous groups. It's not like bin Laden wrote the checks."[80] Russian military analysts Dmitri Trenin and Aleksei Malkashenko suggest that the word "terrorism" rarely appears in Russia without the adjective "Islamic."[81]

Yet they are also clear when they state that the Chechen conflict *does not* represent an "attack of international terrorism on Russia."[82]

In March 2005, Aslan Maskhadov was killed as Russian security forces surrounded his position and tried to take him alive in Tolstoy-Yurt. The Russian newspaper *Kommersant* reported that Viskhan Khadzhimuratov, Maskadov's nephew and bodyguard, fired the *coup de grace* to prevent Russian security forces the opportunity to torture or humiliate the former president of the Chechen Republic of Ichkeria.[83] Yet with Maskhadov's life went many hopes for a peaceful or negotiated solution to the conflict in the Northern Caucasus. Although Deputy Prime Minister Ramzan Kadyrov, son of the assassinated president and former Imam of Chechnya Akhmad Kadyrov, declared that the resistance movement was 99 percent finished after Maskhadov's death, many feared that the elimination of Yeltsin's preferred candidate in the 1997 Chechen presidential elections would represent the loss of a political center, without whom it might prove impossible to negotiate a settlement.[84] Raising the political stakes, the Kremlin decided to bury Maskhadov in an undisclosed location. Deputy State Prosecutor Nikolai Shepel said that in strict accordance with the law on terrorism, "the place of his burial is to be kept secret."[85] Many Western journalists understood that Moscow wanted to equate Maskhadov with Basayev in order to justify the elimination of both. Yet the question remained: How much of this portrayal was a construction of the Kremlin's?

LINKAGES TO THE GLOBAL WAR ON TERRORISM

Part of the difficulty in evaluating the conflicts in the Caucasus arises from the equations used by the Kremlin and reproduced by the news media and governments in the West. Muslim equals jihadist equals agent of Osama bin Laden. Either part of the equation may be correct, but not its totality. It is important to evaluate the role of Islam in the conflicts in the Northern Caucasus, as well as the politics of the region.

Following Maskhadov's death, Abdul-Khalim Sadulaev stepped forward saying that he was in fact the Chechen vice president and that he would succeed his fallen comrade. In a written response to questions presented by Radio Free Europe/Radio Liberty, Sudulaev said that in 2001 Maskhadov signed a decree making him vice president, but Sadulaev requested that the decision not be made public.[86] He went on to say that "the resistance will continue to try to inflict the maximum damage on the Russian armed forces" but they will "not attack peaceful civilians, women, and children, and not take them hostage."[87] Sudulaev made clear his commitment to democracy saying, "When peace comes

... we shall hold elections and elect a new president." He also made clear his contempt for Chechens who cooperate with the Russians. Referring specifically to Ramzan Kadyrov, he said of collaborators, "there is nothing human and nothing Chechen left in them." Sudulaev placed the blame for the violence in the region at the feet of Putin, claiming his lack of humanitarian policy in Caucasus made the situation increasingly worse. He said, "Explosions and killings in Dagestan have become as frequent as in Grozny, because Putin has no cohesive Northern Caucasus policy. ... [T]he situation is just as bad in Ingushetia and only a little better in Kabardino-Balkaria. Sudulaev blames Putin for trying to 'install his own people everywhere.'"[88] It is this very betrayal of democratic practice and the recognition of self-determination that exacerbates the conflict in the Caucasus.

The Chechen resistance Vice President Doku Umarov, who seconded Sadulaev's comments, has gone so far as to denounce terrorism. He said terrorism "has not undergone any legitimization in the eyes of the Chechen Resistance."[89] Just as the Russian authorities considered Maskhadov to be as much of a terrorist as Basayev, so too did the authorities consider Sadulaev and Umarov to be terrorists. Perhaps a way out of the Chechen-cum-Northern Caucasus conflict is for the Kremlin to take the resistance leaders seriously. The United States would also do well not to equate political Islam with al Qaeda.

Differentiated Islams

Moscow has made much of Wahhabism in the Chechen conflicts, pointing to Amir al-Khattab as proof of the participation of foreign fighters and the infiltration of the strict Saudi religious influence. Islam, like Christianity, is not monolithic. Nor is every reference to Islam or invocation of it the proof of religious conviction. The declaration of "jihad" or "ghazawat" can also be part of an ideology of a national liberation movement, suggesting the rightness of the nationalism and that God sanctions the attempts (much like the Western tradition of "just war"). The struggle in Chechnya, which has grown to encompass many people in the other republics as well, is far more an example of national liberation than religious fundamentalism. Further, declaring Chechnya to be the Chechen Republic of Ichkeria, complete with Shari'a and communiqués that begin "In the name of Allah, the Merciful, the Munificent!" becomes a means of distinguishing the Chechen Resistance government and administration from the one established by Moscow, which for 70 years repressed religious expression.

When Islam made its way into the Caucasus in the eighth and ninth centuries, the four Mazhabi, or schools of religious thought, followed: Khanbalite, Maslikite, Khanafite, and Shafiyite. Shafiyism and Khanafism are the more liberal trends within Islam and generally are the tenants held to by Russia's Muslim population.[90] Both schools are present in the Caucasus, as is Muridism, a variety of Sufism found in the eastern Caucasus, Ingushetia, Chechnya, and Dagestan.[91] The combination of Sufism and Khanafism creates a religious environment that welcomes syncretic elements, ethnic or traditional practices, into Islam. Wahhabism is associated with the strict interpretation that the Koran and Shari'a are unique gifts, and therefore prohibits the borrowing of non-Islamic practices or the blending of local traditions with Islam. This intolerant practice of Wahhabism is also associated with Salafitism in the Northern Caucasus.

According to Trenin and Malashenko, because Chechens possess such a linguistic homogeneity compared to the rest of the region, they are disinclined to welcome non-natives, even Muslims. They suggest that Basayev's lieutenant Khattaab, who was killed in 2002, was very unpopular, saying he was accused of arrogance and reluctance to recognize local traditions.[92] They quote V. Voronov's article Genie on a Jeep (Djinn na djipe): "For all of the people of Ickheria, Khattab remains a wandering alien, who is barely tolerated. [Even] his appearance is an irritant."[93] Similarly, Andrew Jack suggests that "most ordinary Chechens hated the Wahhabis as outsiders who brought terror and a form of religious extremism far from their own traditional Sufism."[94] Trenin and Malashenko concluded that this coldness toward traditional Sufism excluded Wahhabis, who then often worked separate from the traditional Sufi Chechens. Since the aim of many of the Chechen commanders was to make the Chechen cause a wider Caucasian cause, there were very few foreign fighters among the Chechen Resistance forces.

Andrei Babitskii, a correspondent with Radio Free Europe/Radio Liberty, reported that a new relationship is emerging within the Resistance movement, as Wahhabis are integrating into units commanded by traditional syncretic Muslims. This is not the case of growing Wahhabism or infiltration but rather a new demonstration of tolerance on the part of the Wahhabis. Babitskii notes, "If earlier the Wahhabis formed separate djamaats (communities) and fought independently of those Chechens who practice traditional Islam, today you can find men of diverging religious persuasions within a single armed formation, and this does not give rise to conflicts as it used to do when the Salafits branded adherents of traditional Islam as pagans and tried to convert them."[95]

Even Basayev himself, who was reported to have converted to Wahhabism after he began spending more time with Khattab between 1998 and 2001, suggested that he preferred the military campaigns to be waged by Caucasians and not outsiders. Liz Fuller reports that in a July 2005 interview with Al-Jazeera, Basayev said, "In my database I have extensive lists of people all over the world who want to participate in the jihad in Chechnya, tens and hundreds of thousands of them, and not all Muslim." He rejected all such offers, saying "we have quite enough volunteers in Chechnya."[96] Basayev repeated his many denials of any links to al Qaeda and adamantly denied that his ranks include any foreign mercenaries.[97]

A growing concern regarding the radicalization of Islam in Chechnya and the region stems from the Kremlin's politicization of religion in the conflict. After elevating Akhmad Kadyrov from the position of Mufti of Chechnya to head the clearly pro-Moscow government, many in Chechnya came to see the official Muftiate as nothing more than an extension of President Putin's office. Traditionally issued Sufi tariqats began to compete with decisions and interpretations from the Muftiate. This tension increased as many Chechens were disposed to reject the Muftiate and its opinions, because the Russian governmental authorities selected the leaders of the Muftiate. Rather than allowing Chechens to select their own religious leaders, the Kremlin appeared to be pushing believers toward a more radicalized interpretation than they might otherwise be disposed to adopt.[98]

As late as the winter of 2006, many within the Chechen resistance leadership were still actively distancing themselves from those who call for an "Islamic Caliphate." Akhmed Zakayev, the Chechen resistance minister of culture and former deputy prime minister, opposed any such calls, saying the goal of the resistance movement is the liberation of Chechnya from Russian colonial rule and that "there is not and cannot be any national freedom without national sovereignty, without a national state."[99] He wrote on the official Chechen Resistance government Web site:

> [D]emands to dismantle the Chechen state system before the Northern Caucasus has been liberated from the Russian colonial rule are both irresponsible and absolutely damaging to our cause. ... Let me remind the reader that in 1990 Chechens restored its national statehood, not an Imanate, and in 1994 they started fighting against Russian aggressors not because they wanted a "Caucasian Caliphate" but because they wanted to free our country from occupation.[100]

Abdul-Khalim Sadulaev made similar comments when he came to power in 2005. "The path we have chosen is the only one and we have one single goal. Freedom is impossible in an unfree country, and in an unfree country, human rights are worthless and cannot be protected. Russia has shown us this ... and continues to do so. ..."[101]

The fighters ask for the freedom to select their own leaders, both secular and religious. The Chechen separatists boycotted the November 2005 elections, calling them a charade. An eight-member election observer team from the Council of Europe agreed. Andreas Gross, head of the mission, spoke of a climate of fear in relation to the elections, stating that real power in Chechnya is not democratic. Likewise, Russian and international human rights groups criticized the polls, calling them only a pretense of a free and fair political process.[102] Basayev has offered to radically change his tactics if the Russians would abide by the Geneva Conventions, saying, "We want to wage war according to international law."[103] Yet Human Rights Watch continues to monitor abuses and asserts that Russian security forces engaged in forced disappearances on a massive scale. During 2002–2003 Human Rights Watch estimated that at least three disappearances occurred each day and that 1,700 people disappeared in 2004.[104] The Organization also denounces the Kremlin's strategy of "Chechenization," stating that the replacement of federal forces with Kremlin-sanctioned Chechen ones only leads to the same abuses.[105]

PROGRESS AND PROSPECTS

Although there was no domino effect of other republics trying to secede from Russia in the northern Caucasus, many men are joining the ranks of the fighters to oppose what they perceive as hostility toward Muslims and Caucasians in general. This sentiment was reinforced when the North Ossetian minister for nationality affairs, Taymuraz Kasaev, suggested on September 25, 2005, that anyone who "actively practices Islam" would be seen as an "enemy,"[106] even though Islam is recognized as a "traditional belief" within Russian law.[107] Russia's senior mufti, Ravil Gainutdin, who is also politically appointed to the official Russian Muftiate, complained, "Politicians and the mass media are equating us, the Muslim faithful, with armed groups."[108] This treatment appears to engender resentment and hostility within the Northern Caucasus. The Council on Foreign Relations suggested this was why so many fighters participated in attacks in Nalchik: "Dozens of men, frustrated by the harassment of Muslims and the closing of mosques, [took] up arms in Nalchik."[109] The growing ranks of fighters are a statement about the sense of neglect from Moscow, and the lack of a future for many young people in the region. The never-ending quality of the conflict has led to great despair. The Kremlin speaks of "black widows," women who become suicide bombers because they have lost everything. Either they lost their men as brothers, husbands, or fathers, or they lost themselves as victims of rape. The continuing battle brings more soldiers of despair to the ranks of the rebels.

The journalist Andrei Babitskii reported that the resistance moved more freely throughout Chechnya than it did on his previous visits to the region. He said that the unit he was with seemed "less apprehensive of being tracked down and apprehended by Russian Forces."[110] Yet it appears that Chechnya has become the Russian military's raison d'être, requiring ever more resources to fuel the ongoing skirmishes in the mountains.[111] With all of the money invested, with all of the young Russian soldiers' blood and lives committed, with all of diplomatic favor dispensed, Russia seems as far from solving this crisis as it has been at any point since 1994.

This is a conflict not of international terrorism but of ethnic separatism, or perhaps even regional autonomy. It is also not a conflict about Islam, as the Chechen separatists have failed to obtain broad-based support from Russia's wider Muslim community of 15–20 million. There is "no organized movement of Russian Muslims in support of the Chechens."[112] This conflict is also not about Russia's disintegration, which was perhaps a viable concern for Yeltsin's Kremlin until the middle 1990s. On the other hand, the continued Russian military presence does appear to have a destabilizing effect. The continued Russian presence in Abkhazia and South Ossetia may ignite larger regional instabilities that involve Georgia and the Organization for Security and Cooperation in Europe. The Russian air forces have penetrated Georgian airspace numerous times to bomb the passes along the Pankisi Gorge, often spoken of as a haven for Chechen fighters, Wahhabis, and Islamists. However, Basayev has categorically denied that his men have used the Gorge as a base.

The region desperately needs rebuilding and a reinvigoration of its economy. The infrastructure of the entire Caucasus needs to be developed if not entirely rebuilt. Real democracy and the exercise of self-determination must be introduced, not only to the Northern Caucasus but also to all of Russia. When discussing religion in the Caucasus, Sebastian Smith wrote: "Many people across the region were so ignorant about Islam that this was less a renewal than a rediscovery. The middle aged grew up in an atheist state, while their children were just as likely to be inspired by the thought of making money and becoming post-Soviet consumers as they were by the mosque."[113] Material wealth never came to the region. In fact, Basayev says he is never in the Pankisi Gorge because "there are better conditions to relax in Chechnya than impoverished Georgia."[114] For the region to prosper, conditions throughout the Northern Caucasus should be better than in a republic that has been scarred by war for 12 years.

NOTES

1. Andrew Jack, *Inside Putin's Russia: Can There Be Reform Without Democracy?* (Oxford 2004), p.94.
2. Bombings in Moscow in August 1999 have been cited by the Kremlin as the proximate cause for the renewal of fighting. On October 23, 2002, guerrilla fighters stormed the Dubrovka Theatre in Moscow and held nearly 900 people for two days. Buynaksk was the scene of the September 4, 1999, bombing of a military garrison housing complex that killed 62, mostly military family members. An earlier bombing in Kaspiysk on November 16, 1996, also targeted an apartment block for military families. Two hundred Chechen rebels seized and held the city of Nazran for a day, on June 22, 2004; 24 people were killed when militants attacked police, security, and military installations in Nalchik on October 14, 2005. Sixty-four people died in the bombing of the central market in Vladikavhaz on March 19, 1999. The raid on Beslan may be the most infamous attack thus far. More than 1,300 hostages were taken when guerrillas attacked the Beslan School No. 1. on the "Day of Knowledge" at the beginning of the academic year. After the hostages were held for three days, the security forces assaulted the school. In the ensuing gun battle and blasts, 31 of the 32 militants were killed, 11 members of the Russian security forces died, and 344 civilians—186 of them children—perished.
3. Susan Glasser and Peter Baker, "Putin, Bush Weigh New Unity Against Common Foe," *Washington Post,* p. A25, September 13, 2005.
4. Ibid.
5. Dmitri V. Trenin and Aleksei V. Malashenko, *Russia's Restless Frontier: The Chechen Factor in Post-Soviet Russia* (Carnegie Endowment for Peace, 2004), p. 63
6. Jeremy Bransten, "Seeing the Chechen War through Moscow's Eyes," RFE/RL Newsline, September 26, 2001.
7. "Putin Scores Coup Over Chechnya," *Moscow Times,* September 27, 2001. http://www.themoscowtimes.com/stories/2001/09/27/001.html.
8. RFE/RL Newsline "Russian Political Leaders Endorse Tactics vis-à-vis Chechnya," October 4, 1999; RFE/RL Newsline "While Moscow Denies Any Battle Took Place," December 16, 1999.
9. RFE/RL Newsline "Yeltsin, Jiang Call for Non-Interference," December 10, 1999.
10. RFE/RL Newsline "Moscow Lashes Out ... At NATO Commander," December 14, 1999. Clark's statement was important because NATO had just concluded its air operation against Serbia for its abusive policies in Kosovo just two months before Russia launched a new military offensive against Chechens.
11. RFE/RL Newsline "Council of Europe May Suspend Russia Over Chechnya," December 14, 1999; RFE/RL Newsline "EU Threatens to Pull Russia's MNF Status Over Chechnya," December 17, 1999.
12. Sebastian Smith, *Allah's Mountains: The Battle for Chechnya* (I. B. Tauris, 2001), p.7.
13. Ibid.

14. At the time of the 1989 Census, Ingushetia and Chechnya were a single Autonomous Soviet Republic. U.S. Central Intelligence Agency, "Russia's Ethnic Republics" Map, 1994, in University of Texas' Perry Costeñeda Map Library, Chechen Map Collection. http://www.lib.utexas.edu/maps/commonwealth/russia_ethnic94.jpg.

15. Dagestan was also part of the Roman Protectorate system then known as Caucasian Albania.

16. Dzhokhar Dudaev, Chechen President from 1991–1996, had a portrait of Mansur on his office wall.

17. Mansur also means Victor in Arabic. Smith op. cit., p. 40.

18. Ibid., p.40.

19. Ibid., p.42.

20. Jack, op. cit., p.91.

21. The successor to Groznaya is the Chechen capital city Grozny. Anna Politkovskaya, *A Dirty War: A Russian Reporter in Chechnya* (Harvill Press, 2001), p.1.

22. There are various spellings of his name, including Abd al-Qadir. He was a significant leader of the Algerian resistance against the French attempts to supplant Ottoman rule in North Africa.

23. The Caucasian Wars continued until Tsar Alexander II declared them finished by decree in June 2,1864. After his capture, Shamil was taken to Tsar Alexander II who was so impressed, he allowed Shamil to live under house arrest in Kaluga until 1869 when he was allowed to retire to Mecca. Shamil died in Medina in 1871.

24. Emil Souleimanov, "History of Russian-Chechen Relations: Attempt at a Polemic View," *Prague Watchdog,* January 4, 2004, http://www.watchdog.cz.

25. Ibid.

26. Smith, op. cit., p. 55.

27. The western territories formed the North Caucasus Soviet Republic in July 1918. By the end of the year, the Republic was abolished after it been overrun by Anton Denikin's White army.

28. Smith, op. cit., p. 56.

29. Ibid., p. 56.

30. Chechen-Ingushetia Autonomous Soviet Socialist Republic.

31. Carl Savich, "Sandzak's Nazi Past: Still Forgotten," in Serbiana, February 15, 2006, http://www.serbianna.com/columns/savich/072.shtml.

32. Savich claims that number to be 75,000 Soviet Muslims who went to the German side. Other Muslim "Legions" were also formed, including the Legion Freies Arabische and the Turkestanisch Legion, which had 40,000 soldiers and 30,000 military workers from 1941–1945.

33. Mikhail Heller and Aleksandr M. Nekrich, *Utopia in Power: The History of the Soviet Union from 1917 to the Present* (Summit Books, 1986), p. 533.

34. The NKVD, or the People's Commissariat for Internal Affairs, was the predecessor to the KGB, the State Security Committee, which is now the FSB, the Federal Security Service. Stalin combined security and police functions within the NKVD; the most ruthless element was the GUGB, the Main Directorate for State Security, which replaced the GPU, the State Political Administration, and the Checka as the secret police.

35. Heller and Nekrich, op. cit., p.534.

36. The Volga Germans and the Tatars were still left out.

37. Heller and Nekrich include the statistics for the other deported people as from Nekrich's book *Nakazannye narody (The Punished People)*, 1978, p.116., in Heller and Nekrich, op. cit., p.535. The Ingush population declined by 9 percent, the Kalmyks by 15 percent, the Balkars by nearly 27 percent, and the Karachai people by almost 30 percent.

38. Ibid., p.536.

39. Ibid., p.536.
40. BBC News, http://news.bbc.co.uk/onthisday/hi/dates/stories/january/12/newsid_4059000/4059959.stm.
41. Jeremy Bransten, "USSR Breakup: Tracing the Collapse of the World's Last Great Empire," RFE/RL Newsline December 14, 2001, http://www.rferl.org/features/2001/12/14122001094030.asp.
42. Ichkeria refers to the more mountainous regions of Chechnya. The name Chechen Republic of Ichkeria (ChRI) is to distinguish it from any references that Moscow makes regarding what constitutes Chechnya.
43. Emil A. Payin and Akardy Popov, "Chechnya" in U.S. and Russian Policymaking in Respect to the Use of Force, Jeremy R. Azreal and Emil A. Payin, eds. (RAND Corporation, 1995), http://www.rand.org/pubs/conf_proceedings/CF129/CF-129.chapter2.html.
44. Politkovskaya, op. cit., p. 324.
45. Trenin and Malshenko, op. cit., p.55.
46. The FSK or Federal Counterintelligence Services became the FSB in April 1995.
47. Payin and Popov, op. cit.
48. Nearly all of the sources consulted describe a similar course of events. The decision was clearly not made by the Defense Ministry, although in the end they would go along with the plan. C.f. Smith, Allah's Mountain, pp. 139–140; Trenin and Malashenko, Russia's Restless Frontier, pp. 53–54, and Payin and Popov, Chechnya, et al.
49. Chechen Times, No. 2, November 29, 2002, http://www.chechentimes.org/en/chechentimes/2.
50. PBS Newshour, http://www.pbs.org/newshour/bb/europe/chechnya/timeline_2.html.
51. Jack, op.cit., p.95.
52. Ibid., p.96.
53. Jack, op. cit., p.96.
54. National Counterterrorism Center, Russia Overview: 1998, http://www.tkb.org.
55. National Counterterrorism Center, Russia Overview: 1999, http://www.tkb.org.
56. Jack, op. cit., p. 102.
57. National Counterterrorism Center, Russia Overview: 1999, http://www.tkb.org C.f. Jack, op. cit., pp.102—103.
58. Quoted in Thomas de Waal in Politkovskaya, op. cit., xxviii.
59. Ibid., p. xxvii. C.f. Jack, op. cit., p.104. On September 22, in Rayzan, east of Moscow, police following-up on a local tip detained two men who were spotted transporting heavy sacks from their car into an apartment block. Local experts who analyzed the sacks found hexagon, a rare and powerful military grade explosive; this was also the substance found in the Moscow blasts. Eyewitnesses also stated that they saw electronic devices in the sacks attached to clocks. Initially, the FSB said that the local police had thwarted a terrorist attack, but when it was reported that the men originally detained were freed after showing FSB identity cards, the agency changed its story and claimed that the events in Ryazan were part of a "training exercise." All of this suggested that it was quite possible the FSB was behind the bombings in Moscow. Boris Berezovsky held a press conference in London in the spring of 2002 to present this accusation and presented evidence to prove the link. Berezovsky also screened a documentary film that analyzed the events and came to the same conclusion: Yeltsin and the Kremlin orchestrated the Chechen War in order to stay in power.
60. Georgi Derlugian, New Left Review, September/October 1999. Quoted in Thomas de Waal in Politkovskaya, op. cit., xix.
61. Politkovskaya, op. cit., 327.
62. BBC News, April 4, 2000, 16:53 GMT "Chechen Visit Mixed Success," http://news.bbc.co.uk/1/hi/world/europe/701590.stm.

63. Human Rights Watch "Chechnya: Renewed Catastrophe," http://www.hrw.org/campaigns/russia/chechnya/.
64. BBC News, April 2, 2000, 18:27 GMT "Explosion Rocks Dagestani Capital," http://news.bbc.co.uk/1/hi/world/europe/699123.stm.
65. Mosnews, "Dubrovka Theatre Siege," http://www.mosnews.com/mn-files/dubrovka.shtml.
66. Ibid.
67. Six people did die, however, including four of Zyazikov's bodyguards.
68. Kadyrov replaced Koshman. June 8, 2000.
69. The date refers to the end of World War II, or the Great Patriotic War, when the Germans surrendered on May 9, 1945.
70. The film Beslan: Siege of School No. 1 is an amazing documentary that is also very disturbing. The Chechan guerrillas shot many hours of videotape that survived the siege. The film presents footage from both outside and inside the school.
71. John Dunlop, *Beslan: Russian 9/11?* (American Committee for Peace in Chechnya and Jamestown Foundation, 2005), p.19.
72. Sunday Telegraph, "Ex-policeman 'master-minded' Beslan Terror," September 12, 2004, quoted in Dunlop, p.19.
73. It has been reported that the "Slant-eyed" person might either be Korean or Irktusk, Ibid., pp, 19-20.
74. Svetlana Meleteva, Beslan bez grifov, part II Moskovskii Komsomolets, May 25, 2005, in Dunlop, p.20.
75. Mosnews, "Russian Prosecutor Says International Terrorists Planed Beslan," September 12, 2005, http://www.mosnews.com/news/2005/09/12/beslanshepel.shtml.
76. Ibid.
77. Scott Peterson, "Al Qaeda Among the Chechens" *Christian Science Monitor,* September 7, 2004.
78. On August 24, 2004, 90 people were killed when two Sabir Air flights from Moscow to Southern Russia exploded nearly simultaneously. Russian security services and investigators concluded that it was the work of two Chechen "black widows"—women who lost their men, either husbands, sons, or both, and became suicide bombers.
79. Ibid.
80. Ibid.
81. Dmitri V. Trenin and Aleksei V. Malashenko, op cit. p. 72.
82. Emphasis mine. Ibid., p. 46.
83. Mosnews, "Chechen Rebel Leader Maskhadov Killed by Bodyguard: Forensic Expert," October 28, 2005, http://www.mosnews.com/news/2005/10/28/maskhadovgun.shtml.
84. Mosnews, "Family of Killed Chechen Leader Asks ASEAN to Help Return His Body," December 15, 2005, http://www.mosnews.com/news/2005/12/15/aseanbody.shtml.
85. Mosnews, "Rebel Chechen Leader Maskhadov Buried in Secret Grave," April 22, 2005, ttp://www.mosnews.com/news/2005/04/22/maskhadovburied.shtml.
86. Liz Fuller, "Russia: New Chechen Resistance Leader Vows No More Hostage Takings," RFE/RL Newsline, June 3, 2005.
87. Ibid.
88. Ibid.
89. Liz Fuller, "Chechnya: Vice President Denounces Terrorism, Basaev [sic]," RFE/RL Newsline July 15, 2005.
90. Trenin and Malshenko, op. cit., p. 84.
91. Ibid., p.84.
92. Ibid., p.97.
93. V. Voronov, "Djinn na djipe," Novae vremia 2000, No. 43 (99) p.13. Quoted in Trenin and Malashenko, op. cit., p.97.

94. Jack., op. cit., p.109.
95. Liz Fuller, "Chechnya: Vice President Denounces Terrorism, Basaev [sic]," RFE/RL Newsline, July 15, 2005.
96. Liz Fuller, "Chechen Warlord Warns of New Terrorist Attacks," RFE/RL Newsline, November 3, 2005.
97. Ibid.
98. Paul Globe, *Russia: A Three-Way Struggle for Chechen Islam.*
99. RFE/RL Caucasus Report, February 10, 2006, Vol. 9 No. 5.
100. Akhmed Zakayev wrote the quoted piece in January 2006 while he was still Vice-Premier of the Chechen government. In early February 2006, Abdul-Khalim Sadu-layev, the Chechen Resistance leader, stripped Zakayev of his title Deputy Prime Minister. Sudulayev also ordered home all ministers outside of Chechnya, except Zakayev, who remained in London as the Chechen representative to Europe and the West. At the time of this writing there were press speculations that Zakayev was demoted to Culture Minister, because his comments went too far and were too moderate. However, Zakayev himself said that the government reshuffle had long been anticipated, and the recall of ministers was to prevent the Russians from ignoring the Resistance government by claiming that it was in exile. Radio Free Europe/Radio Liberty interviewed Zakayev on February 6, 2006. RFE/RL Newsline, "Chechen Envoy Confirms Government Shuffle," February 7, 2006. The quoted material is from Akhmed Zakayev, "Commentary on Certain Ideas and Statements," SIA Chechen-press, http://www.chechenpress.co.uk/english/news/2006/01/03/01.
101. Liz Fuller, "Russia: New Chechen Resistance Leader Vows No More Hostage Takings," RFE/RL Newsline, June 3, 2005.
102. RFE/RL Newsline, "Pro-Kremlin Party leads in Chechen Elections," November 28, 2005, http://www.rferl.org/featuresarticle/2005/11/c9ff1a31-38e9-45cb-98ea-17a350ef58c7.html.
103. Liz Fuller, "Chechen Warlord Warns of New Terrorist Attacks," RFE/RL Newsline, November 3, 2005.
104. Human Rights Watch, "Human Rights Defender Abducted," Russia: Chechnya a Catastrophe Continued, http://www.hrw.org/campaigns/russia/chechnya/.
105. Human Rights Watch, "Human Rights Concerns for the 61st Session of the U.N. Commission on Human Rights." Russia: Chechnya a Catastrophe Continued, http://www.hrw.org/campaigns/russia/chechnya/.
106. Paul Globe, RFE/RL Newsline, "Authorities seek to convert Beslan's Muslims," RFE/RL, September 7, 2005.
107. See Law of Freedom of Conscience and Religious Organization, Lev Krichevsky, "Russian House passes religion bill restricting 'nontraditional' faiths," Jewish Telegraphic Agency, June 26, 1997.
108. *The Economist,* "Russia and Islam: Chaos in the Caucasus," October 9, 1999, Vol. 353, Issue 8140, p. 23.
109. Pan., op. cit.
110. Liz Fuller, "Chechnya: Vice President Denounces Terrorism, Basaev [sic]," RFE/RL Newsline, July 15, 2005.
111. In mid-October 2005, 220 fighters attacked 15 separate police and military targets in the Kabardino-Balkar capital, Nalchik. Units from the Kabardino-Balkar sector of the Caucasus Front led the assault with support from the Ingush and Yarmuk djamaats. Russian security officials had claimed to have wiped out the Yarmuk djamaat, also based in Kabardino-Balkaria, between January and April 2005. Khachim Shogenov, the KBR Interior Minister, acknowledged that 300 police and military personnel had been killed or wounded in the attack. Shogenov also claimed that security forces killed 91 militants—more than the 42 claimed to have been lost in

an October 17, 2005, communiqué from rebel leader Shamil Basayev. Later figures confirmed that 138 people were killed. Basayev explained the discrepancy, saying Russian security forces killed 49 Nalchik civilians, placed guns beside them, and claimed they were militants too.

112. Trenin and Malashenko, op. cit., p.47.

113. Smith, op. cit., p. 75.

114. Liz Fuller, "Chechen Warlord Warns of New Terrorist Attacks," RFE/RL Newsline, November 3, 2005.

The Fergana Valley

6

THE FERGANA VALLEY

Christopher J. Fettweis

NATURE OF THE FLASHPOINT

If, as it is often said, war is God's way to teach Americans about geography, then apparently 9/11 was the beginning of His lesson on Central Asia. Unbeknownst to most of the American public, Washington had already established relations with these new states and had also identified a number of interests in the region, from oil to economic reform to democracy. The terrorist attacks brought the international spotlight to Afghanistan and its neighbors, and introduced many people to these formerly unknown, remote "stans." News about the region's tyrannical leaders, disputes over oil pipelines, and Islamic fundamentalists moved Central Asia from the back pages to the front.

Although few analysts were optimistic about the potential for stability in Central Asia when independence was thrust on these peoples in 1991, the short history of the region has been surprisingly peaceful. Each state had a Soviet autocrat that was able to adopt nationalist trappings, assume power, and bring a measure of stability to his country. Even Tajikistan, where a civil war broke out immediately upon independence, has remained relatively calm since 1994. Just as significantly, Islamic fundamentalist groups did not find willing audiences among the Central Asian people, most of whom seemed to be far more secular, or at least more moderate, than many other Muslim societies.

Ominous signs of change emerged in 2005, however, when two very different uprisings threatened the region's tranquility. The first ended with the abdication of the President of Kyrgyzstan and what may have been the region's first "free and fair" election. The second started and ended more violently, and brought a quite different reaction from the regime. The decade of stability that Central Asia enjoyed after the end of the Tajik civil war may be coming to an end, and Central Asia may be emerging as the next flashpoint in the war on terror.

U.S. Interests in Central Asia

The United States had been encouraging political and economic reform in Central Asia since independence in 1991, and had tried to help the new states avoid becoming vassals of Russia or following Iran down the road to fundamentalism. Central Asia borders on almost all the regions that have the potential to become more important for a variety of reasons as the next century unfolds, since it touches China, Russia, South Asia, and the Middle East (see map at beginning of chapter). Many feared that its position, combined with the relative weakness of the new states, would create a *de facto* power vacuum that would invite intervention from outside powers and spark a "new great game," echoing the struggle for power that took place here between Russia and Great Britain during the nineteenth century.[1]

The Caspian Sea appeared on the radar screen of U.S. diplomatic defense planners in the late 1990s, as estimates of the region's potential fossil fuel reserves began to grow. Central Asia quickly became the cutting edge of international diplomacy and was made "seriously sexy" by the specters of back-room deals and geopolitical machinations, according to one U.S. diplomat.[2] As the discovery of a number of large oil fields fed the impression that Soviet geologists had grossly underestimated the reserves of the region, Washington's concerns with democracy and freedom were placed on hold, and it laid proverbial (as well as literal) red carpets in front of visiting Central Asian leaders. These new estimates were not ignored in Moscow and Beijing either, as they also increased their interest and presence in the region. For a time, the situation seemed to have the potential to become somewhat volatile. "If we clash," wrote one Russian analyst at the time, "it will be on the Caspian."[3]

Such pessimistic projections have thus far proven fortunately inaccurate. The pull of oil has not been as powerful as previously expected. Although current estimates of Caspian fossil fuel reserves still vary widely, they are significantly lower than the unbridled optimism of a decade ago. According to the U.S. Department of Energy, the region's proven oil reserves are between 17 and 44 billion barrels, which is somewhere between those of Qatar and the United States.[4] Although a good deal of oil may still await discovery, the current estimates are a far cry from the 200 billion barrels that many optimistic analysts initially predicted would be found.[5] Negotiations over the construction of pipelines that brought Caspian oil to world markets occurred without even the threat of violence, even if they were not always entirely cooperative. With the opening of the U.S.-supported Baku-Tblisi-Ceyhan pipeline, export issues appear to be all but settled. Therefore, the most dangerous period in the development of Central Asian international politics may well have passed.[6]

September 11th immediately changed the priorities of the United States' Central Asian policy. The interests previously identified in the region, from oil to democracy, quickly became secondary to the struggle against extremists. Washington found the secular autocrats of Central Asia to be quite willing partners in the struggle against both Islamic fundamentalism and with the terrorist groups crossing Central Asian borders to fight in Afghanistan, central front in the war on terrorism. Uzbekistan and Kyrgyzstan opened their doors to U.S. military forces shortly after the attacks, allowing bases to be established in former Soviet territory to support the attack on the Taliban. Regional cooperation against fundamentalism increased, and U.S. aid poured into the region as a result.

Uzbekistan became the central partner of the United States in the region's antiterrorist struggle. As part of the Strategic Partnership and Cooperation Framework that the two countries signed in March 2002, the United States averred that it would "regard with grave concern any external threat to the security and territorial integrity of the Republic of Uzbekistan." The two countries pledged to "develop cooperation in combating transnational threats to society" and expand military-to-military cooperation.[7] In addition, Islam Karimov, president of Uzbekistan, was given $500 million in aid and credit (more than a 15-fold increase), $25 million in military assistance, $18 million for border security, and $1 million for his internal security and police. President Bush called him one of America's "foremost partners in the fight against terrorism," which, as one observer points out, is a "sentiment that's been repeated by a parade of dignitaries that have made the trek to Tashkent, including Generals Tommy Franks, Richard Myers, and Anthony Zinni, and Senators McCain, Lieberman, and Daschle."[8] Karimov had become "our man" in Central Asia.

In that March 2002 meeting, both sides also renewed their commitment for political, economic, and legal reform in Uzbekistan, pledges that unsurprisingly do not seem to have had much effect on behavior in Tashkent. Although opinions are quite mixed about the seriousness with which Washington has ever approached issues of democracy, freedom, and economic liberalization with its new allies, the United States has consistently pressed Karimov to make good on his promises to reform.[9] The pestering has at the very least become loud enough to serve as an irritant in relations between the two nations, culminating in the nadir that occurred after the Andijan incidents, which will be discussed below.

Central Asians' opinions of the United States are fairly difficult to gauge, since reliable public opinion analyses are few and far between. Anti-Americanism does not often rear its head, perhaps partially because the issues that seem to cause the most ill-will among Muslims in the 1990s—such as the permanent Israeli-Palestinian crisis and the sanctions on Iraq—had little resonance among the Turkic peoples of the region. The extent to which the war in Iraq might affect feelings toward America, for better or worse, remains to be seen.

Sources of Instability? Regional Leaders versus Islam

The collapse of the Soviet Union, so celebrated in Riga and Kiev, met little glee in Central Asian capitals, where more than a few people felt that the region's ill-defined national identities, poorly drawn borders, and semi-buried ethnic tensions were kept quiet only by Moscow's iron fist. Outside observers like Zbigniew Brzezinksi feared that the region was destined to become the "Eurasian Balkans," torn by strife, lawlessness, and ethnic cleansing.[10] The bloody civil war in Tajikistan seemed to be the harbinger of even worse things to come.

However, regional leaders proved able to replace Moscow's stabilizing influence with iron fists of their own. The last Soviet governors of these SSRs became the first presidents of four of the five new Central Asian states. The lone exception, Kyrgyzstan, was led by a university professor who seemed to espouse democratic ideals at first, but soon abandoned them as the advantages of power became apparent. Since these men were all products of the Soviet system, perhaps it should be no surprise that they brought a similar leadership philosophy to their new countries. Before long each was a virtual fiefdom.

The career path of Islam Karimov is exemplary in this regard.[11] A dedicated, lifelong communist, Karimov was first secretary of the Communist Party in Uzbekistan (or *de facto* provincial governor) in 1991 when the great socialist experiment unraveled. Like most leaders of Central Asia, Karimov was in no rush to see independence come to his native land. "If we remain part of the Soviet Union," he said as the regime in Moscow was collapsing, "our rivers will flow with milk. If we don't, our rivers will flow with the blood of our people."[12] Nonetheless, independence was thrust upon them. In December 1991, Karimov won the first in a series of rigged national elections and has ruled over Uzbekistan ever since.

Many observers feel that Uzbekistan holds the key to the future of the region.[13] Uzbeks are not traditionally nomadic, as are many of the other peoples of Central Asia. They are "people of oases," and have developed a culture and national identity that makes them simultaneously the most coherent state in the region and the envy of their neighbors, for better and for worse.[14] Uzbekistan is the home to both the largest population and the only active fundamentalist groups in Central Asia, and is thus a lightning rod for terrorism, international attention, and foreign aid. It is not much of an exaggeration to say that as goes Tashkent, so goes the region.

Karimov's regime is secular, which has helped make it a sworn enemy of political Islam. He is also, by all measures, a tyrant. The levels of political and religious freedom in Uzbekistan are quite low, and show no signs of improving. Uzbekistan is but an extreme example of the many illiberal, undemocratic, tyrannical regimes across the region.

The people of Central Asia are divided by nationality and tribe but are largely united by religion. The vast majority are Muslims, and, as is the case with nearly every majority Muslim community, a homegrown fundamentalist minority has emerged with Saudi backing to press secular regimes for reform. Some of those groups have shown a willingness to use violence and terrorist tactics in pursuit of their goals, and have helped move Central Asia from a post-Soviet backwater onto the front lines in the war on terror.

The epicenter of both the population and fundamentalism of Central Asia is the Fergana Valley, which is a large oasis split among three states. It is the most fertile, the most vibrant, and by far the most important region in Central Asia. It is the heart of the intellectual, cultural, and spiritual life of its people, and the home of the growing fundamentalist movements that threaten the stability of the region. It is worth noting that the Fergana Valley is shared by four states. This division was created intentionally. Joseph Stalin, the Soviet Minister of Minorities in the 1920s, drew borders based not on a logical division of existing peoples or coherent natural features, but rather to divide the local people and maximize the efficiency of imperial control. The Fergana Valley may stretch across multiple states, but its people are a mixture of local tongues and cultures; they are tightly intermingled throughout an area whose boundaries are often not respected.

Many longtime Central Asia watchers are now warning that the brand of Islam being practiced in the region is beginning to shift in ominous directions. Muslims of the Fergana Valley have traditionally followed Sufi teachings, which is a mystical and tolerant form of religious expression that does not lend itself well to the support of extremist violence. After achieving independence, the region did not appear a likely destination for the emergence of radical Islamic organizations.[15] The stark separation between church and state that existed in Soviet times seemed likely to continue in the successor states.

The influx of both Saudi money and veterans of the 1980s war in Afghanistan have brought a new conceptualization of religion to the Fergana Valley. Since 1985, the Saudis have spent nearly $75 billion promoting Wahhabism, their more conservative brand of Islam, across the region.[16] In many communities, including those in the Fergana Valley, Saudi money replaced Soviet aid in the 1990s, paying for the construction of mosques, schools, and basic social infrastructure. Although many religious scholars object to the manner with which Wahhabism is often equated with violent extremism, Karimov routinely labels all his enemies "Wahhabis," which is generally more conservative than the Sufism in Central Asia. The activist, even militant nature of much of the preaching that goes on in Saudi-funded Wahhabi mosques has proven popular with many disadvantaged groups throughout the world, and those of Central Asia are no exception. It is no coincidence that the majority of Islamic militants emerge from Wahhabi roots.

Many returning veterans of the Afghan war brought with them not only their training and battlefield knowledge, but also a conservative brand of Islam that they saw practiced in Afghanistan. "Deobandism" is the atavistic form of Islam that was practiced by the Taliban and their ideological allies in the mountainous regions on both sides of the Pakistan-Afghanistan border. Deobandis reject Westernization and modernization, and instead encourage Muslims to live their lives in similar ways to the Prophet Mohammed, to the point of mimicking socio-economic conditions of the seventh century.[17]

The staying power of the detachment between religion and politics in Central Asia, therefore, is by no means assured. The depressed Central Asian regions may prove to be fertile soil for the growth of both Wahhabism and Deobandism. Thanks in part to the Saudi billions, Wahhabism has found a receptive audience in some quarters, especially in the Fergana Valley. The extent to which Sufism can recover and provide a philosophical and theological counterweight might be the deciding factor for the future of radical, violent Islamic groups in the Fergana Valley.

LINKAGES TO TERRORISM

Political Islam has never been a monolithic movement. Instead, it is made up of a large number of disparate groups that vary widely in attitudes toward democracy, the West, and violence in the pursuit of political goals. Many violent groups have religious and social agendas that outweigh their political goals. Nonetheless, since the end of the Cold War the anti-democratic regimes throughout the Muslim world tend to group all of their political opponents together under one label—fundamentalists—in order to evoke the specter of Iran (and now al Qaeda) in the capitals of the West. As one analysis argued, Central Asian authorities have proven "unable or unwilling to distinguish between ordinary Sunni Muslims and the Wahhabis and Deobandis who were in league with the militants."[18] Openly practicing Islam has become hazardous for the people of the Fergana Valley—merely wearing a beard is often enough to draw attention from the police.[19]

Two major radical Islamic movements emerged in the Fergana Valley during the first decade of independence. The Islamic Movement of Uzbekistan (IMU) was the more violent of the two, at least until its apparent evisceration by recent fighting in Afghanistan. Since a variety of splinter and successor groups seem to be in the process of emerging in its wake, few believe that terrorist violence died with the IMU. The other group, the Islamic Party of Liberation, or HT (from its Arabic name, Hizb ut-Tahrir al-Islami), is powerful, growing, and far more controversial. Unlike the IMU, which from its inception espoused the violent overthrow of apostate governments, the HT has consistently denounced violence and sought peaceful regime change. Although Karimov lumps both movements together as terrorist enemies of the state, the variance in tactics among the two major movements suggests that Islamic fundamentalism in Central Asia is quite a bit more complex than he would have outsiders believe.

The Islamic Movement of Uzbekistan (IMU)

Although the HT is the largest fundamentalist organization in Central Asia, it is overshadowed in the headlines and in counterterrorist planning by the Islamic Movement of Uzbekistan. Founded in 1997 with the express purpose of overthrowing the secular apostate government in Tashkent, the IMU distinguished itself from Hizb ut-Tahrir with its aggressive espousal of violence. The IMU announced its existence with an attempted assassination of Karimov in February 1999, and during the next four years the group executed a variety of rather small-scale operations across the Fergana Valley from bases in Tajikistan and

Afghanistan. Overall, however, only three attacks during a seven-year period claiming fewer than 20 casualties each can be attributed to the IMU.[20]

The primary base of operations for the IMU in its early days was among the Uzbek minority in northern Afghanistan. Several hundred IMU members received sanctuary, training, and funding from the Taliban and its other guests, including al Qaeda, throughout the late 1990s.[21] This connection with Osama bin Laden, combined with the IMU's radical rhetoric and espousal of violent tactics, resulted in international notoriety for the IMU and a permanent place on international terrorist watch lists.

This alignment with the Taliban and al Qaeda may well prove to have been a strategic mistake for the IMU. The IMU decision to stand and fight alongside its allies against the U.S. and Northern Alliance counterattacks of late 2001 may have effectively broken the back of the IMU, resulting in the majority of its fighters killed, captured, or scattered. Juma Namangani, its military leader and primary motivator, is believed to have been among the hundreds of IMU fighters killed during the siege of Mazar-e-Sharif in October 2001.[22] Namangani was a former Soviet soldier and veteran of the war in Tajikistan, as well as a charismatic and effective leader. Whether or not he is dead and despite its modest successes in its first eight years of existence, the IMU appears to have been severely weakened since 9/11. At the very least the pace of its attacks has fallen considerably.

Other minor incidents have taken place across the region during the past few years, some of which seem to have connections to terrorist groups while others seem more politically motivated. Both Nazerbayev of Kazakhstan and Niyazov of Turkmenistan have been targets of assassins, but given the wide range of enemies that such men tend to produce, it is impossible to place blame on political Islamists without evidence.[23] Reliable information is a precious and rare commodity in Central Asia.

The erosion of IMU capabilities, if true, does not spell the end of trouble for the Central Asian regimes. Other groups seem poised to take their place. In April 2004, the Islamic Jihad Group (IJG) made its existence known with a series of bombings across Uzbekistan that resulted in 47 deaths. Three months later, the group masterminded largely ineffectual attacks on the U.S. and Israeli embassies, and on Uzbek officials. Washington added the IJG to the State Department's list of Foreign Terrorist Organizations (FTOs) in May 2005. Little has been heard from either the IJG or the IMU since the summer of 2004, but as usually the case with such groups, it is not clear whether silence is the result of counterterrorist actions or strategic decisions made by the group.

To this point, neither the IMU nor its inchoate successor groups have demonstrated much interest in affairs outside of their region. Their goals are fairly specific: they see the Karimov regime to be no better than the communists that came before, and they support its overthrow by any means necessary. Although these groups may share many of the same tactics and ideology of al Qaeda, there is no evidence that they have ever directly attacked or even threatened any targets outside of Central Asia. To date, they remain religiously oriented revolutionary groups with national, not international, goals.

The identity and organization of antiregime fundamentalist groups in Central Asia will no doubt continue to evolve in coming years as groups are smashed, splinter, and reform, and as copycats rise in their stead. These days it seems that any tiny group of malcontents with access to the right kind of fertilizer can become a terrorist group. The extent to which such groups represent a larger movement and the will of the people of the region is in some ways far more significant than the precise identification of which group of malcontents caused which devastation.

The Islamic Party of Liberation (Hizb ut-Tahrir al-Islami, or HT)

The Islamic Party of Liberation is far larger than the IMU in both membership and influence throughout Central Asia, and its status as a terrorist organization is much murkier and controversial. The movement was born in Saudi Arabia and Jordan in the early 1950s, and spread to Central Asia inside Saudi-funded mosques shortly after the collapse of the Soviet Union.[24] Today, the HT is the largest and most influential radical movement in the region, and as a predictable result, there are far more of its members in Central Asian jails than any other group. As Pakistani journalist and author Ahmed Rashid explains, the goals of the HT "are probably the most esoteric and anachronistic of all the radical Islamic movements in the world today."[25] It seeks to unify Islam, from Morocco to Xinjiang, under a renewed and righteous caliphate. The organization is quite secretive—there are no extant photographs of the leadership, no information on how the chain of command operates, or where exactly they are based. Although the HT is an international movement, with headquarters in London and as many as 10,000 members scattered across Pakistan, Indonesia, Turkey, and the Middle East, its primary base of operations these days is the Fergana Valley.[26]

The HT differs from other radical groups that hold similar beliefs in its choice of tactics. Unlike the IMU or other pan-Islamic groups like al Qaeda, the HT has always denounced violence, relying instead on the power of mass opinion to overthrow heretical Muslim governments. The movement has proven to be quite popular among many of the peoples of Central Asia, which has brought the HT into direct conflict with its authoritarian rulers. To analysts of terrorism in Central Asia, the HT is like an Islamic avian flu: although to date it has not engaged in violence, it seems to have the potential to mutate into a far more deadly form. If that mutation happens, if young firebrands convince their colleagues to take up arms (or if they splinter off to form their own group), violence might swiftly spread to infect the entire region.

No such pathological mutation has yet occurred. Since U.S. intelligence has been unable to make definitive connections between the HT and international terrorist activity, the group remains off the official State Department terrorist list. Not all allies in the global war on terror agree. The German government, for example, became the first to ban HT activity inside its borders in January 2003, largely because of the group's consistent and virulent anti-Semitic rhetoric (its literature refers to Karimov as a Jew and a "stooge" of Israel).[27] One month later, the Russian Supreme Court followed suit, adding the HT to Moscow's list of banned terrorist organizations.[28]

As of late 2005, HT rhetoric is fiery, divisive, fundamentalist, anti-Semitic—and almost exclusively focused on Central Asia. Although the group has members in many countries and espouses international goals, apparently it has calculated that the first steps toward a renewed caliphate should be taken in the Fergana Valley. The unjust caliphs that draw most of its ire are the strongmen of Central Asia, not those in the West, Middle East, or Russia. In return, the Uzbek leader argues that the HT is integrated into the overall global jihadi movement and is an illegal terrorist organization. Karimov's government has taken great pains to link the group to every act of violence that has occurred in the region since independence. Most observers find his efforts inconclusive at best, and utterly unconvincing at worst.[29] Its regional focus and opposition to violence seem to make the HT unlikely to become much of a factor in the global war on terror.

In May 1998, Uzbekistan began a widespread crackdown on the HT in particular and Wahhabi Islam in general. Its police questioned any man with a beard or "more than one wife," as well as anyone traveling frequently to Afghanistan or Pakistan.[30] Human Rights Watch estimates that between 5,000 and 7,000 people were arrested in the sweep, which may have included as many as 2,000 HT members, many of whom remain in Uzbek jails and have been subjected to a variety of painful unpleasantries.[31] Karimov seems to have calculated that he can crush the HT virus before a mutation takes place that could turn the organization into the largest terrorist organization the region has ever seen. The sagacity of his strategy is debatable; the outcome, as yet unclear.

Turmoil in 2005

The struggle against violent political Islamists does not seem to have had an appreciable effect on overall levels of human development across the region. At least to this point, it is hard to identify ways in which the violence, which has of course been fairly minor, has affected the daily lives of the people. Private investment in the region has not slowed since the IMU first reared its head, especially in the oil-producing areas, and foreign government-to-government assistance has increased since 9/11.[32] A 2005 UN report examining the trajectory of human development in Uzbekistan does not even include the war on terrorism as a factor in its analysis. In fact, it does not mention terrorism at all, but rather devotes its 97 pages to the desultory economic decentralization under Karimov since independence.[33] Civil war had of course hampered the development of Tajikistan, but the peace brokered there in 1994 has proven to be less precarious than some feared. Despite many dire predictions to the contrary, the Central Asian states have experienced very low levels of internal instability in the first decade and a half of independence. Four out of five countries had no significant unrest to speak of. This shroud of stability showed its first signs of weakness in 2005, when rioting in Kyrgyzstan and Uzbekistan brought down one of the region's autocrats, and cast a shadow over the rule of another.

The last few years have produced a good deal of instability in the Soviet successor states. The so-called "Rose Revolution" led to the end of the Scheverdnadze government in Georgia in November 2003. A year later, the "Orange Revolution" toppled Ukrainian President Kuchma. Perhaps most surprisingly, the "Tulip Revolution" of late March 2005, which forced President Askar Akayev to flee Kyrgyzstan, led to the first change of power in Central Asia in a decade. Remarkably, all three of these "revolutions" were relatively bloodless.

The spark for the Tulip protests was a parliamentary election that was widely seen as corrupt and rigged to benefit Akayev's party. The deeper cause, however, was longstanding frustration with the President's 15-year incompetent, nepotistic, and increasingly autocratic rule.[34] In July 2005, presidential elections were held in Kyrgyzstan for the first time since independence, and a new administration led by Kurmanbek Bakiyev took power in Bishkek.[35] These developments could not have sat well with the other leaders of the region. The Karimov regime sealed off its Fergana Valley border with Kyrgyzstan, explaining that it had to "prevent terrorist groups from entering Uzbek territory."[36] What was a popular uprising against a corrupt regime on one side of the border was an extra-constitutional terrorist coup on the other.

As it turns out, Karimov had a reason to be concerned. Violence broke out in Andijan, a Fergana Valley city near the Uzbek-Kyrgyz border, on May 13, 2005. Descriptions of the events that unfolded that spring evening vary widely on a number of important points; what seems fairly incontrovertible is that armed militants attacked a jail in the Fergana Valley city, freed a number of inmates, and transferred others to a downtown cinema where they were kept hostage. Uzbek security forces surrounded and stormed the cinema, and in the melee hundreds were killed. Government sources claim the raid was part of an attempted coup by Hizb ut-Tahrir and other Islamist forces that ended with the death of 150. Other accounts, primarily from journalists and human rights NGOs, describe the violence as a spontaneous local uprising to free unjustly arrested citizens, one that ended with more than 1,000 deaths.

Clearly, government accounts should be met with some incredulity. However, it is not entirely clear that the alternative narrative can be accepted at face value either, since many of the sources have long-standing grievances against the regime in Tashkent. In fact, a scholar of Central Asia at the University of London produced a dispassionate and quite convincing independent assessment of the incidents, and came to the conclusion that the government's account of the incident was probably more accurate.[37] It may well be that the Andijan incidents were an attempt to set off a nationwide revolt against Karimov's rule, mirroring the brightly named "revolutions" that took place across the former Soviet states. It remains possible, however, that this was an entirely local and mostly apolitical event, aimed at freeing prisoners with little forethought given to any national or international impact. Finally, it could have been a revolt carried out by secular enemies of (or within) the regime.

Whatever the cause, the short-term implications of the violence at Andijan seem to be much less ambiguous than were the incidents themselves. The Karimov government interpreted the events as an attempted coup, and cracked down on the scant domestic political opposition that existed in Uzbekistan, as well as religious organizations, NGOs, and independent journalists. When faced with criticism over his government's reaction to Andijan, Karimov responded by accelerating the timetable for the removal of U.S. bases in Uzbekistan.[38] It is perhaps worth noting that Moscow and Beijing were notably silent on the incident, since they may stand to benefit from the cooling of relations between Uzbekistan and the West. Karimov has aired his grievances at meetings of the so-called "Shanghai Cooperation Organization," which includes China, Russia, Kazakhstan, Kyrgyzstan, and Tajikistan. Some observers fear that the group, which has to this point been an ally of the U.S. antiterrorist efforts in the region, may be starting to reconsider the wisdom of continued cooperation with the United States.[39] As U.S. forces were leaving Uzebekistan at the end of 2005, Russia and Uzbekistan signed a mutual defense pact, sending a signal to the regime's critics in Washington.

LINKAGES TO THE GLOBAL WAR ON TERRORISM

Few argue that the HT or IMU were created by post-Soviet autocratic rulers. They are in many respects indicative of the kind of movements that have sprung up wherever Saudi money has funded the establishment of their atavistic brand of Islam. However, the leaders of Central Asia have in some ways become the main ally of the region's violent extremists. By responding to provocation with increased repression, Central Asia's autocrats have helped to create a political atmosphere where political Islam has become the most legitimate voice of opposition. Although the IMU is probably unlikely to put Karimov's likeness on its recruiting posters, there is little doubt that the Uzbek tyrant has been a powerful aid during its membership drives.

Fundamentalism spreads rapidly when the masses perceive homegrown radicals to be the only anti-tyrannical political element in oppressed societies. As the United States discovered on 9/11, international allies of tyrannical rulers often become targets of such movements. As long as Washington remains allied with regional governments that rule with an iron fist, it risks alienating the tyrannized masses and pushing a minority toward anti-Americanism and violence. This is a self-perpetuating cycle. The more that governments oppress dissent, the greater the impetus in the population for rebellion—and the more need for oppression. If the suppression of popular movements becomes linked to the war on terrorism, the United States risks becoming an outlet for anger that cannot be expressed at home.

During this struggle, the United States may well be forced to make tough decisions about tyrannical regimes that are supportive in counterterrorism operations. On the one hand, democracy brings the very real risk of seeing political Islamist groups rise to power. On the other hand, when the U.S. courts anti-democratic leaders, Washington risks alienating the affections of the people, perhaps making terrorism against U.S. targets more likely.

Thus far the United States has resisted the attempts of Central Asian leaders to paint all their domestic rivals as terrorists. For example, despite Karimov's insistence, Washington has refused to add the HT to its list of FTOs. Failure to do this may have eroded support for U.S. basing in the region, but in the long run the benefits probably outweigh the costs, for at least two important reasons. First of all, on a tactical level, the loss of its bases in Kyrgyzstan or Uzbekistan would not be too costly to U.S. objectives as long as there is a friendly leader in Kabul. Bases in Afghanistan can serve many of the same purposes as those in the former Soviet Union, at far less political cost. And secondly, from a strategic perspective, if the United States were to kowtow to regional actors, it would be the equivalent of allowing the Lilliputians to dictate to Gulliver. It is far more important for Uzbekistan to stay in the good graces of the United States than the other way around. Furthermore, in the war on terrorism, Central Asian strongmen are bereft of viable political alternatives—all major players in and out of the region have similar policies toward Islamic fundamentalist terrorism. No matter what its policy is toward the region's autocracies, or if they "lean" toward Beijing or Moscow, Washington does not risk losing support for the War on Terror. China and Russia are of course just as militantly anti-IMU as is the United States. During the Cold War, if the United States alienated Third World leaders, it accepted the risk that they would throw their lot in with the communists. Today, there is no chance whatsoever that any regional tyrant will align his nation with the terrorists. In this instance, rhetorical support for democracy is risk-free and can help affect the crucial battle for the "hearts and minds" of the oppressed masses.

What is needed, therefore, is a regional policy that balances the needs of law enforcement with the will of the people. By steadfastly supporting the transition to democracy, the United States can deflect the anger of the tyrannized population away from the West. At the same time, law enforcement cooperation can help locals root out the threats to their regime. By remaining engaged, but not to the point of full cooperation in the agendas of the regional tyrants, the United States can affect regional policymaking while simultaneously maximizing the effectiveness of the war on terror. In other words, when dealing with oppressive regimes in Islamic countries, Washington wins as long as it does not choose—or, at the very least, as long as it never appears to choose a leader over the people.

As the aftermath of the Andijan incident makes clear, the rather odious nature of the Karimov regime is beginning to serve as a significant irritant to U.S.-Uzbek relations. The next few years may well prove to be decisive. Soon Washington may feel forced to choose between supporting an unpopular but secular regime or its democratic, and perhaps fundamentalist, opponents. The only thing that can be said with any certainty at this point is that the road ahead will not be an easy one to travel.

PROGRESS AND PROSPECTS

The first decade of Central Asian independence passed without much violence; the second may not be as quiet. The combination of increased U.S. presence and growing unhappiness with local leaders may be sowing the seeds for unrest in the years ahead. The extent to which the people of Central Asia are predisposed to accept the kind of conservative, Wahhabi, or Deobandi Islam that seems to fuel violent movements remains to be seen. If indeed political Islam emerges as the only alternative to oppression, as the legitimate voice of the people, then the supporters of those regimes will risk becoming targets of popular ire. Unless these illiberal regimes allow the rise of responsible, moderate opposition, fundamentalism will remain the only alternative to tyranny.

Few issues seem to be as urgent for Washington in the coming century than heading off that Hobson's choice. The war on terrorism cannot be won while the legitimate concerns of the masses are suppressed. As the West discovered to its horror in 1979 Iran, when fundamentalists provided the only avenue for popular outrage, oppressive secular regimes can be toppled by equally unjust, atavistic Mullahs. Although political Islam may be unpalatable to the majority of Central Asians at the beginning of the twenty-first century, continued oppression may change minds as the century goes on. God may be preparing a new geography lesson, to help Americans become more familiar with the remote Fergana Valley.

NOTES

1. For representative samples of fears about a new "great game," see Ariel Cohen, *The New 'Great Game': Oil Politics in the Caucasus and Central Asia* (Washington, DC: Heritage Foundation, Backgrounder No. 1065, January 25, 1996); Diane L. Smith, *Central Asia: A New Great Game?* (Carlisle, PA: U.S. Army War College, Strategic Studies Institute Report, June 17, 1996); and Lutz Kleveman, *The New Great Game: Blood and Oil in Central Asia* (Washington: Atlantic Monthly Press, 2003). The original Great Game is retold in stirring fashion by Peter Hopkirk in *The Great Game: The Struggle for Empire in Central Asia* (New York: Kondasha International, 1994).

2. Quoted by Anatol Lieven, "The (Not So) Great Game," *The National Interest*, No. 58 (Winter 1999–2000), p. 80.

3. Pavel Bogomolov, "If We Clash, It'll Be on the Caspian," *The Current Digest of the Post-Soviet Press*, Vol. 47, No. 21 (1995), pp. 21–22.

4. From the Energy Information Agency, "Caspian Sea," Country Analysis Briefs (Washington, DC: U.S. Department of Energy, September 2005), Online. Available HTTP: < http://www.eia.doe.gov/emeu/cabs/Caspian/Oil.html>.

5. Charles Clover and Robert Corzine, "Treasure Under the Sea," *The Financial Times*, May 1, 25, 1997. The 200-billion-barrel estimate was made by the U.S. State Department at the height of the optimistic period.

6. Martha Brill Olcott, *Revisiting the Twelve Myths of Central Asia* (Washington, DC: Carnegie Endowment for International Peace), Working Paper No. 23 (September 2001), p. 9.

7. A fact sheet describing the declaration can be found on the State Department Web site, Online. Available HTTP: <http://www.state.gov/r/pa/prs/ps/2002/8736.htm>.

8. The figures and quotation are from Joe Bob Briggs, "Behind the Silk Curtain," *The National Interest*, No. 76 (Summer 2004), p. 132.

9. For a skeptical view, see the report by the Institute for War and Peace Reporting, "Will U.S. Policy Backfire in Central Asia?" March 30, 2004, available at http://www.iwpr.net/index.pl?archive/rca/rca_200403_273_1_eng.txt; for a good explanation of the opposing view, see the testimony by Zeyno Baran to the House International Relations Subcommittee on the Middle East and Central Asia, "Building a Democracy in Uzbekistan," June 15, 2004.

10. Zbigniew Brzezinski, *The Grand Chessboard: American Primacy and its Geostrategic Imperatives* (New York: Basic Books, 1997), esp. pp. 123–150.

11. It would be hard to devise a more ironic name, since from the outset Karimov has been openly hostile to the faith of the vast majority of his people.

12. Quoted by Briggs, "Behind the Silk Curtain," p. 130.

13. See, for instance, S. Frederick Starr, "Making Eurasia Stable," *Foreign Affairs*, Vol. 75, No. 1 (January/February 1996), pp. 80–92.

14. For interesting discussions of the cultural identities of Central Asian peoples by knowledgeable regional observers, see Ahmed Rashid, *The Resurgence of Central Asia: Islam or Nationalism?* (New Jersey: Zed Books, 1994); and Dilip Hiro, *Between Marx and Muhammad: The Changing Face of Central Asia* (New York: HarperCollins, 1995).

15. For more on the evolution toward extremism, see Tiffany Petros, "Islam in Central Asia: The Emergence and Growth of Radicalism in the Post-Communist Era," in Daniel L. Burghart and Theresa Sabonis-Helf, eds., *In the Tracks of Tamerlane: Central Asia's Path to the 21st Century* (Washington, DC: National Defense University Press, 2004), pp. 139–155.

16. The $75 billion figure can be found in David E. Kaplan, "Hearts, Minds, and Dollars," *U.S. News and World Report*, April 2005, p. 29.

17. Named after the town of Deoband, where it originated, the movement was built around Islamic schools.

18. Daniel Benjamin and Steven Simon, *The Age of Sacred Terror: Radical Islam's War Against America* (New York: Random House, 2003), p. 207.

19. Human Rights Watch and other NGOs have been particularly vociferous about the "appalling" human rights situation in Uzbekistan. For information on the dangers of growing a beard in Uzbekistan, see their "Crackdown in the Fergana Valley: Arbitrary Arrests and Religious Discrimination," *Human Rights Watch Report*, Vol. 10, No. 4 (May 1998).

20. Data compiled predominantly from the RAND Terrorism Chronology and the MIPT-RAND Terrorism Incident databases. Online. Available HTTP: <http://www.tkb.org/Home.jsp>.

21. The "Terrorism Project" at the Center for Defense Information is a very good source of information on and analysis of individual terrorist groups. Online. Available HTTP: <http://www.cdi.org/terrorism/imu.cfm>.

22. Benjamin and Simon, *The Age of Sacred Terror*, p. 208.

23. The cult of personality surrounding the Turkmen leader is well-documented, and would be amusing if it were no so tragic for his people. It needs little review here. Recently the Turkmenbashi ("leader of the Turkmen") reluctantly acceded to the will of the people and added "The Great" to his official title. The people are consulted over few other matters.

24. For more on the origins and philosophy of the HT, see Ahmed Rashid, *Jihad: The Rise of Militant Islam in Central Asia* (New York: Penguin, 2002).

25. Rashid, *Jihad*, p. 115.

26. These numbers are from a report written by the Heritage Foundation's chief Central Asia hawk. They certainly do not underestimate Hizb ut-Tahrir's numbers. See Ariel Cohen, "Research: Russia and Central Asia." Online. Available HTTP: <http://www.heritage.org/Research/RussiaandEurasia/BG1656.cfm#pgfId-1028397>.

27. Rashid, *Jihad*, p. 123.

28. See the article on Hizb al-Tarir al-Islami on the GlobalSecurity.org Web page. Online. Available HTTP: <http://www.globalsecurity.org/military/world/para/hizb-ut-tahrir.htm>.

29. In addition to Human Rights Watch, Amnesty International, and the Institute for War and Peace Reporting, the list of skeptics includes the U.S. State Department. See its "Uzbekistan: Country Reports on Human Rights Practices, 2004," February 28, 2005. Online. Available HTTP: <http://www.state.gov/g/drl/rls/hrrpt/2004/41717.htm>.

30. Rashid, *Jihad*, p. 125.

31. Human Rights Watch, "Creating Enemies of the State: Religious Persecution in Uzbekistan," March 2004, pp. 3–4. Online. Available HTTP: <http://hrw.org/reports/2004/uzbekistan0304/uzbekistan0304.pdf>.

32. See the analysis by the Asian Development Bank, "Asian Development Outlook 2005: Uzbekistan." Online. Available HTTP: <http://www.adb.org/Documents/Books/ADO/2005/uzb.asp>.

33. It is of course possible that the omission of consideration of terrorism was mandated by Tashkent in order to procure their cooperation. However, given its history, it seems equally possible that the Karimov government would have sought to exaggerate the threat from the IMU and the HT if its input was necessary for completion of the report. United Nations, Human Development Report, "Uzbekistan 2005: Decentralization and Human Development." Online. Available HTTP: <http://hdr.undp.org/docs/reports/national/UZB_Uzbekistan/Uzbekistan_2005_en.pdf>.

34. For more, see Karl Vick and Peter Finn, "Protests Topple Kyrgyzstan's Government: Revolt is the Third in Former Soviet Republics in 16 Months," *Washington Post*, March 25, 2005, p. A1.

35. Krygystan's future is therefore probably brighter than its neighbors. However, there are reasons beyond mere regional precedent to believe that democracy may prove to be just a moment. For one, although outside observers have reported that these elections were largely "free and fair," the outcome—89 percent of the vote was cast for one candidate, Kurmanbek Bakiyev—suggests otherwise. And, although many have supported the move as necessary and long overdue, it is noteworthy and ominous that one of Bakiyev's first official acts was to dissolve the parliament. It is therefore perhaps a bit early to pronounce the end of tyranny in Kyrgyzstan.

36. Filip Noubel, et al., "A Shock to the System for Kyrgystan's Neighbors," Institute for War and Peace Reporting, March 27, 2005. Online. Available HTTP: <http://www.iwpr.net/index.pl?archive/rca2/rca2_363_2_eng.txt>.

37. Shirin Akiner, "Violence in Andijan, 13 May 2005: An Independent Assessment," *Silk Road Paper* (Washington, DC: Central Asia-Caucasus Institute), July 2005, esp. pp. 30–33.

38. See Robin Wright and Ann Scott Tyson, "U.S. Evicted from Air Base in Uzbekistan," *Washington Post*, July 30, 2005, p. A1.

39. Stephen Blank perhaps best represents the power-balancing, realist school of thought on Central Asian politics. For a review of the Shanghai Cooperation Organization, see the analysis by the Center for Defense Information, "Here There Be Dragons: The Shanghai Cooperation Organization," September 26, 2005. Online. Available HTTP: <http://www.cdi.org/friendlyversion/printversion.cfm?documentID=3153>.

III
Asia

Thailand

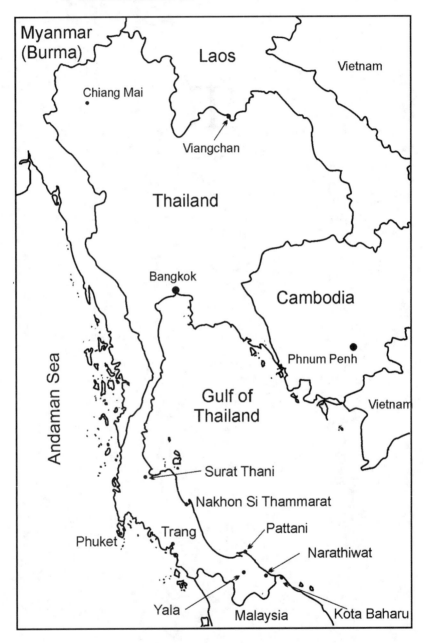

7

THAILAND

Rohan Gunaratna and Arabinda Acharya

NATURE OF THE FLASHPOINT

Since January 2004 the insurgency in the southern Thai provinces of Narathiwat, Pattani, and Yala has taken a violent turn and is now at its bloodiest stage in the entire history of the Kingdom with about 1,000 people being killed in the simmering violence. Insurgents in southern Thailand have targeted almost everyone: the security forces, government officials, civilians, and especially Buddhists. Thailand's security forces have also responded in kind, killing insurgents in significant numbers. On one notable occasion, Thai authorities were perceived to have taken a particularly heavy hand; during the October 25, 2004, riot in Tak Bai, 78 Muslim protesters were taken into custody and later died from suffocation. That incident brought a new dimension to the conflict.

Some separatist groups now threaten to bring the violence to other parts of the kingdom, which thus far has been localized to the south. A period of relative calm followed the February 2005 elections, during which the government adopted a series of measures for a lasting solution to the problems in the south. Most notable was the creation of the National Reconciliation Commission, headed by former Prime Minister Anand Panyarachun. Yet even as the National Reconciliation Commission was to submit its reports and recommendations, near simultaneous and coordinated bombings in Yala on July 14, 2005, brought the specter of violence, fear, and intimidation once again to the fore. These multiple bombings in Yala preceded a spate of brutal killings, including the beheadings of numerous members of the Buddhist community. In response, Prime Minister Thaksin Shinawatra moved swiftly, declaring a state of emergency in the southern provinces, vesting the responsibility for security matters and the power to deal with insurgent violence directly in the office of the Prime Minister.[1] There is, however, a perception that the emergency measures would be counterproductive, which further exacerbates the conflict.

Unrest and violence have never been alien to Thailand's southern provinces. Muslim separatism in that region has been present to some degree or another since the 1940s, which was transformed into insurgent violence in the 1960s. However, in the late 1990s, insurgency and violence abated somewhat. The current phase of insurgent violence, especially since January 2004, and Bangkok's response mark a departure from the previous separatist movements in the south.

HISTORICAL CONTEXT

The unified Thai kingdom dates back to the mid-fourteenth century. In 1782, King Rama I founded the Chakri dynasty with Bangkok as its capital, which continues to the present. The southern Thai provinces of Narathiwat, Yala, and Pattani, together with Songkhla, Satun, and the northern Malay states of Kelantan, Terengganu, and northern Kedah, were all part of what was known as Patani Raya (Greater Patani[2]), a domain of the earlier Sultanate of Pattani. It was in the mid-thirteenth century that the kingdom adopted the name "Pattani" under the rule of Sultan Ismail Shah. After the fall of Malacca in 1511, the kingdom's stature as a major trading center grew with Indian-Muslim traders competing vigorously with the kingdom of Sumatra in Aceh.

In 1786, the forces of Rama I invaded Pattani. Its ruler, Sultan Muhammad, was killed and the city was destroyed. Many Malays were taken to Bangkok as slaves. Thai rule over the southern provinces continued since then, with intermittent periods of rebellion and unrest. In the later part of the nineteenth century, Thai rulers responded more vigorously to these periodic rebellions, thereby weakening the Pattani Sultanate.[3] In May 1897, the Thai Provincial Administration Act (Phraratchabanyat Laksana Pakkhrong Thongthi) was enacted with the goal to integrate the southern provinces within Thailand.

In 1902, Siam formally annexed Pattani. The seven provinces of Pattani—Pattani, Nong Chik, Saiburi, Yala, Yaring, Ra-ngae, and Reman—came under the Area of the Seven Provinces, which in turn was placed under a centralized administrative structure governed by Siamese-appointed bureaucrats.[4] In 1906, the seven Malay provinces were brought even closer together under a single administrative unit called Monthon Pattani. Following the Anglo-Siamese Treaty of 1909, which drew a border between Patani and the Malay states of Kelantan, Perak, Kedah, and Perlis, Siam's absolute suzerainty over Pattani was formally established.[5] Since then, there have been systematic attempts to develop a mono-ethnic Buddhist Thai character in the entire kingdom, which was seen by southern Muslims to be at odds with the Islamic identity in the provinces of the Pattani.[6]

At present, the Thai population is predominantly Buddhist (95 percent), with Muslims comprising 4.6 percent of the population. The majority of the Muslim population is Sunni with a miniscule Shiite minority. Geographically, the Muslim population has been concentrated in southern Thailand, particularly in Narathiwat, Yala, and Pattani, now collectively known as the Southern Border Provinces. These provinces now constitute the restive segments in Thailand.

Islam in Thailand

Southeast Asia's initial contact with Islam was through Arab traders in the region as early as the eighth century CE. Between the twelfth and fifteenth centuries, Islam spread extensively, with large numbers of people converting, including the king of Pattani, who declared an "Islamic kingdom" in 1457.[7] Islam in Southeast Asia drew heavily from the beliefs and practices of Hinduism and animism. In Thailand, Islam had been largely inclusive, as elsewhere in Southeast Asia. Like Buddhism, it integrated many beliefs and practices, which were not central to the Islamic faith.[8] However, since the seventeenth century, Islamic scholars educated in Saudi Arabia and Egypt introduced more orthodox and scripture-based interpretation of the faith.[9] The insistence on ethnic and religious solidarity was reinforced by the status of Islam as a pillar of the Malay identity.[10]

The Pattani Kingdom was at that time considered the "cradle of Islam" in Southeast Asia,[11] due to its status as a major center for Islamic learning, comparable to the prestigious Sultanate of Aceh in Indonesia.[12] The Islamic teachings affirmed the traditional virtues and greatness of the kingdom of Pattani (Patani Darussalam), the identification with the Malay race, and a religious orientation toward Islam.[13] The centralization of the Thai state since the eighteenth century sought to bring the Pattani Kingdom under Buddhist influence, with controls exerted in taxation, education, and through the *Thaification* of the local culture, language, and religion. Measures were introduced to abolish "backward" customs and dialects and to enforce uniformity in social behavior as part of strategies to integrate the southern Muslims into mainstream Buddhist Thai society. The Education Act of 1921 forced Muslims to attend Siamese schools to receive a secular education. State-run schools were forced to impart teachings in Buddhist ethics, with monks often serving as teachers.[14] Under the Act's provisions, the Koran was translated in the Thai language. This was considered an insult to Muslims, as it is not permissible in Islam to reproduce the Koran in any other language except its original Arabic.

One of the primary reasons why Bangkok attempted to integrate the southern provinces into Thai culture has been a sense of vulnerability rising out of its proximity to the northern Malay border states of Kelantan, Trengganu, and Kedah. Despite administrative separation, people on both sides share the same language, political culture, social structures, customs, and values, with a high level of cross-border contact.[15] This has reinforced the ethnic affinity of the Malay Muslims with their Muslim brethren in southern Thailand.[16]

Origins of the Southern Insurgency

Discontent against what the southern Muslims call "Thai imperial dominance" began to manifest as early as 1903 when Tengku Abdul Kadir Qamaruddin, the last sultan of Patani, revolted against Bangkok. He was defeated and imprisoned. In 1910, two Sufi preachers—To'tae and Haji Bula—led protests against the Thai government, which the military put down and arrested the leaders.[17] After another failed attempt in 1915, Tengku Abdul Kadir fled to Kelantan and regrouped his forces with the help of Sultan Muhammad IV, launching one of the biggest campaigns against Bangkok in response to the Education Act of 1921. The education reform was seen as an attempt to erase Pattani-Malay identity through coerced conversions to Buddhism.[18] It also undermined the influence of Islamic religious teachers who mobilized the community against the reforms. This rebellion, like so many before, failed when many key leaders were either captured or killed.

In 1939, Bangkok introduced the Thai Customs Decree (Thai Ratthaniyom) which forced all Thai citizens—including the minority groups—to conform to a set of common cultural norms.[19] Muslims were prevented from adopting Muslim names or using the Malay dialect. Thai Buddhist laws on marriage and inheritance replaced Shari'a.[20] In some cases, Muslims were even forced to participate in the public worship of Buddhist idols, and men were required to wear Western-style trousers.[21] This process challenged the ethno-cultural identity of the Muslims and led them to rebel against the central government;

the resulting rebellion was harshly quelled with Pattani leaders killed, arrested, or exiled to Malaysia.

During World War II, the Malay Muslims fought alongside the British with an assurance that after the war, Pattani would be granted independence. When the war ended in 1945, Bangkok allowed the sultanates of Kelantan, Trengganu, Kedah, and Perlis to rejoin Malaya. Muslim leaders under Tengku Abdul Jalal petitioned the British to grant independence to four southern provinces from Thailand. However, the British reneged on their "gentlemen's agreement." For the British, a unified Thai state was a strategic counterweight to the communist insurgency in China, Indochina, and Malaya. This marked the beginning of militant separatism in 1946.

From the 1960s to the 1980s, there was a massive transmigration of Thai-Buddhists from other parts of Thailand to the south to "balance up" the racial and religious demography of the southern provinces.[22] Though there was an attempt by the central Thai administration to be more conciliatory in the post-war period, centuries of marginalization, suppression, state penetration of Muslim civil society, and the absence of political participation stood in the way of any meaningful cultural assimilation of the southern provinces with the rest of Thailand. The process of social and cultural assimilation was very much resented by ethnic Malays, who saw it as cultural colonization by the Bangkok government.[23]

This led to the development of radical Islamist movements in southern Thailand. One of the earliest groups to engage in armed rebellion was Barisan Nasional Pembebasan Patani or the Patani National Liberation Front (BNPP) formed by Adun Na Saiburi from among the remnants of Gabungam Melayu Pattani Raya (GAMPAR, the Greater Pattani Malayu Association). GAMPAR was established in Madrasah Muhammadiyyah, Kota Baru, Kelantan (now in Malaysia) in March 1948, with the avowed objective of uniting the four provinces of Pattani, Yala, Narathiwat, and Satun as a Malay Islamic state.[24] Other groups subsequently emerged, such as the Barisan Revolusi Nasional (BRN) or the National Revolutionary Front, and the Pattani United Liberation Front (PULO). The objectives of these groups were to establish an independent Islamic state in the three provinces of Pattani, Yala, and Narathiwat. These groups were, however, different in their ideological orientation and did not foster any unity among themselves.[25] According to some scholars, the Pattani resistance movements developed a more radical Islamist character following the Islamic revolution in Iran in 1979, with groups like the BNPP moving closer to the global current of Islamist radicalism.[26] In 1985, the more radical and insurgent elements of the BNPP broke away and formed the Barisan Bersatu Mujahideen Pattani (BBMP, United Mujahideen Front of Pattani or Bersatu) under the leadership of Wahyuddin Muhammad. In 1986, the BNPP renamed itself the Barisan Islam Pembebasan Pattani (BIPP, Islamic Liberation Front of Pattani) with a view to "underline its stronger commitment to Islamist politics."[27] Between the late 1980s and early 1990s, new configurations and groups emerged, such as New Pattani United Liberation Organisation (New PULO), Gerakan Mujahideen Islam Pattani (GMIP), and Pusat Persatuan Tadika Narathiwat (PUSAKA).[28]

The nature and the number of attacks since January 2004 in southern Thailand make it difficult to determine which of the groups is responsible for each particular incident. At the beginning of the crisis, the Thai government maintained that the violence and unrest in the south were the handiwork of criminal elements engaged in illegal trafficking—including drugs—rather than ideologically motivated extremism.[29] Many analysts maintained that some of the attacks were "due to political rivalry." While other analysts suggested the reason for the resurgence in violence was that some groups might be working together, there appears to be no real coordination among the groups. A very disturbing development could be found in the overlapping nature of the group membership. For example, Masae Useng, one of the key masterminds behind the southern unrest, simultaneously belonged to many groups. He was a primary member of BRN. However, reports also suggest that he is a member of the GMIP as well as the new group PUSAKA. Thus, the insurgency could very well be the handiwork of a group of free-floating cadres actually owing allegiance to none of the groups. This makes them more amorphous and more difficult to apprehend.

Role of Religious Educational Institutions

During the simmering violence since 2004, the Islamic religious schools in southern Thailand have become loci of suspicion, fear, and violence. In the provinces of Pattani, Yala, and Narathiwat, schools have been repeatedly burnt. Teachers—both Muslim and Buddhist—have become prime targets for assassination. Security forces have raided Islamic schools in search of insurgents, further angering the Muslims. The Thai prime minister has accused the pondoks (Islamic religious schools)[30] of being a breeding ground for Muslim insurgents bent on causing disturbances in the South. The government has repeatedly asserted that "distorted" Islamic teaching has now become an ideological catalyst for unrest. It asserts that some young Islamic teachers (ustaz) are recruiting and training volunteers for jihad.[31] It may be noted that pondoks have long been symbols of resistance against the centralized educational system imposed by the government.[32]

Since the 1990s, many separatist groups have systematically targeted the education system for recruitment, training, and indoctrination. BRN has been particularly active in targeting schools and recruiting both teachers and students into its network. Documents seized in 2003 from the house of wanted BRN leader Masae Useng indicated an interest in expanding propaganda activities into even the primary school levels. Since January 2004, the role of these schools has come under even sharper scrutiny. Four religious schoolteachers were arrested in December 2004 in a government attempt to demonstrate a link between militancy and religious educational institutions.

Interrogations of suspects arrested after the April 28, 2004, government raids revealed that a number of religious leaders, including Islamic provincial committee members with links to local politicians, played a key role in the uprising in the southern provinces. After the incident, a 34-page booklet titled "The Fight for the Liberation of Pattani" (Berjihad di Pattani) was found on the bodies of some of the 108 insurgents killed by government forces. The handbook, written in Yawi, a Malay dialect written in Arabic script, urged Muslims to fight for the greater autonomy of Pattani and outlined steps that the author said would lead to the Pattani state gaining independence. It is now believed that the handbook was written by Issamul Yameena (alias Isamail Jaafar or Pohsu), who was a resident of Malaysia's Kelantan state.[33] Isamail Jaafar was arrested by the Malysian authorities in August 2004. However, the Malaysians refused to extradite him to Thailand since he held dual-citizenship.[34] A co-author of the book is Abdul Wahab Data (alias Babor Wahab), principal of Malayu Bangkok Ponoh School in the Muang district in southern Thailand.

Explaining Insurgency

The conflict in southern Thailand is rooted in the perceived injustice of nonfulfillment of minority needs and interests that prevent their integration. Exacerbating this situation is Bangkok's failure to address minority groups' fundamental needs, provide for participation in governance, and ensure an equitable distribution of resources and benefits.[35] Malay Muslims have perceived attempts to promote an integrated polity in Southern Thailand through the promotion of the Buddhist religion, the Thai language, and a uniform assimilative education as direct threats to the region's particular ethno-religious identity and cultural imperialism.[36] Some analysts believe that the resurgence of violence is the result of government policies that have not only been insensitive to Muslim values, but also repressive and frequently irrelevant.[37] The prevalent attitude of the local Thai government officials and the security personnel has been one of ignorance of the southern Thai Muslim culture, which might be better thought of as northern Malaya.

In addition, the southern provinces are marked by fundamental abjection like poverty, unemployment, lack of public infrastructure, lack of capital, low levels of living standards, lack of markets for agricultural products, and environmental disasters.[38] There is great income disparity between the center and southern provinces. For example, as of 2002, the average monthly household income per capita in Bangkok was 28,239 baht (US$735); by contrast, it was 2,224 baht (US$58) in the Narathiwat. Unemployment increased from 1.9 percent in 1998 to 2.3 percent in 2003 in the three provinces.[39] Although the southern provinces boast popular tourist spots, the government controls a major share of the tourism sector, and most of the revenues and job opportunities available are in the hands of non-Muslims.[40] Left vulnerable, the unemployed have been preyed upon by thriving criminal-narcotics networks, leading to the proliferation of drugs and drug-related crimes.[41] This situation, which is compounded by locals rejecting financial assistance programs offered by the government, has been largely due to inherent complexities and religious biases.

The surge in violence is also related to Thailand's foreign policy and its alignment with the United States in the war on terrorism. Thailand has been very supportive of U.S. efforts, especially in Afghanistan and in Iraq, where it sent a contingent of 420 soldiers. The United States reciprocated Thailand's support by declaring the kingdom a "Major Non-NATO ally," along with Pakistan and the Philippines.[42] However, many Muslims in the south are not supportive of Bangkok's alliance with Washington or its stand on Iraq. Moreover, measures adopted by Thailand to combat terrorism after 9/11, namely the People's Protection and Internal Security Act 2002 and the Executive Decree amending the Anti-Money Laundering Act 2003, have been regarded not only as draconian and repressive, but also as unnecessary. Many analysts contend that Bangkok adopted these measures under pressure from the Bush administration.[43]

LINKAGES TO TERRORISM

There is as yet no evidence of outside terrorist groups being directly involved in the conflict in southern Thailand. Moreover, given the current nature of the attacks, it is reasonable to conclude that there has not been any significant exchange of logistical support between the groups in Thailand and those outside. At present, the capabilities of the Thai insurgents are rudimentary, as evidenced from the nature of the attacks, which involve low-grade explosives, drive-by shootings, and the use of basic weaponry such as knives and machetes. The death toll from bombings in the south is usually small, with very few people killed in each attack. The insurgents seem to be lacking the sophistication necessary for large-scale escalation of violence or to bring the violence to other parts of the Kingdom.

Leading members of PULO were known to have connections with the Free Aceh Movement in Indonesia, particularly regarding training.[44] For example, the getaway plan used by the insurgents in January 2005 attacks on an army camp was quite similar to those used by Aceh rebels.[45] The Indonesian group Front Pembela Islam (FPI) is known to be keenly interested in the developments in southern Thailand. After the deaths of many Muslims on April 28, 2004, FPI issued a call for volunteers from Indonesia to join their co-religionists in jihad in southern Thailand.

Some analysts believe that regional or international Islamic insurgents and local separatists could have been working together to stir up unrest in southern Thailand. In June 2003, Thai authorities arrested four Muslims, three from Thailand and one from Singapore, allegedly from the regional terrorist group Jemaah Islamiyah (JI). They were apparently plotting to stage terrorist strikes in Bangkok that targeted, among others, the embassies of the United States, Britain, Israel, Australia, and Singapore, coinciding with the APEC summit in October 2003. This followed the arrest in Bangkok on May 16, 2003, of Arifin bin Ali, a Singaporean alleged to be a senior member of JI.[46] Arifin, also known as John Wong Ah Hung, received military training in a Moro Islamic Liberation Front (MILF) camp in the Philippines in 1999.

Another JI link to southern Thailand was Hambali, the mastermind of the 2002 Bali bombings in Indonesia. He had taken shelter in Narathiwat before going to Cambodia, and later returned to Thailand and went into hiding in Ayutthaya province until his arrest in August 2003.[47] Apart from Hambali, other JI elements were found in Cambodia, some of them Thai. In June 2003, Cambodian authorities clamped down on a religious school run by Umm al-Qura (UAQ), headed by an Egyptian, Esam Mohammad Khidr Ali. They also ordered the expulsion of 28 teachers, including some from Thailand. Two Thais were arrested on suspicion of having links with the JI.[48]

However, in southern Thailand, direct involvement of the al Qaeda terrorist network has not yet been evidenced. The U.S. 9/11 Commission has provided very few details of the al Qaeda connections to Thailand in its final report. Contrary to other assumptions, the Muslim separatist movement in southern Thailand is largely local. The most recent example that the southern Thai insurgency does not follow the global jihad movement can be found in the booklet found on the bodies of some of the insurgents killed on April 28, 2004; it was titled "Berjihad Di Pattani" (The Fight for the Liberation of Pattani). In it, the author sought to employ Islam primarily for the preservation of material possessions—wealth, freedom, peace, and security—and then religion:

> Our struggle is also for the liberation of our beloved country, one which is continuously under the occupation of heretic imperialists and their alliances. That is why we need the support and sacrifices from the believers. ... [E]very possession that belongs to an individual legally belongs to that individual. These include housing estates, material possessions, financial wealth, children and wives, country, and cultural traditions, and the most important thing of all, is the religion. Thus, let us work together to protect all these, even if it costs us our life.[49]

This is quite unlike the rhetoric used by leaders of global jihadi movements such as al Qaeda or even JI. An analysis of this text indicates that the movement is still largely a separatist one, devoid of the international jihadist ideology that is propagated by al Qaeda. It is not in the same vein as al Qaeda literature and is not pan-Islamic. It instead has a nationalist character. Thus, the insurgency has yet to develop an external dimension since the insurgency has largely been a resistance to Thaification.

Given Thailand's geo-strategic significance for the United States, its troop commitment for Afghanistan and Iraq, and its Major Non-NATO ally status, jihadi elements would have little difficulty in identifying common purpose with the cause of Muslims in southern Thailand. Anti-Americanism has already begun to manifest in the south, especially commercially and economically. In the province of Yala, for example, people have boycotted American commercial products following the directives of the National Association of Muslim Youth (NAMY). NAMY has erected billboards declaring the province as "U.S. product-free zones."[50] There has also been a strong reaction against the U.S.-Thailand Free Trade Agreement. The handover of Hambali, who was captured in Thailand in August 2003, to the United States has inflamed the Islamic sensitivities. Southern Muslims are also very sensitive about the Counterterrorism Intelligence Centre (CTIC), a joint U.S.-Thai initiative that was instrumental in the capture of Hambali. Local residents allege that CTIC is manipulating the violence in the region to push the Thai government closer to the United States.[51]

Understanding the Threat

During the most recent phase of insurgency the perpetrators used a number of unconventional methods. Such methods reflect both the unusual nature of the insurgency and the depth of indoctrination that the masterminds of the unrest have instilled in the disaffected population. One strategy is the use of agitprop methods similar to those used by the communists in the past. The leaders, in this case Muslim clerics and community leaders, build up confrontational situations with the security forces in order to provoke overreaction. Such methods were used on April 28, 2004, outside the Krue Se Mosque, and again on October 25, 2004, at Tak Bai. Thai security forces are known to take heavy-handed measures to control the violence, which the present administration endorses as legitimate and necessary. The overreaction by the security forces, however, fueled further Muslim anger. It is apparent that the separatist leaders are exploiting the age-old Muslim anger and resentment against the security forces and the government.[52] Muslim clerics denounce the use of force by the security agencies as serious incidents of state terrorism to attract international attention.[53]

Currently, the indoctrination of the Muslims in the south appears to be very intense, and this can be exploited. An example was an incident on April 28, 2004. While the youths were told that they would be impervious to bullets if they chanted the holy Koran and truly had faith in their cause, some also showed an understanding that they may end up sacrificing their lives in the fight for God.[54] This willingness to die was apparent in they way they fought: They appeared almost suicidal in their motivation. It was as if they wanted to die in order to send a message about their beliefs to their fellow religionists. Here, death was seen not as a cause for mourning. Instead, it was to be respected and celebrated. As the study of radical movements suggests, political and religious revisions of history, and the interpretations of present situations based on such revisions, exacerbate the conflict with fanatic intensity.[55] It is interesting to note here that the author of Berjihad di Pattani glorified death in combat in order to use it as a potent motivational tool:

> Let us realize ... how glorious we will be if we fall as warriors of our land. O Brothers, understand! When the martyrs were killed, they are not dead, but they are alive next to God. Allah placed them to rest temporarily. Allah will place them in the most honorable place. They will continuously receive sustenance from Allah.

They will watch and listen to every piece of news, if their children will follow in their footsteps.

The martyr blood flows in every one of us fellow Muslims who believe in Allah and the Prophet, which we inherited from our ancestors who had sacrificed their lives in the path of Jihad. This blood is eager to be spilled onto the land, to paint it red and illuminate the sky at dawn and dusk, from east to west. So it is known that the Pattani land produce Jihad warriors.[56]

This level of indoctrination suggests Islam's potential to increasingly become the organizing principle of the resistance. Southern Thailand has indeed become a fertile recruiting ground for groups willing to exploit it for producing suicide volunteers. This could then close the gap in the insurgents' capability to bring jihad to the doorsteps of Bangkok and spread it to other parts of the kingdom in a very real way.

Government Response

Over the years, successive Thai governments contained separatist violence using various methods. Between 1968 and 1975, Bangkok launched a series of military operations in the south code-named "Operation Ramkamhaeng" and the "Special Anti-Terrorist Campaign" to destroy the networks of the Pattani liberation movements.[57] During that seven-year period, Thai security forces and Pattani insurgent groups clashed on 385 occasions, resulting in nearly 329 insurgent deaths, 250 insurgent camps destroyed, and 1,208 people arrested.[58]

The Thai government also initiated a number of administrative and political initiatives for the socioeconomic development of the provinces in southern Thailand. In 1981, the Prem Tinsulanond administration formed the Southern Border Provincial Administration Committee (SBPAC, sau-aor-bau-tau), a special unit of the army, police, and Interior Ministry and the Civilian-Police-Military Task Force 43 (CPM 43), to oversee security in the region and to work as an advisory body to the policymaking establishment in Bangkok.[59] Economic and industrial development packages were also implemented to eradicate poverty and backwardness in the south. Democratization was used as a means to allow the Malay-Muslim community to enter parliamentary democratic politics, with the hope that this would release some of the radical steam in their political agenda. The Democratic Party and the New Aspiration Party reinforced their presence in the south, incorporating several Malay-Muslim politicians and providing them with new public space in national politics.[60]

The Thai government vigorously pushed the tourism and entertainment industry with a view to attract foreign tourists and much-needed revenue. Bangkok perceived that tourism would be the major catalyst in the economic transformation of the region, creating new job opportunities and consequently lessening the deprivation. The overall impact of the policies was that popular support for Muslim separatism "waned past a point at which separatism could be considered a credible and sustainable option for Muslim political elites."[61]

Between March and April 2002, Prime Minister Thaksin Shinawatra overhauled the Southern Border Provinces Administrative Committee (SBPAC) and replaced it with the Southern Border Provinces Coordination Centre (SBPCC), a step that marked the beginning of the end of good governance in the southern provinces. This was seen as yet another manifestation of the centralization of power, police misadministration, and corruption.[62] Officials associated with the SBPAC claimed that the committee was able to calm the southern unrest significantly by being responsive to and accommodating the region's unique security and social needs.[63] SBPAC served as an "interface between Bangkok and local provincial administrations while acting as a watchdog on errant officialdom and liaising with local communities."[64] Similarly, CPM 43, under the Internal Suppression Operations Command (ISOC), coordinated different elements of the government and the military. "[It] maintained several very large and effective agent networks, which were tied into many of the Muslim and criminal communities located throughout the region."[65] The dismantling of the SBPAC infrastructure "created an environment conducive for the rise of power struggles among the many groups in the southern provinces." It enabled organized criminal gangs in connivance with corrupt local politicians to proliferate.[66] Local Muslims gradually lost confidence in the new administrative setup.

On February 16, 2005, Thaksin announced the introduction of a zoning scheme according to which villages in the three southern provinces would be divided into red, yellow, and green zones, depending on the level of violence;[67] the number of core insurgent leaders suspected of involvement in the violence; and the extent to which villagers cooperate with officials to provide information.[68] Bangkok modified the plan in June 2005, doing away with the green, yellow, and red zones. In its place were "pacified" and "contested" areas. The contested areas were deemed to be areas heavily targeted by militants. In these areas, the military would mount security sweeps to preempt terror attacks and protect local officials and citizens.

Not long after the new zoning scheme was in place, the coordinated attacks in Yala on July 14, 2005, prompted the Thai government to take harsher measures in an attempt to control the insurgency. All three of the southernmost provinces were declared to be in a "severe state of emergency" on July 19, 2005. Notwithstanding the measures adopted by the government, there has been no reduction in violence.

It now appears that the character of the insurgent campaign is changing from guerrilla warfare into urban terrorism. Insurgent ideologues are increasingly politicizing and mobilizing their target audiences, using religion rather than nationalism as a motivational tool. Religiosity, a more powerful ideology, is steadfastly replacing ethnonationalism. Although the insurgents are largely driven by domestic grievances, they are drawing inspiration, finance, and training from external sources. Most Islamist conflicts in Southeast Asia—such as Mindanao in the Philippines and Ambon (Maluku) and Poso (Sulawesi) in Indonesia—have attracted foreign Mujahedin. It may be just a matter of time before the insurgency in southern Thailand attracts Malaysians, Indonesians, Filipinos, Singaporeans, and other nationalities.

LINKAGES TO THE GLOBAL WAR ON TERRORISM

The U.S.-Thai relationship is now based on implicit and explicit support for each other's economic and military goals. Besides the U.S.-Thai free trade agreement, Washington has conferred Major Non-NATO Ally status on Bangkok, largely because of Thai support of U.S.-led military operations in Iraq. Both countries also share the common objective of security and stability in Southeast Asia.

The U.S.-Thai bonhomie nevertheless has produced tensions among the insurgents in Southern Thailand. There is an inherent suggestion that Bangkok's aggressive policies in dealing with the unrest in the south is encouraged and sponsored by a wider American pressure to exhibit more aggressive strategies on counterterrorism. Bangkok has been more proactive and persistent in its efforts to counter the unstable security environment in the southern provinces in particular and war on terrorism in general. Some of the measures taken by the Thai government, such as the enactment of the Peoples Protection and Internal Security Act of 2002 and the Executive Decree amending the Money Laundering Act of 2003, are perceived as invasive and excessive. Bangkok's uncritical acceptance of some of the multilateral initiatives at the behest of Washington is seen as intervention into its domestic political agenda.

Underpinning the current violent environment is the extent of Washington's support to the administration under Thaksin. Unlike some other countries in the region, especially Indonesia, anti-U.S. sentiment in the Muslim-dominated provinces of Narithwat, Pattani, and

Yala in Southern Thailand is not very pronounced. The perceived grievances that the insurgents in Southern Thailand currently exploit are
mostly about local issues and are not yet about U.S. policies, as with
conflicts elsewhere involving the Muslim community. This is not discounting the fact that the U.S. involvement in the region has often been
used to incite Muslim anger.

Therefore, it is essential for Washington to keep as low a profile as
possible regarding Bangkok's efforts to come to terms with the situation
in Southern Thailand. Washington's increased visibility in Thailand has
the potential to radicalize the community and convert sympathizers
into active participants in the extremist violence. This has the potential
to undermine Bangkok's credibility in dealing with the unrest in the
south. And it could provide a platform for the insurgents to denounce
Bangkok as a puppet that is conditioned by an American agenda.

PROGRESS AND PROSPECTS

As the analysis of incidents in southern Thailand indicates, Thai national
security apparatus suffers from a chronic inability to develop its intelligence dominance in the south. After the January 4, 2004, attacks,
Prime Minister Thaksin Shinawatra himself admitted that "intelligence
was flawed and underutilized." The situation remains the same in 2005,
especially as the security agencies failed to anticipate simultaneous
bombings in Yala in July 2005. The problem has also been exacerbated
by an undercurrent of tension and competition among various security
agencies for influence and resources. As a result, the security agencies
appear to have little understanding of the organizational composition,
command structure, or the nature and extent of international connections of the insurgent groups operating in the south.[69]

The essential ingredient to effectively combat the terrorist threat is
to develop high-quality intelligence. It is also crucial to maintain the
flow of intelligence and operational effectiveness on the ground to deter
attacks and to prevent insurgency to cross the threshold to become terrorism. This would mean a combination of smart technology as well as
a pool of professional undercover agents with some degree of compe-
tence in the local Malay dialect. They must be able to embed themselves
into the community and relate to Malay-Muslim culture.[70]

In Southern Thailand, especially after the January 2004 incidents,
as the security situation rapidly deteriorated, the Thai government lost
significant public support from the local Muslims. The overreaction by
security agencies, abuse of authority, corruption, intimidation tactics,
and lack of sensitivity to local religious and cultural values aggravated

the situation further. This led to what some analysts call the hardening of identities through blatant injustice, such as torture and abductions, inflicted by the security forces in the south.[71] Of particular significance was the disappearance, now believed murder, of the lawyer Somchai Neelahphaijit, who defended the suspects in the January 2004 raid. Interestingly, the policies of repression were contributing to the violence more blatantly than the separatists themselves. The climate of fear and suspicion has distanced even the moderate Muslims from the government's policies and actions.

To retain and nurture public support, it is essential for the government to win over the mainstream community leaders and influential religious teachers. To win public confidence, it is essential to empower the Muslims by co-opting Muslim leaders to join the decision-making structures in the south. The government must invest in forming trust-building relationships through an advocacy campaign and continuous dialogue. Muslims should be allowed to express the insurgency problem as they perceive it.

Traditionally, religious institutions in the south have been the centers used by local Malay-Muslims to reinforce their identity. Islamic education in pondoks has been extensively used to revive and sustain pan-Malay nationalism. At the same time, these are the centers that can train "a future leadership that offers hope for the region."[72] It is therefore imperative to encourage the schools to modernize general Islamic education in a manner that not only fosters knowledge of religion, but also practical skills that will empower and equip graduates from the Muslim education system for mainstream life.[73] The creation of avenues and opportunities for higher education would prevent Muslim students from going abroad, especially to Middle Eastern, Pakistani, and Indonesian universities to get radicalized.[74]

CONCLUSION

The current strategy adopted by Bangkok, which privileges the use of force to improve the situation in Southern Thailand, is flawed. It must be understood that insurgency in Southern Thailand is an unconventional threat and not a military one. A group of power-hungry Islamist leaders are using and misusing religion to politicize and mobilize the masses through the religious schools and mosques. A conventional military response to a political and ideological threat is likely to worsen the problem.

To discourage and dissuade extremism, the government should strengthen existing infrastructures and build new institutions with resources and authority, set deliverable goals, and monitor progress. As there is no standard textbook for restoring normalcy in the south, the government should develop sound and timely policies and practices that will encourage moderation and instill toleration—the hallmark of traditional Thai norms and values. Previous efforts to forcibly assimilate the Muslim Malaya population have provoked violent nationalist backlashes.

The government should open more space for the local Muslims in political, social, and administrative matters; this would undermine the perceived grievances of the local population to a great extent. At the same time, the Muslims in the south must break themselves free from the appeal of violence to legitimize their cause. They must ensure that the unique culture, traditions, and identity and the institutions associated with them are not hijacked by a handful of preachers of hate whose agenda transcends Thai nationality. They must in their own interest undercut the appeal of radical ideology, which finds in violence and death the answer to all the problems that beset the Muslim community today.

NOTES

1. Kavi Chongkittavorn, "Thaksin's Emergency Power: A Kiss of Death," *The Nation*, July 18, 2005.
2. "Pattani" is the Anglicized spelling, whereas "Patani" is how it is written in Malay.
3. Uthai Dulyakasem, "Muslim Malay in southern Thailand: Factors underlying the political revolt," in Lim Joo Jock and Vani S., eds., *Armed Separatism in Southeast Asia* (Singapore: Institute of Southeast Asian Studies Regional Strategic Studies Program, 1984), pp. 220–222.
4. Grandson of Haji Sulong, "Colonisation reason for southern Thai conflict," *Malaysiakini*, November 9, 2004. Online. Available HTTP: <http://www.malaysiakini.com/letters/31339>.
5. Though most of Kedah was ceded to British Malay, Satun, a Muslim majority area, was retained as a Thai province that was successfully assimilated into Thai Culture and language. See Moshe Yegar, *Between Integration and Secession* (Boulder: Lexington, 2002), pp. 79–80.
6. Syed Serajul Islam, "The Islamic Independence Movements in Pattani of Thailand and Mindanao of the Philippines," *Asian Survey*, Vol. 38 (May 1982): 441–56.
7. Ibid.
8. "Thailand Islamic Insurgency", GlobalSecurity.org. Online. Available HTTP: <http://www.globalsecurity.org/military/world/war/thailand2.htm>.
9. Angel M. Rabasa, et al, *The Muslim World After 9/11* (Santa Monica, CA: RAND Corporation, 2004), p. 378.
10. Ibid, p. 379.
11. Carlo Bonura Jr., "Location and the Dilemmas of Muslim Political Community in Southern Thailand" (paper presented at the First Inter-Dialogue Conference on Southern Thailand, University of Washington, Seattle, June 13–15, 2002), p. 15. Online. Available HTTP: <http://mis-pattani.pn.psu.ac.th/registra/grade/temp/speech/Bonura/Bonura's%20paper%20(panel%2016).html>.

12. Clive Christie, *A Modern History of Southeast Asia: Decolonization, Nationalism, and Separatism* (London: Tauris Academic Studies, 1996), p. 174.
13. Connor Bailey and John Miksic, "The Country of Patani in the Period of Re-Awakening: A Chapter from Ibrahim Syukri's Serjarah Kerajaan Melayu Patani," in *The Muslims in Thailand, Volume II: Politics of the Malay-Speaking South*, Andrew Forbes, ed. (Bihar: Centre for South-East Asian Studies, 1989), p. 151.
14. Moshe Yegar, *Between Integration and Secession: The Muslim Communities of the Southern Philippines, Southern Thailand, and Western Burma/Myanmar* (Lanham, Maryland: Lexington Books, 2003), p. 89.
15. See W. K. Che Man, *Muslim Separatism: The Moros of Southern Philippines and the Malays of Southern Thailand* (Manila: Ateneo de Manila University Press, 1990).
16. Peter Chalk, "Separatism and Southeast Asia: The Islamic Factor in Southern Thailand, Mindanao, and Aceh," *Studies in Conflict and Terrorism*, Vol. 24 (July 2001): 241–269.
17. Moshe Yegar, *Between Integration and Secession*, p. 87.
18. Che Man, *Muslim Separatism*, pp. 63–64.
19. Ibid.
20. Andrew D.W. Forbes, "Thailand's Muslim Minorities: Assimilation, Secession, or Coexistence?" *Asian Survey* 22 (November 1982): 1056–1073.
21. Che Man, 1990, p. 65.
22. Grandson of Haji Suliong, "Colonisation reason for southern Thai conflict."
23. Moshe Yegar, *Between Integration and Secession*, p. 125. Also see Linda J. True, "Balancing minorities: A Study of Southern Thailand," SAIS Working Paper 02/04, May 2004, p. 5.
24. Chidchanok Rahimmula, cited in ICG report, p. 6.
25. See the analysis of R. J. May, "The Religious Factors in Three Minority Movements," *Contemporary South East Asia*, Vol.13, no. 4 (1992): 403–404; Chalk, "Separatism and Southeast Asia"; and Dan Bristow, "Porous Borders Aids Muslim Insurgency," *Jane's Intelligence Review Pointer* 005/003 (March 1998).
26. Farish A. Noor, "The Killings in Southern Thailand: A Long History of Persecution Unrecorded," *Just International,* May 15, 2004. Online. Available http: <http://www.just-international.org/article_print.cfm?newsid=20000634>.
27. Ibid.
28. For a more detailed information about the groups, see Rohan Gunaratna, Arabinda Acharya, and Sabrina Chua, *Conflict and Terrorism in Southern Thailand* (Singapore: Marshall Cavendish Academic, 2005), Appendix 7, pp. 157–204.
29. "Army, police on high alert for cabinet meeting in South," *The Nation*, March 16, 2004.
30. Pondok is also locally known as ponoh, a corruption of the Malay word pondok. For a discussion on the educational system in Thailand and the religious educational system, see Rohan Gunaratna, et al (2005), pp. 46–53.
31. "I joined to liberate Pattani," *The Nation*, May 5, 2004.
32. One of the biggest resistance movements against Bangkok was in response to the educational reforms imposed under the Education Act of 1921. Pasuk Phongpaichit and Chris Baker, *Thailand: Economy and Politics* (Kuala Lumpur: Oxford University Press, 1995), p. 273.
33. "Imam admits to contact with separatists," *The Nation*, September 1, 2004.
34. "Principal admits co-writing book," *Bangkok Post*, September 1, 2004.
35. John Paul Lederach, *Building Peace—Sustainable Reconciliation in Divided Societies* (Washington, DC: United States Institute of Peace Press, 1997), p.8.
36. Thailand Ministry of Foreign Affairs, "Thai Muslims" (Bangkok, 1979) 5–6; Muthiah Alagappa, *The National Security of Developing States: Lessons from Thailand* (Massachusetts: AcornHouse, 1987), pp. 204–207.

37. Ibid.

38. See Prinya Udomsap, et al., *The Findings to Understand Fundamental Problems in Pattani, Yala and Narathiwat* (in Thai) (Bangkok: National Research Council of Thailand, 2002), pp. 62–66.

39. NSO (National Statistics Office), "Statistics of Household Income and Expenditure and Their Distribution" (2002). Online. Available HTTP: <http://www.nso.go.th/eng/pub/keystat/key03/key.pdf>.

40. Kazi Mahmood, "Poverty Grips Muslims In Southern Thailand," *Islam Online*, February 12, 2004. Online. Available HTTP: <http://www.islamonline.net/English/News/2004-02/12/article04.shtml>.

41. Uttrasin, The Local Administration of the Special Area, pp. 5–6.

42. Title 10 U.S. Code, Section 2350a, authorizes the Secretary of Defense, with the concurrence of the Secretary of State, to designate MNNAs for purposes of participating with the Department of Defense (DOD) in cooperative research and development programs. MNNA Status does not entail the same mutual defense and security guarantees afforded to NATO members. Status makes a nation eligible for priority delivery of excess defense articles; to buy depleted uranium ammunition; to have U.S.-owned War Reserve Stockpiles on its territory; to enter into agreements with the USG for the cooperative furnishing of training on a bilateral or multilateral basis under reciprocal financial arrangements; to use U.S.-provided Foreign Military Financing for commercial leasing of certain defense articles; to make a country eligible for loans of materials, supplies, and equipment for cooperative R&D projects and testing and evaluation; and for expedited processing of export licenses of commercial satellites and their technologies, components, and systems.

43. Marwaan Macan-Markar, "Thai Gov't Faces Political Storm over Anti-Terrorism Law," *One World US*, August 13, 2003. Online. Available HTTP: <http://us.oneworld.net/article/view/65553/1>.

44. Peter Searle, "Ethno-Religious Conflicts: Rise or Decline? Recent Developments in Southeast Asia," *Contemporary Southeast Asia*, Volume 24, Number 1, April 2002.

45. Peter Searle, "Ethno-Religious Conflicts: Rise or Decline? Recent Developments in Southeast Asia," *Contemporary Southeast Asia*, Volume 24, Number 1, April 2002.

46. "Thailand Islamic Insurgency," GlobalSecurity.org.

47. Joe Cochrane and Mark Hosenball, "Inside the Hunt for Hambali," *Newsweek International*, August 2003.

48. "Cambodia meets Islam head on," *Asia Times*, June 3, 2003. Online. Available HTTP: <http://www.atimes.com/atimes/Southeast_Asia/EF03Ae02.html>.

49. "Berjihad di Pattani" (The Fight for the Liberation of Pattani), translated by the International Centre for Political Violence and Terrorism Research (ICPVTR) at the Institute of Defence and Strategic Studies (IDSS).

50. Surat Horachaikul, "The far south of Thailand in the era of the American empire, 9/11 version, and Thaksin's 'cash and gung-ho' premiership," paper presented at MSRC-KAF Intercultural Discourse Series, Dealing with Terrorism Today: Lessons from the Malaysian Experience (Kuala Lumpur, July 23, 2004).

51. "CIA-backed unit 'may be involved in violence,'" *The Nation*, April 19, 2004.

52. "Plan to capture province," *The Nation*, January 14, 2004.

53. Similarly, the insurgents may well be using one of the tactics that Thai security has been known to adopt to stir up more feelings of distrust. This involves the abduction and subsequent disappearance of suspects picked up by the police. In some cases, after the police have released the suspects, many of them were immediately abducted by masked persons, never to be seen again. One of the so-called disappearances that provoked much popular resentment and outcry involved Somchai Neelapaijit, a

Muslim lawyer. While all the "disappearances" may not be the work of the security agencies, with its past reputation, the blame almost invariably lands at their feet, prompting further backlash.

54. Nirmal Ghosh, "Shadowy group behind violence," *Straits Times*, May 1, 2004.
55. Rona M. Fields, Salman Elbedour, and Fadel Abu Hein, "The Palestinian suicide bomber," in *The Psychology of Terrorism, Volume Two: Clinical Aspects and Responses*, Chris E. Stout, ed., (Westport, CT: Praeger, 2002), p. 208.
56. Berjihad di Pattani, ICPVTR translation.
57. Farish A. Noor, "The Killings in Southern Thailand."
58. Ibid.
59. See Surat Horachaikul, "The Far South of Thailand in the Era of the American Empire."
60. Ibrahim Syukri, "Sejarah Kerajaan Melayu Patani," in *The Muslims in Thailand, Volume II: Politics of the Malay-Speaking South*, Andrew Forbes, ed. (Bihar: Centre for Southeast Asian Studies, 1989), p. 151.
61. Carlos Bonura, "Location and the Dilemmas of Muslim Political Community in Southern Thailand—An Essay for the First Inter-Dialogue Conference on Southern Thailand," University of Washington Department of Political Science, Seattle, June 13–15, 2002. Online. Available HTTP: <http://mis-pattani.pn.psu.ac.th/registra/grade/temp/speech/Bonura/Bonura's%20paper%20(panel%2016).html>.
62. "Thai Opposition Leader Slams Government's Scrapping of Previous Mechanisms in South," *Nation*, July 18, 2002.
63. See Horachaikul, "The Far South of Thailand in the Era of the American Empire."
64. Anthony Davis, "Thailand Confronts Separatist Violence in Its Muslim South," *Jane's Intelligence Review*, March 1, 2004.
65. "Primer: Muslim Separatism in Southern Thailand," Virtual Information Center, July 22, 2002. Online. Available HTTP: <http://www.vic-info.org/Regionstop.nsf/0/e42514a843d9a3260a256c05006c2d84?>.
66. "Latest Violence Highlights Tense Relations between Bangkok, Muslim South," channelnewsasia.com, January 11, 2004. Online. Available HTTP: <http://www.channelnewsasia.com/stories/afp_asiapacific/view/65764/1/.html>.
67. Responding to the January 2004 armory raids, Bangkok imposed martial law in troubled areas of the provinces of Yala, Pattani, and Narathiwat that was subsequently extended to other areas in June 2004. The martial law gave the military powers to search and arrest "suspects," which inflamed local sentiments further.
68. Anucha Charoenpo, "Sirichai: Zoning idea military's brainchild," *Bangkok Post*, February 19, 2005.
69. Tony Davis, "Are Thailand's Southern Insurgents Moving to Soft Targets?" *Jane's Terrorism and Intelligence Centre*, April 5, 2004.
70. Joseph C. Y. Liow, "Violence and the Long Road to Reconciliation in Southern Thailand" (paper presented at the Conference on Religion and Conflict in Asia: Disrupting Violence, Arizona State University, October 14–15, 2004).
71. Linda J. True, "Balancing minorities," p.16.
72. Surin Pitsuwan, "Abode of Peace," *Worldview Magazine*, Vol. 17, No. 2 (June–August 2004), p. 3.
73. Hasan Madmarn, *The Pondok and Madrasah in Patani* (Bangi: Penerbit Universiti Kebangsaan Malaysia, 1999), p. 66.
74. S. P. Haris, "Conflict in Southern Thailand: Removing Education from the Security Agenda," *IDSS Commentaries* (33/2004), August 25, 2004.

Indonesia

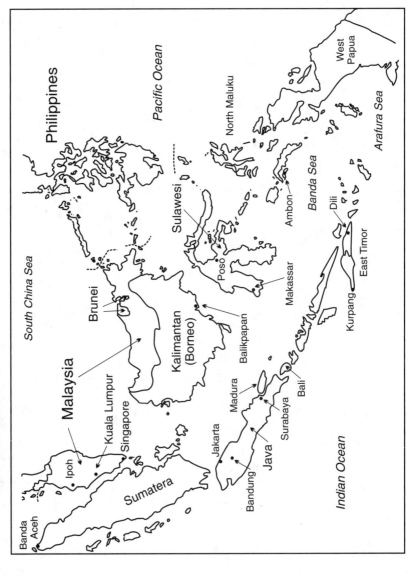

8

INDONESIA

Arabinda Acharya and Rohaiza Ahmad Asi[1]

NATURE OF THE FLASHPOINT

Indonesia, the fourth most populous nation in the world, is an archipelago consisting of more than 17,000 islands. The country has about 360 tribal and ethno-linguistic groups who speak 25 languages and more than 250 different dialects. Roughly 45 percent of the population is Javanese; another 14 percent are Sundanese concentrated in western Java. A third significant group, Malays, constitute nearly 7.5 percent of the population. With regard to religion, Indonesia is the world's most populous Muslim state. Eighty-eight percent of the population identify themselves as Muslims, 8 percent are Christians, 2 percent are Hindus, and 1 percent is Buddhist.[2]

Indonesia makes a very interesting yet complex case study for a student of conflicts. Communal conflicts, secessionist demands, and Islamist political violence and terrorism proliferate in the country. While these conflicts did not appear overnight, the end of the "New Order"[3] under Soeharto's rule and the instability associated with political transitions seem to be contributing factors for their emergence. With the fall of Soeharto's regime in 1998 and the initiation of democratization, weak government institutions, and the absence of charismatic leadership paved the way for dissent and bold secessionist demands. The heterogeneous Indonesian population and the peculiarly isolating and separating geography also contributed to the problems of governance.

Although the West is particularly concerned about Islamist terrorism, not all political conflicts or ideological contestations lead to terrorism in Indonesia. In a majority of cases, violence is associated with resource competition, issues of political participation, or regional autonomy. In addition, there is a high propensity for these issues to be layered over communal concerns; this eventually leads to greater political and ideological involvement.

HISTORICAL CONTEXT

Conflicts in Indonesia may be categorized into three types: those associated with issues of self-determination, those that might be called "communal conflicts," and conflicts that arise from the democratization process itself. Indeed, most of the conflicts overlap as the democratization process that followed the ouster of Soeharto led to open dissent and the more assertive articulation of secessionist demands.

The demand for self-determination has been a major source of conflict in Indonesia. These include demands for independence and/or for significant autonomy, which have been most pronounced in Aceh, West Papua and East Timor. Almost all cases involved armed combat with insurgents combating Indonesian security forces. East Timor was successful in gaining independence after a period of violent struggle in which an estimated 100,000 to 250,000 individuals lost their lives.[4] In other cases, the demand for self-determination involves a desire for greater autonomy from central governmental control. These include demands by the local population to have provincial status or distinct political units of their own, to have the right to choose their leaders without interference from Jakarta, to have a more generous share of national government revenues, and to have more authority to determine how local resources are used.

Grievances over resource allocations and usage have often been expressed in violent terms in many regions for two reasons. Historically, violence has been more common in regions that were not deeply integrated into the former Dutch colonies such as Aceh, which was only weakly integrated into the Netherlands East Indies. Since Indonesia's independence, the Acehnese have been engaged in a campaign to establish a separate state that may also be Islamic. In fact, at the time of independence, East Timor and West Papua were not even parts of Indonesia. There were armed secessionist movements in East Timor and are still ongoing in West Papua.[5]

Communal conflicts in Indonesia are along the lines of ethnicity, religion, and culture, and they are distinct from the conflicts of self-determination because they regularly do not include separatist elements or demands for autonomy. For example, the violence against the Sino-Indonesian community in Malukus and Poso in Central Sulawesi[6] do not involve issues of self-determination. But separatist conflicts such as those in Aceh have often been on communal (religious) lines.

More often than not, both types of conflicts involve struggles over economic, environmental, and political resources, with most of the grievances over the distribution of economic resources. Locals often complain about the exploitation of regional economic resources by the central government in Jakarta and over the unfair distribution of the proceeds of such resources. This is manifested in centralized and elite ownership of and control over natural resources, displacement, and transmigration.[7]

Communal conflicts in different parts of Indonesia have different dimensions. For example, in West Kalimantan, communal violence preceded economic crisis. The violence was about economic resources and political power, layered over a communal conflict. There were no serious allegations about political maneuvering at either the national or local levels instigating the violence, although there were accusations that the military did not act quickly to stop the violence once it had broken out.[8] In this case, the violence involved two communities: the Dayaks (who may be Muslim or Christian) and the Madurese (who are Muslim). Other ethnic groups such as the Javanese and Chinese were not affected.[9] The Dayaks, who are the indigenous population in Kalimantan, felt displaced and threatened by the large migration of the Madurese. The former were also unhappy with the economic policies of the central government, which appeared to put them in a disadvantaged position as elaborated later in the chapter. This further worsened the already tense relations between the Dayaks and the Madurese.

In the Malukus, a small group of Christian separatists loyal to Dutch colonial rule declared the South Maluku Republic (RMS) in 1950. And while most of the RMS activists are now living in the Netherlands, they continue their campaign for international recognition. Renewed communal strife in the Malukus began in January 1999 with economic, ethnic, and religious undertones that quickly polarized into Christian-Muslim conflict. During the Soeharto era, a large number of Muslims were relocated to the Malukus from other parts of the country, displacing Christians and altering the religious balance. The situation was exacerbated by the intervention of Islamist militias such as Laskar Jihad (Islamic militia), most of whom are from Java. These militias recruited locals, most of them being criminals with a history of violence. In addition, the militias fueled the anti-Christian sentiments among the Muslims in Maluku.

During the Soeharto regime, challenges to the territorial integrity of Indonesia were dealt with primarily through repression. Public discussion of racial, ethnic, and religious issues—SARA (Suku, Agama, Ras, and Antar-golongan)[10] was banned. Subsequently, the legal basis for the banning of oppositions such as the Indonesian Communist Party (PKI) and Darul Islam (DI)[11] was removed with the scrapping of the 1963 Anti-Subversion Law in 1998.[12] This created a powerful legacy of conflict between the national government and a very broad range of local society, not just small, radical groups. As the society became more open after the end of the New Order regime in 1998, the legacy of excesses became a powerful mobilizing force for these groups.[13]

Flashpoints in Indonesia

In a report prepared in April 2002, the London-based Asia Pacific Foundation identified six security "trouble spots" with regard to the threat of Islamist terrorism in Indonesia. They were Aceh, Maluku, Papua, Kalimantan, Poso in Central in Sulawesi, and West Timor. Although most of the conflicts in these areas are rooted in local grievances, there have been attempts by external elements to "Islamize" them. The following will highlight some of these conflicts.

Aceh: A Demand for Self-Determination   Aceh, located on the northern tip of the island of Sumatra, is known for its strong Islamic influence and fierce demands for independence from the central government, led by the Free Aceh Movement (GAM). The conflict in Aceh has often been mistaken as a religious conflict; it is in fact a war of independence. The signing of the August 2005 peace accord between the GAM and the Indonesian government signals a better future for the Acehnese. By far, this agreement has made the most significant inroads into the stalemate between the two sides. Both sides have compromised on certain issues, and the subsequent surrender of weapons by GAM proceeded smoothly. Many Acehnese, who were the last to fall to Dutch colonial power in the nineteenth century, joined the DI rebellion across Indonesia to set up an Islamic state in the 1950s when the incipient Indonesian nation failed to give Aceh a provincial status as promised.[14] The Aceh revolt ended temporarily when the government in Jakarta gave Aceh the status of a "special territory" in 1959.[15] However, in 1976, GAM emerged to fight for an independent Aceh following the Acehnese disillusionment with what they perceived as Javanese economic and political domination. Fighting between GAM and the Indonesian military has continued, with intermittent ceasefires and breakdown of peace agreements.

A component of GAM's strategy is to target sectors of the economy from which Indonesia and particularly the security forces benefit.[16] GAM's grievance with multinational companies is twofold: first, they are seen as exploiting Aceh's resources; second, they are perceived as collaborating with the Indonesian military, which secures their premises. For GAM this makes corporations legitimate targets. In fact, GAM goes so far as to invoke the Hague and Geneva conventions, which recognize the right of warring parties to eliminate those economic facilities of the enemy that can be used to strengthen the muscle of the military.[17] GAM focuses on the domestic and foreign corporations in the Lhokseumawe industrial complex, whose workers have been living under the threat of intimidation, kidnapping, or death since the early days of armed resistance. In general GAM targets Aceh's industrial infrastructure: the oil and gas production facilities and pipelines.

Besides economic infrastructure, GAM also targets civil servants in Aceh, particularly politicians who support Jakarta. The group has also been known to target the country's education system by burning schools and intimidating and killing the teaching staffs. According to GAM, the Indonesian educational system actively destroyed Acehnese history and culture while promoting "the glorification of Javanese culture."[18]

Even though one of GAM's strategies has been to gain international attention and sympathy for the plight of the Acehnese people, the conflict itself has largely been a local affair. For a long time, Aceh was closed to foreigners until the December 2004 tsunami destroyed much of the region. There were speculations by security analysts that GAM had been seriously undermined by the tsunami to the extent that its networks and logistical supplies had been damaged and its support in the coastal areas was severely disrupted.[19] However, the group retains a significant presence.

Opening Aceh to international relief efforts came to be exploited by the Islamist militant groups in Indonesia. Islamist groups, such as the Islamic Defenders Front (FPI). The Indonesian Mujahidin Council (MMI)—allegedly the political wing of Jemaah Islamiyah (JI)—set up a command post at an air force base in Aceh to help bury the dead and distribute aid.[20] These groups also claimed that they provide counseling and religious lessons to the victims of the disaster. It is a disturbing development, because it can be assumed that they are also spreading an intolerant, radical brand of Islam. These groups are rabidly anti-American in their outlook. They are critical of Western assistance that they perceive as being Christian-oriented. In light of this development, GAM's exiled leaders in Sweden issued a statement that the presence of FPI and MMI is unhelpful to the cause of a free Aceh, and that their objectives differ from those for which GAM is fighting. If these groups persist in operating in Aceh, however, they might eventually be able to gain support from the Acehnese through their propaganda, even if only from a minority.

The signing of the peace accord in Helsinki between GAM and the Indonesian government on August 15, 2005, is a watershed in the peace process between the two sides.[21] During the talks preceding the signing of the peace accord, both sides reached agreement on almost all of the issues on the agenda, including amnesties, political participation, and economic, legal, and security arrangements. Under the agreement, the GAM leaders have decided to put aside their demand for full independence, accepting instead a form of local self-government and the right to eventually establish a political party.[22] The government has agreed to allow GAM to form Aceh-based political parties and within 18 months to change the law banning local political parties. In addition, GAM agreed to disarm in return for the withdrawal of Indonesian troops from Aceh.

Having seen the breakdown of previous peace agreements between GAM and the Indonesian government, it is not too conservative to think of this as just providing provisional peace to the region. A few months after the signing of the peace accord, disagreements have emerged on the future of Aceh and over the demands for Aceh's partition into three provinces to facilitate governance. If the demands for Aceh's partition proceed in the near future, it will undermine the peace accord and threaten the fragile peace as it runs counter to the border of Aceh as specified in the truce.[23] However, if the agreement does proceed smoothly, it may be a model for defusing other trouble spots in Indonesia. If it does not, it will just confirm the unyieldingness of all sides.

Kalimantan: Competition over Resources   The Dayaks are the indigenous occupants of the Kalimantan, while the Madurese first arrived in West Kalimantan in the 1930s. The term Madurese refer to the original inhabitants of Madura, an Indonesian island off the northeastern coast of Java, near the port of Surabaya. Since the sixteenth century, the population of Madura is predominantly Muslim. The transmigration of the Madurese to Kalimantan was part of the national relocation policy from high-density areas of Java to islands that were sparsely populated.[24] The violence in Kalimantan followed several decades of dislocation of the Dayak community. As in many other settlement areas, a manifestation of discontent was the violence between settlers and indigenous populations in Kalimantan. Apart from the dilution of the demographic mix due to spontaneous migration, the Dayaks were also disturbed by the Soeharto regime handing out vast parcels of Kalimantan's forests to logging companies, many of which were connected to members of the Soeharto family, his cronies, or the military. The result was that many forest-dwelling Dayaks were driven from their traditional environment. A 1979 law, which provided for uniform structures of local government throughout Indonesia, had the effect of undermining the authority of traditional village leaders and the cohesion of Dayak communities. Accompanying this dislocation was a widespread feeling among Dayaks that they were often looked down on by other communities as "backward" and "uncivilized."[25]

There was a particularly large outbreak of riots in 1987 in which hundreds allegedly died. A few ethnic riots also broke out in the 1990s. During 1999–2000, this area witnessed some of Indonesia's most vicious ethnic killings. The initial conflict had been between Madurese and Malays—both Muslim communities—with the non-Muslim Dayaks joining in later on the Malay side.[26] It was only after virtually all Madurese had fled from Sambas that order was restored.

Besides the communal conflict, there have been indications of increasing terrorist activities in Balikpapan in East Kalimantan and other areas of Kalimantan. On January 8, 2005, a bomb exploded in Balikpapan in East Kalimantan in Indonesia. The explosion was a minor one and the bomber himself was injured in the blast. Police arrested the bomber identified as Sujono, alias Sugiono. In February 2005, Indonesian police chief General Da'i Bachtiar told a Commission of the House of Representatives dealing with security affairs that police found a copy of what may be the constitution of Southeast Asian terrorist group Jemaah Islamiah (JI) from the possession of Sujano.[27] The document—Nidhom Azasi—consisting of 15 chapters and 34 articles, contains, among others references to fundamentalist teachings, hostilities between Islamic and Western countries, terrorist movements in Indonesia, and a section on bomb-making and shooting skills. Security experts believe that when a training camp maintained jointly by JI and al Qaeda in Poso was disrupted, they shifted the infrastructure to Balikpapan. However, the camp was not static and large and could not be maintained due to pressure from the Indonesian authorities. There have been lingering suspicions that JI and DI maintain some infrastructure in Balikpapan and other areas of Kalimantan, including several schools, using them as clandestine safe houses and training bases. Of particular importance is the Hidyatullah pesantren, a religious boarding school in Balikpapan, which was used by Omar al-Faruq, who was the representative of al Qaeda in Southeast Asia before his arrest. Similarly, Ali Imron and Mubarok—two key JI members implicated in the October 2002 Bali bombings—were arrested on an isolated island near Balikpapan.[28] East Kalimantan has been further implicated as a major transit route for terrorists belonging to JI and other groups for travel to the southern Philippines for training.[29]

Increasing terrorist activities in Balikpapan are particularly worrisome for foreign investors, as Balikpapan is home to several multinational oil, gas, and mining firms. While terrorist groups such as JI have been known to attack foreign interests in Indonesia, such foreign investment, particularly from the United States, has become highly controversial following shootings and beatings in Unocal's East Kalimantan oil and gas operation in late 2000 in which 300 local residents blockaded access to Unocal's transportation lines. This violence followed the construction of a special landing strip near the Unocal operation to allow the rapid transport of Indonesia's "Mobil Brigade" security forces directly to the region in order to defend the company's operations. The community that was negatively impacted by Unocal's operation felt frustrated that their demands were never addressed and thus, organized the blockade. Security forces were called in. Several people were shot and severely beaten at the site, effectively crushing the blockade.

The Indonesian Mining Advocacy Network, JATAM, alleged that Unocal's operations in East Kalimantan over the past 30 years have created huge environmental and, more importantly, social problems.[30] This involved forced seizure of land and crops with no prior dialogue, consent, or compensation for local communities. According to JATAM, the October 2000 blockade was the outcome of decades of frustration.[31] Although it was just a single incident, the radical Islamic groups and their members who are vehemently anti-United States could easily take advantage of issues such as the exploitation of local resources by foreign companies to promote their own agenda.

Maluku: Inter-Religious Rivalry The Maluku archipelago, in eastern Indonesia, consists of 1,208 islands.[32] In October 1999, the previously single province was divided into two: North Maluku with Ternate as its capital and Maluku with its capital Ambon. The formation of North Maluku was ostensibly to prevent the violence in Ambon from spreading north. However, its formation only exacerbated the conflict. North Maluku comprises a Muslim majority whereas Maluku is made up of a Christian majority. An estimated 54 percent of the population professes Islam as their religion while 44 percent identify as Christians.[33] The Malukan have had a relatively peaceful relation with one another for centuries. Disputes are often mediated and solved by the local rulers. A few factors contributed to the disruption of these peaceful relations. Among the sources of conflicts are traditional regional rivalries, the separatist legacy of some of Maluku's Christians, the undermining of traditional conflict management practices and leadership structures, government policies under Soeharto's regime, and migration.[34] A last factor was the chaos that hit the streets of Indonesia following the collapse of Soeharto's regime, which increased ethnic and religious tensions in many parts of the country.

Two events set the stage for the outbreak of open hostility in Maluku. The first occurred on November 22, 1998, when anti-Christian/Chinese riots broke out in Ketapang, Jakarta. Six Ambonese Christians were killed and 22 churches were burnt or damaged.[35] In retaliation, reprisals took place in predominantly Christian Kupang, West Timor. The second trigger event occurred as Muslims were celebrating the end of the fasting month on January 19, 1999. A fight broke out between a Christian public transport driver and a Muslim youth and subsequently escalated into a war between the Christians and the Muslims.[36] As the violence between the two sides persisted, Muslim groups throughout Indonesia, particularly in Java, called for jihad. Foremost among these groups was Laskar Jihad, which was created as a response to the conflict in Ambon.[37] Laskar Jihad, under the leadership of Ja'far Umar Thalib, subsequently issued a declaration of jihad on the Christians and sent its members into Ambon and Maluku in 2000. The influx of the Laskar Jihad paramilitary tipped the balance in favor of the Muslims.

Laskar Jihad was not the only Islamic militant group that participated in the conflict. Also in Maluku was Laskar Mujahideen, the military wing of the Indonesia Mujahedin Council (MMI), which in turn has been alleged to be the political wing of JI. Other smaller Islamic militant groups were also present in Maluku. Al Qaeda dispatched its men to Maluku, namely Omar al Faruq, al Qaeda's Southeast Asia's representative. The presence of these external radical Islamic militant groups in Maluku did more harm than good. In most instances, their presence exacerbated the conflict.

The conflict in Maluku has produced many jihadists who have the ability to pose a security threat anywhere in Indonesia. Personal bonds forged through joint training and shared combat experiences in areas of communal conflict have helped perpetuate violence.[38] These personal bonds in turn lead to fluidity and overlapping group memberships, which can be easily tapped for any future terrorist operations.

LINKAGES TO TERRORISM

Jemaah Islamiah (JI) was officially founded in 1993 with the objective of establishing a pan-Islamic state in Southeast Asia that centers in Indonesia but would include countries such as Singapore, Malaysia, and the southern Philippines.[39] Even though the JI network was only uncovered by the Southeast Asian authorities in 2001, the group has been implicated in terrorist attacks prior to that. One of its large-scale, pre-2001 attacks was the Christmas Eve bombings, on December 24, 2000. A series of bombs exploded in 38 places, mostly targeting churches, in various cities throughout Indonesia.[40] Westerners and Western symbols were hardly the target before 2001. The discontent of the group was localized or contained within the region.

The first crackdown on JI came in December 2001 when the Singaporean authorities arrested 15 JI suspects in the country. A videotape was later discovered in Afghanistan that confirmed the Singapore connection.[41] With the unraveling of the members' connections, Malaysia too cracked down on the terrorist network in its territory. In contrast to the response of these two countries, Indonesia persistently denied the existence of JI in its territory. It was, however, rudely shaken to realization with the October 2002 Bali bombings, which claimed 202 lives. The increased international pressure following the blasts forced the Indonesian government to take harsh measures against the members of JI. Since then, most of the violence in Indonesia and in other parts of the region has been increasingly attributed to JI.

The JI phenomenon cannot be understood in isolation. Often, communal conflicts provide a conducive ground for operations and training, as well as a justification to promote their own agenda by highlighting the plight of the Muslims in those conflict areas. To the extent that JI is an offshoot of Darul Islam (DI), the much more extensive and one of the most penetrative movements in Indonesia, it is also necessary to study the movement in its entirety. Most significantly, the DI milieu in Indonesia has now become the recruitment base of JI factions interested in achieving their objectives through violent means. It is noteworthy that after the Marriott hotel bombing in 2003, in which a number of Indonesian Muslims were killed, many in JI questioned the rationale of violent jihad in support of a pan-Islamist cause that has little to do with Indonesia's problems. As the discontent grew, the so-called Afghan veterans of the group found it difficult to mobilize support for the group. This was the time for them to look to the old but hitherto largely dormant ties with the parent movement—DI—for recruitment of volunteers for jihad and other logistical support. The second Bali bombings, which took place on October 1, 2005, demonstrated how even if JI has been seriously weakened by arrests and other counterterrorism measures put in place since the October 2002 Bali bombings, parts of the organization, or even individuals, continue to function.

Jemaah Islamiah has its roots in the struggle of Darul Islam (DI) since the 1940s.[42] DI was an anti-colonial organization that in turn became a political opponent of the Indonesian government.[43] Abu Bakar Ba'asyir and Abdullah Sungkar, the prominent founders of JI, were both members of DI. The duo joined DI in 1976 and subsequently went on to hold important positions. In 1985, both men went to Malaysia to escape subversion charges against them.[44] It was in Malaysia that they arranged for mujahedin to go to Afghanistan, turning Malaysia into a transit point for those heading to Afghanistan.

All of JI's top leaders and many of the men involved in JI bombings trained in Afghanistan over the 10-year period from 1985 to 1995. The jihad in Afghanistan had a huge influence in shaping their worldview, reinforcing their commitment to jihad, and providing them with terrorist and guerrilla training. It was here that JI separated from DI. Abdullah Sungkar was influenced by Osama bin Laden's global jihad approach and wanted to embrace this new concept. In his capacity as the shadow Minister of Foreign Affairs,[45] Sungkar contacted many Arab jihadists to seek financial and military assistance for DI. Thus, he was consistently exposed to the concept of a global jihad. One may even argue that Sungkar's Arab descent made him more sympathetic to their cause. However, the then leader of DI, Ajengan Masduki, was not interested in involving DI in external affairs. For him, DI's objective was to create an Islamic state in Indonesia and to overthrow the central government. According to Masduki, DI should not get itself entangled in the affairs of others, resulting in an irreparable break between Sungkar and Masduki. After the split, Sungkar brought many DI members into JI.

In many ways, the emergence of JI as a formal organization created by Sungkar on January 1, 1993,[46] merely institutionalized a network that already existed.[47] By May 1996, Sungkar and some of the Afghan veterans consolidated the structure of Jemaah Islamiyah and documented it in a book, *General Guidelines for the Jemaah Islamiyah Struggle, PUPJI*.[48]

With the return of most of the JI leadership to Indonesia after the end of the Soeharto government in 1998 during the Reformasi transition,[49] the total number of core Jemaah Islamiyah members has been estimated to range from 500 to several thousand. Its influence, however, transcends these numbers. JI has avidly sought out alliances—which at times have been ad hoc—with a loose network of like-minded organizations, and JI-run training camps have upgraded the military skills and ideological fervor of smaller, localized groups.

Jemaah Islamiyah supposedly has a highly formalized command structure. Several functional committees and four mantiqis (loosely translated as regional brigades) that were defined not only by geography but also by functional roles, including fundraising, religious indoctrination, military training, and weapons procurement, were led by a five-member Regional Advisory Council. Mantiqi 1 was composed of West Malaysia, Singapore, and Southern Thailand and was initially led by Riduan Isamuddin aka Hambali. But he was replaced by Ali Ghufron aka Muklas in 2001 when the region's security forces were hot on the heels of the former. The main function of these territories was to provide financial support, as business and employment opportunities are plenty in these countries. Mantiqi 2, composed of most parts of Indonesia except Sulawesi and Kalimantan, was led by Abdullah Anshori aka Abu Fatih. He later relinquished his leadership to Zuhroni aka Nu'im. These territories are used for the main operation of JI because the majority of the members are based in these territories; it is the most efficient and the fastest in recruiting members and also has a vast network of sympathizers and supporters.[50] Mantiqi 3 is composed of Kalimantan, Sulawesi, and Mindanao. It was led by Abu Tholut aka Mustofa, who was arrested in July 2003. These territories were used for paramilitary training purposes, which include infantry skills and bomb-making classes and to provide ammunition, weapon, and explosives materials for the group's use. Mantiqi 4 is composed of Australia. It was led by a man name called Abdul Rahim Ayub, who was arrested in Indonesia in July 2004.[51] The function of this mantiqi was solely to provide financial support.

In practice, however, JI appears to function in a much less centralized fashion than this structure might imply, particularly after a recent crackdown by the Malaysian and Singaporean authorities on the group's members. Many of the individual cells were compartmentalized from one another. This means that no single individual is indispensable. The arrest of many if not most of JI's top leaders appears to have accentuated these decentralized tendencies by disrupting the network's command and control structure. As JI's leadership structure is dismantled, institutional identities become less important with greater emphasis being placed on personal bonds. This essentially meant that individuals in JI might decide to go off on their own without reference to the central command structure.[52] They can pull together the foot soldiers required in an ad hoc fashion, cobbling together the critical mass for an operation from their own personal networks. The breakdown of JI's hierarchy has exacerbated tensions between two factions over the best strategy for waging jihad. A minority group is interested in focusing on a broader anti-Western agenda similar to al Qaeda, and in effecting change in the near term.[53] Opposing this faction is a majority group within JI, depicted as the "bureaucrats," that sees these tactics as undermining its preferred, longer-term strategy of building up military capacity and using religious proselytization to create a mass base sufficient to support an Islamic revolution.[54]

Despite the internal dissensions, JI has demonstrated remarkable resilience. This stems from the vast network of Islamic militant groups that it can tap into specifically from the DI movement. One of the suicide bombers in the October 2002 Bali bombings (i.e., the Sari Club suicide bomber), Arnasan (aka Jimmy, Acong, and Iqbal 1[55]), was a former member of DI West Java. He was purportedly recruited by Imam Samudera, the operations coordinator in the October 2002 Bali bombings who is currently imprisoned for his impending death sentence. The suicide bomber in the September 2004 Australian Embassy bombing, Heri Golun, was also a member of DI West Java, and he was recruited by Rois, who is believed to be the right-hand man of Noordin Mohd Top. Some intelligence sources have claimed that the bomb carriers in the October 2005 Bali bombings were also DI members.[56] However, this information has not been verified (investigations were still going on at the time this chapter was written).

As mentioned earlier, DI started with an objective that was localized within the Indonesian context. But it has been JI that has successfully internationalized these local goals by injecting anti-U.S. and anti-West sentiments into the group's message. The growth of local resentment has led many other indigenous radical Islamist groups to likewise target Western interests. An example was the bombing of the McDonald's restaurant and car showroom in Makassar in Sulawesi in December 2002, carried out with the involvement of two South Sulawesi-based groups, Wahdah Islamiah and Laskar Jundullah.[57] All targets of the terrorist attacks in Indonesia since the 9/11 attacks in the United States by al Qaeda have been associated with foreign interests. These include an explosion at the Kentucky Fried Chicken (KFC) outlet in the Panakku-kang Mas area in Makassar in October 2001; the October 2002 Bali bombings where 88 Australians died; blasts at the McDonald's Ratu Indah Mall in Makassar, South Sulawesi, in December 2002; the failed attempt to bomb a KFC outlet in the Pengayoman area of Makassar in December 2002; the Marriott hotel bombing in August 2003; the Australian Embassy bombing in September 2004; and the October 2005

Bali bombings, where foreigners were clearly the target of attacks. The U.S. invasion of Afghanistan and Iraq has further fueled the anti-U.S. sentiments of these radical groups, a trend similarly emerging among radical Islamist groups elsewhere in the world.

Critical in helping JI to survive is a group of Islamic boarding schools, or pesantren, which harbor JI members on the run from police and sympathize to some extent with the aim of JI to create an Islamic state. This solidarity has helped JI replenish its ranks with young jihadists recruited from Indonesian Islamic boarding schools that are spread across the archipelago. The common thread that runs through these boarding schools is the teachings of Salafism, a movement that seeks to return to what its adherents perceived as the purest form of Islam, asserted to have been practiced by the Prophet Muhammad and the two generations that followed him. They reject what they see as unwanted innovations brought to the religion in the later years.[58]

In Indonesia, pesantrens, mosques, and university campuses have been the main vehicles for spreading Salafi teachings, with the pesantrens being the most important. The Afghan veterans of Southeast Asia set up small networks of pesantrens to espouse jihad. Similarly, the JI directly owns a number of pesantrens and Islamic boarding schools, and has been affiliated with a number of others. The most important of them in Indonesia is the Al Mukmin (Pondok Ngruki of Abu Bakar Ba'asyir) pesantren in Solo, Indonesia. Others are Pesantren Hidayatullah in Balikpapan, Kalimantan, Pesantren Darul Aman, Gombara, Ujung Pandang, and the al Islam School. These schools, besides spreading Salafist teachings, became the centers of recruiting, indoctrination, and operations for the JI. The Hidayatullah pesantren was used as a training camp for JI recruits after Abdul Hadi and Syawal Yasin (Abdullah Sungkar's son in law) had gone to Balikpapan to establish a training school for terrorists. This school was also used by Omar al-Faroq for training for the Laskar Jundullah members. It is also alleged that the Hidyatullah pesantren became a place of shelter or transit for JI members at different times.[59] It is this network of Salafist schools that has now become an important resource for the recruits of different violent groups.

LINKAGES TO THE GLOBAL WAR ON TERRORISM

The United States has intensified its engagement with Indonesia after 2001, particularly following the Bali bombings in October 2002. President Bush's visit to the country in October 2003 and his open-ended discussion with the cross-section of the community, along with commitment for assistance and cooperation in the fields of defense and education, laid the foundation for a turnaround in perceptions about the United States in Indonesia. The tsunami disaster in Aceh, in December 2004, gave Washington a two-pronged strategic opportunity. Washington got the opportunity to enhance its presence and engagement in the region through its contribution to relief and rehabilitation efforts. At the same time, it got the chance to repair its image in the country, especially among the Muslims. It could demonstrate that it used its economic wealth and military capability to bring aid to Indonesia, the largest Islamic country (in terms of population) in the world.[60] Jakarta and Washington are now moving closer together toward more defense cooperation, which had been on ice due to the legacies of the East Timor era. More recently, the willingness of the moderate Muslims to speak out against the radicals offers opportunities for closer cooperation between the two countries.

However, the greater willingness on the part of Indonesia to work with the United States does not signal greater latitude for the U.S. actions in the region, particularly with regard to countering terrorism. Suspicions of U.S. motives in the region are still deep. The radical elements in Indonesia project Washington's assistance to Jakarta as interference in Indonesia's domestic affairs. This is compounded by Washington's actions against Iraq. Muslim and non-Muslim elites throughout the region continue to be critical of U.S. support for Israel, which they consider to be one of the root causes of terrorism.

Thus, Washington needs to be more sensitive in managing its relations with the world's most populous Muslim nation. The United States will have to build on its now cordial relations with Indonesia and continue to provide assistance to the latter to deal with myriad problems that Indonesia faces as a country making a painful transition to democracy. Additionally, Washington should be sensitive to the fact that Jakarta has to take into account the prevailing sentiment of the Muslim community, as its legitimacy to rule depends on the support of its Muslim majority population. If handled properly, Indonesia can become a model for other Islamic countries, by demonstrating that democracy and Islam are not necessarily incompatible as the radicals now project.

PROGRESS AND PROSPECTS

Radical Islamist terrorism will continue to pose a threat to the security of Indonesia and the region if the authorities do not deal effectively with communal conflicts and inter-religious/interethnic conflicts in the country effectively. Conflicts such as those in Poso and Maluku have produced many jihadists, who continue to pose a security threat even if those conflicts have ceased.[61] It is disturbing that the Muslims in some of those conflict zones have turned to these Islamic militant groups for protection rather than to the police. This owes largely to the perceived failure of the police to carry out their functions in those areas. The government of Indonesia has to review the role and the operational procedures of their regional police. Most importantly, the government has to address the root causes of those conflicts in negotiations of a ceasefire or a peace agreement, which in turn will appease the parties involved. The resolution to such conflicts in Indonesia is important, as they not only provide the militant groups or the terrorist groups with bases from which to operate, but also with political and economic issues to exploit to further their cause.

This can be demonstrated from an incident that occurred on October 29, 2005, in which three Christian teenage girls were beheaded in the sectarian divided town of Poso, Central Sulawesi.[62] Poso has been relatively peaceful since a government-mediated truce succeeded in ending the conflict in early 2002. Beheadings were a signature atrocity then and this latest development sparked fears of a renewed violence between the Muslims and non-Muslims. If the violence resumes, it will certainly attract Islamic militant groups from outside, specifically Java, and may even revive the allegedly defunct Laskar Jihad, which was known to have sent its members to Poso previously. This spells danger for the future security and stability of Indonesia.

NOTES

1. We wish to thank Dr. John Harrison and Ms. Sarah Jamie Burnell for reviewing the manuscripts and providing their feedback on the structure, as well as the contents of the chapter.

2. The World Factbook 2005, CIA. Online. Available HTTP: <http://www.cia.gov/cia/publications/factbook/geos/id.html> (accessed November 20, 2005) and data from Badan Pusat Statistik in "Setahun SBY-JK: Kerukunan Umat Beragama Masih Diwarnai Kesalahpahaman," *Departemen Agama Republik Indonesia*. Online. Available HTTP: < http://www.depag.go.id/Ber_kub_keslhphmn.php> (accessed December 10, 2005).

3. The period from 1966 to 1998, in which then-President Soeharto ruled Indonesia, was known as the New Order regime. It was generally characterized by the repression of oppositions and public opinion, heavy-handed measures of the government, and the monopoly of the government and businesses in Indonesia by Soeharto's family and cronies. See *Gerry van Klinken*, "The End of the New Order—How Would We Know?" *Inside Indonesia*, Digest 62, May 27, 1998. Online. Available HTTP: <http://www.insideindonesia.org/digest/dig62.htm> (accessed December 8, 2005).

4. Many lives were lost following a UN-supervised popular referendum on August 30, 1999, in which an overwhelming majority of the people of East Timor voted for independence from Indonesia. Between the referendum and the arrival of a multi-national peacekeeping force in late September 1999, anti-independence Timorese militias—organized and supported by the Indonesian military—commenced a large-scale, scorched-earth campaign as reprisals. The militias killed approximately 1,300 Timorese and forcibly pushed 300,000 people into West Timor as refugees. Most of the country's infrastructure was also destroyed. This continued until September 20, 1999, when the Australian-led peacekeeping troops of the International Force for East Timor (INTERFET) were deployed to the country. They subsequently brought an end to the violence. On May 20, 2002, East Timor was internationally recognized as an independent state. The World Factbook 2004, CIA. Online. Available HTTP: <http://www.cia.gov/cia/publications/factbook/geos/tt.html> (accessed November 10, 2004).

5. John Gershman, "Indonesia: Islands of Conflict," *Asia Times*, October 26, 2002.

6. There are slight variations to the causes of the conflict in Poso. It started in 1999 when then-regent Arif Patanga, a Muslim, proposed that one of his family members succeed him instead of a Christian. The custom in Poso over many years was for the regent to alternate between Christian and Muslim office-holders. There were also reports that corruption involving the Patanga family surfaced during his bid for a third term and triggered a conflict. Whatever the causes were, it later steered into a religious conflict. Since 2001, religious conflict has been officially blamed for the violence in Poso. See "Money and Military: A Coalition in the Poso Conflict," Laksama, November 11, 2005. Online. Available HTTP: <http://www.malra.org/posko/malra.php4?nr=40220> (accessed November 20, 2005).

7. Until recently, natural resources were owned and controlled by the central government, and access to resources and the distribution of benefits from their exploitation was determined by alliances within the ruling elites in Jakarta. Since 1999, local and regional governments have more control regulating access to and sharing of the benefits from natural resources. In many cases, however, local elites have simply displaced national elites as the beneficiaries, and basic inequalities have not been addressed. The decentralization of control over local resources has also raised the stakes of competition for local office.

8. "Communal Violence in Indonesia: Lessons from Kalimantan," *ICG Report*, No.19, June 27, 2001, p. iii.

9. John Gershman, "Indonesia: Islands of Conflict."

10. "SKB Rumah Ibadah," *Republika*, November 29, 2004. Online. Available HTTP: <http://republika.co.id/ASP/kolom_detail.asp?id=179560&kat_id=17> (accessed October 29, 2005).

11. DI was an anticolonial movement with religious overtones that still exists today, albeit in different forms. It aims to establish an Islamic state in Indonesia.

12. John McBeth, "Indonesia's Battle with Terrorism: Outlawing JI No Simple Matter," *The Straits Times*, October 24, 2005.

13. John Gershman, "Indonesia: Islands of Conflict."

14. Yang Razali Kassim, "Post-Tsunami GAM and the Future of Aceh," *The Straits Times*, February 12, 2005.

15. Lesley McCulloch, "Aceh: Then and Now," *Minority Rights Group International Report*, April 2005.

16. Kirsten E. Schulze, "The Free Aceh Movement (GAM): Anatomy of a Separatist Organization," *Policy Studies Issue 2*, East-West Center Washington, p. 37.

17. *Ibid*, p.38

18. Interview with Malik Mahmud, February 23, 2002, in *Ibid.*, p. 37.

19. Potengal Mukundan, the Director of the International Maritime Bureau, cited in John S. Burnett, "The Next 9/11 Could Happen at Sea," *The New York Times*, February 22, 2005.
20. Yang Razali Kassim, "Post-Tsunami GAM and the Future of Aceh."
21. "Aceh Rebels Sign Peace Agreement," BBC News, August 15, 2005. Online. <http://news.bbc.co.uk/go/pr/fr/-/1/hi/world/asia-pacific/4151980.stm> (accessed August 15, 2005).
22. "Aceh Rebels Sign Peace Agreement," *BBC News*, August 15, 2005. Online. Available HTTP: <http://news.bbc.co.uk/go/pr/fr/-/1/hi/world/asia-pacific/4151980.stm> (accessed August 15, 2005).
23. Tiarma Siboro and Muninggar Sri Saraswati, "Aceh Partition Could Derail Peace Accord, Warn GAM, Scholars," *The Jakarta Post,* December 9, 2005.
24. "Communal Violence in Indonesia: Lessons from Kalimantan," *ICG Report*, p. 14.
25. *Ibid.*, p. ii.
26. A detailed account can be found in Edi Peterbang and Eri Sutrisno, *Konflik Etnik di Sambas* (Jakarta: Institut Studi Arus Informasi, 2000).
27. "Indonesian Police Seize "JI Manual," *The Sydney Morning Herald,* February 15, 2005.
28. "Humanitarian Move for Bali Bomb Seven," *The Sydney Morning Herald*, August 2, 2004.
29. "Indonesia Backgrounder: How the Jemaah Islamiyah Terrorist Network Operates," *ICG Asia Report*, No. 43, December 11, 2002, p. 18.
30. The Dark Story Behind UNOCAL's Operations in East Kalimantan. Online. Available HTTP: <http://www.jatam.org/english/case/unocal/effect.html> (accessed August 1, 2005).
31. Since October 2000, Unocal assigned a full-time senior management official to work with the community to identify and resolve community concerns. A community council (Marangkayu Society Commitee) was formed to identify priority issues and approve plans for community assistance efforts to be financially supported by Unocal. However, According to JATAM, however, this "community council" was not at all a community initiative, but rather was proposed four days after the shootings during a meeting between Unocal representatives, the notoriously corrupt Indonesian parastatal oil and gas company; Pertamina, a senior official of the East Kalimantan House of Representatives; the East Kalimantan head of police; and a military commander.
32. Building Human Security in Indonesia, Humanitarian Policy and Conflict Research. Online. Available HTTP: <http://www.preventconflict.org/portal/main/maps_maluku_overview.php> (accessed November 2, 2005).
33. Gary Dean (June 2000), "Ethno-Religious Conflict in Maluku." Online. Available HTTP: <http://www.okusi.net/garydean/works/maluku.html> (accessed October 21, 2005).
34. Building Human Security in Indonesia.
35. Gary Dean, "Ethno-Religious Conflict in Maluku."
36. "Indonesia: The Violence in Ambon," *Human Rights Watch Report*, Vol. 11, No. 1, March 1999, p. 2.
37. Jamhari and Jajang Jahroni, *Gerakan Salafi Radikal di Indonesia* (Jakarta: PT Raja Grafindo Persada, 2004), p. 85.
38. "Weakening Indonesia's Mujahidin Networks: Lessons from Maluku and Poso," *ICG Asia Report*, No. 103, October 13, 2005, p. 1.
39. "The Jemaah Islamiyah Arrests and the Threat of Terrorism," Singapore Ministry of Home Affairs, White Paper, January 7, 2003, p. 6.
40. "Indonesia Backgrounder: How the Jemaah Islamiyah Terrorist Network Operates," *ICG Asia Report*, No. 43, December 11, 2002, p.5.

41. "Al Qaeda in Southeast Asia: The Case of the 'Ngruki Network' in Indonesia," *ICG Indonesia Briefing*, August 8, 2002, p. 2.
42. "The Jemaah Islamiyah Arrests and the Threat of Terrorism," Singapore Ministry of Home Affairs, p. 6.
43. Ibid.
44. "The Jemaah Islamiyah Arrests and the Threat of Terrorism," Singapore Ministry of Home Affairs, p. 6.
45. DI was created as a parallel government to the Republic of Indonesia. Thus, its members hold ministerial positions.
46. JI detainee debriefs both in Singapore and Indonesia. Also, see Sidney Jones, "Indonesia Backgrounder, Jihad in Central Sulawesi," ICG Asia Report, No. 74 Jakarta/Brussels, February 3, 2004, p. 2, where she authenticates the "Official Statement of al-Jamaah al-Islamiyah" (Pernyataan Resmi al-Jamaah al-Islamaah al-Islamiyah) of October 6, 2003, which cites the date of founding.
47. "Jemaah Islamiyah in South East Asia: Damaged but Still Dangerous," ICG Asia Report, No. 63, August 26, 2003, p. 2.
48. Pedoman Umum Perjuangan al-Jamaah al-Islamiyah (PUPJI).
49. "The Jemaah Islamiyah Arrests and the Threat of Terrorism," Singapore Ministry of Home Affairs, p. 6.
50. Ahmad Asi, Rohaiza, "JI Tapping Islamist Groups for Recruits," *The Straits Times*, July 8, 2005.
51. Michael Vincent, "Australian Terrorist Suspect Questioned in Indonesia," transcript taken from The World Today, ABC Local Radio, July 16, 2004. Online. Available HTTP: <http://www.abc.net.au/worldtoday/content/2004/s1155486.htm> (accessed October 19, 2005).
52. Derwin Pereira, "JI Cells 'Still as Deadly,'" *The Straits Times*, April 1, 2005.
53. "Divisions over Jakarta bombing 'could destroy JI,'" *The Straits Times,* September 13, 2004.
54. Ibid.
55. The suicide bomber who died in Paddy's club was known as Iqbal 2.
56. Agung Rulianto, A. Manan, Tjandra, and Rofiqi Hasan, "Another Bali Tragedy," *Tempo Interaktif,* No. 05/VI/Oct 04–10, 2005.
57. Wahdah Islamiyah's goal is to establish Islamic law first in Sulawesi and subsequently in other parts of Indonesia and to spread the true teachings of Islam. Laskar Jundullah is the security arm of the Preparatory Committee for the Implementation of Syariah Islam (KPPSI). KPPSI's objectives are the attainment of special autonomy status in South Sulawesi, similar to that granted to Aceh, and the implementation of Islamic law in South Sulawesi provinces.
58. "Indonesia Backgrounder: Why Salafism and Terrorism Mostly Don't Mix," *ICG Asia Report,* No. 83, September 13, 2004, p. i.
59. Matthew Moore, "Rising Ranks of JI Killers Uncovered," *The Sydney Morning Herald,* August 27, 2003. Online. Available HTTP: <http://www.smh.com.au/articles/2003/08/26/1061663795866.html?oneclick=true> (accessed June 12, 2005).
60. Arabinda Acharya, "The Second Bush Presidency: Priorities and Issues for Asia," UNISCI Discussion Papers, January 2005. Online. Available HTTP: <http://www.ucm.es/info/unisci/Arabinda.pdf>.
61. "Weakening Indonesia's Mujahidin Networks: Lessons from Maluku and Poso," *ICG Asia Report,* p. 19.
62. "Three Christian Schoolgirls Beheaded in C. Sulawesi," *The Jakarta Post*, October 30, 2005.

Kashmir

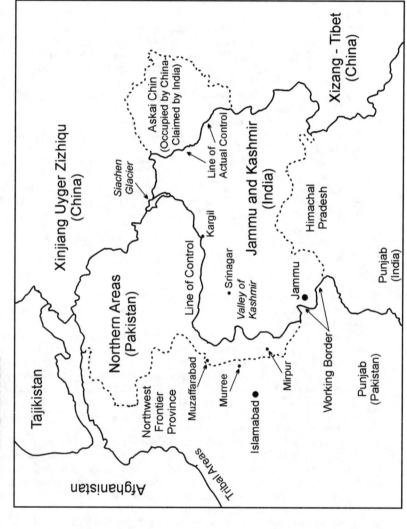

9

KASHMIR

Samina Raja[1]

INTRODUCTION

Nestled in the Himalayan mountain range in South Asia, the region of Kashmir remains a contested territory. Home to multiple ethno-linguistic and religious groups, the region has been the site of a struggle for autonomy that is rooted in a set of complex issues related to failed post-colonial efforts at nation building, inadequate and corrupt political processes, poor development strategies, and burgeoning ethnic claims. A princely state until 1947, nearly 45 percent of Kashmir's area is currently administered by India and 35 percent by Pakistan; about 18 percent of the state's largely uninhabited area is currently controlled by China. India-administered Kashmir, formally known as the "State of Jammu and Kashmir," comprises three districts: the Valley of Kashmir, the southern plains of Jammu, and the mountainous region of Ladakh to the North. The Pakistan-administered Kashmir comprises "Azad (free) Jammu, Kashmir (AJK)", and the Northern territories.[2]

In the most recent two decades, India-administered Jammu and Kashmir—henceforth referred to as IAJK—has become a flashpoint for violence by insurgent groups clashing with and provoking responses from the armed forces of the government of India. The violence has left thousands dead. The nuclear-muscle flexing by India and Pakistan, combined with the growing influence of violent political Islamist ideology among separatist groups in Kashmir, makes this conflict central to international peacemaking discussions.[3] This chapter argues that failed

179

development processes and outcomes within India-administered Kashmir are steering the trajectory of the Kashmir conflict toward greater intractability. It examines the intertwining trajectories of development and conflict in IAJK over the last five decades, and offers insight into how failed development efforts promote an identity of resistance and push conflicts toward intractability.

NATURE OF THE FLASHPOINT

Scholars define a conflict as "a struggle, between individuals or collectivities, over values or claims to status, power, and scarce resources in which the aims of the conflicting parties are to assert their values or claims over those of others."[4] Conflicts are not a problem per se, since their existence can positively contribute to maintaining or changing social systems, but when accompanied by destructive behavior (such as physical violence) they can deprive individuals of their freedoms and drastically reduce their quality of life. The emergence of the Kashmir conflict, for instance, reflects the aspirations of a significant portion of the Kashmiri population to change their political system in the hope of promoting khudmukhtari or self-rule.[5] The emergence and escalation of violence in recent decades has turned Kashmir into a flashpoint where the population has paid dearly with loss of life and property.

Flashpoints are sites of complex conflicts that threaten to escalate into increasing violence or war. Kashmir is increasingly recognized as a flashpoint in the media, policy, and academic world.[6] Hoyt identifies three key features that classify Kashmir as a flashpoint: The region is the site of a long-standing political conflict, the conflicting parties are in relative physical proximity, and the conflict involves, or threatens to involve, international actors. Concerted efforts to increase nuclear capacity since the 1970s that accelerated into nuclear muscle flexing in the 1990s by India and Pakistan also establishes Kashmir as a "nuclear flashpoint."[7] As such, the failure to diffuse the Kashmir flashpoint carries serious ramifications for the subcontinent as well as the international community.[8]

What pushes conflicts along a trajectory such that they become more resistant to resolution and ultimately transform a place into a flashpoint? Conflicts exist along a continuum, some more resistant to resolution than others. Caton Campbell identifies several traits that push conflicts along this continuum toward intractability,[9] which is likely to increase as conflicts get protracted, although the passage of time is not necessarily a causal factor.[10] In fact, in some protracted conflicts that involve violence, such as Northern Ireland or Kashmir, conflict-weary populations may eventually push for a change in the status quo and pro-vide a basis for resolution or at least diffusion of a flashpoint.[11] Conflicts based on differences in fundamental values, beliefs, rights, and world-views are more resistant to resolution, or at least display greater degrees of intractability, particularly when individuals or groups adhere to their beliefs and value systems with rigidity. If the benefits and the risks (perceived or otherwise) to the parties are high, the degree of intrac-tability tends to be likewise higher. Most important, conflicts that are embedded within a context of power imbalances—where individuals or groups may perceive a threat to their core identity—tend to move toward intractability.[12] Therefore, processes that accentuate power imbalances in a conflict, increase the stakes for the parties involved, and threaten their core identity is likely to more readily push a conflict toward intractability. The development processes since 1947 have con-tributed to the Kashmir conflict in exactly this manner.

Development and Conflict

Some scholars critique development as an exercise in disempowerment that creates the very idea of the "underdeveloped."[13] Amartya Sen offers a more hopeful and pragmatic view.[14] Development, he argues, should be concerned with the expansion of human freedoms and capabilities of all kinds that enable individuals to lead a life that they have rea-son to value. This notion of "development as freedom" emphasizes the reduction or removal of "unfreedoms," including premature mortality, disease, hunger, and lack of political and civil liberty rather than focus on the achievement of narrowly defined (and much critiqued) indica-tors such as gross domestic product or per-capita income.[15] To achieve these rather ambitious freedom goals, development practice requires adequate public investments as well as efficient public processes and institutions that empower people to articulate and pursue the kind of life they value.

Framing "development as freedom" is particularly relevant for regions experiencing conflict. In such regions, it is not only the lack of access to resources per se, although those may be limited as well, but what individuals are able to do with their resources within the conflict environment is what determines their true quality of life. For example, even if there are an adequate number of schools in a conflict area, the freedom to obtain an education is mediated by the potentially fatal risk that children face while traveling from their homes to their schools. Kashmir provides numerous examples of this quandary. On May 12, 2005, several children boarding their school bus at the end of a day died as a result of a grenade blast, apparently intended for an Indian army vehicle driving by the school.[16] In conflict regions, therefore, the freedom to education requires that one must go beyond measuring the number of schools (or teachers) as an indicator of development. It must also be determined whether the education infrastructure is supplemented with adequate provisions to ensure that children travel to and attend schools in safety.

Like Sen, I argue that in conflict regions it is important to redefine development broadly in terms of the enhancement of human freedoms and capabilities as well as understand how the ongoing conflict mediates the relationship between the means (resources such as the access to public education infrastructure) and the ends (such as the freedom to receive an education) of development.[17] It is helpful to examine two specific aspects of development vis-à-vis their influence on the trajectory of conflict in Kashmir. First, the adequacy of public investments and resources in Kashmir and second, the adequacy of political processes as a means of regulating and safeguarding public and private investments and resources such that they serve to equitably enhance people's freedoms and capabilities. Before outlining the influence of development on pushing the Kashmir conflict toward intractability, it is important to trace the emergence of the conflict and explore how its nature has changed over the past six decades, focusing on how failures in development, through inadequate public investments and failed political processes, have contributed to steering the conflict toward intractability.

HISTORICAL CONTEXT

Conflicts in the contemporary world rarely have a clear beginning; the same is true with Kashmir. Some scholars point to 1988, when a bomb blast rocked the capital city of Srinagar, as the start of the Kashmir conflict. The 1988 blast, however, was an echo from decades of repression, dating back to autocratic regimes well before the departure of Great Britain from India in 1947. In concert with those regimes, the hastily designed policies for post-colonial transfer of powers in 1947 by Great Britain to the newly independent states of India and Pakistan became a trigger for the emergence of a conflict in Kashmir.

Prior to 1947, Kashmir was a princely state ruled by a Maharaja whose family had been in power since the 1800s. The ruling family—belonging to the Dogra ethnic group from the Southern district of Jammu—was ethnically and linguistically different from a majority of the population in Kashmir. The ruling family was composed of Dogri-speaking

Hindus, while a majority of their subjects were Kashmiri-speaking Muslims. By most historic accounts, the Dogra Maharajas led a repressive regime, characterized by economic hardship, severe political repression, and a lack of public infrastructure.[18] The conditions for the Kashmiri-speaking Muslims, in particular, were markedly worse than their non-Kashmiri-speaking counterparts in the rest of the state. Discriminatory practices restricted opportunities to gain employment in the civil service or military, and public organizing and freedom of the press were severely restricted.[19]

On July 13, 1931, Dogra Maharaja Hari Singh's forces opened fire on unarmed civilians during a public protest over hikes in electricity fees, killing 21. Bose marks this as a turning point in the history of Kashmir's political mobilization.[20] Subsequent mass-organizing campaigns in the late 1930s and early 1940s spearheaded by Sheikh Abdullah, an articulate young Kashmiri from the Valley, fueled aspirations for better government, self-rule, and the overthrow of autocratic repression in the entire state. The lineage of a few present-day insurgent groups in Kashmir is traceable back to the days of resistance to the repressive Dogra regime.[21] This continuity is often overlooked or ignored.

In any event, in 1932 Abdullah and his fellow activists formed a political organization called the All-Jammu and Kashmir Muslim Conference, which in response to the left-leaning and secular tendencies among its leaders including Abdullah, morphed into the All-Jammu Kashmir National Conference (NC) in 1938. A more religious faction of the original party regrouped as the Muslim Conference in 1941. In the time leading up to independence in India, representatives of NC continued to organize popular and political resistance against the Maharaja's regime in Kashmir. Two events merit particular attention. In 1942, the party published the "Naya Kashmir" manifesto, which presented a progressive political and economic vision for Kashmir's future, and called for reducing the Maharaja to a titular head of state. This was followed by the more aggressive "Quit Kashmir" movement launched in 1944—similar to the 1942 "Quit India" movement against the British in India—asserting the Kashmiri right to self-rule and the overthrow of the Maharaja. Leaders of the All-Jammu Kashmir National Conference, particularly Abdullah, played a significant political role in negotiating and steering the tumultuous relationship of Kashmir and Kashmiris with the Indian Union in the post-1947 era.

Before their departure, the British fully controlled nine provinces within the Indian subcontinent and were responsible for the defense and foreign relations of nearly 600 relatively autonomous princely states. To implement the transfer of powers in accordance with the

Indian Independence Act, Britain appointed an independent commission[22] to determine the distribution of land from the nine provinces between India and Pakistan, ostensibly according to the religious affiliation of people living in those territories. Pakistan was to receive the Muslim-majority areas, while India was to receive the Hindu-majority areas.[23] The fate of the autonomous princely states, however, was not spelled out. According to the Indian Independence Act, all powers previously resting with the British crown returned to the independent princely states. However, scholars agree that Lord Mountbatten, the British Viceroy at the time, encouraged the states to accede to one of the two nations, possibly for the pragmatic reason that the small princely states stood little chance at independence in the face of the new nations of India and Pakistan.[24]

The territory of the undivided region of Kashmir (222,236 sq. km) was the largest among these princely states, covering an area slightly smaller than that of the United Kingdom (241,590 sq. km). Unlike the vast majority (approximately 99 percent) of the subcontinent's princely state rulers, who acceded to India or Pakistan within days of the partition, Maharaja Hari Singh did not immediately accede to either of the two nations, possibly holding out for an arrangement that would best guarantee retention of his princely powers. Indeed, imagining an autonomous state was not unreasonable, given the large size of the state. Hari Singh's indecisiveness was also possibly prolonged because of the dilemma that, although he was a Hindu, a majority of the people in his state were Muslim. In any event, on August 15, 1947, the Maharaja signed with the government of Pakistan a "standstill agreement," which, among other agreements, delegated responsibility to Pakistan of administering Kashmir's postal system and supplying essential commodities.

In the meantime, trouble was fomenting within the state. Along the border with Pakistan, Muslim rebels led a popular uprising against the Maharaja's rule and gained control of large sections of the district of Poonch in the Jammu area. On October 13, 1947, rebel leaders from Poonch declared the area—which made news as the site of the 2005 South Asian earthquake—as "Azad (Free) Jammu and Kashmir." Simultaneously, communal violence in the wake of the partition spread along the borders of Kashmir. Historic records of the letters between representatives of India, Pakistan, and the Maharaja reveal a fascinating account of the Maharaja's despair at the deteriorating conditions in Kashmir, Pakistan's rejection of its involvement in the looting and rioting along the borders, and India's firm belief that the violence was being incited at the behest of Pakistani government.[25] Bose also points out that these letters could just as well describe the conditions in the state today, six decades later.[26]

A final blow to the standstill agreement between the Maharaja and the Government of Pakistan came in the wake of a massive tribal incursion on October 21, 1947. The invaders, who came from the northern tribal areas, drove out the Maharaja's forces in several towns along the Baramulla-Srinagar Highway, reaching within a short distance of the state's summer capital, Srinagar. Although there are some dissenting opinions, scholars generally agree that the tribal incursion was successful in part due to logistical support provided by the newly formed Pakistani military. However, widespread looting and mayhem by the tribals prevented the incursion from receiving popular local support. Daunted by the prospect of losing Srinagar to the tribals, Maharaja Hari Singh turned to the government of India on October 24, 1947, for emergency military assistance. India agreed to intervene on the condition that the Maharaja sign an Instrument of Accession with the government of India. He signed it on October 26, 1947, delegating certain powers— foreign and military affairs, among others—to India.

The Instrument of Accession was accepted and ratified by General Mountbatten on October 27, 1947, followed by Indian troops landing in Srinagar, fighting the invaders, and with the aid of significant local support, eventually retrieving a significant portion of the state's territory. Fighting continued until a UN-brokered cease-fire line was finally established in January 1949. The cease-fire line was subsequently renamed the Line of Control (LOC) in 1972, after the end of yet another war between India and Pakistan in 1971, during which India gained additional territory. The LOC, which divides the erstwhile princely state of Jammu and Kashmir, and serves as the de facto border between India and Pakistan, has remained relatively unchanged over the ensuing years.[27]

As political alliances between the Maharaja and the state leaders of the newly independent India and Pakistan were shaping and shifting between August and October of 1947, what became of the popular National Conference party? Under Abdullah's leadership, NC led the "Quit Kashmir" protests to overthrow the Maharaja's regime in the summer of 1946.[28] Following the aggressive "Quit Kashmir" protests, in the summer of 1946 the Maharaja arrested Abdullah, who was eventually released in September of 1947, possibly in response to growing unrest in the state. In a turn of events, after acceding to India, Hari Singh appointed Abdullah as the head of an interim administration. Intermittently clamoring for self-rule, Abdullah governed the state from 1948 until 1953, when he was dismissed from office and put under arrest by Karan Singh, the heir apparent to the deceased Hari Singh, ostensibly at the behest of the Government of India. Subsequently, Abdullah was in and out of jail for nearly 20 years; he was finally released by the government in 1972 after he agreed to forsake his demand for self-rule in Kashmir.[29] Following his release, he ran for and was elected to the post of Chief Minister in 1975, which he held until his death in 1982.

Abdullah's contribution to the political psyche of Kashmir was profound. His early days as a feisty supporter of self-rule gained him immense popularity among Kashmiris. Bose suggests that most Kashmiris would be unlikely to accept his dropping the demands for self-rule in the 1970s had they come from anyone but Abdullah.[30] His complex political dance of alternately aligning with and resisting the government of India over the decades fostered a legacy of uncertainty in the psyche of an entire generation of Kashmiris vis-à-vis their subnational identity and relationship with the Indian Union.

As the fighting on the ground continued following the signing of the Instrument of Accession, the government of India complained to the UN Security Council about Pakistani interference in Kashmir, hoping to gain the Security Council's support against Pakistan. The Security Council appointed the UN Commission on India and Pakistan (UNCIP), which passed several resolutions recommending, among other things, that a plebiscite be held to determine the will of the Kashmiri people. However, such a plebiscite was never implemented. While some point to the UNCIP resolution as a basis of legitimacy for the pro-Pakistani and pro-independence positions,[31] others point to the Instrument of Accession as the basis for why Kashmir is an integral part of India. Decades of autocratic repression, the simplistic two-nation theory imposed in the wake of Great Britain's departure, the modern nation-building aspirations of Pakistan and India, and the failure of international organizations such as the UN to successfully resolve the Kashmir conflict laid the groundwork for what has become one of the longest-standing unresolved conflicts. The United Nations has maintained an observer group in Kashmir since 1949.

Development Failures and Conflict

In the decades following the de facto alignment with the Indian union, how India-administered Kashmir fared is a crucial question, because its answer sheds light on why the Kashmir conflict has become increasingly intractable and the positions of various stakeholders further entrenched.

Some argue that Kashmir enjoys a special status within the union of India and receives resources disproportionate to the rest of the country.

Hence, its claims of a disenfranchised region within the Indian Union are less than credible. However, this overlooks two issues. First, the very complex relationship between India and Kashmir lends considerable support to the argument that Kashmir's relationship is indeed different from that of other states and therefore it deserves "unique" institutional and political arrangements within the Indian Union. Second, the fiscal aid from the central government in IAJK is simply insufficient when compared to the needs of the region. For example, a public rupee spent in Kashmir does not guarantee elementary education to a child as it would in another state. Development policies in Kashmir, particularly fiscal decisions of the central government, must re-focus on development outcomes (e.g., level of education), and not just the inputs to development (e.g., public rupees spent on education). Otherwise, as described below, Kashmir will continue to lag behind the Indian Union in development terms despite possessing abundant natural resources.

Perhaps the most worrying outcome of failed development is the low access to education in the region. Slightly over half (54 percent) of the population is literate (Census of India 2001). Access to higher levels of education is also difficult due to a limited number of openings in the few publicly funded colleges and universities serving more than 10 million residents of the state, of whom nearly 60 percent are less than 24 years old.[32] Access to good quality and higher education is particularly limited for lower-income students who must compete for the few openings in the face of backdoor admissions brokered by politicians and the wealthy. Those who are fortunate to have been admitted have faced their own challenges in the last two decades. As mentioned previously, students, like many civilians, are caught in insurgent-Indian armed forces violence. Schools and colleges are also frequently closed. Curfews imposed by the government, particularly in the early 1990s, and calls for "civil curfews" by the insurgent groups, often on different days, delayed graduation times of several youth cohorts. A lack of educational opportunities undermines Kashmiris' ability to share in economic progress like the rest of the country.

Physical infrastructure, such as electricity, is essential for the development of regions. In the Indian Union, electricity is regulated, managed and sold by the government. In Kashmir, despite tremendous potential for hydropower (which requires extensive capital investments), inadequate electricity-generation capacity and misappropriation of the existing electricity supply is commonplace. Kashmir is subject to extensive "load-shedding" regimes, during which electricity is turned off in neighborhoods three times a week for 12 hours a day despite the demands of harsh winters.[33] Consequently, the per-capita electricity consumption in the state is a mere 223 kWh, an astounding 40 percent less than the per-capita consumption of electricity in India.[34] The lower electricity consumption could be attributed to the lack of electric wiring and fixtures in the houses, a situation not entirely uncommon in developing countries. However, the vast majority (80 percent) of houses in Kashmir are fitted for electricity (as compared to only 55 percent of houses in the Indian Union). Therefore, the lower per-capita consumption of electricity in IAJK is a direct result of disinvestment by the government.

Not surprisingly, the lack of consistent and adequate electric supply seriously hampers the region's industrial and economic development, which has stagnated over the past two decades.[35] As of 2001, the number of industrial units per 100,000 persons in IAJK was one, compared to 13 per 100,000 persons in the Indian Union.[36] Low budgetary allocations from India's central government for industrial development during the 1950s and 1960s did little to spur industrial development in the state.[37]

Employment opportunities within a stagnating economy are limited as well. The 2001 census of India reported a mere 37 percent of the total Kashmiri population as "workers"; this figure is 2 percentage points lower than that for the rest of the Indian Union (Census of India 2001). Distribution of income among the population is inequitable as well; a small percentage of households controls a majority of the wealth in the region, despite the wide distribution of land. An entire day's wages of an unskilled worker in Kashmir in November 2005 was 100.00 Rupees (Rs) (approximately US$2.50)—an amount insufficient to buy a single full meal at an eating establishment in the region.[38] According to the Plan Commission of India, in the 1990s, the average per-capita annual income earned in the state was Rs 11,591 (approx. US$289.77). As of 2001, over a quarter of the Kashmiri population lived below the poverty line, earning less than Rs 300 (approximately US$7.50) per month (Plan Commission). With increasing disparity in the quality of life among people, a sense of disenfranchisement among the poor is not beyond reason.

The Valley's ground transportation infrastructure is dismal. After nearly a half-century of being part of the Indian Union, the state ranks at the bottom in terms of road mileage per area.[39] The public-run railway system barely exists in the state, as railway lines from India extend only to the city of Jammu located in the Southern Jammu district. In the 1990s, rail lines were extended a few miles north of Jammu to the town of Udhampur, but the remainder of the state still relies heavily on the scanty roads. This lack of infrastructure inhibits a flow of goods and people to any degree of efficiency. In effect, this inadequate ground transportation disconnects the state and its people, physically and perceptually, from the Indian Union.

Local lore has it that every family in Kashmir owns a house. Whether or not this rosy picture is true, available data suggest that the quality of housing in Kashmir, most of which is privately built and owned, is certainly better than the rest of the country; 55 percent of the houses in Kashmir are permanent structures compared to 51 percent of the houses in India. Despite this, the region lags behind the country in terms of publicly provided amenities related to housing, such as adequate water supply within the premises of the house (as opposed to community wells). Compared to 39 percent of houses in the Indian Union, only 31 percent of houses in Kashmir had access to water on their own premises.[40]

A rare, positive traditional indicator of development is in the Valley's land-tenure arrangement. The average landholding in the state is 0.73 hectares, which is the second smallest landholding size in the Indian Union, after Kerala.[41] Smaller landholding size suggests that, contrary to the rest of the country, land is not as consolidated among a few rich, feudalistic rent-seeking landholders. This is particularly important because the economy rests on the agriculture sector, which constitutes 60 percent of the state's gross income.[42] This equitable distribution of land, however, is a result not of reforms advanced by the central government of India, but of the implementation of the Naya Kashmir manifesto when NC (under Abdullah) ran the state in the 1950s.[43]

Public disinvestment is not the only failure of development in Kashmir. Indeed, if this were the only reason for disenfranchisement, perhaps other poor regions in India would be witnessing similar insurgent movements. The lack of political freedoms in post-1947 Kashmir compounds the failures of public disinvestments in the state and contributes to making the conflict intractable.[44] Since 1947, political freedom in Kashmir has existed largely in name only. After NC's ascension to power in IAJK in 1947, there were several elections for State Legislature Assembly and for the Indian parliament. However, most public officials in Kashmir after 1947 rose to power with a significant backing from New Delhi evident through rigged elections or the outright dismissal and replacement of appointments to governments.[45] Voting happens under significant threat from the Indian armed forces (to participate) and by the insurgent groups (to not participate). On the other hand, some scholars have suggested that the participation in these elections indicate a Kashmiri willingness to integrate with the Indian political system.[46] On balance, the post-1947 IAJK political regime, while loosely following the letter of the legal framework, is far from a fully practicing democracy. At the end of 2005, Freedom House rated Indian-controlled Kashmir as "partly free" compared to an overall "free" ranking for India.

Consequently, it is not surprising that the 1988 bomb blast mentioned at the beginning of this chapter came on the heels of the 1987 local elections, when a popular candidate from the Muslim United Front was "defeated" through vote rigging. A candidate from the National Conference—an organization that had turned fairly despotic since its heyday in the 1950s but was then in the good graces of the central government of India—was declared the "winner." The widespread disillusionment among other MUF candidates and their supporters triggered a violent uprising that has since held the Valley in a deathly grip. Since 1988, a multitude of insurgent organizations has rallied against Indian control. Roughly half of those seek an independent Kashmir (and most claim a secular ideology), while the remaining groups (most of which are interested in establishing an Islamic state) seek a union of Kashmir with Pakistan.[47]

Kashmiri civilians have paid dearly in the struggle between the insurgents and the Indian armed forces. The reports of civilian fatalities in the last two decades, the magnitude of which varies widely, are nonetheless quite high. From 1989 to 2005, estimates of civilians killed or injured ranged from several thousand to more than 90,000.[48] Under significant threat to their lives and property, any participation of Kashmiri civilians in political processes is highly constrained and extremely limited. Not surprisingly, the opportunities to make any economic- or development-related claims within a fair political process are nonexistent in Kashmir.

If the purpose of development is to enhance individuals' ability to lead a life that they have reason to value, neither the modern nation-building efforts in the wake of British departure nor the failed development processes in IAJK provided this opportunity. Instead, development failures in Kashmir have worsened its already uneasy relationship with the Union of India. These conditions have kindled ethno-nationalistic aspirations and pushed the Kashmir conflict toward intractability.

ETHNIC RESISTANCE AND CONFLICT

Scholars point to real or perceived threats to ethnic identity as factors that push conflicts toward intractability.[49] For centuries, Kashmiris have been unified by Kashmiriyat—a distinct culture embodied in a distinct language, dress, food, architecture, and Sufi spiritual tradition.[50] Kashmiriyat has reemerged, with force, as an identity of resistance in the face of persistent development "unfreedoms."[51] In particular, the systematic lack of employment opportunities for educated urban Kashmiri-speaking youth (most, but not all, of whom were Muslims) in recent decades has created a wider base of support for insurgency in the Valley. Unfair admissions to a limited number of colleges and universities within the state also cause immense frustration among the Valley's college-eligible, particularly because education is widely perceived to be the only way to improve one's lot in life. Not surprisingly, disillusioned student-recruits among insurgent groups carried out the earliest known militant actions in the Valley. An overall perception of inequitable public investments and dysfunctional public processes have contributed to a sense of alienation and fueled Kashmiriyat as an identity of resistance.

This is particularly so among the thousands of displaced Kashmiris who remain in insular refugee camps.[52] Many Muslim refugees displaced from IAJK in the aftermath of partition continue to live in camps on the other side of the Line of Control, imagining a "reunification" of Kashmir. More recently, displaced populations of mostly Kashmiri-speaking Hindus (who left the Valley due to the threat of insurgent violence) live in refugee camps in the Jammu district and in other states of the Indian Union still see Kashmir as their homeland, while preferring a political alliance with India.[53]

Although the calls for Kashmiriyat stem largely from the Kashmiri speakers from the Valley, it is important to note that idea of Kashmiriyat is not universally accepted.[54] Madan, for example, rejects the idea of a Kashmiri ethnicity, arguing that Kashmiris lack "a key symbol of collective identity other than religion to mobilize support across the religious boundary."[55] He offers the lack of a written script within the Kashmiri language as an evidence of this vacuum.[56] However, oral traditions are as much a symbol of collective ethnic identity as a written language.

Further complicating the question of Kashmiriyat is the fact that the state is also home to a number of other subethnic groups (of various religious affiliations). The population of Jammu comprises mostly Dogri-speaking Hindus and a smaller percentage of Dogri- and Pahari-speaking Muslims. Ladakh, which is the least populous district of the state, is inhabited by Ladakhi speakers, most of whom are Buddhists, although some are Shiite Muslims.[57] In other words, linguistic traits interlock with religious affiliation and ethnic identity in a complex tangle in Kashmir's geography.

Recently, ethno-nationalistic claims by insurgents for an independent state have been imbued with calls for an Islamic state, particularly among groups seeking Kashmir's accession with Pakistan. However, the insurgent groups operating in Kashmir are diverse, with various religious ideologies and distinct political aspirations.[58] A number of groups seek independence from both India and Pakistan, including the Jammu and Kashmir Liberation Front (JKLF), which claims a secular ideology and whose leaders have publicly renounced violence. Two umbrella organizations of separatist groups, the All Parties Hurriyat Conference (APHC) and the Muttahida Jihad Council, seek independence from India and Pakistan.[59]

On the other hand, the Hizbul Mujahideen, Al-Faran, Harkat-Ul-Ansar, and Jayash-e-Muhammad seek the creation of an Islamic State through accession to Pakistan. The Pakistan-based Lashkar-e-Toiba (LeT), which also supports these dual goals is also active in Kashmir and is reportedly responsible for a majority of militant actions in the Valley. The activity of the various insurgent groups in the last decade has varied, in part due to the shifting level of support received from across the Line of Control in Pakistan. Irm Haleem suggests that many of these insurgent groups, including HM and LeT, have been infiltrated by fighters from outside of Kashmir (including Afghani fighters as well as members of al Qaeda's network) who bolster the ranks of and receive support from local groups.[60] Scholars argue that although the call for pan-Islamization among some insurgent groups reflects the efforts by fundamentalists to establish a vast Islamic Caliphate with Kashmir as an integral part, several secular insurgent groups and the civilian population of Kashmir soundly reject this trend.[61] This resistance is not surprising given the plurality of practices within and among religions in Kashmir as well as the moderating influence of the age-old, mystic Sufi tradition common to the region.

LINKAGES TO THE GLOBAL WAR ON TERRORISM

India has consistently framed Kashmir as a bilateral issue, while Pakistan has been more interested in international mediation on the Kashmir issue. This is not surprising given that the status quo in Kashmir rests largely in favor of India. So far, the United States has remained relatively quiet on the issue, as it juggles its allegiance with Pakistan (from Cold War days and more recently during the war on terror) against the emerging economic ties with India. However, the United States cannot afford to remain a passive observer for two reasons: the possession of nuclear weapons by India and Pakistan have exponentially increased the risks associated with the Kashmir conflict; second, the insurgency has the potential of attracting foreign fighters who could recast the conflict as part of a global extremist agenda.[62] As the site of an increasingly intractable conflict, accompanied by a nuclear threat, Kashmir should be on the top of the U.S. and international agenda.

Although a political solution is ultimately necessary to settle the Kashmir conflict (the terms of which are beyond the scope of this chapter), such a solution is impossible without reducing the intractability of the conflict through extensive and meaningful confidence-building measures. What is the role of U.S. foreign policy, if any, in facilitating such measures? In his book, *Kashmir: Roots of Conflict, Paths to Peace*, Sumantra Bose makes recommendations for promoting peace that offer a useful starting point for U.S. foreign policy. He writes, "Low-key, indirect, and discreet facilitation by credible third parties—which is not styled as intrusive mediation—may yet be both necessary and efficacious. ..."[63] While it is unlikely that the United States, or any other country, can steer the Kashmir conflict toward resolution single-handedly or in a belligerent manner, the United States can certainly play a more strategic and considered role than its current non-stance on Kashmir.

Perhaps the single most urgent shift in U.S. foreign policy vis-à-vis Kashmir has to do with recognizing the Kashmiris as stakeholders of comparable standing to the national governments of India and Pakistan. Kashmiris have little or no say regarding their future, which is an extremely significant factor in their disillusionment with India and to a lesser degree with Pakistan. This marginalization of Kashmiris repeatedly has made the Kashmir conflict intractable. Any efforts to find a solution or reduce intractability will ultimately require a commitment from the Kashmiris themselves.

Diffusing protracted strife requires policies that unwedge conflicts—or shift the conflicting parties from their entrenched positions—and do so patiently. Bose proposes that the role of a mediator in Kashmir "would probably be most effectively played by an informally constituted consortium of influential countries, possibly in collaboration with multilateral organizations, which does not preclude any one country or countries ... playing a more substantial role behind the scenes."[64] A consortium of (disinterested and influential) countries is likely to have better successes in reducing the conflict because such a consortium will have considerably more leverage than a single country, even the United States, in unwedging the conflict to any degree.

An international consortium can also facilitate much needed confidence-building measures between IAJK and India, and across the Line of Control. Such a consortium can also serve as a watchdog group on pledges frequently made (generally in the popular media and accompanied by much fanfare) by leaders of both India and Pakistan. Given recent conciliatory gestures by Pakistan's President Musharraf and India's Prime Minister Manmohan Singh, including the opening of a new railway service between India and Pakistan, this might be an opportune time for such a consortium to be initiated.

As John Overton writes, development must not avoid or follow conflict but engage with conflict. The chronic lack of development—inadequate infrastructure, poor employment opportunities, and corrupt government—has fomented an alienation among Kashmiris that has contributed to developing an identity of resistance against India.[65] It is not only a moral imperative but also a judicious one that the state and central governments respond by promoting accountability and transparency in public institutions. They should also rethink public-investment strategies to focus on the removal of development "unfreedoms" from the lives of ordinary Kashmiris. The United States could consider directing development resources to support such investments. Given the past allegations of corruption within the state and central governments, it may be prudent for the United States to seek partners among the local Kashmiri nonprofits as well.

It is imperative to safeguard public expression and discourse without the threat of retribution from national armed forces and various insurgent groups in Kashmir. In Kashmir, public expression and discourse will be limited unless there is significant international pressure on the Indian and Pakistani governments and on insurgent groups to reduce human rights violations and ultimately honor a cease-fire. As long as civilians live under the threat of violence, any question of a public discourse or expression is nonexistent. An international consortium of countries, including the United States, can lean on the national government of India to prevent civilian casualties and on the Pakistan government to reign in support for those insurgent groups who espouse violence toward civilians. Locally, the international consortium can support emerging civil society groups that look beyond the entrenched positions on Kashmir that are held by many in the subcontinent. The Coalition of Civil Society, which includes people from IAJK and India, appears to be a particularly promising group to watch. The coalition recently facilitated a public event where an insurgent leader, representatives of the state government, and young Kashmiri civilians had a chance to talk and listen to the others' vision for Kashmir—a rare event in the troubled region.

U.S. intervention to diffuse conflicts must be based on an understanding of the complexity of the internal fabric of the society where it chooses to intervene. In a multilayered flashpoint such as Kashmir, it is crucial to recognize and involve multiple stakeholders while steering a conflict away from intractability. In Kashmir, these stakeholders include the national governments of India, Pakistan, and the residents of various ethnicities and religious affiliations living in IAJK and PAK.[66] Any plans or policies to diffuse the flashpoint must consider the intricacies of population subgroups, their loyalties, affiliations, and aspirations. Failure to recognize and involve *all* stakeholders in the resolution process will force them to find other, perhaps violent, avenues for expressing dissent; in fact, such failures are likely to sow the seeds of new and lasting civil conflicts.

NOTES

1. I would like to acknowledge Jodi Bryon for her meticulous assistance in finding papers and rare documents on Kashmir.
2. A. S. Anand, "Accession of Jammu and Kashmir State—Historical & Legal Perspective," *Journal of the Indian Law Institute* 43, No. 4 (2001): 455-468; R. S. Saini, "Is the Right to Self-determination Relevant to Jammu & Kashmir," *Indian Journal of International Law: Official Organ of Indian Society of International Law* 38, No. 2 (1998): 157–181.
3. F. Khan, "Nuking Kashmir: Legal Implications of Nuclear Testing by Pakistan and India in the Context of the Kashmir Dispute," *Georgia Journal of International and Comparative Law* 29, no. 2 (2001): 361-394; A. Khan, "The Kashmir Dispute: A Plan for Regional Cooperation." *The Columbia Journal of Transnational Law* 31, (1994): 495-550.
4. J. Goodhand, and D. Hulme, "From wars to complex political emergencies: understanding conflict and peace-building in the new world disorder," *Third World Quarterly* 20, no. 1 (1999): 14.
5. See T. K. S. Group, *1947-1997, The Kashmir Dispute at Fifty: Charting Paths to Peace.* (New York: NY, The Kashmir Study Group, 1997), p. 72; D. Taylor, "The Kashmir Crisis," *Asian Affairs* 22, no. 3 (1991): 303-324.
6. Sumantra Bose. *Kashmir: Roots of Conflict, Paths to Peace* (Cambridge, MA: Harvard University Press, 2003); Sumantra Bose, "Kashmir: Sources of Conflict Dimensions of Peace," *Survival* 41, no. 3 (1999): 149-171; Sumantra Bose, "Kashmir, 1990-2000: Reflections on Individual Voices in a Dirty War." *Development* 43, no. 3 (2000): 99-102; Sumantra Bose, "Kashmir at the Crossroads: Problems and Possibilities," *Security Dialogue* 32, No. 1 (2001): 41–64; Timothy Hoyt, "Politics, Proximity, and Paranoia: The Evolution of Kashmir as a Nuclear Flashpoint," *India Review* (2003).
7. See Hoyt (2003) for a fuller discussion of the nuclear threat.
8. See L. Cliffe and R. Luckham, "Complex political emergencies and the state: failure and the fate of the state," *Third World Quarterly* 20, No. 1 (1999): 27–50.
9. M. Caton Campbell, "Intractability in Environmental Disputes: Exploring a Complex Construct," *Journal of Planning Literature*, 17, No. 3 (2003): 360–361.
10. L. Putnam, and J. M. Wondolleck, "Intractability: Definitions, Dimensions, and Distinctions," in *Making Sense of Intractable Environmental Conflicts.* R. Lewicki, B. Gray, and M. Elliot, eds., (Washington, DC: Island Press, 2002); M. Caton Campbell, "Intractability in Environmental Disputes: Exploring a Complex Construct." *Journal of Planning Literature* 17, No. 3 (2003): 360–361. L. Kriesberg, T. A. Northrup, et al. Intractable Conflicts and Their Transformation (Syracuse, NY: Syracuse University Press, 1989).
11. Sumantra Bose, *Kashmir: Roots of Conflict, Paths to Peace.* (Cambridge, MA: Harvard University Press, 2003).
12. M. Caton Campbell, "Intractability in Environmental Disputes: Exploring a Complex Construct." *Journal of Planning Literature*, 17, No. 3 (2003): 360–361.
13. A. Escobar, *Encountering Development: The Making and Unmaking of the Third World* (Princeton, NJ: Princeton University Press, 1995)
14. Amartya Sen, *Development as Freedom* (New York: Anchor Books, 1999).

15. Ibid.

16. BBC. "Grenade Blast Near Kashmir School," May 12, 2005. Online. Available HTTP: <news.bbc.co.uk/1/hi/world/south_asia/4541499.stm>.

17. See S. A. Bollens, "On Narrow Ground: Planning in Ethnically Polarized Cities," *Journal of Architectural and Planning Research* 13, No. 2 (1996): 120–138; S. A. Bollens, "Urban Planning and Intergroup Conflict: Confronting a Fractured Public Interest," *Journal of the American Planning Association*, 68, No. 1 (2002): 22–42.

18. Premnath Bazaz, *Inside Kashmir* (New Delhi, India: Kashmir Publishing Co, 1941); Tyndale Biscoe, *Kashmir in Sunlight and Shade* (London: Seeley Service Co., 1922).

19. Sumantra Bose, *Kashmir: Roots of Conflict, Paths to Peace* (Cambridge, MA: Harvard University Press, 2003).

20. Ibid.

21. J. G. Cockell, "Ethnic Nationalism and Subaltern Political Process: Exploring Autonomous Democratic Action in Kashmir," *Nations and Nationalism* 6, No. 3 (2000): 319–345.

22. The Radcliffe Commission was composed of representatives of India and Pakistan, and was headed by a British attorney. Prior to his appointment, the Commission Chair, Mr. Radcliffe, had neither traveled to the subcontinent nor had prior experience with its politico-legal affairs. His appointment was ostensibly based on his reputation for fairness and honesty.

23. B. Farrell, "The Role of International Law in the Kashmir Conflict," *Penn State International Law Review* 21, No. 2 (2002): 293–318; S. Ilahi, "The Radcliffe Boundary Commission and the Fate of Kashmir," *India Review* 2, No. 1 (2003): 77–102.

24. B. Farrell, "The Role of International Law in the Kashmir Conflict." *Penn State International Law Review* 21, No. 2 (2002): 293–318.

25. Sumantra Bose, *Kashmir: Roots of Conflict, Paths to Peace* (Cambridge, MA: Harvard University Press, 2003).

26. Ibid.

27. Ibid.

28. Oddly enough, Jawahar Lal Nehru, a top-ranking leader in the Quit India movement against Great Britain who became the eventual Prime Minister of independent India, was a supporter of NC, perhaps in a mutual show of solidarity in favor of the rule of the people. C.f. G. Rizvi "Nehru and the Indo-Pakistan rivalry over Kashmir (1947-64)," *Contemporary South Asia* 4, No. 1 (1995): 17–21.

29. Sumantra Bose, *Kashmir: Roots of Conflict, Paths to Peace* (Cambridge, MA: Harvard University Press, 2003).

30. Ibid.

31. Some scholars argue that the UNCIP Resolution does not hold any legal stature under international law and hence does not provide a legitimate basis for a plebiscite. See B. Farrell, "The Role of International Law in the Kashmir Conflict," *Penn State International Law Review* 21, No. 2 (2002): 293–318.

32. Higher education in public institutions is heavily subsidized; students pay a nominal fee, if any. See Planning Commission. *State Development Report: Jammu and Kashmir* (New Delhi: Planning Commission, Government of India, 2003).

33. Author field notes (November 2005).

34. Planning Commission, *State Development Report: Jammu and Kashmir* (New Delhi: Planning Commission, Government of India, 2003).

35. S. Prakash, "The political Economy of Kashmir Since 1947," *Contemporary South Asia* 9, No. 3 (2000): 315–337.

36. Planning Commission, *State Development Report: Jammu and Kashmir* (New Delhi: Planning Commission, Government of India, 2003).

37. S. Prakash, "The Political Economy of Kashmir Since 1947," *Contemporary South Asia*, 9, No. 3 (2000): 315–337.
38. Author field notes (November 2006)
39. Planning Commission, *State Development Report: Jammu and Kashmir* (New Delhi: Planning Commission, Government of India, 2003).
40. Ibid.
41. Ibid.
42. Ibid.
43. Sumantra Bose, *Kashmir: Roots of Conflict, Paths to Peace* (Cambridge, MA: Harvard University Press, 2003).
44. I. Hilton, "Letter from Kashmir: Between the mountains India and Pakistan are caught in a dangerous struggle over Kashmir. But what do its people want?" *The New Yorker* (2002): 64.
45. Sumantra Bose, *Kashmir: Roots of Conflict, Paths to Peace* (Cambridge, MA: Harvard University Press, 2003).
46. A. S. Anand, "Accession of Jammu and Kashmir State — Historical & Legal Perspective," *Journal of the Indian Law Institute*, 43, No. 4 (2001): 455–468.
47. Irm Haleem, "Micro Target, Macro Impact: The Resolution of the Kashmir Conflict as a Key to Shrinking Al-Qaeda's International Terrorist Network," *Journal of Terrorism and Political Violence* 16, No. 1 (Spring 2004): 18–47.
48. Kashmir Media Services. Online. Available HTTP: http://www.kmsnews.com; Memorial Institute for the Prevention of Terrorism (MIPT), Terrorism Database. Online. Available HTTP: <http://www.tkb.org/AnalyticalTools.jsp>; Amnesty International.
49. M. H. Ross, "Creating the Conditions for Peacemaking: Theories of Practice in Ethnic Conflict Resolution," *Ethnic and Racial Studies* 23, No. 6 (2000): 1002–1034; M. Caton Campbell, "Intractability in Environmental Disputes: Exploring a Complex Construct," *Journal of Planning Literature* 17, No. 3 (2003): 360–361; M. Ranganathan, "Potential of the Net to Construct and Convey Ethnic and National Identities: Comparison of the Use in the Sri Lankan Tamil and Kashmir Situations," *Asian Ethnicity* 4, No. 2 (2003): 266–279.
50. R. Punjabi, "Kashmir: Realizing the Dream of an Islamic Caliphate," *World Affairs* 4, No. 2 (2000): 58–73; R. Punjabi, "Kashmir Imbroglio: The Socio-Political Roots," *Contemporary South Asia* 4, No. 1 (1995): 39.
51. E. Desmond, "The Insurgency in Kashmir (1989–1991)," *Contemporary South Asia* 4, No. 1 (1995): 5–12; Amartya Sen, *Development as Freedom* (New York: Anchor Books, 1999).
52. P. Ellis and Zafar Khan, "Kashmiri Displacement and the Impact on Kashmiriyat," *Contemporary South Asia* 12, No. 4 (2003): 523–538.
53. Sumantra Bose, *Kashmir: Roots of Conflict, Paths to Peace* (Cambridge, MA: Harvard University Press, 2003).
54. B. Puri, "Kashmiriyat: The Vitality of Kashmiri Identity," *Contemporary South Asia* 4, No. 1 (1995): 55–64; P. Ellis and Zafar Khan, "Kashmiri Displacement and the Impact on Kashmiriyat," *Contemporary South Asia* 12, No. 4 (2003): 523–538.
55. T. N. Madan, "Coping with Ethnicity in South Asia: Bangladesh, Punjab, and Kashmir," *Ethnic and Racial Studies* 21, No. 5 (1998): 986.
56. Ibid.
57. Sumantra Bose, *Kashmir: Roots of Conflict, Paths to Peace* (Cambridge, MA: Harvard University Press, 2003).
58. Iffat Malik, *Kashmir: Ethnic Conflict, International Dispute* (Karachi, Pakistan: Oxford University Press, 2002).

59. Sumantra Bose, *Kashmir: Roots of Conflict, Paths to Peace* (Cambridge, MA: Harvard University Press, 2003); Irm Haleem, "Micro Target, Macro Impact: The Resolution of the Kashmir Conflict as a Key to Shrinking Al-Qaeda's International Terrorist Network," *Journal of Terrorism and Political Violence* 16, No. 1 (Spring 2004): 18–47.

60. See Irm Haleem 2004 for a discussion of the possible links between global fundamentalist groups and Kashmiri insurgent groups.

61. R. Punjabi, "Kashmir: Realizing the Dream of an Islamic Caliphate," *World Affairs* 4, No. 2 (2000): 58–73.

62. Irm Haleem, "Micro Target, Macro Impact: The Resolution of the Kashmir Conflict as a Key to Shrinking Al-Qaeda's International Terrorist Network," *Journal of Terrorism and Political Violence* 16, No. 1 (Spring 2004): 18–47.

63. Sumantra Bose, *Kashmir: Roots of Conflict, Paths to Peace* (Cambridge, MA: Harvard University Press, 2003), p. 220.

64. Sumantra Bose, *Kashmir: Roots of Conflict, Paths to Peace* (Cambridge, MA: Harvard University Press, 2003), p. 221.

65. John Overton, "Three worlds, Two Worlds, One World, or Many? Geographies of Global Inequalities," *Southeast Asia: A Multidisciplinary Journal* 2 (2000): 47–54.

66. H. B. Schaffer, "Reconsidering the U.S. Role," *The Washington Quarterly* 24, No. 2 (2001): 201–209; R. Ganguly, "India, Pakistan, and the Kashmir Insurgency: Causes, Dynamics, and Prospects for Resolution," *Asian Studies Review* 25, No. 3 (2001): 309–334; R. Kumar, "Untying the Kashmir Knot," *World Policy Journal* 19, No. 1 (2002): 11–24; B. Merck, "International Law and the Nuclear Threat in Kashmir: A Proposal for a U.S.-led Resolution to the Dispute Under UN Authority," *Georgia Journal of International and Comparative Law* 32 (2004): 167–197.

Philippines

10

PHILIPPINES

Toshi Yoshihara

NATURE OF THE FLASHPOINT

The Philippines occupies a unique regional position in the global war on terrorism. The Philippines is the only predominantly Catholic nation among the sizable states in Southeast Asia. This demographic reality combined with disparities in political power has historically pitted the dominant Christian majority against the disenfranchised Muslim minority. In addition, the sources of Manila's strategic outlook, including its colonial past under the Spanish and then, later, American rule coupled with a strong contemporary political and sociocultural identification with the United States, and a treaty-based alliance with Washington, make the Philippines a distinctly Western-oriented country in the region. Together these factors have sharpened the ideological and cultural divides between the largely secular Christian political center and the Muslim minority in pursuit of Islamist autonomy operating on the periphery.

The roots of the conflict far predate the radical Islamist movements that emerged in the 1990s. Mindanao, an epicenter of terrorism in the southern Philippines, has long suffered violence between the authorities and local resistance movements. Indeed, the struggle can be traced as far back to the Spanish colonial era. Geographic isolation and political grievances stem from long-enduring socioeconomic inequities, which were exacerbated by decades of government-sanctioned Christian migration to ancestral Muslim lands and Manila's cultural insensitivity, have ensured continuity in the vicious cycle of violence and repression. However, a significant discontinuity emerged as the anger over the persistence of inequity began to find expression in violent political Islam. Most worrisome, some factions of the separatist movement reject the entire notion of the nation-state and embrace visions of a pan-Islamic union over large swaths of Southeast Asia. As a result, radical ideology could potentially transform a simmering local problem into a dangerous transnational phenomenon.

The severity of the extremist menace and its ability to spread unpredictably across state borders in the region and beyond underscore a pressing analytical need to understand the nature of radical political Islam in Mindanao and the policies required to manage and reduce the terrorist threat created by this flashpoint.

HISTORICAL CONTEXT

Mindanao, the historical epicenter of Muslim insurrection, is the Philippines' second largest island positioned at the southern end of the archipelago. Among the 20 million inhabitants on the island, approximately 15 percent are Muslim.[1] Muslim populations are concentrated primarily in central and southwestern Mindanao. The ethnic conflict zone also encompasses the smaller Basilan and Sulu islands west of Mindanao, which are both predominantly Muslim. Mindanao's resource abundance once earned the island a reputation for being "the land of promise" and remains an area ripe for agro-industrial development. As such, the island's value as an economic prize cannot be divorced from the broader political disputes over sovereignty and autonomy. Moreover, given the island's proximity to Malaysia and Indonesia, its potential as a steppingstone into and out of the Philippines confers geopolitical significance to Mindanao that has certainly not gone unnoticed in Manila and in neighboring capitals.

The Colonial Roots of Discontent

The current Mindanao conflict traces its roots through a long history of repression, discrimination, and violence. Indeed, its longevity, spanning some 450 years, is rivaled only by the ethnic struggles that began nearly a millennium ago in Sudan.[2] The religious and ethnic character of the conflict in the southern Philippines was locked into place almost as soon as the Spaniards arrived to claim the archipelago in the late-sixteenth century. Boasting an Islamic tradition dating back to the fourteenth century, the inhabitants of Mindanao or the Moros—a Spanish reference to the North African Moors of an earlier era—fiercely resisted

Spain's efforts to establish political control over the island and to convert locals to Christianity. Although the Spaniards launched numerous military expeditions to defeat the Moros, they were never able to exercise unchallenged dominion over the course of Spain's 350-year colonial rule. In the meantime, populations in northern parts of the Philippines converted to Catholicism. Over time, Filipino Catholics inherited the Spanish animosity toward Muslims and benefited from educational and economic opportunities that were not made available to the unconquered southern regions.

The American colonial experiment in the Philippines did little to redress the deeply embedded social disharmony; in fact, U.S. policies may have aggravated the Spanish legacy of ethno-religious divisiveness. Preferring a decentralized form of governance, the United States chose to administer Mindanao as a separate area of responsibility after the U.S. military subdued the Moros through a brutal pacification program.[3] Despite efforts to develop and integrate the southern provinces and to "attract" the inhabitants through education programs to accept colonial administration, the locals were largely left out of the economic and political processes that the United States advanced. Among the most damaging policies, the colonial power promoted land ownership schemes that spurred a major migration of Christians to the Moro Province. As the authorities handed over administrative powers to Catholic Filipinos in preparation for self-governance, Muslims became a politically disenfranchised minority.[4] In short, U.S. colonial rule largely failed to improve the poisoned atmosphere between Christians and Muslims.

Rise of the Post-Colonial Moro Insurgency

The independence of the Philippines in 1946, which for the first time united the two communities under one national entity, inaugurated a new phase in ethnic tensions. The predominantly Catholic Filipino government oversaw discriminatory policies that explicitly targeted the country's rural south. Government-sanctioned migration programs inherited from the U.S. colonial era forcibly displaced indigenous populations that eventually evicted hundreds of thousands of Muslims out of their ancestral lands. Entire communities became refugees. Worse still, the weight of the migration flows tilted the demographic balance increasingly in favor of Christians. As Muslim grievances mounted, violence between the locals and Christian settlers became a common phenomenon. By the 1960s, the gathering momentum of resistance coincided with the wave of post-colonial nationalism that swept through Asia. Indeed, an emerging national Moro identity provided a durable basis for a more coherent insurgency.

Against this backdrop, three major developments bolstered the Moro cause in the late 1960s. First, a fledgling separatist movement emerged in the form of the Moro National Liberation Front (MNLF) in 1968. Under the leadership of Nur Misuari, the MNLF sought the full independence of Mindanao. Second, the internal conflict began to exhibit inklings of internationalization. As early as 1969, Moros militants reportedly received guerrilla training in Malaysia to develop the skills necessary to defeat the heavy-handed tactics of the Philippine Army.[5] As the confrontation escalated, the MNLF received political and financial support from Iran and Libya, which trained and armed nearly 30,000 Moro fighters.[6] Third and ironically, President Ferdinand Marco's 1972 martial law decree in the face of rising resistance fully galvanized the secessionist movement.[7] Repression did little to stamp out rebellion. Indeed, the MNLF waged a war of attrition and managed to fight Marco's forces to a bloody stalemate.

From Insurgency to Politics

By 1976, the mounting costs of the insurgency and external pressures exerted by Libya and the Organization of Islamic States—representing a region from which the Philippines received most of its oil and over-seas remittances from a massive Filipino expatriate workforce—forced Marcos to sign the Tripoli Agreement that promised limited autonomy in exchange for a cease-fire. However, Marcos refused to implement the terms of the agreement, which were under dispute, and sporadic attacks on both sides continued. To complicate matters, general inattention from Manila and mismanagement by Marcos' corrupt local authorities further diminished the credibility of the peace accord.[8] The ceasefire quickly crumbled and a new round of internal unrest ensued. The fail-ure of the Tripoli Agreement gradually sidelined the MNLF as a viable vehicle to attain outright independence through armed struggle. Fac-tions of the organization would split off to carry out further violence.

In the meantime, the promise of autonomy as stipulated in the Tripoli Agreement became the basis for a negotiated political process between the government and MNLF. But it was not until 1986 that President Corazon Aquino implemented a plebiscite to establish the Autonomous Regions in Muslim Mindanao (ARMM). Unfortunately, the Christian migrations created many pockets of Catholic majorities in key regions of Mindanao. For instance, Christians constitute over 75 percent of the Davao region. Due to demographic realities across large parts of the island, only three of Mindanao's 13 provinces opted to join the ARMM. Not surprisingly, the MNLF rejected the legitimacy of the autonomous region and pledged to continue its resistance movement. Another 10 years passed before President Fidel Ramos and the MNLF entered into a peace agreement. The 1996 accord empowered the MNLF to oversee economic development projects covering all provinces of Mindanao (designated as the Special Zone for Peace and Development). Manila's efforts to negotiate and grant (at times, unilaterally) autonomy to the region in the 1980s and 1990s had the effect of co-opting the main MNLF faction into a political process. By the late 1990s, the military dimension of the MNLF largely receded into the background—with the exception of splinter militant groups—as leaders of the organization joined the political and administrative apparatus at the national and local levels.

The New Dynamics of Rebellion

As Manila drew the MNLF into negotiations, the perception grew that the ultimate goal of independence was being compromised. This widespread disillusionment fractured the secessionist movement. Hashim Salamat, an Egyptian-educated cleric, broke away from the MNLF in 1978 to form an alternative organization, the Moro Islamic Liberation Front (MILF). Rejecting secularism and the more modest goals of autonomy for the homeland, Salamat sought an independent Islamic state. The religious orientation of MILF and the promise of an Islamic way of life armed the organization with a compelling political agenda that attracted many willing recruits. As a result, the MILF grew rapidly, and at the height of its power, the organization boasted 12,000–15,000 well-armed guerrillas. Salamat's refusal to compromise over the goal of independence and the MILF's military prowess set the stage for a protracted conflict against the government. After more than two decades of warfare and sporadic negotiations, MILF remains a formidable insurgent force motivated by legitimate political grievances. The inability of either side to decisively break the stalemate has led to inconclusive peace talks and a fragile ceasefire that is currently in place.[9] Notwithstanding the apparent breakthroughs in negotiations between the government and MILF in late 2005, the irreconcilable goals of the two parties—conditional autonomy compared with state independence—suggest that prospects for a meaningful and permanent resolution remain far from certain.[10]

In the meantime, the MNLF's unity cracked further in the mid-1980s as more members defected to form another splinter group. By 1989, the Abu Sayyaf ("Bearer of the Sword") emerged under the leadership of Abdurajak Janjalani, a Muslim scholar and a veteran of the Soviet-Afghan conflict. An ultra-fundamentalist, Janjalani advocated jihad as the means to establish an independent state based on Salafi Wah-habism, a highly intolerant and austere strain of Islam.[11] Moreover, Abu Sayyaf tied its national objectives to a broader agenda that envisioned an armed struggle to establish Islamic dominance on a global scale.[12] Janjalani's extremist views stood in sharp contrast to the MILF's more moderate brand of political Islam. His training experiences in Afghanistan in the late 1980s and contacts with the mujahedin, including Osama bin Laden, most likely hardened his radical political aspirations.[13] During this same period, Janjalani also established contact with Mohammed Jamal Khalifa, bin Laden's brother-in-law, who reportedly provided Abu Sayyaf with financial and logistical support, including funding for Islamic education in Pakistan, through a network of front businesses and a charitable organization.[14]

Throughout the 1990s, the Abu Sayyaf gained international notoriety for its vicious attacks against Christian targets, series of kidnappings for ransom, bombings, and assassinations.[15] In 1998, Janjalani was killed in a police raid, and his younger brother, Khaddafy Janjalani, took over as the titular head of Abu Sayyaf. Following the founder's death, the group quickly lost its unity of command and ideological coherence, and devolved into a loose confederation of gangs sustained by profits from criminal activities on the island strongholds of Basilan and Sulu.[16]

Several pertinent themes emerge from this historical overview of the Muslim insurrection in the southern Philippines. First, the familiar adage that the past is prologue applies quite appropriately to this conflict. Unresolved political and economic grievances stemming from a very long history of Catholic-Muslim antagonism provided the basic ingredients for the secessionist movement. Moreover, the demographic shift that increased the Christian population in Mindanao from 15 percent in 1900 to 85 percent a century later aggravated socioeconomic disparities. The original incarnation of resistance was primarily a secular response—underwritten by fledgling Moro nationalism—to the inequities that the Muslim communities suffered over centuries.

Second, the struggle for the autonomy or outright independence of Mindanao featured foreign intervention on behalf of the Moros as soon as a national movement began to take shape in the late 1960s. The ability of foreign powers to intervene, particularly Libya, was largely derived from economic leverage and partly drew upon the Marxist-nationalist ideological appeal that Tripoli actively promoted. The Philippines' dependence on oil and remittances from the Middle East forced Manila to permit a prominent role for outside mediators. Religious doctrine of the kind found in today's radical political Islam, then, did not occupy a major strategic place in the secessionist movement during the 1960s and early 1970s.

Third, the Islamic dimension of the conflict did not emerge until disillusioned members believed that the MNLF could not deliver on its promises of a liberated homeland. More importantly, the splintering of the MNLF in the late 1970s and 1980s coincided with the rising tide of political Islamist extremism. The Iranian revolution, the export of Saudi-funded Wahhabism, and the Afghan-Soviet war all provided the external impetus for the emergence of ideologically motivated organizations in the Philippines.[17] It is against this backdrop of internationalization and radicalization that the linkages between local resistance in Mindanao and the broader global phenomenon of Islamist terrorism require further scrutiny.

LINKAGES TO TERRORISM

The rise of radical political Islam and al Qaeda have produced a new dimension to the insurgency and domestic terrorism within the Philippines. The ideological appeal and organizational reach of global terrorist networks have raised fears that members of al Qaeda could exploit local grievances as a method to penetrate weak states or undermine government control over its territories. As such, a great deal of contention continues to animate the debate over the extent to which the secessionist movements and criminal groups in Mindanao are linked to the threat of global terrorism. Greater clarity on the local-global interface is critical because any judgment rendered on this issue will determine both the scope and scale of the resources required to address the Mindanao conflict as a part of the global war on terrorism. In this context, there is some disturbing evidence that local actors in the Philippines have been plugged into the global and regional networks of Islamic terrorism since the 1990s.

The Abu Sayyaf–al Qaeda Connection

As noted, Osama bin Laden's brother-in-law, Khalifa, played an important financing role in support of Abu Sayyaf operations. As Khalifa consolidated his relations with Janjalani, another important al Qaeda figure entered the scene in the Philippines. Ramzi Yousef, a veteran of the Afghan war and the mastermind behind the World Trade Center bombing in 1993, met with Janjalani in 1991 and 1992.[18] Yousef's uncle, Khalid Sheikh Mohammad, who was the third highest-ranking member of al Qaeda and the alleged architect of the 9/11 terrorist attacks, apparently provided assistance for some time.[19] After a period of refuge in Pakistan following the 1993 World Trade Center attack, Yousef returned to the Philippines with the intent of using the country as a base from which to launch an international terrorist campaign. During his stint in the Philippines, he planned but failed to carry out (1) the bombing of trans-Pacific flights to Los Angeles, (2) an operation that would crash an explosives-laden aircraft into CIA headquarters, and (3) assassination plots against Pope John Paul II and President Bill Clinton during their respective visits to Manila. He did, however, succeed in the bombing of a Philippines airline jet in December 1994 as a dress rehearsal for executing more destructive plots. In the mid-1990s, Yousef and his confederates reportedly visited Mindanao to establish terrorist cells and to train members of Abu Sayyaf in the art of using explosive devices.[20] After he was arrested in Pakistan in 1995, interrogations uncovered additional plans to kill the president of the Philippines and to poison the country's water system.[21] Yousef was ultimately extradited to and imprisoned in the United States.

The MILF–al Qaeda Connection

Khalifa did not limit his contacts to Abu Sayyaf. Osama bin Laden reportedly instructed him to recruit Filipino Muslim fighters for the Afghan campaign against the Soviet army. Khalifa apparently persuaded Salamat, the chief of MILF, to dispatch hundreds of his fighters in support of the jihad.[22] Salamat probably calculated that the returnees would provide him with additional skilled manpower for his insurgency. Indeed, many of the current commanders of the MILF are experienced combat veterans of the Afghan conflict.

Beyond individual contacts with al Qaeda operatives, the local insurgency also developed complex ties with homegrown regional networks in Southeast Asia. Particularly noteworthy, MILF enjoyed close links to the Indonesian-based Jemaah Islamiyah (JI). Founded by two Indonesian clerics in the mid-1990s, JI established a regional terrorist network with cells across Southeast Asia.[23] JI's main objectives resemble al Qaeda's agenda on a regional scale: to radicalize Islam and to create a pan-Asian Islamic union in the region. To achieve these ambitious goals, JI's operations were divided into four sub-regional commands or mantiqi.[24] The Philippine cell operating in Mantiqi 3 acquired explosives and forged ties with MILF to gain access to training camps for JI operatives.[25] It is important to note that while JI is a discrete organization from al Qaeda, it has served as a convenient conduit for bin Laden's operations in the region. These overlapping and layered relations, then, link al Qaeda to the MILF.

The viability of MILF training camps situated in the inaccessible jungles of Mindanao is perhaps the most prized asset for both JI and al Qaeda. In the early 1990s, al Qaeda provided generous funding to MILF in exchange for access to training facilities where al Qaeda trainers offered expertise in terrorist tactics to MILF and JI members. Camp Abubakar, which the Philippine army overran in 2000, provided a wealth of information on the extensiveness of the training activities. In the mid-1990s, the camp was a regular destination for veteran mujahedin from Pakistan, Afghanistan, and Algeria. In 1998, bin Laden dispatched a Sudanese expert in commando techniques to Mindanao.[26] Abubakar became such an important gathering place that it was divided into permanent sub-camps for JI and other nationalities. The loss of Abubakar proved to be only a temporary setback as MILF was able to reconstitute its capabilities.[27] There is evidence that new camps have been established.[28] As long as the global war on terrorism persists, the need for a safe sanctuary will likely ensure MILF's continuing links to and patronage from regional and global Islamist groups. According to Zachary Abuza, "Without the MILF camps and a secure base area, JI cannot train effectively."[29] Indeed, JI has been able to replenish its ranks despite mass arrests of its members throughout Southeast Asia.

While the evidence linking domestic players to regional and global terrorism clearly exists, several caveats are in order. First, at the local level, the terrorist threats are not identical to each other. There are significant qualitative differences between MILF and Abu Sayyaf, in terms of ends and means. The mainstream factions of the MILF are motivated primarily by the promise of an independent homeland while Abu Sayyaf, at least in its current incarnation, is still largely driven by greed. MILF seeks to redress genuine political injustices and has thus been involved in negotiations with the government. This basic difference in core principles has led to divergences in modus operandi to achieving their respective objectives. According to Alfredo Filler, "The MNLF and MILF, in separate moves, have distanced themselves from the group [Abu Sayyaf] and, on certain occasions, even joined the government and civil society in denouncing and condemning the ASG as not Islamic."[30] Thus, the distinct and constantly evolving qualities of each organization should be the basis for judging the nature and seriousness of the threat to Filipino national security.

Second, observers have cautioned that the connection between the local players and regional/global actors remains rather tenuous. Indeed, some historical accounts suggest that the significance of early contacts between the indigenous groups and al Qaeda are weak.[31] More importantly, the strength of these ties today is still under dispute. The

Philippine government's attrition of Abu Sayyaf, prior to its resurgence in the past two years, and the weak internal control over the loosely organized group after the founder's death may have deprived the leadership's ability to establish meaningful links to pan-regional Islamic organizations or al Qaeda.[32] The fractured nature of the MILF suggests that contacts with JI and al Qaeda may not be centrally directed. As Peter Chalk argues, "It would be perfectly conceivable for semi-autonomous local commanders to make operational decisions that do not necessarily reflect the thinking or wishes of the central command structure."[33] The International Crisis Group postulates three possibilities: (1) MILF could be deliberately pursuing a Maoist "fight and negotiate" strategy; (2) hardline factions could be acting independently with or without the MILF leadership's acquiescence; or (3) MILF leaders could be unaware of terrorist activities and links to JI and al Qaeda.[34] As such, some caution is required when extrapolating the policy significance of the reported transnational linkages.

Third, and closely related to the previous point, there are probably limits to the degree of political congruence between the insurrection in the Philippines and al Qaeda's global threat. The extent to which al Qaeda and JI have tapped into and co-opted the insurgency in the Philippines remains unclear. For example, it is not entirely obvious whether the MILF-JI/al Qaeda nexus was a marriage of convenience based on a supply (bases for international terrorists) and demand (financial support for MILF) relationship or a genuine ideological convergence regarding the prospects of a pan-Asian Islamic union. Given MILF's long-standing goal of establishing an independent Islamic state for the Moro communities, the latter scenario seems less likely. As such, conflating the unique local circumstances unfolding in Mindanao and al Qaeda's apocalyptic global ambitions could prove misleading. It is within this ambiguity over the local-global terrorism nexus that the United States became directly involved in the intractable conflict of the southern Philippines.

LINKAGES TO THE GLOBAL WAR ON TERRORISM

The U.S.-led global war on terrorism, at least rhetorically, treats Southeast Asia as the second major front in the "long war." In late 2001, the discovery of terrorist cells across Southeast Asia, particularly in countries with reputations for robust internal security, such as Singapore and Malaysia, seemed to confirm the global scale of terrorism. The deadly bombings in Indonesia, in October 2002, August 2003, and October 2005 testified to the reach and resilience of radical Islamic movements.

Fears that the terrorist hotbed in the southern Philippines could further feed this transnational threat compelled Washington to designate Mindanao a major theater of operations for the U.S. military.

U.S.-Philippines Security: Cooperation Since 9/11

The September 11, 2001, terrorist attacks dramatically revived American-Filipino security ties,[35] which remained largely dormant for nearly a decade following the unceremonious withdrawal of U.S. forces from the Philippines in 1992.[36] Seizing upon a historical opportunity, Manila quickly and decisively aligned itself with the United States on the global war on terrorism, distinguishing itself as the first Asian nation to do so. Shortly after 9/11, President Gloria Macapagal-Arroyo offered access to Clark and Subic bases, overflight rights, and logistical support to U.S. forces operating in the region.[37] The United States for its part promised to assist Manila's ongoing military campaign against Abu Sayyaf.

At a Washington summit meeting in November 2001, Arroyo declared her nation's strong support for U.S. antiterrorism activities. In exchange, President George W. Bush pledged a generous assistance package totaling over $1 billion aimed at fighting terrorism, alleviating poverty, promoting trade, and "addressing Mindanao's root economic and social problems."[38] On the security front, Washington agreed to provide equipment and training worth $100 million. According to David Capie, the Philippines became "the single largest beneficiary of American largesse in the region"[39] virtually overnight.

The level of cooperation deepened with the joint military exercise dubbed Balikatan 02-1. Between January and July 2002, the United States deployed 1,200 troops, including 150 Special Forces and 300 Navy engineers.[40] These forces provided training, intelligence, and civil engineering assistance in support of Filipino military operations against Abu Sayyaf on the island of Basilan.[41] American military personnel observed strict rules of engagement, limited their activities to assessing the progress of their Filipino counterparts, and avoided direct involvement in combat operations. After the exercise ended, the majority of U.S. forces pulled out of Basilan while a small contingent of Special Forces personnel stayed behind to conduct counterterrorism training. In another sign of closer ties, Manila and Washington signed the Mutual Logistics Support Agreement (MLSA) in November 2002.[42] The agreement permits U.S. forces to stockpile vital supplies, such as ammunition, food, water, and fuel, and to request logistical support from the Philippine government.[43]

During Arroyo's state visit to the White House in May 2003, the United States designated the Philippines as a "Major Non-NATO Ally,"[44] thus opening the door to higher levels of assistance, including greater access to defense equipment. This was an unprecedented status granted to a developing nation in Asia.[45] In addition, President Bush announced a $95 million program to train several battalions and to provide economic aid to Mindanao. In October 2003, during an appearance before the joint session of the Philippine parliament (the first in more than 40 years), Bush praised the Philippines as a "great light" of democracy in Asia and committed the United States to a five-year plan to modernize the Armed Forces of the Philippines (AFP).[46]

Arroyo's narrow electoral victory in May 2004 initially augured well for policy continuity and stability in U.S.-Philippines relations. However, two months following the elections, bilateral security ties made an unexpected plunge. A hostage crisis in Iraq involving the kidnapping of a Filipino truck driver by insurgents forced President Arroyo to pull out Philippine troops from Iraq despite numerous pleas and warnings from Washington. Not surprisingly, the decision to withdraw had an immediate, chilling effect on the relationship. Washington openly questioned and criticized Manila's reliability as an ally in the war on terror. Subsequently, in a series of retaliatory steps, the United States either stopped or scaled back military and economic aid to the Philippines. Washington dropped its $30 million pledge to revive Mindanao's economy and backed out of plans to play a mediating role between Manila and Muslim rebels.[47] It remains uncertain whether Arroyo's controversial step had permanently unraveled the advances that the alliance made in the aftermath of 9/11.[48]

Benefits and Risks of Cooperation

In the post-9/11 era, the security relationship experienced both dramatic successes and disappointments. The highs and lows of this period reflected both the common motivations and divergent interests within the alliance. Washington treated Manila as a partner within the broader framework of its global antiterror strategy. This approach tended to overlook the unique local circumstances unfolding in the Philippines. Manila for its part sought U.S. support to meet the demands of its national security interests and of broader concerns related to regional stability. At the same time, the Philippine government had to be mindful of powerful local stakeholders who sought to constrain further cooperation with the United States.

For the United States, several variations on the geopolitical imperative compelled its intervention in the southern Philippines. Taken at face value, the U.S. involvement was part of a second front in the global war on terrorism—following the collapse of the Taliban in Afghanistan—designed to deny al Qaeda sanctuary and resources (both material and financial) in other parts of the world. According to Renato Cruz De Castro, the U.S. forces in the Philippines were intended "to help a regional ally untangle the links between terrorist groups and transnational criminal organizations that converge within the so-called "seam of lawlessness"—a geographic area that stretches from Afghanistan to Southeast Asia."[49]

In contrast to the Cold War model, whereby massive U.S. forces were deployed forward to directly repel external threats, the United States' new strategy has focused on the capacity building of vulnerable states. The Philippines demonstrates a case in which Washington has sought to professionalize and enhance the effectiveness of friendly armed forces as a proxy for American power to fight terrorism. Moreover, the revitalization of American alliances in Asia, which has long been a major foreign policy priority for the Bush administration, dovetailed closely with the greater strategic importance attached to the Philippines.

Other less charitable (and even conspiratorial) interpretations of American realpolitik deserve mention as well. Still others assert that broader imperial ambitions and balance-of-power designs—underwritten by a neo-conservative agenda—have animated U.S. policy in Southeast Asia. Relying exclusively on a series of think tank reports, Jim Glassman claims:

> [T]he clearly stated project of the neoconservatives in Southeast Asia since before 9/11 is to restore military relations with key countries such as the Philippines (bases) and Indonesia (aid and training to the TNI), while expanding regional defense alliances to include other countries (Singapore, Malaysia, Thailand). These goals have everything to do with U.S. neoconservatives' military and economic ambitions in East and Southeast Asia—including vis-à-vis China—and little or nothing to do with real or imagined Islamic terrorist threats.[50]

While Glassman may have overstated his case, perceptions that the United States is acting out of narrow self-interest bearing little connection to terrorism do enjoy real currency in the Philippines. Indeed, reservations about U.S. intentions are fairly widespread. The Bush administration's inattention to Abu Sayyaf prior to the 9/11 attacks fed public suspicions at the outset that ulterior motives lurked. Some

Filipinos suspected that the U.S. military exploited the joint exercises in 2002 to secure a permanent presence in Mindanao.[51] Even high-level policymakers in Manila "believed that the United States was attempting to gain greater access to the 'southern backdoor' of the Philippines, ostensibly to monitor developments in Southeast Asia's more volatile spots,"[52] such as Indonesia and Malaysia. Still others feared that the U.S. presence might be a prelude to a more expansive plan that would eventually incorporate logistical hubs in the Philippines for a China-Taiwan conflict.[53]

For the Philippines, the rapprochement with the U.S. military enhanced the country's ability to contain terrorist activities and the ongoing insurgency while heightening Manila's geo-strategic profile that had languished for nearly a decade. The United States rewarded Arroyo's open and enthusiastic support for the global campaign against terrorism with a massive infusion of much-needed U.S. assistance. Yet, Arroyo's drive to solicit Washington's involvement quickly ran afoul of public opinion. The presence of U.S. forces on Philippine soil energized anti-Americanism not seen since the acrimonious debates over basing rights a decade earlier. Memories of U.S. colonial rule, heightened sensitivity over sovereignty, fears of a widening war in the southern Philippines due to American involvement, and anxieties over the permanence of U.S. military presence all stirred strong emotions and suspicions. Ironically, just as Americans seemed to have overcome psychological barriers inherited from the Vietnam War, which cautioned against military intervention in quagmire-prone Southeast Asia, Filipinos retreated into history. Indeed, stakeholders across the political spectrum ranging from leftists to nationalists to civil society groups found common cause in forestalling a deepening of security ties. Buckling under tremendous pressure from domestic players long opposed to the invasion of Iraq, Arroyo ignored American entreaties not to withdraw Filipino forces from Iraq during the hostage crisis. She was apparently willing to risk a severe deterioration in bilateral ties to shore up her political survival at home.

Most problematic for the alliance's counterterrorist agenda, internal preoccupations in the Philippines continue to prevent a common alliance-based definition of the threat. The ongoing bilateral differences (and tensions) over the ambiguous organizational status of the MILF demonstrate how Manila's domestic concerns take precedence over Washington's position. To keep alive the fragile ceasefire and on-and-off peace negotiations that remain between the MILF and the Philippine government, Arroyo consistently resists American requests to formally label the MILF as a terrorist entity.[54] Indeed, despite its alleged linkages to regional and global terrorist networks, the MILF (in contrast to Abu Sayyaf) is conspicuously missing from the State Department's annual report on international terrorism.[55] The Philippines' domestic priorities, then, do not always conform with America's global strategy, which in turn increases Washington's vulnerability to charges of inconsistency or double standards. Manila thus faces the daunting task of carefully navigating between the pressures from its most important security guarantor and the demands of domestic constituents crucial for sustaining regime legitimacy.

PROGRESS AND PROSPECTS

How does one make sense of the dizzying array of actors, threats, interests, and events at the local and international levels surrounding the Mindanao problem? One way is to measure the progress and effectiveness of the counterinsurgent/terrorist threat in the southern Philippines. As one analyst points out, there are two distinct levels of activity that can be assessed: counterterrorist versus counterterrorism policies.[56] The former seeks to hunt down individuals, deprive the adversary from gaining access to resources (financial, material, manpower, etc.), uncover and break up terrorist cells, and ultimately liquidate the organizations and leaders behind the terrorist activities. The objective is to close down the "functional space" of the enemy with law enforcement, military, and intelligence mechanisms. The latter provides the basis for undermining the powerful political incentives for and ideological appeal of terrorism. The method for weakening the sources of terrorism requires long-term commitments designed to address the "root causes"—usually centered on political and socioeconomic grievances—that fuel the energy of extremist ideology.

Thus far, the most visible and preferred option seems to be counterterrorist campaigns. This phenomenon partially stems from a confluence of the rise in Abu Sayyaf violence with the responses to 9/11. The series of high-profile crimes in 2000 and 2001, including the kidnapping of Americans, drew the attention of the United States. Subsequently, the widely publicized joint U.S.-Philippine military operations to root out Abu Sayyaf in 2002 further added to the counterterrorist tinge that predated the American arrival on the scene. A primarily military option to eradicate the Abu Sayyaf Group thus became the standard modus operandi for the alliance. While euphoric reports of Abu Sayyaf's imminent demise circulated following the joint exercise, the threat level and violence did not noticeably decrease. Indeed, the record of success on this front thus far has been mixed at best. The pattern has been consistent: official claims of progress are quickly overturned by fresh attacks and other setbacks.

Consider the conflicting accounts between official sources and actual events in 2004–2005. The U.S. State Department issued glowing reviews of Philippine counterterrorism campaigns in its most recent annual report on international terrorism. The document recounted a series of successes in arresting and killing Abu Sayyaf members.[57] Yet, the Philippines suffered its worst terrorist strike in February 2004 when Abu Sayyaf sank a ferry in Manila Bay, killing 130 people onboard. Soon afterwards media reports indicated that the Bush administration had quietly warned Manila of a new tide of terrorist attacks and chided its counterpart for not doing enough to combat terrorism.[58] Steven Rogers, a longtime observer of the Philippines, noted that the Abu Sayyaf Group may be morphing back into an ideologically-driven group. The group, he argues, is enjoying growing links to other extremists and equipping itself with the reach to threaten the entire country.[59] These warnings appeared prescient when in December 2004 a bomb blast in a crowded market in the largely Christian port city of General Santos killed at least 15 people.[60]

Two months later, three coordinated bombings ripped through the southern Philippines and Manila, killing four and wounding more than 100 people.[61] A leader of Abu Sayyaf claiming to avenge the crackdown on his group audaciously described the blasts as a "Valentine's gift" to President Arroyo. In the following month, a bungled jailbreak involving Abu Sayyaf detainees in a maximum-security facility led to the deaths of 22 militant political Islamists.[62] In response, Janjalani personally declared in a newspaper interview that he would seek revenge for the deaths of his jailed comrades. (His appearance ended months of speculation about his reported death in a raid by Filipino authorities.) In the meantime, Filipino police claimed that the Abu Sayyaf Group no longer possessed the capacity to carry out strikes in Manila or other major metropolitan areas.[63] Such declarations flew in the face of unfolding events and added a surreal quality to Manila's counterterrorist efforts. As of this writing, government claims that Abu Sayyaf has been reduced to a spent force have proven premature.

Counterterrorism Activities

Counterterrorism deals with the sources that generate political violence. In the case of the Philippines, one of the key causes of terrorism has been the radicalization of political Islam. The original mandates of MILF and Abu Sayyaf attest to such a trend. According to one study:

> Alienation and humiliation appear to be key concepts for under-
> standing the Islamic resurgence in Asia and for understanding why
> individuals are drawn to terrorist groups ... [F]rustration from
> diminished expectations driven by economic malaise, the lack of
> effective political participation, and a sense of humiliation are at
> the core of why many Asian Muslims have become radicalized.[64]

Thus, two main remedies characterize counterterrorism: a socioeconomic recovery that generates equitable wealth and a political process
that genuinely addresses local concerns. Both pose daunting challenges
to Manila. Indeed, progress on this front has lagged far behind government efforts to diminish the operational space of terrorist groups.

From an economic perspective, it is important to note that poverty
per se does not lead to terrorism. The correlation is ambiguous and
subtle at best. However, poor socioeconomic conditions are conducive
to heightening the appeal of violent recourse to political grievances.
According to the World Bank, the socioeconomic costs of the Mindanao conflict have been substantial over the past three decades. Based
on measures such as productivity loss, capital flight, and depressed agricultural investment, the total economic cost of the war is estimated at
$10 billion from 1975 to 2002.[65] While this figure is insignificant com-
pared to the overall size of the national (or Mindanao's) economy, most
of the losses were concentrated in the poorest southwestern region of
the island. Moreover, given the low economic baseline of the afflicted
areas, the costs were prohibitive. The conflict also exacted a high social
toll. Since 1970, the conflict killed 120,000 people, displaced two million
more, spawned Muslim ghettos, increased crime, worsened poverty (to
more than 70 percent of the population in 2000), undermined the rule
of law and security, and disrupted much-needed social services.[66]

These conditions continue to persist as a result of local governance
problems, weak external aid, and poor policy implementation. As noted,
the 1996 peace agreement created an economic zone that permitted
autonomous development under the auspices of the Southern Philippines Council for Peace and Development (SPCPD). However, opposition from national lawmakers prevented the distribution of adequate
resources, including the power to collect local taxes.[67] Lacking a local
resource base and the authority to initiate development projects on
its own, the SPCPD was (and still is) dependent on Manila's goodwill.
Political intrigue and ineffectual leadership within the MNLF, whose
key leaders were charged with administering the Special Zone for
Peace and Development, worsened matters. Moreover, the central government dispersed funds to the SPCPD for major infrastructure (high

impact and high visibility) projects that failed to reach the local communities. The absence of accountability and oversight over the SPCPD's activities suggests that corruption is rampant. Even international aid from the United Nations and the World Bank did not significantly impact the poorest segments of society. From 1996–2001, development aid amounted to a paltry annual average of $6 per person compared to $543 in Northern Ireland.[68]

More than economics are at work. The root causes fueling radicalism and terrorism are inherently political. First, the peace process is structurally flawed. The 1996 settlement granted limited economic authority only to the MNLF, an organization with diluted ambitions for a Muslim homeland. Not surprisingly, the MILF rejected the legitimacy of the agreement. Not only did the accord pit the MNLF against MILF due to overlapping jurisdictional claims, but Manila also negotiated away whatever bargaining chips it had with the latter. As such, the lack of progress in the peace negotiations reflects the legacy of an incomplete political process. How the government will be able to offer political incentives that would adequately meet MILF's demands remains unclear. Moreover, the half-measures of autonomy that characterized the agreement undermined the credibility of Manila in the eyes of local authorities and communities.

Second, sheer government incompetence, corruption among the political elite in Manila, and the fragility of Filipino democracy are contributing to the problems in Mindanao. There is, for example, evidence that the establishment colluded with the terrorists. Indonesian terrorist Fathur Rothman al-Ghozi escaped imprisonment in 2003 under suspicious circumstances suggesting an "inside job" that embarrassed the Philippine government and enraged the United States. Two weeks after his getaway, Filipino soldiers staged a mutiny and seized a famous shopping complex. They justified the "coup" with accusations that senior military officers had sold arms to the rebels and staged bombings in the south to sustain U.S. military support. While such allegations remain unproven, they resonated with public perceptions that the military was part of the terrorist problem.

Third, Filipino civil society, though far more vibrant compared to its Southeast Asian neighbors, remains weak. Civil society groups and nongovernmental organizations (NGOs) have not been able to fully mobilize grass-roots support to pressure the government and the rebels for a sustainable peace process in Mindanao. Conflicting ideologies and interests among the disparate groups, the absence of adequate funding, and the lack of professional and technical expertise continue to hobble peace advocacy groups.[69] However, a civil society network has gradually emerged, providing critical social services, such as relief and rehabilitation, that otherwise would have been the government's responsibility. Indeed, Manila appears to appreciate the benefits of NGOs and has generally not interfered with their work. Civil society is perhaps the one political arena in which prospects for positive change are bright.

CONCLUSION

A lasting settlement of the Mindanao conflict remains a distant proposition. Three major disconnects stand in the way of an enduring peace. First, the linkages between the local terrorist and regional/global terrorist networks remain unclear. Even if the local-global nexus existed, an excessive focus on the transnational dimension distracts attention from the local conditions that are at the root of the insurrection. Second, a mismatch in ends, ways, and means between Manila and Washington persists. Allied resources committed to the Philippines are often disproportionate (and overly militarized) to the threat on the ground. Consequently, bilateral cooperation heightened anti-Americanism and undermined the legitimacy of the government. Third, the preference for squeezing the operational space of terrorists over addressing the root causes of terrorism has not changed appreciably. A counterterrorist plan unaccompanied by a longer-term counterterrorism strategy ensures that a pool of willing recruits will be available to replenish the ranks of terrorist groups killed during military action. These three disconnects point in one worrisome direction: a continued militarization of the Mindanao conflict at the expense of the political and economic tools designed to address the sources of terrorism. As long as such imbalances in policy priorities remain in place, a vicious cycle of violence and repression will plague the Philippines. Above all, the prospects for peace are not separable from the Philippine political system itself. The culture of neglect, the endemic corruption among the elites, and the fragilities inherent to any new democracy have all exacerbated the poor economic conditions and the absence of local political participation in Mindanao. Painful political and military reforms within the democratic process, then, offer the best promise for resolving this centuries-old conflict.

NOTES

1. Statistics of the Moro population are highly contested. It is generally accepted that Muslims constitute 5 percent of the overall population while 92 percent of the country's population is Christian. According to the 2000 census by the Filipino National Statistics Office, 20 percent of Mindanao's population was Muslim. See *A Special Release on New*

Mindanao Groupings Based on the Results of the Census 2000, Special Release No. 173, June 8, 2005. Online. Available HTTP: <www.census.gov.ph/data/sectordata/sr05173tx. html>. For the low-end figure of 15 percent, see Central Intelligence Agency, *The World Fact Book 2005*, (Washington, DC: Central Intelligence Agency, May 2005). Online. Available HTTP: <http://www.cia.gov/cia/publications/factbook/geos/rp.html>.

2. Salvatore Schiavo-Campo and Mary Judd, *The Mindanao Conflict in the Philippines: Roots, Costs, and Potential Peace Dividend*, Conflict Prevention and Reconstruction Working Papers Series, Paper No. 24, (Washington, DC: World Bank, February 2005), p. 1.

3. For a sense of the brutality on both sides of the U.S.-led counterinsurgency campaigns, see Max Boot, *The Savage Wars of Peace: Small Wars and the Rise of American Power* (New York: Basic Books, 2002), pp. 99–128.

4. Syed Serajul Islam, "Ethnocommunal Conflict in the Philippines: The Case of Mindanao-Sulu Region," in *Ethnic Conflict and Secessionism in South and Southeast Asia*, Rajat Ganguly and Ian Macduff, eds. (New Delhi: Sage Publications, 2003), pp. 198–199.

5. Christopher A. Parrinello, "Operation Enduring Freedom, Phase II: The Philippines, Islamic Insurgency, and Abu Sayaff," *Military Intelligence Professional Bulletin*, Volume 28, Issue 2 (April–June 2002), p. 40.

6. Christopher A. Parrinello, "Operation Enduring Freedom, Phase II," p. 41.

7. Paul A. Rodell, "The Philippines and the Challenge of Terrorism," in *Terrorism and Violence in Southeast Asia: Transnational Challenges to States and Regional Stability*, Paul J. Smith, ed. (Armonk: New York, 2005), pp. 127–128.

8. Steven Rogers, "Beyond the Abu Sayyaf," *Foreign Affairs*, Vol. 83, Issue 1, (January–February 2004), 16.

9. In the latest round of talks hosted by Malaysia in April 2005, both sides failed to reach any formal agreements. "Peace talks in Malaysia 'very encouraging' but no agreement yet: Philippines," *Agence France Presse (AFP)*, April 20, 2005.

10. See Jason Gutierrez, "Negotiations resume, but real peace a long way off in southern Philippines," *AFP*, April 18, 2004.

11. Zachary Abuza, "Al Qaeda Comes to Southeast Asia," in *Terrorism and Violence in Southeast Asia: Transnational Challenges to States and Regional Stability*, Paul J. Smith, ed. (Armonk: New York, 2005), p. 42.

12. Angel M. Rabasa, *Political Islam in Southeast Asia: Moderates, Radicals, and Terrorists* (New York: Oxford University Press, 2003), p. 53.

13. Zachary Abuza, "Al Qaeda Comes to Southeast Asia," p. 42.

14. David Martin Jones, Michael L. R. Smith, and Mark Wedding, "Looking for the Pattern: Al Qaeda in Southeast Asia—The Genealogy of a Terror Network," *Studies in Conflict and Terrorism*, Vol. 26, (June 2003): pp. 443–457.

15. For statistics on the strength and criminal activities of Abu Sayyaf in the 1990s, see Alfredo L. Filler, "The Abu Sayyaf Group: A Growing Menace to Civil Society," *Terrorism and Political Violence*, Vol. 14, No. 4 (Winter 2002), pp. 142–144.

16. Peter Chalk, "Militant Islamic Extremism in Southeast Asia," in *Terrorism and Violence in Southeast Asia: Transnational Challenges to States and Regional Stability*, Paul J. Smith, ed. (Armonk: New York, 2005), 21.

17. Angel Rabasa, *Political Islam in Southeast Asia*, pp. 9–10.

18. David G. Wiencek, "The Philippines: Searching for Stability," in *Asian Security Handbook: Terrorism and the New Security Environment*, William M. Carpenter and David G. Wiencek, eds. (New York: M.E. Sharpe, 2005), p. 249.

19. Emma Chanlett-Avery, Richard Cronin, Mark Manyin, and Larry Niksch, *Terrorism in Southeast Asia* (Washington, DC: Congressional Research Service, February 2005), p. 4.

20. MA. Concepcion B. Clamor, "The Philippine Perspective," in *Terrorism in the Asia-Pacific: Threat and Response*, Rohan Gunaratna, ed. (Singapore: Eastern Universities Press, 2003), p. 204.
21. Wiencek, "The Philippines," p. 250.
22. Rommel C. Banlaoi, "The Role of Philippine-American Relations in the Global Campaign Against Terrorism: Implications for Regional Security," *Contemporary Southeast Asia*, Volume 24, Issue 2, (August 2002), p. 294.
23. For the historical background of JI, see Zachary Abuza, *Militant Islam in Southeast Asia: Crucible of Terror* (London: Lynne Rienner, 2003), pp. 125–128.
24. Emma Chanlett-Avery, et. al., *Terrorism in Southeast Asia*, p. 8.
25. Zachary Abuza, "Learning by Doing: Al Qaeda's Allies in Southeast Asia," *Current History*, Issue 103, (April 2004), p. 173.
26. D. M. Jones, et. al., "Looking for the Pattern," p. 446.
27. David G. Wiecnek, "Mindanao and Its Impact on Security in the Philippines," in *The Unraveling of Island Asia? Governmental, Communal, and Regional Instability*, Bruce Vaughn, ed. (Westport, CT: Praeger, 2002), p. 52.
28. Zachary Abuza, "Learning by Doing," p. 174.
29. Zachary Abuza, "Learning by Doing," p. 173.
30. Alfredo L. Filler, "The Abu Sayyaf Group," p. 132. Following a deadly confrontation between Filipino police authorities and Abu Sayyaf members in a jailbreak attempt in March 2005, MILF urged the group to "mend its ways" and act according to the teachings of Islam. See "Philippines Moro groups calls on Abu Sayyaf to mend ways," *The Philippine Star*, March 18, 2005.
31. For details undermining bin Laden's direct role in supporting activities undertaken by Khalifa and Yousef, see Carlyle A. Thayer, "Al Qaeda and Political Terrorism," in *Terrorism and Violence in Southeast Asia: Transnational Challenges to States and Regional Stability*, Paul J. Smith, ed. (Armonk: New York, 2005), pp. 86–88.
32. Zachary Abuza, *Militant Islam in Southeast Asia*, p. 112.
33. Peter Chalk, "Militant Islamic Terrorism in Southeast Asia," p. 23.
34. International Crisis Group, *Southern Philippines Backgrounder: Terrorism and the Peace Process*, p. 8.
35. The 1951 Mutual Defense Treaty continues to underwrite the security relationship. A legacy of the Cold War, the treaty provides the legal mechanisms by which the United States commits itself to defend the Philippines should the metropolitan territories of the archipelago come under armed attack by foreign forces.
36. See William J. Crowe, "U.S. Pacific Command: A Warrior-Diplomat Speaks," in Derek S. Reveron, ed., *America's Viceroys: The Military and U.S. Foreign Policy* (New York: Palgrave, 2004), pp. 86–94.
37. Renato Cruz De Castro, "The Revitalized Philippine-U.S. Security Relations: A Ghost from the Cold War or an Alliance for the 21st Century?" *Asian Survey*, Vol. 43, No. 6 (November/December 2003), p. 980.
38. Joint Statement Between the United States of America and the Republic of the Philippines, November 20, 2001, *Weekly Compilation of Presidential Documents*, November 26, 2001, Vol. 37, Issue 47, pp. 1697–1701.
39. David Capie, "Between hegemon and a hard place: the 'war on terror' and Southeast Asian-US relations," *Pacific Review*, Vol. 17, No. 2 (June 2004), p. 233.
40. Emma Chanlett-Avery, et. al., *Terrorism in Southeast Asia*, p. 20.
41. Renato Cruz De Castro, "The Revitalized Philippine-U.S. Security Relations," p. 984.
42. However, controversy still managed to erupt over this relatively innocuous document when leaders of the Filipino opposition objected to the absence of public disclosure over the agreement's content and disputed the constitutional legality of the process by which the parties concluded the MLSA.

43. In late 2002, both sides engaged in negotiations for a follow-on training exercise. However, Filipino sensitivities to the potential U.S. role, including rules of engagement and differences over the nature of the joint operation, prevented a rapid conclusion of an agreement. In particular, the parameters of the proposed exercise went far beyond those of Balikatan held earlier in the year. The military operation would have involved a direct combat role for U.S. Special Forces, an offshore naval presence—including rapid-reaction U.S. Marine units and fighter aircraft—capable of projecting significant firepower, and an indefinite timeline for the operation's duration. A premature announcement of these details by the Pentagon generated a firestorm of public controversy in the Philippines. The uproar centered on the country's constitutional restrictions against combat roles for foreign troops on Filipino soil. The intensity and scale of the political backlash forced Washington and Manila to shelve the plan in February 2003.

44. Title 10 U.S. Code Section 2350a authorizes the Secretary of Defense, with the concurrence of the Secretary of State, to designate MNNAs for purposes of participating with the Department of Defense (DOD) in cooperative research and development programs. MNNA Status does not entail the same mutual defense and security guarantees afforded to NATO members. Status makes a nation eligible for priority delivery of excess defense articles; to buy depleted uranium ammunition; to have U.S.-owned War Reserve Stockpiles on its territory; to enter into agreements with the USG for the cooperative furnishing of training on a bilateral or multilateral basis under reciprocal financial arrangements; to use U.S.-provided Foreign Military Financing for commercial leasing of certain defense articles; for loans of materials, supplies, and equipment for cooperative R&D projects and testing and evaluation; and to expedite the processing of export licenses of commercial satellites, their technologies, components, and systems.

45. David Capie, "Between hegemon and a hard place: the 'war on terror' and Southeast Asian-US relations," p. 233.

46. Raissa Robles, "Bush heaps praise on the Philippines," *South China Morning Post*, October 19, 2003, p. 7.

47. Al Labita, "Washington seeking to teach Manila a lesson," *The Business Times*, November 10, 2004.

48. David Wiencek, "The Philippines," p. 245.

49. Renato Cruz De Castro, "The Revitalized Philippine-U.S. Security Relations," p. 982.

50. Jim Glassman, "The 'war on terrorism' comes to Southeast Asia," *Journal of Contemporary Asia*, Vol. 35, Issue 1 (March 2005), p. 8.

51. Steven Rogers, "Beyond the Abu Sayyaf," p. 18.

52. Noel M. Morada, "Philippine-American Security Relations After 11 September: Exploring the Mutuality of Interests in the Fight Against International Terrorism," in *Southeast Asian Affairs*, Daljit Singh and Chin Kin Wah, eds. (Singapore: Institute of Southeast Asian Studies, 2003), pp. 228–238.

53. Rommel C. Banlaoi, "The Role of Philippine-American Relations in the Global Campaign Against Terrorism," p. 303.

54. For a recent flare-up in bilateral tensions over this issue, see, "Arroyo dismisses reports linking MILF with JI as old hat," *Asia Pulse*, March 11, 2005; "US warns Philippines about militant ties of main Muslim rebel group," *AFP*, March 31, 2005, and "Malaysia FM tells US not to undermine Philippines peace talks," *AFP*, April 13, 2005.

55. For the latest report, see Office of the Coordinator for Counterterrorism, *Country Reports on Terrorism 2004* (Washington, DC: U.S. Department of State, April 2005).

56. Kumar Ramakrishna, "Countering Radical Islam in Southeast Asia: The Need to Confront the Functional and Ideological 'Enabling Environment,'" in *Terrorism and Violence in Southeast Asia: Transnational Challenges to States and Regional Stability*, Paul J. Smith, ed. (New York: Armonk, 2005), pp. 145–168.

57. Office of the Coordinator for Counterterrorism, *Country Reports on Terrorism 2004*, p. 38.

58. Raymond Bonner and Carlos H. Conde, "U.S. Warns the Philippines on Terror Groups," *New York Times*, April 11, 2004, p. 4.

59. Steven Rogers, "Manila must counter the return of Abu Sayyaf," *International Herald Tribune*, May 21, 2004, p. 6. See also Anthony Davis, "Philippines fears new wave of attacks by Abu Sayyaf," *Jane's Intelligence Review*, May 1, 2005.

60. Simon Montlake, "In Philippines, a renewed bid to drive out terror factions," *Christian Science Monitor*, December 14, 2004, p. 4.

61. Richard C. Paddock and Al Jacinto, "Coordinated Blasts in Philippines Kill Seven, Wound More Than 100," *Los Angeles Times*, February 15, 2005, p. 3.

62. Hrvoje Hranjski, "Abu Sayyad, very much alive, threatens retaliation for bloody prison assault," *Associated Press*, March 16, 2005.

63. Luige del Puerto, "Philippine police: Abu Sayyaf's ability to carry out attacks now 'almost nil,'" *Philippine Daily Enquirer*, March 27, 2005.

64. Bruce Vaughn, *Islam in South and Southeast Asia* (Washington, DC: Congressional Research Service, February 2005), p. 6.

65. Salvatore Schiavo-Campo and Mary Judd, *The Mindanao Conflict in the Philippines*, p. 6.

66. Ibid, pp. 5–7

67. Syed Serajul Islam, "Ethno-communal Conflict in the Philippines," p. 214.

68. Kim Cragin and Peter Chalk, *Terrorism and Development: Using Social and Economic Development to Inhibit a Resurgence of Terrorism*, (Santa Monica, CA: RAND, 2003), pp. 8, 18.

69. Rufa Cagoco-Guiam, "Mindanao: Conflicting Agendas, Stumbling Blocks, and Prospects Toward Sustainable Peace," in Searching For Peace in Asia Pacific: An Overview of Conflict Prevention and Peacebuilding Activities, Annelies Heijmans, Nicola Simmonds, and Hans van de Veen, eds. (Boulder, CO: Lynne Rienner, 2004), pp. 492–493.

Xinjiang

11

XINJIANG

Dru C. Gladney

NATURE OF THE FLASHPOINT

In the summer of 2002, both the United States and the United Nations supported China's claim that an organization known as the East Turkestan Islamic Movement (ETIM) should be recognized as an international terrorist organization and that China deserved international support for fighting a war against terrorism that had been going on in the region known as Xinjiang for some time.[1] Despite widespread incidents of Uyghur-related violence in the late 1990s, this announcement took many by surprise, as there had been no documented incidents of violence or large-scale civil unrest in Xinjiang since 2000.

Indeed, Xinjiang Party Secretary Wang Lequan, now a member of the Chinese politburo, was quoted nine days prior to the 9/11 attacks by foreign reporters that Xinjiang was a stable place for tourism and investment, adding, "Although national separatists and religious extremists have never stopped their efforts for launching destructive activities, their efforts never affect Xinjiang's stability." During the opening of the international trade fair at the Kunlun Hotel in Urumqi where these remarks were given, the Uyghur governor of Xinjiang, Abluhat Abdurishit, proclaimed that Xinjiang was "better than ever in history," while both stressing that "society is stable" and boasting that Xinjiang was a safe place to go out at night until "two or three a.m."[2] Less than one month after 9/11, however, China's *People's Daily* proclaimed that Xinjiang faced serious terrorist threats.[3]

What accounts for the change? Is Xinjiang a flashpoint for domestic and international terrorism? Or is it simply a publicity flash to bolster China's rule? Are there terrorism and civil unrest in the Xinjiang Uyghur Autonomous Region (XUAR) or is it a ploy to gain international support for China's increasing integration of the region, what *Oxford Analytica* termed, "scapegoat terrorism"?[4] And what will the future bring? The truth, as in all things of value in this western region, lies somewhere beneath the desert, and increasingly, in the international arena of nonstate organizations.

Xinjiang: Restive Region or under Arrest?

After denying the problem for decades and stressing instead China's "national unity," official reports and the state-run media began in late 2001 to detail terrorist activities in the regions officially known as the Xinjiang Uyghur Autonomous Region, and on January 21, 2002, issued the first White Paper addressing this issue: "East Turkestan Terrorist Forces Cannot Get Away with Impunity."[5] Prior to the release of this document by the State Council and the subsequent media reports, the term "Eastern Turkestan" was not allowed to be used in the official media. Anyone found using the term or referring to Xinjiang as Eastern Turkestan could be arrested, even though this is the term most often used outside China to refer to the region by Uyghurs and other Turkic-speaking people.

In May 2003, China released another more detailed White Paper on Xinjiang, which not only detailed continued control of the region by the Chinese state since the Han Dynasty, but also listed numerous incidents of terrorism and violence attributable to East Turkistan independence movements.[6] In the northwestern Uyghur Autonomous Region of Xinjiang, China's State Council and the official media discussed a series of incidents of terrorism and separatism since the large riot in the Xinjiang town of Yining in February 1997. Troop movements to the area, related to the nationwide campaign against crime known as "Strike Hard" launched in April 1996 that included the call to erect a "great wall of steel" against separatists in Xinjiang, were reportedly the largest since the suppression of the large Akto insurrection in April 1990 (the first major uprising that initiated a series of unrelated and sporadic protests).[7] Multiple crackdowns and arrests have rounded up thousands of terrorist suspects, seized large weapons caches, and confiscated printed documents allegedly outlining future public acts of violence.[8] Amnesty International has claimed that these roundups have led to hurried public trials and summary executions of possibly thousands of locals. One estimate suggested that in a country known for its frequent executions, Xinjiang had the highest number, averaging 1.8 per week, most of them Uyghur.[9]

International campaigns for Uyghur rights and possible independence have become increasingly vocal and well organized, especially on the Internet. Repeated public appeals have been made to Abdulahat Abdurixit, the Uyghur People's Government Chairman of Xinjiang in Urumqi. International organizations are increasingly including Uyghur indigenous voices from the expatriate Uyghur community. Notably, the 1995 elected chair of the Unrepresented Nations and People's Organization (UNPO) based in The Hague is a Uyghur: Erkin Alptekin, son of the separatist leader, Isa Yusuf Alptekin.[10] Supporting primarily an audience of mostly expatriate Uyghurs, there are at least 25 international organizations and Web sites working for the independence of "Eastern Turkestan," based in Amsterdam, Munich, Istanbul, Melbourne, Washington, DC, and New York. Following 9/11, the vast majority of these organizations disclaimed any support for violence or terrorism, pressing for a peaceful resolution of ongoing conflicts in the region. Nevertheless, the growing influence of "cyber-separatism" is of increasing concern to Chinese authorities seeking to convince the world that the Uyghurs do pose a real domestic and international terrorist threat.

It is clear that the so-called separatist activities are not new and that China is taking advantage of the United States' declared global war on terrorism to attempt to eradicate a domestic problem. What is not clear is whether occasional violent incidents carried out by Uyghurs are examples of "terrorism" or merely expressions of civil unrest and discontent. It is significant that since 1998, not one incident reported in the Chinese documents has been directed against civilians.[11]

HISTORICAL CONTEXT

The post-Cultural Revolution period in the region was welcomed by most Xinjiang residents due to the harsh treatment of minorities and religious practitioners from 1966 to 1976. Indeed, many Muslims point to the 20 years of discrimination against religious practice since the initiation of the Religious System Reform Campaign in 1958, which led to the further consolidation and restriction of religious practice.[12] With Deng's liberalization of the marketplace, cultural and religious practices also flourished, leading to widespread mosque building and the revival of religious education in the region. It was during this period that most of the mosques in the region were built or reopened, Islamic training of young Imams was permitted, and pilgrimages to Mecca resumed.

Indeed, there are many residents of Xinjiang, Uyghurs included, who continue to strongly support the Deng Xiaoping reforms as they have been continued under Jiang Zemin and now Hu Jintao. As loyal citizens, they see the dramatic progress made since the end of the Cultural Revolution and generally share in the government's vision of a modernized, developed Xinjiang region. Working not only in the state sector as cadres, teachers, production crops farmers, and factory workers, but also in the growing private sector, these supporters of the state's development program are generally quite unwilling to listen to any criticism of state policies, especially from outsiders or disgruntled minorities. Given the lack of public polling or uncensored media in the region, it is difficult to ascertain if these supporters are a silent majority or a tiny minority, speaking out in support of state policies because it serves their interest. Nevertheless, the Deng reform era in general can be characterized as a period of heightened loyalty to the state and new-found optimism after the previous 20 years of internal chaos and repression, similar in many respects to the period of relative loyalty when Xinjiang was first brought into the PRC and established as an Autonomous Region.

However, in the late 1980s and mid-1990s, this period of "loyalty" gave way to increasing expressions of "voice," not only among Uyghur, but also among a wide cross-section of local residents that felt the northwest was not keeping pace with the rapid development of the rest of the country. Many Uyghurs were particularly disappointed that the independence of the former Soviet Central Asian Republics in 1991 did not lead to independence or at least increased autonomy in their own state-declared Autonomous Region. Throughout the early and mid-1990s, increasing expressions of "voice" demonstrated these concerns from university protests to greater ethnic and civil unrest. Alternative histories and stories of Uyghur origins and heroes proliferated, radically different from what had been presented in official Chinese documents. Whether there were smaller, unreported expressions of voice in the past, the mid-1990s witnessed a number of public expressions of contrary views and dissatisfaction with state policies in the region.

In spring 1996, the *Xinjiang Daily* reported five serious social eruptions in the region that resulted in a crackdown that rounded up 2,773 terrorist suspects, 6,000 pounds of explosives, and 31,000 rounds of ammunition. Overseas Uyghur groups claimed that more than 10,000 were arrested with over 1,000 killed.[13] The largest protest, from February 2–8, 1996, was sparked by a Chinese raid on an evening Mashrap cultural meeting, where young Uyghur men and women gather for prayer, sing religious and folk songs, and feast.[14] Police actions in response to protests against the arrests made during the meeting led to 120 deaths and more than 2,500 arrests. Perhaps related to anger over the crackdown, the press reported on February 12 a bombing and train derailment, which was claimed to have been coordinated by the United Revolutionary Front based in Kazakhstan.[15] Following an uprising and crackdown in Yining, on February 25, in a well-coordinated operation, three bombs exploded simultaneously on three buses in downtown Urumqi, leading to 20 civilian deaths and scores of injured (including some Uyghurs). The Chinese government subsequently executed eight Uyghurs allegedly responsible for the bombings.[16] The United Revolutionary Front led by Yusupbek (Modan) Mukhlisi based in Almaty denied responsibility for the bombing.[17]

Later that spring, the United Revolutionary Front claimed responsibility for the bombing of a police building in Urumqi that was meant to disrupt anti-separatist security measures.[18] Then the violence came to Beijing. During March 7–8, two separate bombs exploded on public buses in the nation's capitol.[19] The first bomb in the Xidan district claimed three lives with 10 injured, while the second bomb killed two. The bombs were timed to take place during the Chinese National Peoples Congress and were widely attributed to Uyghur separatists, though this has never been independently verified and no group has ever claimed responsibility.[20]

The world's media heavily covered the Yining uprising on February 7, 1997, and the subsequent bombings in Urumqi and Beijing.[21] This distinguishes the late 1990s events from the events during the mid-1980s that met with little media coverage. One report suggested several incidents of violence in Xinjiang throughout late 1997 and early 1998 that ranged from "wanton killing of Han people," to assassination attempts on police, to various bomb blasts in the southern Tarim region were carried out by Xinjiang separatists, yet none of these incidents were independently verified or claimed by Uyghur organizations.[22] In addition, there were at least two major incidents in Xinjiang widely believed initially to have been carried out by Uyghur separatists, but later to have been found to be completely unrelated: the poisoning of elementary schoolchildren in Ghulje on May 8, 1998, and the explosion of radioactive material in downtown Urumqi, which was later determined to be due to PLA mishandling of weaponry.[23] Many Uyghur outside of China point to these events as proof that many events widely attributed to Uyghur separatists are either mistaken or deliberately instigated by saboteurs to provide the government with excuses for further crackdowns in the region.

In the late 1990s, the government responded with a host of arrests and new policy announcements. In Spring 1998, the National Peoples Congress passed a New Criminal Law that redefined "counterrevolutionary" crimes to be "crimes against the state" that are subject to severe prison terms and even execution. Included in "crimes against the state" were any actions considered to involve "ethnic discrimination" or "stirring up anti-ethnic sentiment."[24] Many human rights activists have argued that this is a thinly veiled attempt to criminalize "political" action and to make them appear as illegal as traffic violations, supporting China's claims that it holds "no political prisoners." Since any minority activity could be regarded as "stirring anti-ethnic feelings," many ethnic activists are concerned that the New Criminal Law will be easily turned against them.

In previous years, China denied any serious social or political problems in the region and followed the old Soviet "divide-and-rule" strategy, which sought to limit all references to Turkestan or even Turkology that might link the Uyghurs, Kazakhhs, and other Turkic-speaking minorities to broader pan-Turkic movements in the region. Yet certainly since early 2001, due to the desire to receive international support for its domestic war on terrorism, China's Foreign Ministry and the *People's Daily* have documented an ongoing series of incidents of "terrorism" and separatism since the large riot in the Xinjiang town of Yining of February 1997.

In June 2002, under U.S. and Chinese pressure, Pakistan returned one Uyghur activist to China, apprehended among hundreds of Taliban detainees, which follows a pattern of repatriations of suspected Uyghur separatists in Kazakhstan, Kyrgyzstan, and Uzbekistan. This detainee was supposedly one of several hundred Uyghurs arrested fighting with the Taliban, with up to 20 Uyghurs placed in the Guantanomo Bay detention facility.[25] Clearly, domestic responses to Chinese rule have changed dramatically in the last 20 years for there to be large groups of Uyghur militant Muslims fighting abroad, and for the Chinese government to publicize separatist actions inside and outside the region, launching large-scale suppressions of potential terrorists. Nevertheless, despite China's increasing crackdowns, fewer reports of civil unrest or terrorist acts have been reported since the late 1990s. This suggests a changing pattern of opposition to Chinese rule in the region.

LINKAGES TO TERRORISM

China's Uyghur separatists are small in number, poorly equipped, loosely linked, and vastly outgunned by the People's Liberation Army and People's Police. Though sometimes disgruntled about others' rights and mistreatment issues, China's nine other official Muslim minorities do not generally support Uyghur separatism; there is continued enmity between Uyghur and Hui (Tungan) in the region. Few Hui support an independent Xinjiang, and one million Kazakhs in Xinjiang would have very little say in an independent "Uyghuristan." Local support for separatist activities, particularly in Xinjiang and other border regions, is ambivalent and ambiguous at best, given the economic disparity between these regions and their foreign neighbors, including Tajikistan, Kyrgyzstan, Pakistan, and especially Afghanistan. Many local activists call not for complete separatism or real independence, but generally express concerns over environmental degradation, nuclear testing, religious freedom, over-taxation, and recently imposed limits on childbearing. Many ethnic leaders are simply calling for "real" autonomy according to Chinese law for the five Autonomous Regions that are each led by First Party Secretaries who are all Han Chinese controlled by Beijing.

Freedom of religion, protected by China's constitution, does not seem to be a key issue, as mosques are plentiful in the region and pilgrimages to Mecca are often allowed for Uyghur and other Muslims (though some visitors to the region report an increase in restrictions against mosque attendance by youth, students, and government officials). In addition, Islamic extremism does not as yet appear to have widespread appeal, especially among urban, educated Uyghur. However, the government has consistently rounded up any Uyghur suspected of being "too" religious, especially those identified as Sufis or the so-called Wahhabis (a euphemism in the region for strict Muslim, not an organized Islamic school). These periodic roundups, detentions, and public condemnations of terrorism and separatism have not erased the problem, but have forced it underground and increased the possibility of alienating Uyghur Muslims even further from mainstream Chinese society.

In spite of these structural challenges, most analysts agree that China is not vulnerable to the same ethnic separatism that split the former Soviet Union. But few doubt that should China fall apart, it would divide, like the USSR, along centuries-old ethnic, linguistic, regional, and cultural fault lines.[26] If China did fall apart, Xinjiang would split in a way that, according to Anwar Yusuf, President of the Eastern Turkestan National Freedom Center in Washington, DC, "would make Kosovo look like a birthday party." However, there seems to be very little support for radical political Islam and the term "jihad" is not commonly used.[27] As Rudelson (1997) has noted, many of the Uyghur nationalists are quite secular in their orientation, and overthrow of Chinese rule is related to issues of sovereignty and human rights, rather than those of religion. By contrast, Uyghur expatriates with whom I have spent time in the U.S., Canada, Turkey, and Europe tend to be quite religious, yet I have rarely heard them call for a holy war against the Chinese. Again, their concerns are more related to historic claims upon their ancestral lands, Chinese mistreatment of the Uyghur population, and a desire to return home to a "free East Turkestan."[28]

Since 9/11, very few groups have publicly advocated terrorism against the Chinese state, and most have denied any involvement in terrorist activities, though they may express sympathy for such activities. The East Turkistan National Congress, based in Munich, recently published a brochure entitled "Help the Uyghurs to Fight Terrorism."[29] In an interview with Enver Can, director of the ETNC in Munich on November 10, 2003, he reiterated the view that Uyghurs were depicted as terrorists in order to allow further Chinese consolidation of the region, and that as Muslims, Uyghurs were peaceful and opposed to violence. One exception is the "Islamic Party of Turkistan," which maintains a Web site entirely in Uyghur (in the Arabicized script used in China, not the Cyrillic that is still used in the Central Asian Republics).[30] The site advocates the overthrow of the Chinese government by any means and chronicles atrocities committed against the Uyghur in Xinjiang and Central Asia, with detailed reports on incidents in the region often drawn from BBC and Al-Jazeerah.

Even groups accused of the most violent incidents have backed away from supporting terrorism. A case in point is East Turkestan Liberation Organization (ETLO, also referred to as SHAT for the Turkic name, Shärqiy Türkistan Azatliq Täshkilati), led by the secretive Mehmet Emin Hazret. In a January 24, 2003, telephone interview with the Uyghur service of *Radio Free Asia*, Hazret admitted that there may be a need to establish a military wing of his organization that would target Chinese interests, he nevertheless denied any prior terrorist activity or any association with the East Turkestan Islamic Movement (ETIM). "We have not been and will not be involved in any kind of terrorist action inside or outside China," Hazret said. "We have been trying to solve the East Turkestan problem through peaceful means. But the Chinese government's brutality in East Turkestan may have forced some individuals to resort to violence."[31]

Hazret, a former screenwriter from Xinjiang who migrated to Turkey in his 40s, denied any connection between his organization and al Qaeda or Osama bin Laden. Nevertheless, he did see the increasing need for a military action against Chinese rule in the region: "Our principal goal is to achieve independence for East Turkestan by peaceful means. But to show our enemies and friends our determination on the East Turkestan issue, we view a military wing as inevitable ... The Chinese people are not our enemy. Our problem is with the Chinese government, which violates the human rights of the Uyghur people." Once again, a common pattern to his response regarding Chinese rule in the region was not to stress Islamic jihad or religious nationalism, but to emphasize human rights violations and Uyghur claims on Eastern Turkestan.

Documented separatist and violent incidents in Xinjiang have dropped off dramatically since the late 1990s. Philip Pan reported in a July 14, 2002, *Washington Post* interview that local Xinjiang security officials were only able to cite three relatively small occurrences.[32] Interestingly, few have noted that despite many incidents of ethnic and civil unrest in the region, not one significant terrorist attack against any strategic infrastructural target (oil refinery, pipeline, railroad, dam, or bridge) has ever been fully documented, nor have any local or international incidents been positively identified with any international Uyghur or Islamic organization. In addition, visitors to the region have increasingly reported a sense of disillusionment and disappointment among activists. One acquaintance mentioned to this author in late August 2001, "We've given up on independence; we just want to emigrate."

While violent incidents have declined or almost completely disappeared in Xinjiang since spring 1998, possibly due to the success of the "Strike Hard" campaign or the increasing disillusionment of activists since the peaceful reunification with Hong Kong, a rising number of international incidents involving Uyghurs outside of China have been attributed to organized separatist and terrorist activities. The 2002 White Paper, however, does argue that these incidents support the view that the Uyghurs are engaging in international terrorism directed against Chinese interests. Yet after examining the available evidence of international Uyghur violence, several sources indicate that most of the victims of violence have been other Uyghurs and Central Asians, rather than being directed against Han Chinese or the Chinese State.[33]

It is clear that there is a plurality of organizations, many of which compete for funds and take a wide variety of positions that support increased autonomy or separatism. In a personal interview with Erkin Alptekin in The Hague, he suggested that many of these organizations consisted of "one man" in order to increase the possibilities of asylum for the "leader of an organization banned in China." The list included "The United Revolutionary Front of Eastern Turkestan," whose leader Yusupbek Mukhlisi claims to have 30 armed units with 20 million Uyghurs primed for an uprising; the "Home of East Turkestan

Youth," said to be linked to Hamas with a reported 2,000 members; the "Free Turkestan Movement," whose leader Abdul Kasim is said to have led the 1990 Baren uprising; the Organization for the Liberation of Uighuristan, whose leader Ashir Vakhidi is said to be committed to fighting Chinese "occupation" of the "Uighur homeland"; and the so-called "Wolves of Lop Nor" who have claimed responsibility for various bombings and uprisings.

A U.S. State Department report claimed that all of these groups have tenuous links with al Qaeda, the Taliban, the Hizb-ut-Tahrir ("Islamic Revival"), and the Tableeghi Jamaat.[34] Many of these groups were listed in the 2002 Chinese report, but failed to mention ETIM. It came as a surprise, therefore, when at the conclusion of his August 2002 visit to Beijing, Deputy Secretary of State Richard Armitage identified ETIM as the leading Uyghur international terrorist group.[35] At the time, very few people, including activists deeply engaged in working for an independent East Turkistan, had ever heard of the ETIM group.[36] What was most surprising about the report was that it listed ETIM as responsible for more than 200 acts of terrorism leading to 162 deaths and 440 injuries, but the earlier Chinese reports had never specifically mentioned the organization.

Even the U.S. military did not seem to be aware of the group, as the September 28, 2001, "Special Report: Uighur Muslim Separatists" issued by the Virtual Information Center in Honolulu, which is funded by USCINCPAC (the Asia-Pacific Command), did not mention ETIM. Rather, the report concluded that there is "no single, identifiable group but there is violent opposition coordinated and possibly conducted by exiled groups and organizations within Xinjiang."[37] Significantly, in his study of the legal aspects surrounding the ETIM designation, John Z. Wang suggests that it is not one organization but a "terrorist network" consisting of at least eight "subgroups or forces" and another "five small organizations."[38] The problem is, the UN designation was directed toward one individual organization, not a network, which no one has demonstrated is coordinated at any level. John Z. Wang's case study, based on personal interviews with Chinese organizations and Internet surveys, seemingly takes the earlier reports regarding ETIM at face value, and does not refer to any historical or political studies by specialists on Xinjiang or the Uyghur.[39]

Nonviolent Means

Though silenced within China, Uyghur voices can frequently be heard abroad, and virtually on the Internet. Perhaps due to Chinese restrictions on public protest and a state-controlled media, or the deleterious effect of a war on domestic terrorism begun in the late 1990s, very few Uyghur voices can be heard today in the region that are critical of Chinese policies. Supporting primarily an audience of approximately 500,000 expatriate Uyghurs (estimates differ widely on the number of Uyghurs living outside of China in the diaspora[40]) there are at least 25 international organizations and Web sites working for the independence of "Eastern Turkestan."

Since the early 1990s, Uyghur Diaspora communities have sought without success to organize a single umbrella organization to coordinate international events and publicize their cause. While no single organization has yet to emerge, their continued efforts illustrate the almost insurmountable obstacles facing any single organization representing such a wide variety of communities and individuals with divergent agendas and conflicting views. In December 1992, the first General Assembly of Uyghur Diaspora met in Istanbul, Turkey. This was followed by several smaller meetings, mostly in Europe, but culminating in the December 18, 1998, establishment of the East Turkestan National Centre in Istanbul, with 11 Uyghur organizations participating from Turkey, Central Asia, and Germany. The following year, in Munich, the second East Turkestan National Congress was held from October 13–16, 1999, establishing the by-laws of an umbrella organization under the name of the "East Turkistan (Uyghuristan) National Congress," with a 15-member governing body, and became registered under German laws as a legal association. According to its 2003 brochure, there are 18 international Uyghur organizations belonging to ETNC.[41]

However, there are many other organizations that do not belong to this Congress (including ETIM and ETLO); some regard the ETNC as too pro-West, not Islamic enough, or even too pro-Uyghur (in that the name Uyghuristan is in the title of the organization and several organizations suggest that an independent Eastern Turkestan should be more inclusive of non-Uyghurs, including Kazakhs, Uzbeks, Hui, and even Han Chinese). As yet, there is no single coordinating body, though the Uyghur American Association in Washington, D.C., is increasing in importance.[42] This may have much to do with the important informational role of the Uyghur News Service of Radio Free Asia located in Washington. This follows the rise of the ETNC in Munich, which was established by Erkin Alptekin, followed three years later by Enver Can; they were hired by Radio Liberty to establish the Uyghur language service. Munich now contains the largest community of Uyghurs in Europe.

Although the UN and the United States government have agreed with China that at least one international organization, ETIM, is a

Uyghur-sponsored terrorist organization, the vast majority of the Eastern Turkistan independence and information organizations renounce violence. Supported largely by Uyghur emigres who left China prior to the Communist takeover in 1949, these organizations maintain a plethora of Web sites and activities that take a primarily negative view of Chinese policies in the region.[43] Although not all organizations advocate independence or separatism, the vast majority of them do press for radical change in the region, reporting not only human rights violations, but also environmental degradation, economic imbalances, and alternative histories of the region. In general, these Web sites can be divided roughly into those that are mainly information-based and others that are active advocacy sites. It is difficult to assess who the audience is for Web sites and organizations like these, as they are all blocked in China and mostly inaccessible in Central Asia due to either inadequate Internet access or the high costs of getting on the Web. It is clear, however, that Uyghurs in the Diaspora, particularly in Europe, Turkey, the United States, Canada, and Australia are frequent readers and contributors to these sites.

There are a number of publicly known Uyghur advocacy organizations, which grew to nearly 20 in the late 1990s but seemed to have declined in membership and activities since September 2001.[44] In the United States, one of the most active information and advocacy groups in the Washington, D.C., area is the Uyghur American Association, whose chairmen have been Alim Seytoff and Turdi Hajji.[45] Founded like many advocacy groups in the late 1990s, it supports various public lectures and demonstrations to further raise public awareness regarding Uyghur and Xinjiang issues.

LINKAGES TO THE GLOBAL WAR ON TERRORISM

While there is no evidence to suggest al Qaeda's involvement in Xinjiang and the use of the word "terrorist" to describe the separatist violence in the region is a misnomer, the United States supports Beijing's position on separatist violence. Previous attempts to promote an independent Uyghuristan have not been well received by the United States, which is generally committed to territorial integrity. For example, Mr. Yusuf indicated that the Eastern Turkestan National Freedom Center continued to support a free and independent Xinjiang.[46] On June 4, 1999, Yusuf met with President Clinton to press for fuller support for the Uyghur cause.[47] Subsequent Uyghur organizations have sought to pressure the Bush administration with varying degrees of success. Now many fear that with the United States and China cooperating on the war on terrorism, there is no hope for U.S. support of Uyghur human rights' issues.

As noted above, the East Turkestan Islamic Movement (ETIM) was recognized by the United Nations in October 2002 as an international terrorist organization responsible for domestic and international terrorist acts, which China claimed included a bombing of the Chinese consulate in Istanbul, assassinations of Chinese officials in Bishkek, and Uyghur officials in Kashgar thought to collaborate with Chinese officialdom.[48] This designation, however, created a controversy in that China and the U.S. presented little public evidence to positively link the ETIM organization with the specific incidents described.[49]

The main concern raised by those critical of this terrorist designation is that, with so many identified groups, it has not been made clear why ETIM in particular was singled out, unless it was for the political purpose of strengthening U.S.-China relations. Interestingly, Mukhlisi's United Revolutionary Front was not included with ETIM, despite its frequent claims of responsibility for violent acts in Xinjiang, such as the 1997 train derailment and police station bombings.[50] When I met with Yusupbek Mukhlisi in Almaty on two occasions in August 2003, he continued to advocate violence in the overthrow of the Chinese state in East Turkistan. He stated: "The Chinese government will never peacefully withdraw from the occupied territory of East Turkistan. We have no choice but to use violence." At the same time, many Uyghur have complained to me that although there have been many reported terrorist bombings in Tibet and frequent organized protests against Chinese rule that have led to violence outside of Tibet, they do not see the U.S. ever siding with China in condemning a Tibetan independence organization as terrorist. Therefore, it is unclear why the United States sides with China regarding violations of Uyghurs' rights.

Following Armitage's announcement and the State Department's report, the Chinese State Council issued its own report on January 21, 2002, charging that from 1990–2001 various Uyghur separatist groups "were responsible for over 200 terrorist incidents in Xinjiang" that resulted in the deaths of 162 people and injuries to 440 others. The report, titled "East Turkestan Terrorist Forces Cannot Get Away With Impunity," also dismissed allegations that Beijing had used the U.S.-led war on terrorism as a pretext to crack down on Uyghurs. The report condemned numerous Uyghur groups, including Hazret's ETLO, the ETIM, the Islamic Reformist Party "Shock Brigade", the East Turkestan Islamic Party, the East Turkestan Opposition Party, the East Turkestan Islamic Party of Allah, the Uyghur Liberation Organization, the Islamic Holy Warriors, and the East Turkestan International Committee.

Chinese authorities are clearly concerned that increasing international attention to the treatment of its minority and dissident peoples have put pressure on the region, with the U.S. and many Western governments continuing to criticize China for not adhering to its commitments to signed international agreements and human rights. In 2001, China ratified the International Covenant on Economic, Social, and Cultural Rights. Article One of the covenant says: "All peoples have the right of self-determination. By virtue of that right they freely determine their political status and freely pursue their economic, social, and cultural development." Article 2 reads: "All peoples may, for their own ends, freely dispose of their natural wealth and resources without prejudice to any obligations arising out of international economic cooperation, based upon the principle of mutual benefit and international law. In no case may a people be deprived of its own means of subsistence." Although China continues to quibble with the definition of "people," it is clear that the agreements are pressuring China to answer criticisms by Mary Robinson and other high-ranking human rights advocates about its treatment of minority peoples. Clearly, with Xinjiang representing the last Muslim region under communism, large trade contracts with Middle Eastern Muslim states, and five Muslim states on its western borders, Chinese authorities have more to be concerned about than just international condemnation for human rights abuses.

PROGRESS AND PROSPECTS

The history of Chinese-Muslim relations in Xinjiang has been one of relative peace and quiet, broken by enormous social and political disruptions, and fostered by both internal and external crises. The relative quiet of the last three years does not indicate that the ongoing problems of the region have been resolved or opposition dissolved. The opposition to Chinese rule in Xinjiang has not reached the level of Chechnya or the intifada in Palestine, but is similar to the Basque separatists of the ETA in Spain, or former IRA in Ireland and England. It is a conflict that may erupt in limited, violent moments of terrorism and resistance. And just as these oppositional movements have not been resolved in Europe, the Uyghur problem in Xinjiang does not appear to be one that will readily go away. The admitted problem of Uyghur terrorism and dissent, even in the Diaspora, is thus problematic for a government that wants to encourage integration and development in a region where the majority population are not only ethnically different, but also devoutly Muslim. How does a government integrate a strongly religious minority (be it Muslim, Tibetan, Christian, or Buddhist) into a Marxist-capitalist system? China's policy of intolerance toward dissent and economic stimulus has not seemed to resolve this issue.

It is important to note here that other border regions with large minority populations, such as Yunnan, Guizhou, Guangxi (with 16 million Zhuang), Hainan, and even the Ningxia Hui Autonomous Region, have not had any reported separatist or terrorist activities. In addition, the poorest Muslim groups in China and the least educated are to be found in the Gansu/Qinghai border areas among the Dongxiang, Baoan, and Salar, where there have been no reports of separatism, violence, or even Islamic radicalism. Most significantly, China's 1.2 million Kazakhs, though living in Xinjiang under similar conditions as the Uyghur, have not engaged in any organized resistance to Chinese rule, nor have they sought to align themselves with Kazakhstan. Indeed, recent reports from the region suggest that Kazakhs from China who initially accepted resettlement offers in Kazakhstan over the last 10 years have been returning to China. Clearly, by its own admission, the problems in Xinjiang and the oppositional voices of mostly Uyghur groups must be addressed by the state.

The problems facing Xinjiang, however, are much greater than those of Tibet if it were to become independent. Not only is it more integrated into the rest of China, but the Uyghur part of the population is less than half of the total and primarily located in the south, where there is less industry and natural resources, except for oil. As noted above, however, unless significant investment is found, Tarim oil and energy resources will never be a viable source of independent wealth. Nevertheless, in his book, *The New Great Game: Blood and Oil in Central Asia,* Lutz Kleveman argues that the United States and Britain are "exploiting the 'war on terror' to further American oil interests in the Caspian region."[51] As James Dorian, Brett Wigdortz, and Dru Gladney argued earlier, this "new great game" will have serious consequences for inter-ethnic relations in the region.[52]

Poor past relations between the three main Muslim groups, Uyghur, Kazakh, and Hui, suggest that conflicts among Muslims would be as great as those between Muslims and Han Chinese. Most local residents believe that independence would lead to significant conflicts between these groups, along ethnic, religious, urban-rural, and territorial lines. One well-known phrase heard among Uyghur since the 1930s in the region depicts these tensions: "Kill the Hui, Destroy the Han, and get rid of the Kazakhs!" Given the harsh climate and poor resources in the region, those caught in the middle would have few places to flee. Xinjiang Han would naturally seek to return to the interior of China, since Russia and Mongolia would be in no position to receive them. Yet given the premise that only a complete collapse of the state could precipitate a viable independence movement and internal civil war in Xinjiang, there would be few places the Han would be able to go. Certainly, the bordering provinces of Gansu and Qinghai would be just as disrupted, and Tibet would not be an option. Uyghur refugees would most likely seek to move south, since the Han would dominate the north and Kazakhstan and Kyrgyzstan would close off the western routes. That leaves only the southern routes, and with the exception of Pakistan, no country in the region would probably be equipped to receive them. Certainly, they would not be better off in present-day Tajikistan and Afghanistan. Given the ongoing conflicts in Kashmir, even Pakistan, the most likely recipient of Uyghur refugees, would probably not wish further destabilization of the region. India, despite its poor relations with China, would certainly not want to add to its Muslim population. During many conversations in Xinjiang with local residents, Muslim and Han alike, it became clear that this fact is well known. Most think that in such a worst-case scenario, there would be nothing to do but stay and fight.

China is a sovereign state, and like all modern nations in the era of globalization faces tremendous challenges from migration, economic imbalance, ethnic unrest, and cyber-separatism. The future of this vastly important region, which Owen Lattimore once called the "pivot of Asia," depends on it. Since 2001, the entire region has once again become pivotal to the wider region. The sources of discontent for Uyghur opposition groups remain the same: massive, unrestricted Han migration to the region; the dramatically increasing gap between the wealthy and mainly Uyghur poor; decreasing educational opportunities for poorer residents related to the market economy; higher mortality rates among Uyghur; unresolved health problems due to nuclear testing in the region; and increased restriction on religious and cultural practices.[53] In general, Muslims outside China are convinced that the Uyghurs are being targeted unfairly in order to advance the interest of the state.[54] These international Muslims will be a key factor in helping to transform the occasional "flashes in the pan" in the region into a larger transnational flashpoint that may spill over into neighboring areas of U.S. engagement (such as Afghanistan, Tajikistan, and Kyrgyzstan), or involve the other states of the Shanghai Cooperative Organization.

Although Uyghurs within the region have not engaged in violence since the late 1990s, there is no reason to believe that ethnic and religious tensions will not erupt into violence. This chapter does suggest, however, that given the changes in the region since 9/11, particularly with the increased counterterrorism cooperation between China, the

United States, and the member states of the Shanghai Cooperative Organization, one should not expect the possibility of organized violence or separatism. Disorganized, ad hoc, and random civil unrest will continue to plague the region until China addresses some of the issues raised by its virtual citizens in the Diaspora. The Xinjiang regional government, aware of these challenges, is now seeking to lessen the gap between rich and poor in the region and satisfy local demands for fair treatment and parity in economic development. China's economic boom has proven to be increasingly successful in other formerly tense and poor border areas, such as Yunnan, Guangxi, and Manchuria. Given the vast challenges in Xinjiang, it remains to be seen how successful these efforts will be.

NOTES

1. Erik Eckholm, "U.S. Labeling of Group in China as Terrorist is Criticized," *The New York Times*, September 13, 2002, p. 1. On September 11, 2002, the US, China, Afghanistan, and Kyrgyzstan requested and received the UN Security Council designation of ETIM as an international terrorist organization under UN Security Council Resolutions 1267 and 1390.

2. Bao Lisheng, "Chinese Officials Say not Much Terrorism in Xinjiang" Ta Kung Pao Hong Kong, September 2, 2003.

3. "China Also Harmed by Separatist-Minded Eastern Turkestan Terrorists," *People's Daily*, October 10, 2001.

4. See "China: China Increases Suppression in Xinjiang," *Oxford Analytica*, December 20, 2002. The report concludes: "Distinguishing between genuine counterterrorism and repression of minority rights is difficult and the Uyghur case points to a lack of international guidelines for doing so. In any case, Chinese policies, not foreign-sponsored terrorism, are the cause of Uyghur unrest. China's development and control policy in Xinjiang is unlikely to stabilize the region as long as development benefits remain so unevenly distributed."

5. Information Office of the Chinese State Council, "East Turkestan Terrorist Forces Cannot Get Away with Impunity," January 21, 2002. Online. Available HTTP: <http://english.peopledaily.com.cn/200201/21/eng20020121_89078.shtml>.

6. Information Office of the Chinese State Council, "History and Development of Xinjiang," May 26, 2003. Online. Available HTTP: <http:///www.china-embassy.org/eng/c4755.html>.

7. Charles Hutzler, "Trade is China's Carrot to Muslim Separatists," *Wall Street Journal*, September 21, 2001.

8. Rym Brahimi, CNN News Service, "Russia, China, and Central Asian Leaders Pledge to Fight Terrorism, Drug Smuggling," August 25, 1999.

9. Amnesty International, *People's Republic of China: Gross Violations of Human Rights in the Xinjiang Uighur Autonomous Region* (London, April 21, 1999), p. 24. Online. Available HTTP: <http://web.amnesty.org/library/index/ENGASA170181999>.

10. See writings by Isa Yusuf Alptekin's son, Erkin Alptekin, which also present alternative histories of the Uyghur from that of the Chinese state: Alptekin, Erkin, Uygur Türkleri [The Uyghur Turks]. Istanbul: Boğaziçi Yayınları, 1978; and "Xinjiang: a Time Bomb Waiting to Explode," *South China Morning Post* (Hong Kong), May 29, 2002. For Alptekin's involvement with the Unrecognized Nations and Peoples Organization in The Hague. Online. Available HTTP: <www.unpo.org/member/eturk.html>.

11. See the neibu (internal circulation only) book edited by Ma Dazheng, which rather reluctantly admits: "Since the first half of the year 2000, the situation in Xinjiang has been peaceful (平静), despite my earlier description of the seriousness of this issue, and should be accurately described as dramatically changed since the internationalization of the Xinjiang problem (新疆问题国际化)" see Ma Dazheng (马大正). 2003. 国家利益高于一切: 新疆稳定问题的观察与思考. (Urumqi: Xinjiang People's Publishing House, 2003): 128.

12. See Dru C. Gladney, *Muslim Chinese: Ethnic Nationalism in the People's Republic* (Cambridge: Harvard University Press, 1996), pp. 122–130.

13. *Xinjiang Daily*, April 9, 1997, from *People's Republic of China: Gross Violation of Human Rights in the Xinjiang Uyghur Autonomous Region*, Amnesty International, 1999; Reuters, Beijing, June 26, 1997, citing the *Xinjiang Daily* of July 21, 1997.

14. See Ildiko Beller-Hann, "Making the Oil Fragrant: Dealings with the Supernatural Among the Uyghurs in Xinjiang" *Asian Ethnicity* 2, No. 1 (2001): 9–23; Nathan Light's dissertation, *Slippery Paths: The Performance and Canonization of Turkic Literature and Uyghur Muqam Song in Islam and Modernity* (Bloomington: Indiana University, 1998); Light's informative Web page on Uyghur and Turkic culture and art. Online. Available HTTP: <http://www.utoledo.edu/~nlight/mainpage.htm>.

15. "Xinjiang Uygurs Blast Railway in Retaliation; Lanzhou Train Derails, Casualties Unknown," *Ping Kuo Jih Pao* (Hong Kong), February 17, 1997.

16. "Five 'Counterrevolutionaries' Executed for Bomb Explosions," *Xinjiang Ribao* (Urumqi), May 31, 1995, p. 1; "Xinjiang Government Worker Says Four Killed in Urumqi Blasts," *Voice of Russia World Service* (Moscow), February 26, 1997; "Further on Bomb Explosions in Xinjiang," *AFP* (Hong Kong), February 26, 1997.

17. Pamela Pun. "Officials Say No Links Found Between Separatists, Bombing," *Hong Kong Standard* (Hong Kong), March 11, 1997, p. 8.

18. "Exile Group Claims Bomb Blast in Xinjiang," *AFP* (Hong Kong), March 1, 1997.

19. Tung-chou Kuang, "Zhongnanhai Holds Emergency Meeting to Discuss Explosion Case, Mayor Says It was a Political Incident in Retaliation Against Society," *Sing Tao Jih Pao* (Hong Kong), March 9, 1997, p. A1; "Cracking Down on Separatist Organizations to Become Central Topic of Discussion at NPC, CPPCC Sessions," *Ping Kuo Jih Pao* (Hong Kong), March 3, 1998, p. A20; "Radio Reports Bomb Blasts in Beijing, Guangzhou," *Broadcasting Corporation of China News Network* (Taipei), March 9, 1997.

20. See "A Bomb in Beijing," *The Economist*, March 13, 1997; Patrick E. Tyler, "Chinese Muslims Recount Their Days of Terror," *The New York Times*, November 10, 1996, p.3. Note that many Uyghurs in the Diaspora believe that the bombs were set by Chinese authorities in order to justify a crackdown on Uyghurs in Xinjiang, "Tao Siju Says No Evidence Shows Xinjiang People Commit Crime," *Ming Pao* (Hong Kong), March 11, 1997, p. A15.

21. "China Fears for its Wild West," *The Economist*, November 13, 1997.

22. "Cracking Down on Separatist Organizations to Become Central Topic of Discussion at NPC, CPPCC Sessions," *Ping Kuo Jih Pao* (Hong Kong), March 3, 1998, p. A20.

23. On the poisonings, see "Chinese Doctors Poisoned 150 Children," *Eastern Turkistan Information Center*, May 15, 1998; "China Executes Woman for Fatal Child Poisonings," *Deutsche Presse-Agentur*, January 19, 1999. On the radioactive detonation, said to be due to the sale of dated weaponry by one PLA unit to another based in Guyuan, Ningxia, see Zhao Yu, "Defying Hazard in Five Days of Relentless Pursuit, Police Crack Smuggled Radioactive Case," *Xinjiang Ribao* (Urumqi), November 11, 1998, p. 1.

24. Amnesty International, op.cit, p. 21.

25. There is not a third country willing to accept Muslims suspected of fighting with the Taliban and enemies of the Chinese state. Most informed sources believe the fate of these Uyghur will not be resolved for a very long time. "Uyghur Separatist Sentenced to Death," *Reuters,* October 18, 2001; Craig S. Smith, "Fearing Unrest, China Pressures Muslim Group," *The New York Times*, October 5, 2001; Pamela Pun, "Separatists Trained in Afghanistan, says Official," *The Standard*, October 22, 2001.

26. Dru C. Gladney, "China's Ethnic Reawakening," *Asia Pacific Issues*, No. 18 (1995): 1–8.

27. In terms of content, it is interesting to note that a cursory monitoring of Uyghur Web sites reveals very little that can be associated with militant or radical Islam, and almost no calls for an Islamic "Jihad" against the Chinese state. Most of the issues as noted above involve documenting the plight and history of the Uyghurs under Chinese rule in Xinjiang as opposed to their glorious, independent past and long history in the region.

28. See K. L. Syroezkhkin, *Myths and Reality of Ethnic Separatisms in China and the Security of Central Asia* (Almaty: Daik Press, 2003), p. 719. For an earlier analysis of Uyghur "ethnogenesis" and its relation to Xinjiang history and Uyghur sovereignty issues, see Dru C. Gladney, "The Ethnogenesis of the Uighur," *Central Asian Survey* 9, No. 1 (1990): 1–28.

29. See Eastern Turkistan (Uyghuristan) National Congress. (N.D.) *Help the Uyghurs to Fight Terrorism* (Munich: East Turkistan [Uyghuristan] National Congress).

30. See http://www.turkistan-islam.com.

31. Radio Free Asia, Uyghur service, "Separatist leader vows to target Chinese government (RFA)," January 24, 2003. Online. Available HTTP: <http://www.rfa.org/service/index.html?service=uyg>.

32. Philip Pan "In China's West, Ethnic Strife Becomes 'Terrorism," *Washington Post*, July 14, 2002, P. A4.

33. In a recent detailed overview, James Millward concludes that the international incidents indicate more "expatriate Uyghur fractiousness" than any threat to Chinese interests (see James A. Millward, "Xinjiang: Anti-state Organizations and Violence in International Context" presented at the East-West Center, Honolulu, July 25, 2003, p.27). I am grateful to Prof. Millward for his sharing his paper with me.

34. See Dewardric L. McNeal and Kerry Dumbaugh, "China's Relations with Central Asian States and Problems with Terrorism, CRS Report for Congress" (Washington, DC: Congressional Research Service, Library of Congress, 2002).

35. Conclusion of China Visit Press Conference, Deputy Secretary of State Richard L. Armitage (Beijing, China, U.S. Department of State, August 26, 2002).

36. For example, Mehmet Hazret in a recent interview claimed he had never heard of ETIM. "I hadn't even heard of ETIM until the Chinese government mentioned its name in a report in January 2002," he said. "But I knew the leaders of this group whom the report mentioned. For many years, they were in Chinese prisons for political reasons, and they escaped from China. We don't have any organizational relations with them because politically we don't share the same goals. But I cannot believe they carried out any terrorist attacks as the Chinese authorities say they did, because they themselves are victims of Chinese state terrorism." *Radio Free Asia*, Uyghur service, "Separatist leader vows to target Chinese government (RFA)," January 24, 2003. Online. Available HTTP: <http://www.rfa.org/service/index.html?service=uyg>.

37. See "Special Report: Uighur Muslim Separatists," *Virtual Information Center*, September 28, 2001, p. 6. Online. Available HTTP: <www.vic-info.org>.

38. Wang lists the following "subgroups or forces" of ETIM: East Liberation Organization; East Turkistan International Committee, United Committee of Uygurs' Organizations (Central Asia and Xinjiang), Central Asian Uyghur Hezbollah in Kazakhstan, Turkistan Party (Pakistan), Eastern Turkistan Islamic Movement (Afghanistan), Eastern Turkistan Islamic Resistance Movement (Turkey), and Eastern Turkistan Youth League (Switzerland). Among the "five small organizations" he lists: Eastern Turkistan Islamic Party, Eastern Turkistan Opposition Party, Shock Brigade of the Islamic Reformist Party, Eastern Turkistan Party of Allah, and Uyghur Liberation Organization. John Z. Wang, "Eastern Turkistan Islamic Movement: A Case Study of a New Terrorist Organization in China," *International Journal of Offender Therapy and Comparative Criminology* 47, No. 5: (2003): 568.

39. Wang (ibid, p. 569) cites the "paucity of literature" on the subject but does mention any materials on Xinjiang in Chinese, Western, or Turkic languages, other than the "Encyclopedia of China," Xinjian-Uyghur Autonomous Region [sic] (New York: Dorothy Perkins & Roundtable Press, 1999). He repeats the widely believed, but completely baseless, view that there are 35 million Muslims in China (despite the maximum 20 million figure on which most specialists are agreed).

40. Yitzhak Shichor estimates approximately 500,000 living abroad, about 5–6 percent of the total world Uyghur population. See "Virtual Transnationalism: Uyghur Communities in Europe and the Quest for Eastern Turkestan Independence." Unpublished paper, 2002.

41. Eastern Turkistan (Uyghuristan) National Congress. (N.D.), *Help the Uyghurs to Fight Terrorism* (Munich: East Turkistan [Uyghuristan] National Congress, 2003), pp. 20–22.

42. In his message, Radio Free Asia president Richard Richter notes the goal of RFA is to provide "objective" news reporting for the region: "Our first broadcast was in Mandarin to China on 29 September 1996. Now there are broadcasts in Tibetan, Cantonese, Uyghur, Burmese, Vietnamese, Lao, Khmer (to Cambodia), and Korean (to North Korea). The director of the Uyghur service is Dolkun Kamberi, a Uyghur scholar born in Xinjiang who received his Ph.D. in Central Asian history from Columbia University.

43. One of the best sites in this genre is that by Dr. Nathan Light of the University of Toledo, which not only includes most of his dissertation and useful articles on Uyghur history, music, and culture, but also directs readers to other links to the region. Online. Available HTTP: <http://www.utoledo.edu/~nlight>. See also the *Turkestan Newsletter* (Turkistan-N) maintained by Mehmet Tutuncu of SOTA. Online. Available HTTP: <www.euronet.nl/users/sota/Turkestan.html>, the Open Society Institute's www.erasianet.org, The Uyghur Information Agency's www.uyghurinfo.com, and the virtual library of the Australian National University based "Eastern Turkestan WWW VL" www.ccs.uky.edu/~rakhim/et.html.

44. A list of some of the international Uyghur and East Turkistan organization can be found on http://uyghuramerican.org/Uyghurorganiz.html and http://www.Uyghur.org/adres/Uyghur_organization.htm.
45. See their Web site introduction: http://uyghuramerican.org. "The Uyghur American Association was established on May 23, 1998, in Washington, D.C., at the First Uyghur American Congress.
46. Anwar Yusuf, President of the Eastern Turkestan National Freedom Center, Washington, DC. Personal interview, April 14, 1999.
47. Turkestan News & Information Network, "Press Release," June 8, 1999.
48. The East Turkestan Islamic Movement (ETIM) is known only as a shadowy group that was previously active in Afghanistan and founded in the mid-1990s by Hassan Mashum. Mahsum had served three years in a labor camp in Xinjiang and had recruited other Uyghurs, including his number-three leader Rashid, who was captured with the Taliban and returned to China in Spring 2001. See Charles Hutzler, "China-Iraq Policy Is Risky For US," *Asian Wall Street Journal,* September 10, 2001.
49. "China Also Harmed by Separatist-Minded Eastern Turkestan Terrorists," *People's Daily,* October 10, 2001; Erik Eckholm, "U.S. Labeling of Group in China as Terrorist is Criticized," *The New York Times,* September 13, 2002; Charles Hutzler, "U.S. Gesture to China Raises Crackdown Fears," *Wall Street Journal,* September 13, 2002.
50. "Exile Group Claims Bomb Blast in Xinjiang," *AFP* (Hong Kong), March 1, 1997.
51. Lutz Kleveman, *The New Great Game: Blood and Oil in Central Asia* (New York: Atlantic Books, 2003), p. 21.
52. See James P. Dorian, Brett Wigdortz, and Dru Gladney. "Central Asia and Xinjiang, China: Emerging Energy, Economic, and Ethnic Relations," *Central Asian Survey* 16, No. 4 (1997): pp. 461–486.
53. See "China: China Increases Suppression in Xinjiang" *Oxford Analytica,* December 20, 2002. The report notes: "Uighur desire for self-rule has been strengthened by the political climate in Central Asia, a heightened sense of Islamic cultural and ethnic identity across the new republics, the support of Islamic groups in the new republics, and the radicalizing effect of the war in Afghanistan."
54. See for example, the RIDEP Institute publication, *Militant Islamic Movements in Indonesia and South-East Asia*, in which Kusnanto Anggoro in a chapter on "The Threats of Terrorism in the Post September 11" declares "China has tried to use the international anti-terrorist agenda to justify its broad repression of ethnic Uighurs in Xinjiang, including peaceful activist and Moslem religious groups" (p. 282–283).

IV
Africa

The Trans-Saharan Arc

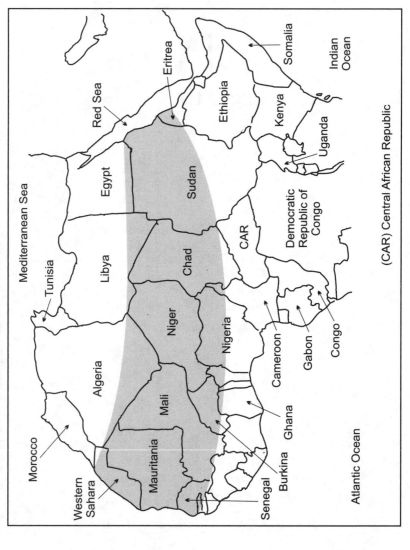

(CAR) Central African Republic

12

THE TRANS-SAHARAN ARC

Stephen A. Emerson

INTRODUCTION

The trans-Saharan region of Africa forms an important strategic arc cutting across the bulk of West Africa—including the northern portion of Nigeria and southern Algeria—and stretches from the Atlantic Ocean in the west to the Red Sea in the east. It is a place where Arab and African cultures begin to merge, of powerful and competing beliefs, and where tradition often clashes with modernity, making it one of the most contentious and conflict-prone areas of the world. Vast, ungoverned spaces; unsecured frontiers; large, uncontrolled population movements; extreme poverty; drought and the resulting famine; and persistent political and socioeconomic conflict are some of the defining characteristics of this region.

Although the trans-Saharan region has great potential (it is in fact home to rich mineral deposits) weak state institutions, authoritarian rule, corruption, and ineffectual conflict-mediation mechanisms perpetuate a climate of distrust and political and social alienation. These and other factors combine to create a vast territory wracked with protracted conflict and political instability, making it highly vulnerable to external interference and manipulation. Given these circumstances it is not surprising that the trans-Sahara and its vast ungoverned spaces has become a major focus of U.S.-African strategy in the global war on terrorism. "We're [the United States] trying to get it under control before it becomes too bad. That's one of the lessons we learned in Afghanistan,

I think that we can't allow environments like that to exist anymore," said General Charles Wald, deputy commander of U.S. European Command.[1] Accordingly, Washington has adopted a proactive approach to the region that seeks to preempt the trans-Sahara from developing into a serious security threat to the United States.

In many ways, the region is a microcosm of the problems besetting the continent. Given its legacy of enduring conflict and severe lack of governmental resources to address its problems, the region is likely to remain dangerously unstable for the foreseeable future. Ironically, the very weakness of national governments will force them and the international community to seek more collective solutions to the trans-Sahara's problems.

NATURE OF THE FLASHPOINT

From the shores of the Atlantic Ocean and cutting a broad swath across the great Sahara Desert and the Sahel of western Africa into central and northern Sudan and skirting the Ethiopian highlands to the Red Sea, the trans-Saharan arc cuts across nine different countries or parts of countries.[2] It encompasses nearly 3 million square miles—or nearly the size of the continental United States (Mali and Niger alone are each nearly twice the size of the state of Texas)—and is home to approximately 120 million people. The region is a foreboding place consisting largely of desert and semi-arid lands, but giving way to brush and grasslands at its southern margins. Much of it is sparsely inhabited by nomadic people eking out a meager existence as their forebears had done for centuries, while the relatively fertile areas are more densely populated and comparatively prosperous. Nevertheless, it is overall a harsh environment that contains some of the poorest countries in the world and is increasingly being seen as a major breeding ground for violent conflict, terrorism, and instability. As such, the region poses a serious challenge to African and global peace and security.

The notion of an all-inclusive region spanning the desert belt of western Africa and the Sudan is not really a new construction. Long before it came to be viewed as strategically important by outsiders, the countries of the trans-Sahara arc were linked together through a common historical legacy and shared socioeconomic bonds. Most of the trans-Sahara is composed of the interior of former French West Africa and the northern part of what was French Equatorial Africa and thus shares a mutual legacy of colonialism and resistance, language, and dependent economic development. A centuries-old Islamic culture in its many manifestations dominates the territory, although significant religious minorities reside in some countries. In the more remote reaches the central government's presence is often weak or even nonexistent, resulting in a de facto reliance on semi-autonomous local rulers and close-knit communities to exercise authority. Traditional caravan routes that once linked the ancient trading kingdoms of West Africa to the northern Mediterranean coast still crisscross the region, as do the pilgrimage routes that transverse the territory from west to east on their way to Mecca. Even today, these corridors bind countries socially and economically together; transnational commerce—both legal and illegal—remains critical to the economy of the region at large.

The legacy of colonialism and subsistence government has left most countries of the trans-Sahara extremely underdeveloped, poor, and ill-governed.[3] They are some of the largest recipients of developmental and humanitarian aid in Africa, and six of nine countries—Burkina Faso, Chad, Mali, Mauritania, Niger, and Senegal—suffer from burdensome international debt and were listed as Heavily Indebted Poor Countries (HIPCs) by the International Monetary Fund in 2005.[4] Although recent oil discoveries in the region, such as in Chad and Mauritania, hold out the prospect for economic improvement, key issues of corruption, mismanagement, and division of revenues need to be effectively resolved first. Politically, the trans-Saharan countries have a long tradition of military coups and authoritarian rule. Nearly all have experienced extended periods of military rule since independence, and only Senegal maintains a strong tradition of democratic governance. There are, however, some positive signs of democratic development emerging in recent years, with Mali and Nigeria making great strides in this area and the ending of Sudan's civil war possibly paving the way for a more representative national government there.

This shared experience, as well as similar political, social, and economic backgrounds, presents the countries of the region with a common set of security problems, which they appear ill-prepared to handle. The primary security challenges facing governments are securing national frontiers and large ungoverned areas, combating domestic and international terrorism, and reducing domestic and regional conflict.

Securing National Frontiers and Large Ungoverned Areas

A fundamental task of government is to guard its borders and administer its territory, yet the majority of the governments of the region lack the basic capabilities and resources to do so. With the exception of Nigeria, their security forces are too small, poorly equipped, and ill-trained to effectively monitor and secure their exceedingly long and often remote borders. Mali has nearly 4,500 miles of border; Chad and Niger each have over 3,500 miles of frontier. This inability also complicates government efforts to control or monitor both benign and malicious population movements—from the migration of nomadic tribesmen and refugees fleeing conflict-torn societies to criminal, antigovernment rebel or terrorist elements seeking sanctuary or easy passage—across and within their countries. The Algerian terrorist group the Salifist Group for Preaching and Combat (GSPC), for example, operates freely across Algeria's southern borders into neighboring states with relative ease, and the smuggling of contraband across international borders is a key part of the region's informal economy. Without the prospect of being able to secure their frontiers and exercise effective administration, trans-Saharan countries will be hard-pressed to deal with illegal activities, such as human trafficking, smuggling of weapons and contraband, and transnational crime, not to mention the challenge of combating international terrorism.

Combating Domestic and International Terrorism

A few countries in the region, most notably Algeria, have a history of domestic terrorism, but increasingly the new threat is seen as coming from the spread of international terrorist networks into the region. With its huge open spaces, unsecured borders, potentially sympathetic Muslim populations, and weak governments and security forces, the region appears ripe for infiltration by radical Islamist extremists. As such, many in the U.S. government view the trans-Sahara as a potential breeding ground for the next wave of international terrorists and believe that it will become the next African battleground in the global war on terrorism. Major General Thomas Csrnko, commander of Special Operations Command Europe, is worried, for example, that al Qaeda is now assessing African groups in the region for "franchising opportunities."[5] With their limited financial and human resources, however, African governments will be hard pressed to effectively combat the unfolding terrorist threat without extensive international assistance.

Reducing Domestic and Regional Conflict

In many respects the trans-Sahara poignantly represents the powerful divide between vastly contrasting cultures, beliefs, and societies on the continent. It is a place where Arab and African cultures meet; of powerful Islamic, Christian, or animist beliefs; of competing nomadic and sedentary societies; and where tradition often clashes with modernity. This makes it ripe for conflict on many levels, as weak governments and fragile institutions lack the means necessary to prevent these divisions from evolving into full-blown, violent confrontations. These sharply contrasting differences present not only a serious threat to national security, but also to regional stability because of the spillover effect of violent domestic conflict onto regional neighbors. The spread of domestic conflict from Algeria to its southern neighbors, the flood of Sudanese refugees fleeing Darfur for Chad, and the spillover of the irredentist struggle in the Casamare territory of Senegal are all indications of this regionalization of conflict. Furthermore, the existence of persistent conflict makes the entire trans-Sahara extremely vulnerable to external exploitation and international actors' competing agendas.

HISTORICAL CONTEXT

Unresolved or chronic conflict situations within the trans-Sahara present the most serious challenge to regional security and stability. Although the underlying causes and factors driving each conflict are unique in themselves, we can usually identify common elements or threads across various conflicts. In doing so, one finds that several very distinct types of conflict situations tend to dominate the region: (a) religious or sectarian; (b) racial, cultural, or ethnic; (c) resource competition; and (d) political power struggles.

Religious or sectarian differences are at the source of many conflicts in the region and are some of the most visible to outside observers. In fact, elements of racial, cultural, or ethnic conflict are all too frequently mistaken for manifestations of religious conflict, as in the case of clashes between African and Arab Muslims. Despite the apparent religious homogeneity across the region given the dominant position of Islam, several countries—including Chad, Nigeria, and Sudan—have significant religious minorities, and the dividing line between Muslims and Christian or animists communities is often quite pronounced.[6] Moreover, when religious conflict does flare up in these societies it often turns extremely violent and deadly; religious violence between Muslims and Christians in northern Nigeria, for example, has left thousands dead over the years.

Often overlooked sectarian divisions within Muslim countries are another significant source of tension. This struggle between various strains or interpretations of Islam is prominent in the trans-Sahara given its tradition of al-Islam al-shabi or "populist Islam." Over the centuries, Islamic communities across the region have developed and nurtured their own blend of religion, tradition, and culture leading to the growth and popularity of mysticism and religious brotherhoods.

Traditionally, populist Islam as practiced in the trans-Sahara has served to temper extremist and fundamentalist appeals by outsiders, who are often viewed with great suspicion. Differences between many of these Islamic sects, however, have often fueled intra-religious conflict in the region. For instance, they have been a chief source of tension within northern Arab political groupings in Sudan since independence.

Stretching as it does across the shadowy divide between North Africa and sub-Saharan Africa, the trans-Saharan arc spans the unique blending of Arab and African peoples, cultures, and traditions that has over time created some of the most dynamic and powerful societies on the continent.[7] Unfortunately, it has also sown the bitter seeds of divisiveness and conflict, and the undertones of racial, culture, or ethnic conflict are constantly present across the region. As a home to thousands of distinct ethnic groups, contrasting languages, lifestyles, and customs, confrontations across racial or ethno-cultural lines are inevitable. As with the rest of Africa, these conflicts are frequently rooted in past colonial policies that resulted in uneven development, ethnic favoritism, and the division of ethnic groups across international boundaries, as well as by African politicians seeking to exploit ethnic divisions for political gain. Likewise, efforts to create a sense of nationhood and national unity through the imposition of "cultural imperialism" have frequently backfired and tended to highlight differences rather than build a common heritage.

Intense competition over resources is at the center of many conflicts, too, as communities try to gain or maintain control over scarce resources. This is especially true of desperately poor countries in the trans-Sahara where access to basic resources, such as land, water, and livestock, is literally a matter of survival. Not surprisingly, these types of confrontations are extremely difficult to resolve, because they involve life and death issues. At the other end of the spectrum, conflict is frequently caused by disputes over the appropriate division of national wealth. For many of the countries of the region these disputes center on the revenue generated from mineral wealth, and oil exports in particular.[8] The most serious of these tend to revolve around what local oil-producing areas see as exploitation by their governments, because the revenue they generate is earmarked for national treasuries. Ironically, many oil-producing areas are some of the most underdeveloped and poverty stricken; this is certainly the case in Nigeria's Niger River delta and in southern Sudan. In these cases, the failure of local populations to reap significant financial benefits has fed violent conflict by reinforcing existing grievances and further alienating the people from their central governments.

Another type of conflict that threatens the security and stability of the region is the struggle over political power within countries and, more precisely the ways in which it manifests itself. Fundamentally, this contest pits competing interests, groups, ideas, and even visions of the future against one another. This type of political competition is a healthy part of the societal debate, but without adequate structures, institutions, and mechanisms to peacefully channel and direct this competition it can turn into highly divisive conflict. This is especially true where there is a winner-take-all attitude and/or where the opposition sees no realistic chance of assuming power from the incumbents through existing political structures. Unfortunately, this latter pattern has been all too characteristic of political power struggles in the region. Although a significant political evolution is underway in a number of countries as they seek to embrace peaceful change, democratic principles, and institutions, this process of transformation will take time.

Conflict arising from political competition in the region tends to fall into two basic categories: (1) the struggle for national power and (2) the fight for greater local autonomy. In the first instance, the stakes are exceedingly high—especially in the poorest countries—because victory in the national political struggle means access to power, money, patronage, and the means of coercion to remain in power. Since this competition is often seen as a zero-sum situation where the winner takes all and the loser gets nothing, the consequences of losing are great and thus too is the level of conflict. Political mobilization of supporters in these contests based on religious, ethnic, cultural, ideological, or regional lines can increase societal divisions and can also serve as catalysts for galvanizing these types of conflicts.

The second type of political struggle involves the contest between central governments and their outlying provinces for control. More and more of these confrontations center on greater demands for political autonomy by local governments. They are frequently in reaction to alienation or even outright hostility to an unpopular regime and a desire to gain more control over their share of national resources and revenues. Thus, the result is a clash between central governments seeking to exercise strong nationwide control and local interests demanding devolution of power. Separatism is the most extreme manifestation of this phenomenon. Separatist demands, either in the form of increased federalism or complete secession, appear to resonate strongly across the region and clearly pose a serious challenge to national unity and stability. The 1990 Tuareg rebellion in Mali, the ongoing Casamance revolt, and of course the recently ended war in southern Sudan are examples of this form of conflict. Somewhat surprisingly, separatist-fueled conflicts, although extremely violent, are also very often amenable to peaceful resolution if the parties are willing to compromise and accommodate each other's demands. Unfortunately, this usually only happens following a period of prolonged warfare.

As we have seen, the factors driving conflict across the trans-Sahara are many, complex, persistent, and dynamic. Rarely can conflict be characterized as a single type, as each unique conflict is usually layered with several reinforcing factors that shape the confrontation over time. Thus, for example, historic tensions between ethnic groups can easily evolve into a fight over resources and end up becoming a violent civil war for self-rule. This mercurial nature makes conflict resolution extremely challenging and strengthens the case for crafting comprehensive solutions to national and regional problems.

LINKAGES TO TERRORISM

Once home to some of the remotest areas on earth, the trans-Sahara now finds itself in a policy debate and is at the center of one of the key security challenges of the twenty-first century.

As destabilizing as the incessant level of conflict is on the region's political and economic development, it is the perceived connection between conflict, weak states, and terrorism that has brought the trans-Sahara into the global spotlight. This representation is evident in public statements. "I am concerned about the large, ungoverned areas of Africa that are possibly melting pots for the disenfranchised of the world, so to speak, the terrorist breeding grounds," says General James Jones, Commander, U.S. European Command, in assessing the regional threat. "I believe that we're going to have to engage more in that theater."[9] The U.S. Director of the Central Intelligence Agency, Porter Goss, has testified that chronic instability in Africa, specifically in Nigeria and Sudan, "will continue to hamper counterterrorism efforts."[10] And finally, a recently declassified Canadian intelligence report cites the combination of religious sectarianism, regional politics, and regional and ethnic rivalries as fueling the terrorist threat.[11]

Terrorism and, more important, fundamentalist proselytization are not new to the region, but long-running civil conflicts, neglected and alienated populations, and an influx of Islamist extremists and extremist ideology from outside the trans-Sahara surely pose a new level of security challenge to the countries of the region. The bloody Algerian civil war—inflamed by the Algerian military's 1992 intervention to forestall an election victory by the Islamic Salvation Front—has spawned several violent extremist terrorist groups, including the Islamic Army Group (GIA) and its offshoot, the GSPC.[12] The al Qaeda-linked GSPC, whose activities have spillover effects from southern Algeria into neighboring Mauritania, Mali, Niger, and Chad, pose the most serious security threat. Likewise, Sudan's Islamist government helped al Qaeda gain a foothold in the region by providing critical sanctuary to Osama bin Laden and his supporters in the 1990s. And some believe Khartoum may still be maintaining ties to international terrorist networks.[13] (More on the Sudanese connection to al Qaeda will be explored in Chapter 14.) In addition, religious extremists from the Middle East and Southwest Asia, often under the guise of Islamic charities, have reportedly established themselves in Mali,[14] northern Nigeria, and other parts of the trans-Sahara. Radical Islamic ideology may be gaining a receptive audience among increasingly politicized African Muslim youth.

Despite the enormous challenges facing trans-Sahara governments that make them highly susceptible to international terrorist exploitation, it appears that except for the GSPC, international terrorist networks—as opposed to individuals—have yet to plant themselves firmly within the region. Likewise, the trans-Sahara (with the notable exception of Algeria) has not become a major exporter of religious extremists bent on joining a global jihad against the United States and its allies. Nevertheless, the threat emanating from the trans-Sahara is real and is rooted in what Jackie Cilliers calls "an awakening" of international terrorism in Africa in which domestic and international terrorism begin to blend together into a single phenomenon.[15] Moreover, it would appear more likely that domestically fueled trans-Saharan terrorism would drive the creation of alliances with international terrorist networks rather than external terrorist elements seeking to impose their presence from outside the region.

Thus, to successfully tackle the problems of the region, more progress needs to be made in breaking the bonds that link conflict, weak states, and terrorism into a deadly cocktail of political instability and violence. A broad-based approach attacking these problems from multiple dimensions and utilizing an array of tools is needed at the local, national, regional, and international level. Furthermore, no one problem area or tool should be emphasized at the expense of the others—an especially difficult task given the current preoccupation with fighting terrorism. The active involvement of the international community and key European allies (such as France, with its historic ties to large parts of the region) is vital, not only in terms of providing resources and skills, but because of the global nature of the problems.

LINKAGES TO THE GLOBAL WAR ON TERRORISM

Recognizing this looming threat and the geostrategic importance of the trans-Sahara in the global war on terrorism, Washington has sought to put in place a preemptive and integrated strategy that addresses governmental weaknesses and the multiple sources of domestic and regional conflict. "For a change, we're trying to get ahead of the power curve in a region that we believe is susceptible to use by terrorists," says Theresa Whelan, deputy assistant secretary of defense for African Affairs.[16]

In light of these concerns, the United States is pouring in millions of dollars, fortifying the military infrastructure of the region, conducting joint training operations with trans-Saharan militaries, and enhancing intelligence collection and cooperation. At the heart of this effort is the newly instituted Trans-Sahara Counterterrorism Initiative (TSCTI) that began in June 2005—replacing the much more modest Pan Sahel Initiative (PSI)—and will infuse $100 million per year over five years, beginning in 2007, to nine North and West African countries.[17] The TSCTI is designed to provide a more comprehensive approach to regional security by enhancing governments' counterterrorism capabilities and by preventing the region from becoming a safe haven where terrorists can train, organize, and plan their operations. As with the PSI, strong attention is being paid to building mutually supporting and collaborative security ties between trans-Saharan countries. The most concrete result of this improved cooperation has been the successful military operations since 2004 by troops from Mali, Niger, and Chad along their northern borders, which has left at least 50 GSPC fighters dead.[18]

In a related effort, the Pentagon is negotiating bilateral access agreements for the establishment of emergency operating bases, known as "lily pads," for the rapid deployment and support of military forces in the region, and is engaging in joint training exercises with trans-Saharan military forces. During Operation Flintlock in June 2005, several hundred U.S. Special Forces troops conducted tactical training exercises with about 5,000 North and West African troops in an effort to enhance their capability to interdict illegal flows of weapons and contraband.[19]

In his remarks at the 2004 opening of Africa Union's counterterrorism center in Algiers, U.S. Ambassador Cofer Black, former Coordinator for Counterterrorism, acknowledged the need to improve the lives of ordinary people as a means of combating the spread of terrorism.[20] Accordingly, a more comprehensive approach to security in the region will be taken that utilizes multiple U.S. organizations, such as the Agency for International Development and the Department of State. These agencies will help direct $70 million a year of TSCTI funds toward promoting democracy and economic growth, with the goal of reaching out to "the disaffected, disenfranchised, or just misinformed and disillusioned," according to a U.S. military spokesman.[21]

Nonetheless, most of the U.S. focus is likely to remain on shoring up the military and security capabilities of trans-Sahara countries. Critics of this approach warn of a dangerous backlash as strengthened regimes exploit the terrorist menace to stifle political dissent and freedoms. The August 2005 military coup overthrowing Mauritanian President Ould Taya was instigated as a reaction to heavy-handed repression of political opponents in the name of fighting international terrorism. As Ambassador Princeton Lyman cautions, "The United States has to be especially careful that we do not become partners in a political process that drives people into the arms of Islamic extremists."[22] A more effective counter-terrorism strategy, according to the International Crisis Group, is for the world community to address the underlying causes of terrorism and conflict by focusing on development rather than security assistance.[23]

PROGRESS AND PROSPECTS

The history of the trans-Sahara is one rooted in the eternal struggle for preeminance between competing societies, identities, values, and ways of life. What makes it unique in this context, however, is the position in Africa that the trans-Sahara occupies and the resulting implications. For this region is a place of some of the most strident religious, cultural, economic, and political confrontations in Africa. Overlying this explosive landscape are fragile and weak national governments, inadequate political and socioeconomic structures, and a multitude of external actors and interests that hinder efforts to peacefully resolve these inevitable clashes. Thus, conflict has clearly become part of the societal dynamic of the region, and this situation is unlikely to change in the foreseeable future.

Several pronounced trends are likely to affect trans-Saharan conflict over the coming decades; some are likely to acerbate and worsen things, while others hold the promise of promoting peaceful resolution. These include the growing militarization of the region, an increasing internationalization of conflicts, more intense and lethal conflicts, and the changing nature of conflict.

Growing Militarization of the Region

Although the trans-Sahara largely remained on the periphery of the Cold War and escaped the military build-ups that characterized other parts of Africa, there are indications that this is changing. Insurgencies in Algeria and Sudan fueled arms build-ups in these countries in the 1990s, and military spending in general is on the rise across the region.[24] A powerful catalyst behind this trend is the intense U.S. focus on countering terrorism[25] and enhancing energy security in the region, which is likely to drive the U.S. security agenda in the region for the foreseeable future. Accordingly, efforts to secure basing rights for American rapid-reaction forces and the substantial amount of military assistance under the TSCTI are encouraging a militarization of the region. While certainly other diplomatic and economic measures will be committed to the region to shore up fragile regimes, the military option will likely be predominant in the years ahead. The danger in this, as International Crisis Group points out, is that heavy-handed tactics will turn those arrested or killed into martyrs and stoke the flames of anti-Americanism in the region.[26]

Increasing Internationalization of Conflicts

Even though trans-Saharan conflicts have invariably spilled over into neighboring countries and regimes have sought to use antigovernment movements as foreign policy tools, the repercussions are reaching farther than ever and becoming more pronounced. Conflict in the region is increasingly globalized and tied to wider international political and security issues, such as international terrorism that may come to be seen by the disenfranchised as an effective tool to advance their domestic demands.[27] This growing internationalization of conflict is likely to be a two-edged sword for the region. It will undoubtedly bring greater external assistance and resources to bear, but at the same time it may turn localized conflicts into rallying points for outside actors.

More Intense and Lethal Conflicts

The political and economic stakes are also rising in many conflict situations across the region as a result of demographic pressures on a fragile environment, growing demands on national resources, and public expectations outstripping the capabilities of the state. Insecure governments and the absence of institutionalized conflict-resolution mechanisms will permit many of these conflicts to intensify and spin dangerously out of control in the years ahead. Easy and widespread access to small arms and light weapons by nonstate actors in particular are likely to fuel not only the ferocity, but also the lethality, of these conflicts and present a severe challenge to governments.

The Changing Nature of Conflict

In the past, religious, racial, and ethnocultural factors have often been the chief underlying source of societal tensions and conflict in the region. While they undoubtedly will continue to play an important role in shaping the regional conflict dynamic, struggles over political power and resources are increasingly likely to take center stage. Moves toward greater political freedoms and participation along with greater economic development probably will be destabilizing for many old-guard governments as they grapple with these new challenges to their authority. Likewise, the struggle to control resources in fragile and impoverished societies is likely to pit the status quo against rising expectations of the society. How governments and societal elites react to this changing situation will be the key to the future of regional conflict. If they are reactionary and repressive, the cycle of violence is likely to continue. If, on the other hand, they embrace the opportunity to reexamine and debate fundamental political and economic issues, the cycle may be broken.

The evolving nature of conflict in the trans-Sahara over the coming years has serious security implications not only for the region, but also for the United States. The region has become critical to Washington policymakers' thinking, because of its impact on the global war on terrorism, energy security, and peacekeeping and humanitarian concerns. Accordingly, the United States and its European allies almost certainly will become even more actively engaged. Given the complexity of the problems feeding conflict, however, this will require delicate handling; there is a real danger in applying "solutions" that may end up inflaming an already tenuous situation. Thus, a few cautionary notes are in order.

First, care must be taken not to overplay the terrorism card when developing security priorities for the region. While the linkages between conflict, weak states, and terrorism certainly exist and need to be addressed, an over-reliance on military and security tools is likely to prove counterproductive and destabilizing in the long run. Throwing large sums of money and equipment at trans-Saharan militaries is likely to provide some short-term and highly visible gains, but it only addresses the symptoms of much larger fundamental societal issues. Such an approach will promote militarization of the region and could serve as a catalyst for additional violence. Furthermore, growing radicalization and internationalization of the region are also likely to be byproducts of any myopic fixation on the terrorist dimension of conflict. The Algerian government's single-minded counterterrorism approach to its security problems, for instance, has ultimately helped produce one of the largest and most radicalized pools of recruits for international terrorist networks. Algerian extremists have become the new foot soldiers in global terrorism and are some of the most violent. Up to 20 percent of the suicide car bombers in Iraq were from Algeria, according to the U.S. military in June 2005, and Algerian militants have once again been implicated in a plot to attack the Paris metro.[28]

Next, lasting stability and security in the trans-Sahara will ultimately depend on the successful political and economic transformation of societies. As we have found, conflict is often fed by disaffected populations and uneven development, and thus it is essential to take a broader view of security. Political pluralism, a vigorous civil society, entrenched civil liberties and respect for the rule of law, and transparency are all hallmarks of democratic trends trying to take root across the region. Progress, however, will be uneven. Setbacks will occur and conflict probably will increase rather than diminish in the near term as societies seek to redefine themselves. By helping to provide the necessary support and encouragement to stay the course, the United States and others can assist countries in making this a more peaceful transformation.

Finally, given the overwhelming challenges, individual governments will be hard pressed to achieve their goals on their own. Therefore, emphasis should be placed on building regional cooperation and coordination as a way to maximize the use of limited human and financial resources. This collective approach is already well underway in the security arena with the TSCTI, but more attention needs to be paid to the non-security sector. Focusing too heavily on the traditional security sector (military, police, and intelligence) at the expense of wider regional economic development objectives, for instance, is likely to shortchange long-term stability. More attention too needs to be paid to the formulation of international arrangements for addressing the issues behind conflict. The United States and a few key allies are currently driving the international security agenda with little room for alternative approaches. A truly multilateral effort is necessary and would bring extensive benefits to the region, Africa, and the United States. Collective and coordinated action would undercut charges of self-serving American unilateralism, strengthen the role of the Africa Union, promote broader international participation and resource commitment, and provide a greater range of options for tackling the region's problems.

CONCLUSION

Given its historic legacy and explosive mix of people, cultures, ideologies, and competing interests, the trans-Sahara is an ideal breeding ground for violent conflict. In the past, however, this conflict tended to be highly localized in nature and rarely had much impact beyond the immediate region. This clearly is no longer the case. Feeling the pressures of globalization and evolving as a central venue for outside rivalries, trans-Saharan conflict is becoming increasingly internationalized. Thus, the future security and stability of the region will be closely linked to the wider international security environment, for better or worse.

While conflict has become an inescapable part of life in the region, much can and should be done to lessen its impact. It is critical to address the sources and underlying causes of conflict in a systematic and comprehensive manner. Issues of political, social, and economic development deserve as much, if not more, attention than traditional security problems, and long-term solutions should be emphasized over short-term fixes. In addition, greater effort needs to be directed at developing more effective conflict resolution mechanisms at the national, regional, and international level. The mere existence of confrontational situations does not necessarily need to result in violent conflict. Rather it is the repeated failure to resolve or defuse the fundamental issues fueling conflict that increases the likelihood of these situations escalating into violent confrontations. The role and responsibility of the international community in this regard cannot be ignored, but the nations of the world must be careful to walk a fine line lest they aggravate an already dangerous situation.

Throughout key periods in African history, the trans-Sahara has played a pivotal role in defining the continent and its relations with the outside world. Whether through the centuries-old trans-Saharan trade with Europe, the spread of Islam, resistance to colonialism, or as an exotic venue for the struggle between great powers, the region's historical legacy and strategic importance in shaping events cannot be underemphasized. Without a doubt, how the region ultimately handles the challenge of coping with deep-seated political, social, and economic tensions in an ever globalized and interdependent world will go a long way in charting the future course of conflict in Africa and beyond.

NOTES

1. Comments of General Charles Wald, deputy commander of U.S. European Command. *Boston Globe*, "U.S.-Trained Forces Scour Sahara for Terror Links," December 12, 2004.
2. The territory covered by the trans-Saharan arc includes Senegal, Mauritania, Mali, the southern part of Algeria, Burkina Faso, Niger, northern Nigeria, Chad, and north and central Sudan.

3. In 2005, Freedom House listed only two of the nine trans-Saharan countries (Senegal and Mali) as "free" and having a high level of political rights and civil liberties. Four of the nine countries scored in the lower third of the UN Human Development Index. Online. Available HTTP: <http://www.freedomhouse.org/template.cfm?page=15&year=2005>; Online. Available HTTP: <http://hdr.undp.org/statistics/data/hdi_rank_map.cfm>.

4. *International Monetary Fund*, "Debt Relief under the Heavily Indebted Poor Countries Initiative." Online. Available HTTP: <http://www.imf.org/external/np/exr/facts/hipc.htm>.

5. *San Francisco Chronicle*, "The Trans-Sahara Counter-Terrorism Initiative: U.S. Takes Terror Fight to Africa's 'Wild West,'" December 30, 2005.

6. For instance, Christians comprise 35 percent of the Chadian and 40 percent of the Nigeria populations, while 30 percent of Sudanese are Christian or animist. Moreover, these religious minorities tend to be geographically concentrated, further reinforcing their differences with the Muslim majorities in these countries. Online. Available HTTP: <http://www.cia.gov/cia/publications/factbook>.

7. Examples of these vibrant pre-colonial states include the Kingdom of Mali, with its great trading and religious centers of Timbuktu and Jenne as well as the Sokoto Empire of northern Nigeria and Chad. For more information about the history and development of these and other states, see A. E. Afigbo, "Chapter One: West Africa to 1800," in *The Making of Modern Africa: Volume 1 (7th Edition)*, eds., R. Palmer, et. al. (London: Longman, 1992), pp. 33–42.

8. Currently Algeria, Chad, Nigeria, and Sudan are oil-exporting countries and Mauritania has signed agreements with international oil companies to develop its newly discovered oil fields.

9. *allAfrica.com*, "Trained African Armies Key to Fight in Africa," March 8, 2004. Online. Available HTTP: <http://allafrica.com/stories/200403090576.html>.

10. Porter Goss, "DCI's Global Intelligence Briefing," Testimony before the Senate Select Committee on Intelligence, February 16, 2005. (Director Goss resigned his position on May 5, 2006.)

11. *Washington Times*, "Africa Seen as Fertile for Islamism," May 24, 2005.

12. The all but defunct GIA was founded in 1993 by former Algerian veterans of the 1980s struggle against the Soviets in Afghanistan, who brought back a highly radicalized and militant form of Islam. The GSPC broke away from the GIA in 1996 and is reported to have about 300 fighters and ties to al Qaeda.

13. *Washington Times*, "U.S. Probes Reported Sudan Link to Terror," June 17, 2005.

14. A senior Malian security official commented on the difficulty in monitoring the activities of more than 1,800 nongovernmental organizations (many of them Islamic charities) that operate in his country. Africa Center for Strategic Studies, "North and West Africa Counter-Terrorism Topical Seminar," Bamako, Mali, October 12–17, 2003, p. 30.

15. Jakkie Cilliers, "Terrorism in Africa," *African Security Review*, Vol. 12, No. 4, 2003: 91–103.

16. *The New York Times*, "As Africans Join Iraqi Insurgency, U.S. Counters With Military Training in Their Lands," June 10, 2005. Online. Available HTTP: <http://www.nytimes.com/2005/06/10/politics/10military.html>.

17. The new program is a dramatic transformation of the $7.75 million Pan Sahel Initiative (PSI) that began in 2003 and was designed to assist Chad, Mali, Mauritania, and Niger with small-scale counter-terrorist training. For details about the Trans-Sahara Counterterrorism Initiative, see U.S. Department of State, "New Counterterrorism Initiative to Focus on Saharan Africa," May 17, 2005. Online. Available HTTP: <http://usinfo.state.gov/xarchives/display.html>.

18. Boston.com, "U.S. Pushes Anti-terror Alliance for North African Nations, April 11, 2004. Online. Available HTTP: <http://www.boston.com/new/world/africa/articles/2004/04/11/us_pushes_antiterror_alliance>; *Boston Globe,* "U.S.-Trained Forces Scour Sahara for Terror Links," December 12, 2004.
19. *San Francisco Chronicle,* "The Trans-Sahara Counter-Terrorism Initiative: U.S. Takes Terror Fight to Africa's 'Wild West,'" December 30; U.S. EUCOM, "2005 Exercises." Online. Available HTTP: <http://www.eucom.mil/english/Exercises/main.asp?Yr=2005>.
20. Cofer Black, "Remarks at the Second Intergovernmental High-Level Meeting on the Prevention and Combating of Terrorism in Africa," in Algiers, Algeria, October 13, 2004. Online. Available HTTP: <http://www.state.gov/s/ct/rls/rm/2004/37230.htm>.
21. *San Francisco Chronicle,* "The Trans-Sahara Counter-Terrorism Initiative: U.S. Takes Terror Fight to Africa's 'Wild West,'" December 30, 2005.
22. *Washington Times,* "Analysis: Quiet on Terror's 'New Front,'" May 13, 2005.
23. *International Crisis Group,* "Islamist Terrorism in the Sahel: Fact or Fiction?" Africa Report No. 92, 31 March 2005.
24. See International Institute for Strategic Studies, *The Military Balance* (London: Oxford University Press, 2003), pp. 205—227, for a country-by-country spending breakdown.
25. "The growing use of the trans-Sahara region in Africa by terrorists threatens the security of the United States and our European allies," according to General James Jones, Commander U.S. European Command, in testimony before Congress. General James Jones, "Statement before the Senate Foreign Relations Committee," September 28, 2005.
26. *International Crisis Group,* "Islamist Terrorism in the Sahel: Fact or Fiction?" Africa Report No. 92, 31, March 2005.
27. The U.S. military, for example, is deeply worried that Iraq is becoming a major training ground for trans-Sahara terrorist groups. "They're getting to use those training skills, hone them, and eventually go somewhere else and use them," according to a Pentagon official. *The New York Times,* "As Africans Join Iraqi Insurgency, U.S. Counters With Military Training in Their Lands," June 10, 2005.
28. *Associated Press,* "North Africans Joining Iraq Islamic Fighters," June 14, 2005. Online. Available HTTP: <http://news.yahoo.com/s/ap/20050614/ap_on_re_af/africa_terrorism>; *Agence France Presse,* "Terror Suspects Eyeing up Paris Metro, Airport," September 27, 2005. Online. Available HTTP: <http://news.yahoo.com/s/afp/20050927/wl_afp/franceattacksarreststargets>.

Sudan

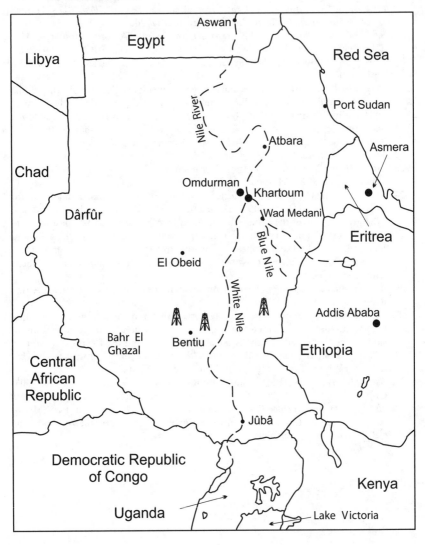

13

SUDAN

Stephen A. Emerson

NATURE OF THE FLASHPOINT

Sudan has always been something of an enigma, with endemic conflict, unrelenting political and social turmoil, and great human suffering becoming its defining hallmarks. It is a place of profound ethnic, religious, cultural, and political contrasts—where Africa begins to fuse with the Middle East, where Christianity meets Islam, and where popular rule clashes with authoritarianism—pulling in opposing directions. Although a sparsely populated and often inhospitable land endowed with few exploitable resources beyond the waters of the Nile (until the discovery of oil in the south in the late 1970s), it has been fought over for generations. Home to one of Africa's longest running civil wars and numerous other smaller conflicts that have destroyed entire communities, left millions dead, and made refugees out of millions more, local rulers and great powers alike have paid dearly in lives and money in an attempt to control the land and its people. Seemingly on the verge of constant anarchy and complete state collapse, Sudan continues to endure.

Although the country has long been at the crossroads of conflict, only recently has its problems become a rising concern to the international community. In an increasingly globalized, post-9/11 security environment, Sudan's chronic domestic instability poses a serious threat to the broader international community. For conflict in Sudan, like in much of Africa, has truly become both regional and international in scope and underscores that there are no longer solely domestic conflicts. Moreover, the United States has come to view Sudan, with its history of violent political Islam and vulnerability to external forces seeking to advance their own self-serving agendas, as a critical player in the global struggle against terrorism. How Washington chooses to respond to the complex issues surrounding Sudanese conflict and the potential linkages to terrorism, however, will ultimately be the decisive factor in determining the success or failure of long-term U.S. security objectives in Africa.

Recent international attention has also served to emphasize the country's strategic importance. With nearly one million square miles of land area, Sudan is the largest country in Africa[1] and lies astride the life blood for some 77 million Egyptians: the Nile River. "The Soudan is joined to Egypt by the Nile, as a diver is connected with the surface by his air pipe. Without it there is only suffocation," noted a young, yet insightful Winston Churchill over 100 years ago.[2] Likewise, Sudan's sheer size and location give it the power to influence events far beyond its borders, from the strategic Horn of Africa to conflict-ridden central Africa and the western deserts of Chad and Libya. As goes Sudan, so goes the region.

Some things, however, may be changing for the better. In January 2005, Sudan's nearly 50-year-old civil war between the government and southern rebels finally came to an end with the signing of a comprehensive peace and power-sharing agreement. The country's oil-driven economy is finally booming and the lives of ordinary citizens are improving. Radical Islamists have been reined in and Khartoum has publicly committed itself to joining the United States in the fight against global terrorism. To be sure, very serious problems still remain in the western region of Darfur[3] and elsewhere. If past experience is any indicator of the future, the road to peace and security will be a long and elusive one that will require persistence, commitment, and the active engagement of the African and wider international community.

HISTORICAL CONTEXT

The sources of Sudanese conflict are highly complex and multifaceted. Moreover, one finds in Sudan an intertwining of seemingly separate conflicts into larger societal ones that raise fundamental questions about the underlying nature of Sudanese nationalism, the survival of the state, and the future of democratic pluralism in a highly divided society. Unlike some of the other case studies explored in *Flashpoints*, however, religious differences between Muslims and non-Muslims are not the defining issue in Sudanese conflict. To be sure, religious differences play a significant role in shaping domestic conflict, but so too do an array of other important factors.

Historically, the genesis of domestic conflict revolves around a handful of social, political, and economic issues related to religion; race, ethnicity, and culture; political autonomy; and resource competition.

Religion. Religious factors, particularly those concentrating on the Muslim-Christian/animist divide, are commonly seen as the focal point of nearly all Sudanese conflict. Moreover, elements of ethnic and cultural conflict are all too frequently mistaken for a manifestation of religious conflict, as in the case of clashes between Sudan's African and Arab Muslims. While certainly an essential part of the conflict dynamic and of the country's historic legacy, inter-religious divisions tend to be overshadowed by other more divisive political, economic, and social issues. Rather, in this overwhelmingly Muslim majority country,[4] it is intra-Islamic sectarian rivalries (and the willingness of their leaders to exploit them) that have characterized the Sudanese religious divide.

Race, Ethnicity, and Culture. In a country like Sudan where Africa begins to blend with the Middle East, the existence of sharp contrasts in race, language, customs, and social norms have made forging a national identity extremely challenging. This situation is further inflamed by the bitter legacy of the southern slave trade that has left an indelible mark on race relations between Sudan's Arab and African communities that lingers to this day. Even more worrisome is the manipulation of these differences by leaders and political parties to stir up passions against their opponents. Rather than emphasizing commonalities across diverse groups, they seek to divide communities to advance their own group's interests. Violent conflict is too often the result.

Resource Competition. At the heart of many conflicts around the globe is the battle between communities over resources. This is especially true where access to basic resources, such as land and water, is literally a matter of survival. With about half the country consisting of desert or semi-desert, fierce competition to control arable land, water (most notably the Nile), and livestock have helped produce extensive conflict throughout Sudanese history. Growing demographic pressure on these fragile ecosystems has increasingly put sedentary farming communities at odds with nomadic pastoralists in a winner-take-all fight over resources. An abundant supply of natural resources, however, is no guarantee of peace either. In fact, it may intensify conflict, because now the stakes have been raised and the victor seeks to reap greater rewards. The discovery of oil in the late 1970s in southern Sudan, while not a direct cause of the civil war, certainly raised the stakes in the ongoing north-south competition and made the conflict much harder to resolve.[5] In addition, this new-found oil wealth has fueled demands from non-oil-producing regions of the country for a more equitable division of national oil revenue.

Political Autonomy. It is not surprising given Sudan's enormous size and distinctive regional makeup that friction between the central government in Khartoum and its outlying regions has been a key factor in conflict. Even under military regimes, the central government's effective control seldom extended very far beyond the capital and a few key towns scattered around the countryside. Disagreements or even outright hostility to unpopular laws or repressive measures, unhappiness with the allocation of scarce national resources, a perceived lack of responsiveness by the central government, and inadequate political representation in national forums are behind the push for greater local autonomy. Southern separatists have long been the most ardent in their demands for enhanced self-rule, but nearly every region of the country has sought a greater political voice. All Sudanese governments have had to grapple with the dilemma of balancing the devolution of political power against the need to maintain strong central control and a sense of nationhood.

Political Islam and the Rise of Sudanese Nationalism

The creation of present-day Sudan can be traced to a religious revolt in the 1880s that ironically laid the foundation for the eventual creation of a modern, secular state. Under the leadership of Muhammed Ahmed bin Al Asyyid Abdullah—the self-proclaimed Mahdi[6]—the fanatical Mahdist movement sought a return to a purified Islam and the expulsion of foreign influences from Sudan. Although the impetus for the rebellion was Egypt's oppressive rule[7] and heavy-handed treatment of the Sudanese, it was Muhammed Ahmed's appeal for a religious revival that united the country's diverse elements of discontent into an Islamic army and later an Islamic state. Starting in 1882, the Mahdi's forces advanced steadily across the country, sweeping aside all Egyptian military resistance, capturing Khartoum in 1885 and killing Governor-General Charles Gordon, and extending the boundaries of the new Mahdist state from Egypt in the north to present-day Uganda in the south, and from the Red Sea in the east to the French colonial frontier in the west.

Although the Madhi would not live to rule the state he had helped create—Muhammed Ahmed died of typhus six months after the fall of Khartoum—his dream of building an autocratic, evangelistic, and puritanical Islamic society that emphasized Muslim unity over tribal diversity was fulfilled by his compatriot and successor, Khalifa Abdullahi. Thus, it is not surprising that many Sudanese Muslims consider the Mahdist state "as having provided the first genuinely Sudanese government and as being an early manifestation of Sudanese nationalism."[8] Nevertheless, the days of the Mahdist movement were numbered as the British government, increasingly alarmed over what it viewed as growing European competition over the Sudan and the British public clamor to avenge the death of Gordon, led London to reverse its policy of noninterference and mount a reconquest of the Sudan.[9] The Anglo-Egyptian army methodically marched its way down the Nile, defeating all in its path and finally decisively crushing Khalifa Abdullahi's Islamic army in 1898 at the battle of Omdurman, on the plains outside Khartoum. The battle of Omdurman, the death of Khalifa Abdullahi a year later, and the destruction of the Mahdi's tomb by the British signaled the end of the Mahdist rule and the beginning of a half century of new foreign domination.

The Anglo-Egyptian Agreement of 1899 officially restored Egyptian sovereignty over the Sudan, while at the same time giving Britain the responsibility for governing the country on behalf of Cairo. This began an era of British hegemony that would last until 1956. The British also sought to limit Egyptian influence and undermine Cairo's claim that Sudan was an integral part of Egypt, thereby indirectly encouraging the maintenance of a Sudanese national identity. In addition, London's policy of indirect rule and paternalism toward the country's three southern Christian and animist provinces increased the power of local African leaders, reinforced north-south divisions, and established a legacy of southern separatism and limited regional autonomy. This policy would have a profound impact in the post-independence period and on Sudanese political stability for decades to come.

The overthrow of Egypt's monarchy in 1952 and the new Egyptian military regime's acceptance of a British proposal granting Sudan the right to self-determination paved the way for Sudanese independence in 1956. Although extended negotiations preceding independence produced a proliferation of Sudanese political parties, the country's two main Islamic sects, the Mahdist-aligned Ansar with their Umma party and the pro-Egyptian Khatmiyya with their National United Party (NUP), would dominate politics. This enthusiastic rush to democratic participation, however, failed to produce a constitution or resolve the issue of southern autonomy prior to independence. Moreover, in an effort to broaden their base of support among the Arab northerners, both the Umma party and the NUP pushed Arabization and Islamization at the expense of national unity and growing southern fears of "Arab imperialism."

Institutionalized Political Instability

The early years of Sudanese independence would establish a pattern of rule alternating between divisive, popularly elected civilian governments and powerful, repressive military regimes that would continue for the next 50 years. Chronic government instability as a result of shifting political coalitions, intra-party factionalism, and personal ambitions produced three different governments from 1956 to 1958. The inability of the Sudanese political system to develop an effective national leadership, growing corruption and economic problems, strained relations with Egypt, and popular displeasure with both the Umma and NUP led to military intervention in late 1958. The new regime of General Ibrahim Abboud, which contained military officers associated with both the Ansar and the Khatmiyya sects, was able to stabilize what had been a worsening political situation, but it proved no more effective than the civilian leadership it replaced. To maintain power, the Abboud regime in the early 1960s turned increasingly to repressive measures, especially in the south. By 1963 the entire southern region was engulfed in widespread fighting between southern rebels and government forces.[10]

By late 1964, overwhelmed by popular demands for a return to civilian rule, Abboud dissolved the government and handed over the reins of power to an interim government. The reappearance of a whole host of narrowly based political parties competing in the 1965 general election (which was limited to the northern provinces because of the poor security situation in the south) produced a return to the pre-1958 political stalemate. Over the next four years, no party would obtain a parliamentary majority and no coalition government—there were five different versions of the Umma-NUP/Democratic Unionist Party (DUP)[11] alliance—survived longer than 13 months. The most serious repercussion of this political atrophy was the failure of every coalition government to address the country's worsening economy and deal with the southern rebellion.

Given these circumstances, it was not surprising that history would repeat itself in the form of military intervention. To the delight of many Sudanese unhappy with the country's ineffectual parliamentary system, a group of relatively unknown military officers led by Colonel Jaffar Nimeiri staged a successful coup d'etat in May 1969 and began what was to become the Nimeiri era. Although faced with the same problems as his predecessors, Nimeiri proved himself adept at ending the southern rebellion, eliminating political factionalism, and reinvigorating the country's slumping economy by turning to Western and Arab donors for increasing levels of aid. An end to the 17-year-old southern war was negotiated in early 1972 with the signing of the Addis Ababa peace accords, which provided amnesty to all antigovernment rebels, granted limited regional autonomy to the south, and established a local executive body and a 60-member southern assembly.[12] Political factionalism was eradicated through the abolition of all political parties and a single political structure, the Sudanese Socialist Union, was formed in 1972 to act "as a union of forces, an organ transcending tribalism, sectarian, and racial divides"[13] to replace the old party system.

In sharp contrast to the decade of the 1970s, the early 1980s were a time of policy drift, growing isolationism, increasingly autocratic rule, and political and economic regression for the regime. In an apparent effort to deflect attention from the country's worsening economic crisis, Nimeiri—against the counsel of many advisers—in September 1983 announced the imposition of Shari'a (Islamic law), his intention to move toward full Islamicization of Sudan, and his plan to redivide the south and abrogate the Addis Ababa accords. By early 1984, amid a foundering economy, increasing concern over his personal security, and faced with a reborn insurgency in the south, Nimeiri declared a state of emergency throughout the country. The situation, however, only deteriorated further and eventually led to Nimeiri's overthrow in April 1985 by military officers seeking to preempt an uncontrolled popular uprising and ease the transition to favorable civilian rule.

Following the first national elections in nearly two decades, the country once again entered a tumultuous period of political turmoil as it sought a return to liberal democratic politics. Despite a proliferation of political parties and calls for setting aside partisan differences in the name of national unity, past patterns and behaviors quickly returned to the Sudanese political scene and the old dormant parties—the Umma and the DUP—held sway in the "new Sudan." Neither party, however, was able to gain an electoral mandate, and the period became characterized by the rebirth of old personal rivalries, party factionalism, regionalism, and the repeated formation and collapse of coalition governments.

One thing that did change, however, was the emergence of Hassan al-Turabi's radical fundamentalist National Islamic Front (NIF) as a significant force in Sudanese politics. Since the return of electoral politics, the NIF built itself into an effective political organization not only by taping support among Islamic fundamentalists, but also by broadening its appeal in Khartoum, the military, and among trade unionists.

This growing political clout, led Umma party leader Sadiq al-Mahdi to oust the DUP and reluctantly form a new coalition government with Turabi's NIF in May 1988.

By 1989, things began to go from bad to worse for al-Mahdi's government. The military situation in the south had seriously deteriorated, with the Sudanese army demoralized and suffering from poor leadership. Moreover, efforts to negotiate an end to the fighting were severely constrained with the government caught between the competing demands (especially on the issue of Shari'a) of the southern rebels and its junior coalition partner, the NIF. So the war dragged on. Increasingly isolated by its repressive domestic policies and combative foreign policy against key neighbors like Ethiopia and Uganda, the regime found itself pushed into a corner. True to Sudan's historical legacy, the military once again intervened. At the instigation of the NIF, military officers led by Brigadier General Umar Hassan Ahmed al-Bashir overthrew the ineffectual, but democratically elected, government and helped establish a radical fundamentalist Islamic regime in Khartoum.

The early 1990s saw the rise to prominence of Turabi and the NIF's Islamist domestic agenda; all political opposition was banned, implementation of strict Shari'a nationwide was pushed, and efforts to create a Sudanese Islamic state were reinvigorated. Meanwhile, the military focused its attention on combating the persistent southern insurgency. Khartoum's vigorous prosecution of the war, which included the unleashing of pro-government militia groups on the civilian population, wanton destruction of life and property, and the withholding of food aid to pro-rebel areas, however, soon provoked a severe international backlash against the regime.[14] Moreover, efforts by Turabi and the NIF to burnish their radical Islamic credentials by supporting extremist elements—including Osama bin Laden's al Qaeda organization—created increasing friction with Sudan's powerful neighbors, as well as Saudi Arabia and the United States.

All this pressure began to take its toll on the shaky military-NIF coalition. In 1997, General Bashir, much to the consternation of Turabi and his supporters, reentered peace talks with the southern rebels. Political maneuvering against Bashir by Turabi lead to Turabi's ouster from the government in 1999, his dismissal as leader of the NIF, the dissolution of parliament, and Bashir's imposition of a state of emergency at the end of the year. The new Bashir government purged itself of the most hardline Islamic elements and reconstituted itself as the National Congress Party. Following questionable elections in December 2000, which Bashir and the National Congress Party easily won, the regime embarked on an ambitious effort to reach a rapprochement with the West, and the United States in particular.

The Southern Insurgency

The southern conflict has been the most persistent, contentious, and destabilizing problem in Sudan. It has also been the most violent and deadly, claiming upwards of 2.5 million lives and making refugees out of some 4 million more.[15] Although the five-decade-old civil war has pitted the majority Muslim north against the minority non-Muslim south, at the heart of the conflict are powerful social, economic, and political issues that transcend the religious divide. The foundation of the north-south confrontation is rooted in the historical legacy of slavery, colonialism, and Anglo-Egyptian rule and in simple geography that aligns southern Sudan with the Bantu-speaking people of tropical central Africa. The late 1970s discovery of large oil deposits in the south added a further complicating economic issue as both sides sought to reap the windfall from this new-found resource. Army mutinies by southern troops in 1963 and again in 1983 proved to be the catalyst for the outbreak of hostilities. But it was the failure of a political system that safeguarded parochial northern interests and exacerbated conflict, as well as the policy of successive civilian and military regimes to force assimilation of the south through the unifying power of Islamic Arab culture, that made civil war inevitable.

Although the 1972 Addis Ababa peace accords had brought an uneasy peace to the country, it failed to resolve fundamental differences between both sides. Thus, it is not surprising that fighting quickly returned in earnest following Nimeiri's efforts in 1983 to tighten his control over the south and curry political favor with Sudan's political Islamists. By redrawing southern administrative boundaries to favor the north, ordering southern army units redeployed to the north, and imposing Shari'a nationwide, Nimeiri abrogated the 1972 agreement. In doing so, he reopened old wounds by striking at the heart of southern sensitivities: regional autonomy and the implied racial and religious superiority of the Arab north. In the wake of such an onslaught, many southern leaders saw no choice but to fight. Several army battalions defected to the rebels and formed the military core of the Sudanese People's Liberation Movement/Army (SPLM/A)[16] under the leadership of former Sudanese army colonel John Garang.

The fighting would steadily escalate with the introduction of more lethal weaponry and expand into central and northeast Sudan, but by 2001 both sides tacitly acknowledged that the war had become hopelessly stalemated. Seasonal military advances by one side were countered by the other, and fresh supplies of arms and material purchased with newly flowing oil revenues—estimated at $500 million per year since 1999[17]— by the government were offset by strong material and political support from the SPLM/A's regional allies. Political pressure was also pushing Bashir and Garang to bring an end to the conflict. Bashir had shored up his internal political position by removing the troublesome Turabi from the government, but other northern opposition elements were demanding an end to the war. Building international pressure over the government's brutal conduct of the war pushed many foreign governments to distance themselves from Sudan and lead to the imposition of an arms embargo and trade ban. Meanwhile, Garang was increasingly concerned about growing southern factionalism, and his regional allies were pressing for a negotiated settlement.[18] After nearly 20 years of fighting, war weariness was taking its toll on everyone.

Thanks to the untiring efforts of the regional grouping of East African states, known as the Intergovernmental Authority on Development (IGAD), efforts to end to the war had been slowly grinding forward since 1997. Once the warring parties finally committed themselves to reaching a negotiated settlement to the conflict, the peace process quickly gained momentum; by the summer of 2004 an agreement had been reached on key power-sharing provisions, the division of oil revenues, the implementation of Shari'a, and the issue of southern autonomy. Under the watchful guidance and timely interventions of IGAD, Kenya, and the United States,[19] the final sticking points in the negotiations were overcome and a Comprehensive Peace Agreement (CPA) signed on January 9, 2005.* Key northern opposition leaders, however, criticized the CPA and the new constitutional arrangements. Sadiq al-Mahdi warned that "there are many problems now in the east, in the west, and in other parts of Sudan whose resolution will require them to be represented in a comprehensive agreement and be represented in the constitution."[20] The fighting may have finally come to an end, but questions remain as to the resolution of the underlying issues that fueled the conflict in the first place.[21]

LINKAGES TO TERRORISM

The use of terror as a tactic to crush rebellious movements has become an inescapable part of Khartoum's military strategy. Whether through the use of pro-government militia groups or regular military forces

---

* For details of the agreement, see International Crisis Group, "Sudan's Comprehensive Peace Agreement," Africa Report No. 106, March 31, 2006.

employing scorched-earth policies, the regime has targeted civilians and other nonmilitary targets as part of a strategy to undermine support for antigovernment rebels both in southern Sudan and more recently, in the western region of Darfur. These tactics, however, tend to spawn an escalating spiral of violence that is difficult to break and makes conflicts harder to resolve as each side grows more intransigent. Furthermore, this escalation in violence can create opportunities for outside intervention by third parties—including international terrorist elements—and a possible spilling over of the conflict into neighboring states.

On a completely different level, rampant political turmoil, violent social conflict, and a legacy of violent political Islamism has long made Sudan a fertile environment for international terrorists to operate, recruit, and seek refuge. Beginning in 1973 with the killings of three Western diplomats (including U.S. Ambassador Cleo Noel) in Khartoum by the radical Palestinian group Black September, the country has attracted international terrorist elements. From 1993 to 2005, Sudan was classified as a state-sponsor of terrorism by the United States, and the United Nations imposed sanctions on the country during the late 1990s because of its involvement with international terrorist groups.[22] The regime was also implicated in supporting an assassination attempt on Egyptian President Hosni Mubarak by a radical Egyptian Islamist group in 1995.[23] However, since at least 2000, Khartoum appears to have distanced itself from violent political Islamist groups as part of its diplomatic rapprochement with the West, and now Sudan is listed as a U.S. ally in the global fight against terrorism.

Al Qaeda in Sudan[24]

The rise of Hassan al-Turabi and the National Islamic Front to political prominence in the early 1990s coincided with Osama bin Laden's search for a new base of operations following his expulsion from Saudi Arabia. Sudan proved to be the ideal fit. Turabi—an old friend of bin Laden[25]—was seeking to burnish his party's fundamentalist credentials, export his version of an Islamic revolution to the region, and transform Sudanese society, whereas bin Laden found in Sudan a secure and isolated venue, supportive government, and ideological compatibility. Bin Laden's newly established government connections and his wealth—estimated at $250 million[26]—instantly made him a powerful force on the Sudanese scene. According to numerous press accounts, bin Laden and his followers relocated to Sudan in 1991, where he began to refine his jihadist ideology and strengthen al Qaeda's organizational and financial infrastructure.[27] By the mid-1990s, bin Laden was reported to have amassed extensive landholdings and business and financial interests in the country, as well as considerable influence within the NIF. It was during this time in Sudan that al Qaeda apparently solidified its ties to other radical Islamist organizations, most notably Ayman al-Zawahiri's Egyptian Islamic Jihad group.

Fears over growing radicalization of the regime and its dangerous flirtation with international terrorism, however, alienated important neighbors, such as Egypt and Ethiopia, and brought it increasingly into conflict with Washington.[28] Charges that the Sudanese government was actively supporting al Qaeda by providing safe haven, granting freedom of movement, and permitting the establishment of training camps in the country would lead Washington to break diplomatic relations with Khartoum in 1995, impose economic sanctions, and institute an arms embargo against the regime. Meanwhile, both Ethiopia and Uganda (with quiet encouragement from the United States) were calling for the overthrow of the Bashir-Turabi government.[29] Clearly, bin Laden had outlived his usefulness and was now a liability to an increasingly threatened and isolated regime. In 1996, under strong American and Saudi pressure, bin Laden and some 300 of his followers were expelled from Sudan.[30]

Despite this setback, al Qaeda might have maintained a low-level presence in the country up to at least 2001 and probably was utilizing Sudanese financial institutions and charitable organizations to move money around the world.[31] This belief in a continuing presence was underscored by the retaliatory U.S. cruise missile attack on suspected al Qaeda targets in Sudan following the 1998 bombings of the American embassies in Nairobi and Dar es Salaam. The real turning point in ending Khartoum's support for radical Islamic groups, however, would be the changed domestic political situation and Bashir's desire to end the war in the south. By removing Turabi and his supporters from the government, abandoning Islamicization, and moving forward on peace negotiations, the reconstituted regime was able to reconcile with Washington and allay its concerns over the terrorism issue. By 2002, Sudan had denounced any ties to international terrorists groups and joined the United States in the global war on terrorism. Nonetheless, lingering doubts remain in some quarters as to Khartoum's sincerity.[32]

LINKAGES TO THE GLOBAL WAR ON TERRORISM

Africa—and particularly the trans-Saharan region of which Sudan is a part—is being increasingly viewed as the next battlefield in the global fight against terrorism. As pressure mounts on their traditional sanctuaries, international terrorists are likely to seek new safe havens among sympathetic populations, in countries with weak (or even supportive) governments, or in areas of high conflict that can be exploited to gain local allies. Accordingly, this makes Sudan a particularly attractive venue. Bin Laden's recent call for his supporters to go to Sudan and "prepare for the long war against the crusader plunders in Western Sudan"* underscores this point. Although his appeal apparently fell on deaf ears, bin Laden was seeking to transform the Darfur crisis into a struggle between the West and Islam. Ultimately, the success or failure of the struggle against terrorism in Africa is likely to be directly tied to the failure or success of reducing conflict and instability in key states, such as Sudan.

The Conflict-Instability-Terrorism Nexus

Overcoming domestic conflict and the resulting instability has been the central challenge to Sudanese governments for the past 50 years. Likewise, across numerous U.S. administrations, conflict and instability in Sudan and the greater Horn of Africa have been seen as posing a serious threat to international peace and security. Terrorism thrives in such a chaotic environment, with the ultimate breeding ground being the failed or failing state as a result of catastrophic internal conflict. The post-9/11 security situation has only served to reinforce this thinking, and the Bush Administration has committed considerable time and energy in helping to bring about peace and stability in Sudan, primarily through a resolution of the north-south conflict. As one report highlighted,

> Sudan is a core country in the U.S. effort to combat failed states, persistent conflict, and terrorism throughout the Horn of Africa/ Red Sea region. If the United States fails to take the necessary steps to ensure against Sudan's falling into the failed-state status, regional instability will continue to threaten U.S. interests in this key region of Africa.[33]

The unique nature of Sudanese conflict is also viewed in Washington as providing fertile soil for the growth and spread of religious extremism that helps fuel international terrorism. Fears that religious extremists may exploit—and distort—religious and cultural conflicts as rallying points and recruiting tools are at the heart of this concern. Furthermore, conflict-driven instability in general weakens government control; creates vast, ungoverned spaces for terrorists to operate, transit, or

---

* Aljazeera.net, "Bin Laden: West Waging a Crusade," April 23, 2006, http://english.aljazeera.net/NR/exeres/FEE6E1E5-DCC0-4E8A-80CF-FFCCA2BC4C2A.htm

seek safe haven; and undermines cooperative security efforts. Although General Bashir appears to have pragmatically distanced his regime from international terrorist groups in the post-9/11 period, there undoubtedly remain significant elements within the Sudanese government that are sympathetic to extremist Islamic ideology and its objectives.

The primary concern for the United States is state collapse—the fear that Sudan could become a failed state and a base for international terrorism. Certainly given the multiple sources of conflict, deep divisions within society, a history of violent religious extremism, and weak political institutions, Sudan is a prime candidate for such a scenario. The repercussions of Sudan becoming a failed state would be felt far and wide—in Egypt, Ethiopia, central Africa, and even parts of the Middle East. Short of the unlikely event of a complete collapse of the state, however, continuing political and social fragmentation and separatist tendencies pose the gravest threats to security and the fight against international terrorism.

Stumbling Blocks to Closer Cooperation

Although Sudan has now joined with the international community in efforts to counter the spread of terrorism, several significant stumbling blocks could disrupt Khartoum's transformation into a full-fledged ally in the struggle. Continuing a long-established pattern, the internal dynamics of Sudanese conflict will almost certainly be the most decisive factor in determining the regime's future course of action. Major domestic obstacles to greater U.S.-Sudanese counterterrorism cooperation include the following:

A collapse of the CPA. Great progress has been made in reconciling north and south, but the peace agreement remains fragile; key groups on both sides feel marginalized, control over the distribution of oil revenues will continue to be a major source of friction, and questions as to the actual extent of southern political autonomy have yet to be answered. High expectations of a peace dividend producing rapid economic improvement in the south are also unlikely to be met, leading to rising popular frustration with the SPLM/A leadership.[34]

The continuing inability to resolve the conflict in Darfur. The longer the crisis in Darfur lingers, the greater the strain in relations between the Bashir government and the international community, undermining the goodwill achieved with the ending of the conflict in the south. Past pledges of American economic assistance to help rebuild the country's war-torn infrastructure may also fall victim to what many in Washington see as the Sudanese government's direct complicity in fueling the ongoing violence. Furthermore, an increasingly hostile international environment may push Khartoum to abandon its policy of rapprochement with the West and retreat inward.

A return of a reconstituted radical Islamic party. Although Bashir effectively undercut the influence of Islamic extremists in 2000 with his purge of Turabi and other NIF hardliners, they still remain a powerful force in the country. Turabi and other religious extremists are active on the political scene, and sympathetic elements undoubtedly remain entrenched in the government and military. A rising domestic religious challenge to the Bashir government could force the regime to cover its political flanks by reducing its cooperation with the West on security issues that are viewed as anti-Islamic.

PROGRESS AND PROSPECTS

In a huge country as diverse and divided as Sudan and with its historical legacy of violence, overcoming conflict and chronic political instability will be a difficult task. In the immediate years ahead, the country will be forced to grapple with contentious issues that focus on expanding regional political autonomy; narrowing the religious, cultural, and racial divide within the society; broadening political participation to include minority elements; regaining civil control of the military; and developing unifying structures and institutions to promote a new sense of Sudanese nationhood. How well it handles these issues will have a direct bearing on the challenge of countering terrorism. Unless the Sudanese can make progress in mitigating domestic conflict, the environment in which terrorism thrives will continue to spawn its deadly offspring.

Just as it was forced to do in the south to resolve conflict, Khartoum will undoubtedly be pressured to grant a greater degree of political autonomy to other regions and decentralize many of the functions of government. This action would go a long way in undercutting a major source of grievances against what many Sudanese feel is an unresponsive and remote national leadership. In doing so, however, Khartoum must take care in crafting this new style of federalism to reflect the long-term goal of promoting national unity and interdependence, lest the country grow even more fragmented. Time is of the essence with the pending 2011 referendum on southern secession providing either an endorsement or rejection of the government's handling of this issue.

The flip side of increased political autonomy is the need to reshape national institutions and political culture to make them more representative of Sudanese society. One such way is to make the political structure more inclusive to minority and marginalized groups and give them a stake in the political system. Likewise, the failure of using Arab-Islamic culture as a unifying political force should be fully acknowledged and replaced with a uniting mechanism that is more reflective of the national ethos. For all its problems, however, Sudan does indeed have the underpinnings of a strong and vibrant democratic society; an emphasis on nurturing political pluralism need not be detrimental to the promotion of national unity. Democracy, however, can be messy. It is essential that the international community—and especially the United States—be supportive of this process and allow Sudanese democracy to chart its own evolutionary course.

Finally, essential to the transformation of the Sudanese political system is the return of the military to its barracks. This certainly will be no easy task in a country that has seen 40 years of authoritarian military rule since independence and whose interventions were often seen as a blessing to a society racked with conflict, political infighting, and gridlock. An essential tenet of democracy is civil control of the military; negotiation, compromise, and accommodation should be the tools of a democratic society, not the fear that comes from looking down the barrel of a gun. The military needs to get out—and stay out—of politics for a new democratic society in Sudan to take shape and grow.

CONCLUSION

Sudan's legacy of violent political Islam, brutal conflict, and incessant instability make it a major flashpoint in the global fight against terrorism. While acknowledging that the country has been burdened with multiple environmental and historical factors beyond its control, it has largely been the failure of Sudanese institutions and leaders to bridge differences that is responsible for the country's plight. This failure is epitomized by the old story of the Sudanese and his visitor who come to gaze on the joining of the Blue and the White Nile at Khartoum, and the visitor remarks that the clear water of one does not seem to mingle with the muddy waters of the other, but appears to maintain its own separateness. The Sudanese host then says that it is not unlike Sudan itself: "We are one country, but some of us are thick and some of us are thin, some come from one direction, some from another, and so far we have not learned to unite."[35]

As has been repeatedly noted, internal conflicts seldom remain that way and quickly become internationalized. Moreover, their very existence makes countries like Sudan extremely vulnerable to outside forces—such as terrorist networks—that seek to exploit the situation and advance their own agendas. Given the linkages between conflict, instability, and terrorism in the region, the continuing existence of violent conflict is likely to be the decisive factor in determining the success or failure of the global war on terrorism in Africa. Addressing the root causes of persistent domestic conflict may, in fact, be the most effective counterterrorism strategy in the long run. Ultimately, a more peaceful and stable Sudan is likely to yield a more stable and secure international community as well.

NOTES

1. Within the 967,243 square miles of Sudanese territory live an estimated 40 million people speaking some 400 languages, with Arabic being the dominate spoken language, although English is widely used in the southern part of the country. Muslims comprise 70 percent of the population, Christians 5 percent, and the remaining 25 percent are animists. Approximately 40 percent of the people identify themselves as "Arabs" and live mainly in the northern part of the country, while black Sudanese account for about half the population and live primarily in the west and south. Important non-Arab Muslim groups include the Nubians in the far north, the Beja in the northeast, and the Fur in the west. The major non-Muslim ethnic group are the Dinka, who comprise about 40 percent of the southern population. Helen C. Metz, ed., *Sudan: A Country Study*, 4th Edition (Washington, DC: Library of Congress, 1992), xv–xvi; CIA World Factbook, http://www.cia.gov/cia/publications/factbook/geos/su.html.
2. Winston S. Churchill, *The River War: An Account of the Reconquest of the Sudan*, Carroll & Graf Edition (New York: Carroll & Graf Publishers, 2000), p. 1.
3. The well-publicized crisis in Darfur, which boiled over into violent conflict in early 2003, has left at least 200,000 dead (some estimates range as high as 400,000), sent 200,000 more fleeing into neighboring Chad, and internally displaced another 1.8 million people. Despite ongoing peace talks between the government and rebel forces and the presence of a 7,000-man Africa Union monitoring force, the situation remains explosive, with no immediate end in sight. For updates, see http://www.usaid.gov/locations/sub-saharan_africa/sudan/darfur.html or http://www.crisisgroup.org/home/index.cfm?id=3060&l=1.
4. It should be remembered that although 70 percent of Sudanese are Muslims, the Islamic community encompasses a wide range of racial, ethnic, and cultural groupings.
5. The politics of oil are increasingly likely to occupy center stage in the years ahead as Sudanese oil production begins to boom. Sudan has been producing 320,000 to 340,000 barrels per day (bpd) of oil, but production is expected to surpass 500,000 bpd in 2006. *Sudan Tribune*, "Sudan Peace to Spur Oil Growth, West Still Wary," January 6, 2005; CIA World Factbook, http://www.cia.gov/cia/publications/factbook/geos/su.html.
6. The coming of the Mahdi (The Guided One) was a long-held Sunni Islamic tradition, whose appearance would presage the second coming of Christ and restore Islam to its true glory. It was prophesied that he would bear the name Muhammed, be descended from the Prophet, and his arrival would be accompanied by violence at the dawn of a new century. For biographic details of Muhammed Ahmed's life, see A. B. Theobald, *The Mahdiya: A History of the Anglo-Egyptian Sudan, 1881–1899* (London: Longmans, Green and Co., 1951), pp. 25–28; Byron Farwell, *Prisoners of the Mahdi* (New York: Harper and Row, 1967), pp. 3–10.

7. Between 1820 and the early 1880s, Sudan was under the control of Egyptian-appointed governor-generals who ruthlessly administered the territory on behalf of Cairo with the assistance of a large locally raised Sudanese army. Egypt's worsening international financial crisis, however, led to the growing influence of European nations. In 1877, Charles Gordon, an Englishman, Christian, and antislavery proponent, was appointed governor-general, much to the consternation of Sudanese Muslims. See E. A. Ayandele, "The Sudan and Ethiopia in the nineteenth century," in A.E. Afigbo, E.A. Ayandele, et. al., *The Making of Modern Africa: Volume One* (London: Longman, 1992), pp. 152–158 for a good overview of this period.

8. Harold D. Nelson, ed., *Sudan: A Country Study* (Washington, DC: U.S. Government Printing Office, 1982), p. 30.

9. For a first-hand account of the British-led military campaign, see Churchill, *The River War*.

10. The rebel forces were a fragmented collection of locally based guerrilla groups (some fighting since 1955), known as the Anya Nya and not under control of any political organization. Older rebels were "joined in the early 1960s by ... policemen, NCOs, and prison warders, who increasingly felt the weight of suspicion and discrimination under the military regime and joined the resistance." Woodward, *Sudan 1898–1989*, p. 107.

11. The Democratic Unionist Party (DUP) came into existence in 1968 with the merging of the core of the NUP, Khatmiyya elements, and the People's Democratic Party.

12. For a detailed discussion of the 1972 peace agreement, see Bona Malwal, *The Sudan: A Second Challenge to Nationhood* (New York: Thornton Books, 1985), pp. 17–20.

13. Mansur Khalid, *Nimeiri and the Revolution of Dis-May* (London: KPI Limited, 1985), p. 38.

14. For a detailed examination of the relationship between the war, famine, and humanitarian relief efforts in the south, see J. Millard Burr and Robert O. Collins, *Requiem for the Sudan: War, Drought, and Disaster Relief on the Nile* (Boulder, CO: Westview Press, 1995).

15. Firm numbers of those killed and displaced since the beginning of the conflict are difficult to verify and estimates range widely, but it would appear that at least 2.5 million people—about 500,000 from 1955–1972 and another 2 million from 1983–2004—have died as a direct or indirect result of the war.

16. The Sudanese People's Liberation Movement (SPLM) and it military wing, the Sudanese People's Liberation Army (SPLA), were two separate structures under John Garang's political and military leadership, but for ease of reference the combined Sudanese People's Liberation Movement/Army (SPLM/A) notation is used throughout this chapter.

17. Institute for Security Studies, "Sudan: Political and Security Information," updated January 12, 2005, http://www.iss.co.za/AF/profiles/Sudan/Politics.html.

18. External military assistance, particularly the establishment of training and logistic bases inside Ethiopia, was vital to the SPLM/A and provided Addis Ababa with an effective tool for punishing Khartoum for its support of Eritrean separatists rebels in their war against Ethiopia. Likewise, strong ties were forged between Garang and the Ugandan government in reaction to what Kampala saw as Khartoum's backing for Ugandan rebels.

19. From the 2001 appointment of John Danforth as Special Envoy for Sudan to the signing of the peace agreement in January 2005, the United States was heavily engaged in the peace process, using a carrot and stick approach (including promises of reestablishing diplomatic relations and the provision of post-war reconstruction assistance) to keep the negotiations moving forward.

20. *BBC News,* "Sudan State of Emergency Lifted," July 11, 2005, http://news.bbc.co.uk/go/pr/fr/-/2/hi/africa/4670231.stm.
21. Time is of the essence for the new coalition government to show results in resolving longstanding north-south differences, because under the terms of the CPA a referendum on southern self-determination and separation is to be held in six years.
22. Council on Foreign Relations, "Background Q&A: State Sponsors [of Terrorism] Sudan," Updated December 2005, http://www.cfr.org/publication/9367/state_sponsors.html.
23. *Ibid.*
24. For an interesting perspective on the al Qaeda-Sudanese connection see, *Jihad Unspun,* "Bin Laden's Life in Sudan: Into the Development of Osama's Viewpoints," Reprinted from London Al-Quds al-Arabi, November 24, 2001, http://www.jihadunspun.com/BinLadensNetwork/background.
25. Former CIA analyst Kenneth Katzman characterized an usually close relationship between bin Laden and Turabi back in 1998 by saying that "bin Laden is inspired by Turabi's expansive vision; he sees eye to eye with him" and bin Laden "is Turabi's alter ego, his field commander, his operations chief." *New York Times on the Web,* "U.S. Sees Bin Laden as Ringleader of Terrorist Network," August 21, 1998; http://partners.nytimes.com/library/world/africa/082198attack-binladen.html.
26. *The New Yorker,* "From the Archives: The Real bin Laden," September 13, 2001, http://www.newyorker.com/archive/content/?010924fr_archive03.
27. *Jihad Unspun,* "Bin Laden's Life in Sudan," November 24, 2001, http://www.jihadunspun.com/BinLadensNetwork/background; *New York Times on the Web,* "U.S. Sees Bin Laden as Ringleader of Terrorist Network," August 21, 1998; http://partners.nytimes.com/library/world/africa/082198attack-binladen.html.
28. For a discussion of Washington's case against the regime, see Marguerite Michaels, *Time,* "Is Sudan Terrorism's Best Friend," August 30, 1993.
29. For the last half of the 1990s, Ethiopia "considered the export of Islamic radicalism from Sudan its greatest security threat" and joined Uganda and Eritrea in "an American-led 'frontline states' policy against Sudan" to counter the threat. *United States Institute of Peace,* "Special Report 113: Terrorism in the Horn of Africa," January 2004, http://www.usip.org/pubs/specialreports/sr113.html.
30. *Observer,* "Resentful West Spurned Sudan's Key Terror Files," September 30, 2001.
31. *BBC,* "Bin Laden's Sudan Links Remain," September 23, 2001, http://www.bbc.co.uk/1/hi/world/africa/1559624.stm.
32. *Washington Times,* "U.S. Probes Reported Sudan Link to Terror," June 17, 2005, http://www.washingtontimes.com.
33. Dina Esposito and Bathsheba N. Crocker, "To Guarantee the Peace: An Action Strategy for a Post-Conflict Sudan," in *Rising U.S. Stakes in Africa,* ed. Walter H. Kansteiner and J. Stephen Morrision (Washington, DC: CSIS Press, 2004), p. 54.
34. The peace agreement appears to have effectively weathered the July 2005 death of John Garang, but Garang's forceful leadership will sorely be missed in the future. See *International Crisis Group,* "Garang's Death: Implications for Peace in Sudan," Africa Briefing No. 30, August 9, 2005, for a detailed analysis.
35. James Morris, *Islam Inflamed* (New York: Pantheon Books, 1957), p. 93.

Nigeria

14

NIGERIA

Michael F. Morris and Charles Edel

In Africa, promise and opportunity sit side by side with disease, war, and desperate poverty.[1]

President George W. Bush

True Muslims should act, incite, and mobilize the nation in such great events ... in order to break free from the slavery of these tyrannic and apostate regimes, which is enslaved by America, in order to establish the rule of Allah on Earth. Among regions ready for liberation are Jordan, Morocco, Nigeria, the country of the two shrines [Saudi Arabia], Yemen, and Pakistan.[2]

Osama bin Laden

NATURE OF THE FLASHPOINT

Nigeria is one of the United States' most important strategic allies in Africa because of its size, large oil reserves, and central role in regional peacekeeping operations, yet instability plagues Africa's most populous country. Because of this growing internal instability, the country is both fertile ground for the radicalization of political Islam and a strategically attractive target for al Qaeda. Home to one out of every four Africans, Nigeria sits atop a wealth of natural resources and holds the key to stability in West Africa. The U.S. Energy Information

Administration has taken note of the deteriorating situation in Nigeria, citing unrest, political instability, and economic disparities as reasons for "violent crime, ethnic and religious strife," calling Nigeria one of its "world energy hotspots."[3] Nigeria's growing economic importance to the world, its struggle with a democratic transformation, and its fight against radicalizing political Islam make it an important test case for U.S. strategy and policy in the early twenty-first century in Africa.

Energy Security

Energy drives U.S. foreign policy in West Africa, which is expected to account for an estimated 20–25 percent of U.S. oil imports by 2015.[4] Nigeria is at the heart, geographically and strategically, of the world's fastest growing energy export region. Nigeria provides access to the potentially large offshore oil deposits in the Gulf of Guinea and has the world's seventh largest proven gas reserves, with 176.4 trillion cubic feet.[5] Nigeria is already a major oil producer that is crucial to the United States' energy needs, and will likely play an increasingly prominent role in U.S. foreign policy toward Africa.

The Gulf of Guinea region is significantly closer to U.S. ports than the Persian Gulf, and oil tankers enroute to and from the region are not subject to the strategic chokepoints of the Strait of Hormuz, the Bab-el-Mandeb, or the Suez Canal. Additionally, Nigerian crude is of the highest quality preferred by U.S. refineries, and Nigerian natural gas reserves are expected to increase in importance as developed countries diversify their energy supplies, impacting regional development. Through a Chevron-Texaco West Africa gas pipeline project, Nigeria will become a regional natural gas supplier to many neighboring countries.

In spite of Nigeria's natural wealth, its growing internal insecurity puts the region's security at risk. Labor strikes are a continuing source of disruption—a strike in March 2003 took 800,000 barrels per day off the world market for months. As late as January 2004 production was still down by at least 200,000 barrels per day. A dispute between the government and labor leaders contributed to a spike in world prices in October 2004. Unrest in the Niger Delta continued to disrupt global oil supplies into 2005; in January, ChevronTexaco announced it was losing 140,000 barrels per day due to closure of its facilities. Additionally, continuing violence in the Niger Delta region threatens overall oil supplies; local militias bunker, or illegally intercept and store, 100,000 to 200,000 barrels of oil per day, reducing the overall global supply of crude oil, and providing more than $1 billion per year to the rebel groups. Underlying these civil disturbances is the unequal distribution of wealth derived from Nigeria's natural resources.

Sources of Religious Tension

Although no official census has been conducted since 1982, reliable estimates place the surging Nigerian population at roughly 140 million people, while more conservative estimates place it at just over 128 million.[6] By either estimate, Nigeria is the most populous country in Africa. There are more than 350 different ethnic groups, the most prominent being the Hausa, Fulani, Yoruba, and Igbo (Ibo). While ethnicity includes strong ancestral and geographic ties, the modernization and urbanization of the country have led many people to leave their traditional homelands and migrate to major cities such as Lagos and Abuja. With this migration, ethnicity is slowly losing its primacy in defining identity, and Nigerians are increasingly defined along religious lines.

While there is much debate about the shifting population balance between Christian and Muslim populations, Nigeria has at least 68.5 million Muslims, the second largest such population in Africa (following Egypt) and the eighth largest Muslim population in the world. While the development and urbanization of Nigeria means that the tribal identities are more in flux, geographically the North is dominated by the primarily Muslim Hausa and Fulani ethnic groups; the Southeast is home to the largely Christian Igbo; and the Southwest is home to the Yoruba. Historically, the Yoruba-dominated southwest has been a pluralistic society, with the population divided more or less evenly between Christian, Muslim, and those who hold animist or indigenous beliefs. This geographic distribution places over 70 percent of the Muslim population in the northern states, with the remaining 20 million living in the Southwest.

While the overwhelming majority of Nigerian Muslims are Sunni, Nigerian religious practices are significantly different from Sunni Islam as practiced in the Arab states. Islam in Nigeria dates to the seventh century, when the Arabs conquered much of North Africa and spread their influence across the desert to the south. This gradual process incorporated the indigenous customs and beliefs, including local tradition and superstition, into religious practices, resulting in a blend unlike that of the Islamic Arab countries. Because of this distinctly Nigerian religion, the country has been largely immune to foreign radicalizing influences; it has only been during the last decade that extremist political Islam has gained ground in Nigeria.

For most of its post-colonial history, Islamic military leaders from the northern regions of the country have ruled Nigeria. In 1993, General Ibrahim Babangida annulled the election when it appeared clear that Moshood Abiola, a Yoruba businessman, was poised to win the presidency, adding to the myth that Islamic generals from the North actually run the country. This led to tension between the resource-rich and predominantly Christian South and the politically powerful Muslim North. This tension was further exacerbated by the 1999 election of former General Olusegun Obasanjo, replacing the corrupt head of state, General Sani Abacha, who died of a heart attack while in office in May 1998. Obasanjo's election restored democratically elected civilian control to a country that had long been run as a harsh military dictatorship. He is generally credited with promoting reforms aimed at alleviating much political and economic oppression, but many sources of tension remain.

Obasanjo, who ruled Nigeria in the late 1970s as the head of a military government before turning power over in 1979 to an elected government, is a born-again Christian Yoruba from the Southwest. He is extremely public in his professions of his Christian faith. For example, every Sunday he attends church and teaches Sunday school. This is widely publicized, and is not well received in the North. Combined with Obasanjo's purge of military officers that began in 1999, most of whom were from the North, and the increasing rate of Christian conversions, many northern Nigerian Muslims feel as if they are losing the power they have long held. This explosive growth of Christianity in Nigeria adds to Northern feelings of anxiety. All across the South, Pentecostal churches have arisen. Conservative American Christians have largely funded this effort, but Nigeria is also a destination for worldwide evangelical organizations. Many Nigerians see a distant president and a corrupt government that has brought them hardship—a sentiment providing some basis for the support of political Islam in the North. Soon after Obasanjo's 1999 election, a northern governor first introduced Shari'a (Islamic law) in Zamfara state. Since that time, 11 other northern states have adopted Shari'a for criminal cases.

Despite widespread electoral irregularities, Obasanjo's April 2003 reelection marked the first civilian-to-civilian transfer of power in Nigeria's history. Obasanjo defeated his primary opponent, General Muhammadu Buhari, a Muslim general from the North. Most of Buhari's support came from the northern states that declared Shari'a law after Obasanjo's election in 1999. Whether this was due to religious, regional, or economic preferences is hard to determine. However, it is worth noting that Buhari received only 32 percent of the popular vote, compared to Obasanjo's 62 percent. Additionally, the level of violence between Christians and Muslims, which peaked in 2002, subsided.

That said, machine-gun-toting youths do nothing to alleviate endemic levels of political corruption. Local and state elections are so violent because the stakes are so high. In regions where unemployment can reach 70 percent, politics is, if not the only game, certainly the most lucrative one in town. Politics is a patronage system where the winners reap the rewards and hoard the riches for themselves and their tribe. Since Obasanjo's election in 1999, at least 11,000 Nigerians have died in communal and sectarian violence between Muslim and Christian communities, with almost all of the violence being concentrated in the North.[7] Kaduna, Jos, and Plateau states have experienced particularly violent conflict, with many churches and mosques being attacked. Often, the implementation of Shari'a has gone hand in hand with calls for sectarian violence. In April 2004, the governor of Zamfara announced plans to destroy all Christian churches and non-Islamic places of worship as part of his religious "duty to subjugate infidels." As of this writing, no such plans have been carried out, though the state may restrict building through regulation.

Economic Stagnation and Political Corruption

BBC journalist Dan Issacs places the responsibility for contemporary conflict on the character of economics in Nigeria. He states that the origin of conflict that appears to be based in religion

> ... most often boils down to competition between those that see themselves as the true "indigens" of an area, and those that are considered to be more recent "settlers." Whatever the historical justifications, the conflict is always and everywhere about access to scarce resources. This might be farmland, or employment, or access to political power. It could even be jealousy over the provision of water or electricity to one village but not to its neighbour [sic]. At their root, these differences are not cultural or religious. They are economic.[8]

In a nation as chronically poor as Nigeria, where the enormous wealth generated by the export of oil and natural gas is held by the political and economic elite while a majority of the citizens subsist below the poverty line, it is not unexpected that much of the conflict centers on gaining or holding resources. However, when those involved in the conflict appear to be segregated along religious lines, it is also understandable to see the conflict in those terms. Yet political corruption and economic mismanagement are at the root causes of conflict.

Despite the discovery of oil and the riches that flowed into the country's coffers, Nigeria's economy continues on a downward trajectory due largely due to corruption and mismanagement. Politically, Nigeria remains one of the most corrupt nations in the world. In Transparency International's survey-based 2005 Corruption Perceptions Index, Nigeria ranked 152 of 158, leading only Haiti, Myanmar, Turkmenistan, Bangladesh, and Chad. Among national institutions, the police are viewed by the populace as the most corrupt, a ranking rivaled only by Nigeria's multitude of political parties.[9] A related metric monitors bribery as an indicator of endemic corruption; in Nigeria, 29 percent of households admitted paying some form of bribe in the last 12 months.[10] While President Obasanjo has taken a strong public stance against corruption, even allowing investigations of his own conduct based on allegations of wrongdoing regarding oil contract commissions and foreign accounts, allegations still abound of money laundering and sequestering of oil revenues outside Nigeria on the part of state governors. In some cases, journalists have been jailed or detained for bringing the charges to light. Nigeria's Economic and Financial Crimes Commission believes up to $17 billion in cash and assets belonging to state governors have been banked outside Nigeria.[11]

In 1975, Nigeria had a $5 billion dollar surplus. By June 2005, Nigeria's external debt was approximately $35 billion, and the Paris Club creditor nations had agreed to $18 billion in debt relief after spirited negotiations.[12] By June 2005, Nigeria's external debt exceeded $30 billion, and the Paris Club creditor nations had agreed to $18 billion in debt relief after spirited negotiations. Thanks to increased oil revenue driven by surging crude oil prices, Nigeria paid back the final $4.5 billion of its Paris Club debt on April 21, 2006, making it the first African nation to do so. With Nigeria's political leaders principally coming from the North, Nigerian leaders used their power to direct oil revenue to their home states. Since almost all of the country's oil and gas reserves are located in the south of the country, competition and anger over the federal government's dispensing of revenue allocation has been and continues to be a large source of regional and ethnic discontent.

In the past decade, per-capita GNP has dropped by two-thirds. Between 70 and 80 percent of Nigerians live on less than a dollar a day; inflation hovers between 17.5 and 20 percent; unemployment might be as high as 70 percent. In almost every measurable way, and by almost all immeasurable accounts, the average Nigerian is worse off today than when the nation gained its independence from the United Kingdom in 1960.

This is particularly apparent in the Niger Delta region, home to the Ijaw people, Nigeria's fourth-largest ethnic group. Traditionally, and most especially since independence, they have been disenfranchised, both economically and politically. There is a long history of abuses of the Ijaw people at the hands of the army. Election fraud and violence, widespread throughout the country, were perhaps worst in the River and Delta states in the 2003 elections. And most grievously to the Ijaws, the federal government disperses the revenues from the Delta's oil wealth throughout the entire country (the Ijaws receive only 13 percent). A recently passed law exacerbates this tension, placing all offshore sites, regardless of location, under federal control.

LINKAGES TO TERRORISM

The United States envisions the possibility of violent political Islamists gaining a stronger foothold in northern Nigeria, a region of the nation dominated by the Hausa and Fulani ethnic groups and populated largely by Muslims (though there is a significant Christian minority). Such an extremist presence would be deeply troubling to the United States, not only for its possible effects within Nigeria, but also for its implications across West Africa, the Pan-Sahel region, and the Gulf of Guinea.

Fully considered, the causes of the apparent conflict between Muslims and Christians in Nigeria are complex in nature and scope, and reach across the whole of Nigerian society. When considering the potential for radical political Islam to arise in Nigeria and the surrounding region, many point to the violent, oftentimes fatal, conflict within the nation as evidence of an underlying religious schism between the predominantly Muslim North and the predominantly Christian and animist South. However obvious this may seem on the surface, the root causes of violence in Nigeria are not that simple. Paul Collier, for example, makes an important point: "Conflicts in ethnically diverse countries may be ethnically patterned without being ethnically caused."[13] This may well be a key to understanding Nigeria's internal conflict and the nation's vulnerability to the intrusion of external elements seeking fertile soil for Islamic extremism. The question is the source of the conflict. Is it the result of ethnic differences, religious disagreement, socio-political disenfranchisement, or economic inequality? And to what degree does the nexus of these factors create an opening for violent political Islamists to gain a foothold in Nigeria?

Unrest is largely confined in the North, Southwest, and the Niger Delta and flows from an increasing sense of economic dislocation and political disempowerment. Poor law and order, increased fragmentation of the country, a heavy influx of Saudi and Pakistani funds, and a growing radicalized political Islam in both the North and the Southwestern regions of the country, as well as an armed uprising in the Delta region, contribute to religious tension. While the North has been historically indifferent to foreign influence, and the manner in which Islam is practiced is at odds with more fundamental interpretations, a sense of helplessness and impoverishment has opened the door to a lingering frustration that is easily exploitable. In the North, poverty is everywhere and increasing. Despite the complaints of those in the South who feel their patrimony is being stolen by lazy northerners, poverty is rapidly accelerating due to deterioration of the infrastructure. Kano is the new center of political Islam in Nigeria and the site of large anti-American gatherings.

As the federal state's control weakens and people's anger rises, the Muslim population in the North is more willing to accept and embrace the influx of foreign money and violent ways. The older, more moderate version of Nigerian Islam is slowly giving way to a newer, more rigorous, and often more extreme version of political Islam. The emirs are losing their power to younger imams who studied in Saudi Arabia.

The terrorism knowledge base of the Memorial Institute for the Prevention of Terrorism (MIPT) records one indigenous religious group that is considered to be "terrorist" in nature: Hisba.[14] This group ensures the enforcement of Shari'a law in portions of northern Nigeria, and their activities are largely intentionally overlooked by Nigerian leaders who are not eager to confront violent political Islamists. In April 2001, the group was credited with destroying several hotels in Christian districts of Kano that were suspected of selling liquor in violation of Shari'a law. They also ensure public buses are segregated by gender. Those "guilty" of infractions of the Islamic law are subject to punishment.

This group, together with Al Sunna Wal Jamma, can prove formidable obstacles to true interfaith tolerance and acceptance. This student-based organization, centered in Maduguri, professes to want a Taliban-like Islamic state in Nigeria. Originally a group of university students, this organization quickly became militant. In December 2003, the group, armed and estimated at 200 strong, attacked two police stations in Kanamma and Geidam. These attacks continued for several weeks until the Nigerian army intervened.

Such religious tactics and studious governmental ignorance of them, are bound to cause friction and discontent, and sometimes even lead to violence. Though economic disparities and the neglect of political leaders to take prompt action exacerbate the violence, one thing is clear: Religious differences still constitute a deep, and perhaps growing, divide in Nigeria.

The lack of an official U.S. presence in the North is a major obstacle to understanding the nature of the militant threat. The United States has only one diplomatic corner in the North. While the Department of State is currently planning three more, all are run by Nigerians and the U.S. employs no native Hausa speakers. Moreover, this is just the area where sustained public diplomacy is needed lest others shape and co-opt the U.S. message.

The Southwest

In southwestern Nigeria, Islam has existed more or less peacefully. Often, more than one religion may be represented in a single family and interfaith marriages are not uncommon. In fact, President Obasanjo's own family is religiously mixed; he is a born-again Christian, while his sister is a Muslim. It is probably this mixing of religions and cultures that has lead to a fairly harmonious balance in the region since independence; it has not suffered the self-determination movements present in the East nor experienced wide-scale sectarian violence as in the North.

For the most part, the Muslims in the country's Southwest are neither violent nor radicalized. Furthermore, this is the most pro-American region of the country; the overwhelming majority of the Nigerian-American community comes from this area and sends both remittances and transmits favorable views of the United States back home to their families. But a highly educated and increasingly interconnected youth culture is tapping into a harsher, more fundamental, and potentially more violent brand of political Islam. In contrast to the North, political Islam is making inroads in the Southwest through the younger, more cosmopolitan educated classes. There, Islam is not a protest movement; it is largely a personal or intellectual movement, and finds its largest expression on the college campuses. A more educated region with more universities, the Southwest offers more connections to the outside world. Because these students have greater access to Internet chat rooms and more familiarity with satellite television programming, they are more informed of global news and trends, and international issues in the greater Islamic world. In short, when students are more connected to the world, they are also more easily contacted and recruited by global jihad networks.

The Niger Delta

Although Muhahid Dokubo-Asari, leader of the Niger Delta Peoples Volunteer Force (NDPVF), claimed to admire Osama bin Laden for fighting "on behalf of all Muslims," Dokubo is not fighting a religious war; it is a fight over access to oil and the revenues it provides. Since the discovery of oil in Nigeria, this predominantly Igbo region has witnessed the value of its resources climb but has seen little, if any, tangible benefits. The fact that revenues are distributed across the entire country (the Niger Delta gets only 13 percent) has led to feelings of exploitation, resentment, and anger. Dokubo has vowed to fight for self-determination for his people, with the understanding that this means control of almost all of the country's onshore oil resources.

The size of Dokubo's force is unknown. He claims 200,000 followers, but this appears to be an inflated number. However, even if his numbers are not reliable, the ongoing violence in the Delta is definitely a threat to stability. Roughly 1,000 lives are lost a year in the Delta region and 100,000 to 200,000 barrels of oil per day are bunkered. Growing unrest in the region often results in violence, kidnapping, and sabotage of oil facilities. Coupled with continuing labor strikes, the major companies involved in the Nigerian oil sector—ExxonMobil, ChevronTexaco, Total, Agip, and ConocoPhillips—have cut back their activity. Although the oil companies did not apparently play a direct role in these conflicts, as they lived in walled compounds, had extensive security on their grounds, and, for the most part, appeared willing to retreat offshore at signs of significant unrest, their unwillingness to disclose financial terms of contracts and other agreements do contribute to the Igbos' sense of frustration and feeds their tendency to resort to violence.

Additionally, almost 40 percent of all oil production in Nigeria was shut down last year due to violence in the region. Dokubo has urged his followers to stand up to the Nigerian government and has claimed that he has received guerrilla training abroad. While there is little chance that Dokubo's NDPVF are actually working with al Qaeda, a large armed insurgency that is at odds with the government opens the door to foreign elements. Like Chechnya, the potential remains for the conflict to move beyond nationalist boundaries, attracting foreign jihadists who attempt to shape the violence into a "clash of civilizations."

LINKAGES TO THE GLOBAL WAR ON TERRORISM

The United States considers Nigeria to be an important country in Africa. Long recognized as a powerful force within the Economic Community of West African States (ECOWAS) and the African Union, Nigeria has gained political leverage through its economic power (largely oil resources), large population, and the regional leadership roles played by its leaders, including President Obasanjo, who at the time of this writing was the seated chairperson of the African Union.

Nigeria is mentioned by name in the 2002 United States National Security Strategy, where the country is noted as an "anchor state" on the continent, along with South Africa, Kenya, and Ethiopia. This combination of Nigeria's economic importance, its growing role in the U.S. war on terror, and its position as both a subregional and regional leader make Nigeria a vital partner of the United States. The U.S. and Nigeria jointly prioritize U.S. assistance, which is administered by the United States Agency for International Development, or USAID. The 2006 budget request for Nigerian aid is $45.7 million, more than half of which ($28.1 million) is dedicated to education and health (non-AIDS/HIV) projects. The remainder is focused on strengthening democratic institutions and civil society, improving governance capability, and enhancing economic performance. AIDS/HIV and tuberculosis efforts receive $1.6 million in funding.[15]

The United States is deeply concerned with the viability and sustainability of Nigerian society, including its political and economic systems. More specifically, the United States has two overriding interests in Nigeria and the broader Gulf of Guinea region: battling the uncertain, but potentially significant terrorist threat and securing the increasingly important energy resources in and near the Niger River Delta.

In the days following 9/11, the threat of terrorism rose to be of paramount importance. United States foreign policy toward other nations was dramatically shaped by how those nations responded to the United States' call to partnership in the global war on terror on which the U.S. was about to embark. In that heated environment, Nigeria quickly supported the American effort to strike back at global terrorists by condemning the terrorist attacks against New York and Washington and supporting U.S. military action, and is credited by the Department of State as playing a "leading role in forging an antiterrorism consensus among states in sub-Saharan Africa."[16] Since that time, Nigeria has been included in ongoing counterterrorism initiatives in the region and continues to play a leading role in subregional and regional security issues, including African Union operations.

Terrorism, and the U.S. government's war against it, shapes the activities of the U.S. Department of Defense. In its Unified Command Plan, the DOD has apportioned responsibility for portions of the continent of Africa to three commands: European Command, Central Command, and Pacific Command.[17] Nigeria falls within the European Command's "area of responsibility," as does most of the continent, with the exception of the easternmost countries in Africa (those east of the eastern borders of Egypt, Sudan, and Kenya). In the command's annual posture statement before the U.S. Senate Armed Services Committee,

Marine General James L. Jones, notes the United States' challenge in the region:

> Violence in West Africa has created ungoverned pockets that extend across national borders and threaten to further destabilize an already fragile region. Broad expanses of marginally governed areas can become havens for terrorists and criminals and have become attractive to terrorist groups increasingly denied sanctuaries in Afghanistan and the Middle East. North Africa, and in particular the Pan-Sahel region of Sub-Saharan Africa, offers opportunities to Islamic extremists, smugglers, and various insurgent groups.[18]

General Jones has called upon both United States Marine Corps and U.S. Special Forces to carry out operations known in military circles as "theater security cooperation" activities. A major defense initiative, the Trans-Sahara Counter Terrorism Initiative (TSCTI), builds upon the earlier successes of the Pan-Sahel Initiative. The TSCTI includes the original PSI countries of Mali, Mauritania, Niger, and Chad, and has expanded in 2005 to include Algeria, Morocco, Tunisia, Senegal, and Nigeria. The TSCTI seeks to equip African partner nations to identify and confront terrorism. This effort to build counterterrorism capacity includes basic tactical training, small-group operations, marksmanship, and communications. Long-term objectives include fostering cooperation and interoperability among the West African and Pan-Sahel nations themselves. This indigenous capacity leverages U.S. capability by enabling partners in the war on terror to assume responsibility for their own territorial defense. A perceived side benefit of this initiative is enhanced bilateral relations between the U.S. and each of the partner nations. Such military-to-military engagements—a "train the trainer" approach—do not in any way obviate the need for direct military action against terrorists when and where they are found. Such initiatives are well supported by most host governments in the region, including Nigeria.

Another military initiative, again spearheaded by the U.S. European Command, is a growing interest and involvement in maritime security in the Gulf of Guinea (GOG). Piracy constitutes a serious and growing threat to international commerce, especially the ships servicing the petroleum industry. EUCOM naval forces are conducting coordinated combined maritime operations with regional partner nations in an initiative called the Gulf of Guinea Guard. This purpose of this initiative, as described by Jones, is to "help GOG nations protect natural resources and use their wealth to develop economically and socially."

The command has already hosted the first Gulf of Guinea Maritime Security Conference in October 2004, with future conferences planned to continue the effort.[19] During the course of the next decade, the U.S. Navy plans to have a more regular presence in the region.

Current and projected congressional funding will enable USAID to lead the U.S. government's efforts to stabilize the Nigerian democracy, continue to fight the scourge of HIV/AIDS and other communicable diseases, broaden the Nigerian economy beyond petroleum exports, and support more effective education initiatives. On June 30, 2004, the government of Nigeria agreed to four "Strategic Objective Grant Agreements" with USAID, marking the beginning of the pursuit of these objectives through 2009. Within this plan, there are a number of specific initiatives to benefit the people of Nigeria. USAID plans include training for elected officials at all levels of government in their roles and responsibilities, conflict prevention and resolution in the Niger Delta region, furthering an understanding of civil-military relations and norms of civil society, and the development of effective political parties. Economically, aid and assistance will be focused on supporting economic management and coordination programs, economic reform, private sector development and diversification (including the agriculture sector), integrating Nigeria more closely into the framework of the U.S. African Growth and Opportunity Act (AGOA), and finding innovative ways to assist small business in Nigeria. Other societal priorities include health, education, transportation, and energy.[20]

This multi-pronged strategy to address both active or potential terrorism through military means and the root societal causes of political and economic instability through focused aid and assistance may indeed prove decisive in locations such as Nigeria where terrorism has not yet been established. Such activities must include curbing corruption at all levels of government; turning law enforcement agencies into trustworthy protectors of the public interest instead of self-seeking political entities; developing a sustainable, more broadly based economy that provides more opportunities for the working-age youth and adults of the nation; and seeking reconciliation and understanding among members of various religious faiths, to include Muslims.

PROGRESS AND PROSPECTS

While religious differences certainly play a role in conflict within Nigeria, economic, political, and societal factors are equally causative. When combined with inadequate leadership, failed and failing governance structures, widespread corruption, and unbalanced economic opportunity, these factors make for a volatile mixture. When considering contemporary Nigerian history, William Reno sees a desire for "ethnolinguistic self-determination" as the objective, a goal that is sometimes sought with threats, intimidation, coercion, and violence. He states that "sectarian politics emerges out of this more immediate political question, not out of a clash of civilizations, or Christianity versus Islam."[21] This situation is only magnified by the strong connection between political power and economic wealth, the basis for much or most of the political corruption so prevalent in Nigeria.

Ironically, the return to civilian rule in 1999 may be part of the reason for the upswing in violence. As the United Nations Human Development Report 2004 notes, the return in 1999 to civilian democratic rule "reanimated regional, ethnic, religious, and local identities" and "led to the social violence that has engulfed the country." The authors conclude that "political stability in Nigeria is still threatened by massive structural socioeconomic inequalities between the North and South, the high level of state dependence on federally collected oil revenues, and the intense competition and corruption of public life linked to its distribution."[22]

Given Nigeria's strategic importance and value to the United States, a broadening and deepening of the relationship is in order. This relationship should be pursued along several paths. It is critical that the Trans-Sahara Counter-Terrorism Initiative begun by the U.S. European Command be continued, emphasizing Nigeria's participation as a leader within the West African community and utilizing U.S. forces to continue training efforts with the Nigerian military. Funding increases may be appropriate to reach a level commensurate with the importance of eliminating possible terrorist safe havens and training grounds. European Command should also consider the expansion of maritime activities in the Gulf of Guinea to secure commercial shipping and operations from piracy and sabotage. Engagement with Nigeria and other nations in the region will be critical to enhancing the capacity of these nations to eventually provide adequate maritime security on their own.

In the interests of greater unity of effort and more effective command and control, EUCOM should consider establishing a Combined Joint Task Force-Gulf of Guinea (CJTF-GOG) along the model of the existing U.S. Central Command CJTF-Horn of Africa (CJTF-HOA). This organizational change would serve to focus the military's operations in the area, uniting land force and maritime force operations under the same joint commander. This greater integration of the counterterrorism operations on land and maritime security operations at sea could prove to be a more effective way to cooperate with the region's militaries and, at a regional level, the African Union. The forces available to the joint task force commander would serve a dual purpose in this regard: building capacity within the national militaries in the region while also addressing the root causes of instability. Such an organizational structure would also be a useful way to engage in coordinated and cooperative operations with allies in the region, including forces from the African Union, the European Union, the United Nations, or NATO. An added benefit would be the example of effective civil-military relations displayed by the U.S. armed forces, particularly as the relationship is enhanced by other, less direct forms of military engagement, such as increased education and training opportunities for Nigerian military officers of all services at United States educational institutions, and programs led by the DoD's Africa Center for Strategic Studies. A logical onshore location for the CJTF headquarters would be in Nigeria, further increasing the military-to-military engagement with the Nigerian armed forces.

USAID should continue its plans to extend U.S. activities beyond those with a narrow focus of directly addressing terrorism and oil, remaining committed to engagement with the Nigerian government across a wide range of bilateral activities designed to build the capacity to oppose radical extremist ideology, secure energy resources, reduce poverty, provide education to all Nigeria's citizens, and reduce disease and infant mortality. A concerted effort by the Agency throughout the years of the Country Strategic Plan could yield significant reduction in such societal ills as corruption and economic inequality. Consideration should be given to making assistance contingent upon implementation of serious governmental and economic reforms designed to prevent a possible slide into political unrest and instability. Although Nigeria, for a number of reasons, does not qualify for Millennium Challenge Corporation funding, U.S. aid should nevertheless be targeted to the most meaningful areas and tied to demonstrable results in Nigerian governance. It is essential that the U.S. address the underlying causes of unrest and instability, particularly the issue of political rights and enfranchisement. These causes affect both the possible rise of radical religious extremists who are more than willing to use terror as a weapon and tactic, and also drive the persistent economic inequality within the country that give birth to indigenous uprisings such as those led by Dokubo and the NDVPF.

As a part of the Plan, it is essential that USAID lead the way, along with other governments and inter- and nongovernmental organizations, to monitor the upcoming 2007 Nigerian presidential election. It is imperative, both for the sake of the people of Nigeria as well as the stability of the continent, that the Nigerian election be full, fair, and free, and be seen as such by Nigerians and those elsewhere in the region. At the time of this writing, supporters of President Obasanjo were seeking a constitutional amendment to allow him to stand for a third term as president. While he has not publicly sought a third term in 2007, neither has he renounced one, if the amendment were to be approved. Early assessments point to a heated race for the presidency, and if past practice is any indicator, the election could well be marked by irregularities, fraud, and violence. It was the 1999 election that sparked the current movement of defining Nigeria along religious lines; efforts should be made to prevent this from strengthening in 2007. It is essential for Nigeria's own internal stability and cohesion, and for its international credibility within the continent and around the world, that the 2007 elections be democratic, legal, ethical, and free of violence and ethnic conflict.

Clearly, democracy alone is not a panacea that can prevent violent, even deadly, conflict within a state. Real or perceived inequalities led to civil strife during the past decade in Nigeria. The elected leadership has not only shown an unwillingness to address the root issues of those inequalities, but in fact exploits religion to explain the disparities. It is this political exploitation of religious identity that makes Nigeria a flashpoint in the war on terrorism.

NOTES

1. George W. Bush, The National Security Strategy of the United States, September 2002, p. 10.
2. CBS News transcript, February 12, 2003. Online. Available HTTP: <http://www.cbsnews.com/stories/2003/02/12/attack/main540297.shtml>.
3. World Energy Hotspots—Nigeria. Online. Available HTTP: <http://www.eia.doe.gov/emeu/cabs/World_Energy_Hotspots/Nigeria.html>.
4. Michael T. Klare and Daniel Volman, "Africa's Oil and American National Security," Current History, vol. 103, Issue 673, May 2004, pp. 226–231.
5. Table of Proved Natural Gas Reserves, 2005. Online. Available HTTP: <http://www.bp.com/liveassets/bp_internet/globalbp/globalbp_uk_english/publications/energy_reviews_2005/STAGING/local_assets/downloads/pdf/table_of_proved_natural_gas_reserves_2005.pdf>.
6. The World Bank estimates the 2004 mid-year population at 139.8 million people, while the Central Intelligence Agency World Factbook estimates the July 2005 population at 128.7 million people.
7. Nigeria: Country Report 2004–2005, The Economist Intelligence Unit, 2004, p. 14.
8. Analysis: Behind Nigeria's Violence. Online. Available HTTP: <http://newsvote.bbc.co.uk/mpapps/pagetools/print/news.bbc.co.uk/1/hi/world/africa/1630089.stm>.
9. Table One: Transparency International's Corruption Perceptions Index 2004. Online. Available HTTP: <http://www.transparency.org/cpi/2004/cpi2004.en.html#cpi2004>.

10. Report on the Transparency International Global Corruption Barometer 2005. Online. Available HTTP: <http://www.transparency.org/policy_research/survey_indices/qcb>, full report, table on p. 23.
11. "NIGERIA: Publisher arrested after newspaper accused governor of corruption," IRINNEWS.org, a publication of the UN Office for the Coordination of Humanitarian Affairs, November 15, 2005.
12. "Nigeria to get $18bn debt relief," BBC News. Online. Available HTTP: <http://news.bbc.co.uk/2/hi/business/4637395.stm>.
13. Paul Collier, "The Market for Civil War," *Foreign Policy,* May/June 2003, p. 40.
14. See <http://www.tkb.org/Incident.jsp?incID=8437> for details on the April 18, 2001 attack.
15. Nigeria Budget Summary, United States Agency for International Development. Online. Available HTTP: <http://www.usaid.gov/policy/budget/cbj2006/afr/ng.html>.
16. Background Note: Nigeria. Online. Available HTTP: <http://www.state.gov/r/pa/ei/bgn/2836.htm>.
17. See Derek S. Reveron, *America's Viceroys: the Military and U.S. Foreign Policy* (New York: Palgrave-MacMillan, 2004).
18. FY07 annual EUCOM posture statement, p. 5.
19. Online. Available HTTP: <http://www.eucom.mil/english/Command/Posture/SASC_Posture_Statement_010305.asp>.
20. Nigeria Budget Summary, United States Agency for International Development. Online. Available HTTP: <http://www.usaid.gov/policy/budget/cbj2006/afr/ng.html>.
21. William Reno, "The Roots of Sectarian Violence, and its Cure," in *Crafting the New Nigeria: Confronting the Challenges*, ed. Robert I. Rotberg (Boulder, CO: Lynne Rienner Publishers, 2004), p. 220.
22. UN Human Development Report 2004, "Building Multicultural Democracies," p. 52, Box 3.2. Online. Available HTTP: <http://hdr.undp.org/reports/global/2004/pdf/hdr04_chapter_3.pdf>.

15

CONCLUSION
Resolving Political Conflicts

Jeffrey Stevenson Murer and Derek S. Reveron

A little more than a year after the 9/11 attacks, a conference titled "Terrorism, the Press, and the Social Sciences" was held at the University of Paris VII. As with so many symposia, this meeting opened with the keynote speaker addressing the participants and audience. A tall, handsome, and distinguished gentleman took the podium and began by announcing, "I am a terrorist." This was neither a rhetorical flourish nor a statement of solidarity. Some 59 years earlier, nearly to the day, the keynote speaker, Raymond Aubrac, was liberated from a Gestapo prison where Klaus Barbie tortured him. Like his wife Lucie, who led the commandos that freed him, Aubrac was a member of the French Resistance.[1] Aubrac explained to the conference audience how he and his colleagues plotted the assassinations of government officials, exploded bombs to disrupt truck and train traffic, cut power and communications lines, and conducted missions that sometimes could only be described as suicidal. To the German occupation authorities, to the Vichy government, to the Gestapo, and to the Milice (the Vichy government's secret police), Aubrac was simply a terrorist.[2]

Aubrac's point was not to suggest that one man's terrorist is another man's freedom fighter. Rather, his talk was intended to remind the audience that terrorism is a tactic employed in a political context. To understand the motivations behind acts of violence it is important to understand the context in which they occur. There have been many times when political activists welcomed the moniker "terrorist."

Nineteenth-century Russian anarchists and anti-monarchists proudly wore the title "terrorist." It was a testament to their commitment.[3] Even today, Shamil Basayev, the leader of the Chechen rebels welcomes the title "terrorist." He said on the U.S. television program *Nightline*, "I admit, I'm a bad guy, a bandit, a terrorist."[4] Yet many politicians of late speak of terrorists as a cohesive whole, often referring to "the terrorists" as a singular construction, implying that they emanate from a single circumstance or that they possess a singular motivation. Currently, that motivation is presumed to be a militant or radical political Islam. Yet as the case studies presented in this volume suggest, this is far from correct. There appear to be many different motivations in many different contexts. Some movements are formed around the expression of Muslim identity, yet these expressions also often employ the idioms of nationalism, separatism, or the agitation for regional or local autonomy. In these cases the practice of Islam as signifier of difference from the ruling population serves as the basis for justifying such claims to self-determination or self-governance. In these cases Islam is deployed as the marker of a difference that warrants the right of self-determination; it is not the motivation of violence itself.

In the struggle for independence, autonomy, recognition, or access to material resources, terrorism may become one of many tools employed. In fact, existing U.S. law recognizes terrorism as a political act.[5] Michael Wieviorka suggests that terrorism is a social product. It is an image, or psychological representation or a social conception that marks a particular phase or theater of a conflict, perhaps even substituting for total war or revolution.[6] While the effects of political violence may at times be repugnant, such disgust should not blind scholars or policy analysts or the public to the fact that there is logic to terrorism. Martha Crenshaw offers in the preface to her wonderful collection *Terrorism in Context* that "terrorism [is] not the result of irrational fanaticism but political calculation; it [is] learned behavior, not the result of primordial forces."[7] Or, as Robert Pape's study of suicide terrorism suggests, religious fanaticism does not explain why the Marxist-Leninist Tamil Tigers are the world's leader in suicide terrorism; rather, suicide terrorism follows a strategic logic.[8] Every suicide terrorist campaign from 1980 to 2001 has been waged by terrorist groups whose main goal has been to establish or maintain a national homeland.[9] The authors of this collection have likewise tried to place the political violence associated with the case studies within a particular context. The violence of terrorism should not be seen as an aberration but rather as a central part of the politics of identity conflict.

Further, terrorism is not born of crisis. As a tool of political action, terrorism is associated not so much with rupture, but with continuity. In this respect, terrorism occurs within the context of a growing/evolving conflict. Often it is a deep conflict in which a range of tactics and stratagems are employed. Different techniques are applied to alter a balance or stasis within which the conflict remains unresolved; this may include the welcoming of foreign fighters or other alien resources. These interventions are often motivated by a very different agenda, the presence of which may, nevertheless, tip the scales of force in favor of resistance or insurgent elements. In this aspect we can discern a common characteristic of terrorist activity: it is a tactic or technique employed in a conflict environment characterized by asymmetrical political engagement. Beyond this, however, it is necessary to identify the motivations associated with specific groups of actors. Just as in a parliament, an opposition may contain elements from both the right and the left, and it would be wrong to assign similar agendas or motivations to such disparate political groups, even when they act in concert. Moreover, while these groups may go far beyond occasional cooperation, it would likewise be wrong to suggest that such an array of political elements constitutes a cohesive whole. To better understand any given political conflict, parliamentary or insurgent, it is necessary to acknowledge the distinct and differentiated qualities of the parties. The guiding premise articulated by Martha Crenshaw could be just as easily applied here: "[T]errorism as a general phenomenon cannot be adequately explained without situating it in its particular political, social, and economic contexts."[10]

THE POLITICS OF TERRORISM

As Raymond Aubrac's declaration reminds us, terrorism is a political label. As a label it immediately qualifies the actions and actors to whom it is applied. The choice to call a political actor a "terrorist" or a political act "terrorism" often has a "prescriptive policy relevance as well as moral connotation."[11] This is as true with the United States as with Russia, or any of the other cases presented in this volume. By evoking the label "terrorist," the speaker seeks to combine descriptive and symbolic elements, creating a kind of shorthand for evil.[12] Such a label implies a preferred policy solution. For example, the association of a political element with terrorism may allow the state to avoid any negotiated settlement to ameliorate the conflict. If terrorists "cannot be negotiated with" or their presence cannot be tolerated, the label rules certain political elements to be outside the bounds of political discourse. Further, the state may claim the right to eliminate such political elements because of the threat they pose to the body politic. State violence may be necessary to deal with terrorists because they are associated with violence.

The use of the terrorist label, however, can be dangerous. By ruling that certain political elements are beyond civil intercourse, it can become tempting for states to expand the list of political elements no longer qualifying for civil engagement. The application of such a label can lead to governments or states becoming blind to the distinction between violent opposition and nonviolent dissent, or the distinction between rebellion and civil disobedience. It was not that long ago when rightist political elements in many South American countries used the broad application of the label "terrorist" to jail, torture, eliminate, and kill political activists associated with leftist movements. The state security apparatuses in the "Dirty Wars" in Argentina and Chile, as well as those in Brazil and Mexico, came to see all of political society as "contaminated" by leftist thought. The efforts to eliminate urban guerrilla organizations led counterterrorism and counterinsurgency units to engage in the types of activities associated with terrorist tactics. The Chilean and Argentine militaries, for example, kidnapped activists and bystanders alike. Late-night raids associated with "disappearances" in both countries were designed to instill fear and a sense of terror within political society.[13] This broad application of the moniker "terrorist" transforms the body politic into an enemy. Such a situation is exemplified today in Russia when the North Ossetian minister for nationality affairs, Taymuraz Kasaev, suggested that anyone who "actively practices Islam" would be seen as an "enemy"[14] even though Islam is recognized as a "traditional belief" within Russian law.[15] Russia's senior mufti, Ravil Gainutdin, politically appointed to the official Russian Muftiate, complained, "Politicians and the mass media are equating us, the Muslim faithful, with armed groups."[16] Although Russian Patriarch Alexy II reminds his followers that "Russian Christians and Muslims traditionally live in peace," the association of "Muslim" with "Terrorist" may be too deeply fixed in the popular mind of the Russian political public. The connection between political oppositions and terrorism in Russia, just as with the connections in South America, serves to justify both continued and escalated state violence.

The application of state violence in these cases begets still more violence, not necessarily in the form of resistance, but in the form of the bureaucratization of state violence. Military, interior ministry, and law enforcement agencies all come to participate in the "war on terrorism." In fact, the word "terrorism" was initially coined to describe acts of state violence perpetrated during the Reign of Terror following the French Revolution. Resources are allocated according to a given agency's ability to contribute to this new state endeavor: the elimination of political opposition identified with terrorism. The state itself and not merely elements within it is also served through the application of the terrorism label to challenging political elements. The proclaimed need to suppress these challenging elements may serve as the basis for the extension of state powers, particularly under the condition of the state of exception.

THE STATE OF EXCEPTION

While acts of terrorism are often depicted as threats to democracy, the real threat may lie in the state's responses to terrorism. In the names of expediency and efficiency, state reactions in the immediate aftermath of a traumatic event often include an alteration in the standing institutional relations of power. This is particularly true in modern parliamentary or democratic presidential regimes, whereby the response of the state entails an extension of executive power, particularly into the sphere of what had previously been seen as legislative power. The delegation of "full powers" allowing the executive to issue and enforce decrees represents a broad alteration of regulatory power, particularly when such an alteration allows for the modification or abrogation by decree laws previously in force.[17] Giorgio Agamben describes this process of expanding executive power as the "state of exception." Through the alteration of the balance of power between the various institutions within a democratic constitutional regime—a structure premised upon the very distribution of power—the "government will have more power and the people fewer rights."[18] What Agamben finds most troubling is that the "state of exception" has in fact become a "paradigm of government" itself, echoing Walter Benjamin's concern that "the state of exception … has become the rule."[19] The essential character of this condition is the provisional abolition of the distinction among the legislative, executive, and judicial powers, which eventually becomes a lasting practice of government.

Agamben revives this notion of the state of exception from Carl Schmitt's *Political Theology* (1922) and *Dictatorship* (1921), with which Agamben examines the cases that both Mussolini and Hitler came to power through parliamentary means, and subsequently eroded parliamentary rule through the use of a series of exceptional circumstance whereby the rule of law was suspended in order to cope with political crisis. Like many European constitutions, the Weimar Constitution provided for special emergency [eccezionali] powers to be granted to the President of the Reich.[20] Herbert Tingsten, Agamben tells us, similarly explored the suspension of the constitutional orders in a number of countries during World War I. Austria, Belgium, England, France, Germany, Italy, and even the United States and neutral Switzerland all declared a "state of siege" or its "full powers" equivalent to a state of emergency, whereby the executive was given special powers to suspend part or all of the constitutional order. Although Tingsten suggests that "temporary and controlled use of full powers is theoretically compatible with democratic institutions," he warns that "a systematic and regular exercise of the institutions [associated with the state of exception] necessarily leads to the liquidation of democracy."[21] This threat is manifest in different ways. While in most circumstances the "state of emergency" ends and decision- and rule-making powers are restored to the legislature, many of the instruments of government depicted as "temporary arrangements" eventually become lasting peacetime institutions.[22]

The simplest and most immediate examples of temporary arrangements becoming permanent institutions come from decrees converted into law. For example, Agamben points out that a whole series of emergency decrees issued by the Prime Minister during a "state of emergency" in Italy in the late 1970s were declared necessary for the "repression of terrorism." Decree number 59 (issued March 28, 1978) was converted into law two months later as the so-called "Moro Law."[23] Likewise, law-decree number 625 (issued December 15, 1979) was converted into law number 15 shortly after its original declaration.[24] These remain operative today. The laws invoked by French President Jacques Chirac by declaring a "state of emergency" (L'état d'urgence) on November 8, 2005, were originally crafted under the René Coty presidency in 1955 in order to quell growing unrest in Algeria. Under the present constitution of the Fifth Republic, the state of exception is regulated by Article 16, which Charles De Gaulle proposed in light of Coty's 1955 crisis. De Gaulle invoked the article in April 1961 in reaction to events in Algeria, although he did not suspend the rule of law as the article allows. Chirac's application of these powers in response to the November 2005 riots demonstrates the tremendous reach associated with the state of exception. Originally declared for 12 days, the powers associated with the state of emergency were granted to the executive for 90 days. These powers include the ability to declare curfews for designated areas, to place individuals under house arrest without arraignment or trial, to censor publications and other news organizations, and to engage in searches and police raids without search warrants. Although the Interior Ministry announced on January 4, 2006, that it was suspending the state of exception 30 days earlier than required, it is worth noting that the street violence and unrest that precipitated Chirac's declaration was subdued by November 18, 2005. The state of exception remained in effect for nearly two months after the street violence subsided.

In the United States the executive branch has lobbied hard for the extension or making permanent many of the powers enacted in the USA PATRIOT Act, passed by Congress in the immediate aftermath of the 9/11 attacks. Written and passed in just seven weeks, many legislators later said that they never read the entire document.[25] Claiming broad powers for the executive, many sections of the act provide for vast presidential discretion to determine whether rights or protections previously afforded under the constitution may be suspended. It included a new power to monitor phones, confiscate property of suspected terrorists, spy on U.S. citizens without judicial review, conduct covert searches, and investigate the reading habits of library users. For example, Section 203 of the International Emergency Powers Act (50 U.S.C. 1702) was amended by the PATRIOT Act to include the following clause, which expands presidential discretion

> when the United States is engaged in armed hostilities or has been attacked by a foreign country or foreign nationals, [to] confiscate any property, subject to the jurisdiction of the United States, of any foreign person, foreign organization, or foreign country that he determines has planned, authorized, aided, or engaged in such hostilities or attacks against the United States; and all right, title, and interest in any property so confiscated shall vest, when, as, and upon the terms directed by the President, in such agency or person as the President may designate from time to time, and upon such terms and conditions as the President may prescribe, such interest or property shall be held, used, administered, liquidated, sold, or otherwise dealt with in the interest of and for the benefit of the United States, and such designated agency or person may perform any and all acts incident to the accomplishment or furtherance of these purposes.[26]

To mollify critics of the act, sunset clauses were included for many of the most sensitive parts of the law, which were to terminate in 2005. Congress initially refused to grant permanent authorization to the PATRIOT Act and negotiations resulted in two short-term extensions to prevent the act from expiring. However, new legislation drafted in conjunction with the Office of the Attorney General would make permanent that which was to expire and expand executive powers in new directions. The Domestic Security Enhancement Act originally proposed in 2003 was designed to "fill in the holes" left by the original

PATRIOT Act, claimed Justice Department spokesman Mark Corallo in a 2003 interview with the *Village Voice*.[27] The Congress passed many sections of the DSEA and President Bush signed them into law on December 13, 2003.[28] For example, the FBI was granted the authority to obtain client records from financial institutions without a warrant by merely requesting the documents in a "National Security Letter."[29] No probable cause need be demonstrated, nor does any executive agent need to appear before a judge, and the bill no longer required the FBI to inform Congress of the frequency and purpose of such National Security Letters. Additionally, the letters are attached with a "gag order" preventing the financial institutions from informing their clients; should any institution breach the order it would face criminal penalties. New executive powers were also articulated in the Intelligence Authorization Act of 2004, which redefined "financial institutions" beyond banks as being stockbrokers, car dealerships, casinos, credit card companies, insurance agencies, jewelers, airlines, the U.S. Post Office, and any other business "whose cash transactions have a high degree of usefulness in criminal, tax, or regulatory matters."[30] At this writing, Congress is investigating enhanced powers the Bush Administration pursued through the executive branch, such as the warrantless surveillance in the United States by the National Security Agency.

CASES FROM THIS VOLUME AS EXCEPTIONS

In nearly every case presented in this volume, a state of emergency has either been recently declared and lifted, or is legally recognized as the de facto condition, with the state of emergency operating even in the absence of a declaration. In Thailand, a state of emergency was originally imposed in July 2005 in reaction to the extensive violence in the south of the country, as described in the chapter by Rohan Gunaratna. The 90-day emergency condition was then extended for another 90 days just as it was about to expire in October 2005; it was renewed yet again for 90 days in January 2006. As under the terms of the French state of emergency, the Thai executive (inclusive of the Prime Minister, Interior Minister, Defense Minister, and Justice Minister) is allowed to declare curfews, ban public gatherings, confiscate property, monitor telephones, and search homes and offices without warrants. Like many other provisions for the state of emergency in other countries, the Thai provisions grant prosecutorial immunity to officials from "civil, criminal, or disciplinary penalties."[31] Civil rights advocates claim that the state of emergency is actually making conditions worse in the south of Thailand. Gunaratna agrees. He states that the Thai strategy of treating the insurgency as a military threat is drastically flawed. By privileging the use of force, the Thai approach worsens the problem by further alienating the Muslim communities. Treating these Thai citizens as if they were enemy aliens reduces the incentives for community involvement in conflict amelioration. Those citizens who might otherwise be indifferent or even opposed to the insurgency give their support or at least tolerate the rebel organizations, because they are seen as an expression of resistance to Thai state violence. Gunaratna suggests that the best way to curb the violence and quell the insurgency is to strengthen infrastructure destroyed by the December 2004 tsunami. Communities must be provided with the means to rebuild themselves, and the Thai government should encourage local political participation rather than stifle it. Political repression through the banning of political organizations only has the effect of driving the most politically active into prohibited groups. Free expression, regional autonomy, and infrastructural support would all signal that the states of southern Thailand are an integral part of the country rather than alienated from it.

In Indonesia, different parts of the country have been under states of emergency, some for considerable periods of time. For example, Aceh was placed under martial law in 1959.[32] That condition was changed with the declaration of a "state of civil emergency" in the province of Nanggroe Aceh Darussalam on May 19, 2003. It was to remain in effect for one year, but was renewed in 2004.[33] In May 2005, the government lifted the declaration but the army has remained in the region to "keep order" and to assist with the clean-up efforts in the aftermath of the December 2004 tsunami.

On the Islands of Maluka, nearly 5,000 people died in clashes between Christians and Muslims in 2000. A state of emergency was declared for the islands on June 6, 2000, and remained in effect for three years. During that time there were serious allegations leveled at the Indonesian security services, army, and special police regarding the use of torture, indefinite detentions, and even state-authorized killings.[34] In their chapter, Arabinda Acharya and Rohaiza Ahmad Asi echo Gunaratna by suggesting the best way to quell the violence across the archipelago is to improve infrastructure, especially by creating new schools, and reforming the police and the army. One of the biggest problems Acharya and Asi identify is that many Indonesians are so distrustful of the state security services that they turn to political organizations with "muscle" to settle disputes rather than turning to the police. Radical Islamic thought is communicated in a select number of pesarten or religious schools. As with the madrasas in Pakistan, many children attend the pesarten because there is no local school. While perhaps far too much has been made in the U.S. media of the link between madrasas and terrorism, the situation in Pakistan and Indonesia exists because of a lack of state resources committed for education. It is this lack of infrastructure that Samina Raja suggests promotes political violence as an identity of resistance against such state neglect in Kashmir.

In the Philippines, Ferdinand Marcos declared martial law in 1972. Though the condition was lifted in 1981, the president kept extensive emergency powers. Even with the coming of democracy the president has still retained those powers. A state of emergency has been declared five times since 1989. In 2003 alone, an emergency condition was declared twice. On the first occasion President Gloria Macapagal-Arroyo declared a "state of rebellion" in response to the mutiny of 296 soldiers, 70 of them officers who were top graduates of the Philippines Military Academy. The soldiers said that they were protesting government-sponsored terror, including a bombing in Davao, Mindano, that killed 12 people. The mutineers said that while the government blamed the terrorist organization Abu Sayyef, the sophisticated bombing was the work of military forces. The soldiers also stated that the government launched these attacks in order to appear active in the "global war on terrorism," to curry favor with the United States, and to obtain more U.S. military aid. At the time, the Philippines had already received more than $100 million in aid.[35] The second occasion in 2003 followed an attempted military coup d'état, whose instigators echoed the claims and concerns of the mutineers. The Philippines' effort to combat the insurgency in Mindano has led to the use of extensive investigatory powers, claimed under the state of emergency. In 2005, in an attempt to stifle media criticism of the government's handling of the fighting in the south, President Arroyo called press freedom groups "enemies of the state." She singled out the Philippines Center for Investigative Journalism, saying that the organization had been "infiltrated by communists."[36] In February 2006, another state of emergency was declared in response to an alleged coup against President Arroyo, which resulted in public protests being banned and several arrests.

Some states of emergency have been in place for many years. The executive had full powers in Sri Lanka from 1983 until 2001, and Israel has had a state of emergency since May 1948. This is not merely a bureaucratic holdover or a vestige of the wars of the founding. Section 9 of the Israeli Law and Administration Ordinance and Article 38(b) of the Basic Law (2001) limit a state of emergency for one year, and thus every year the Knesset renews the special powers for the executive. Another long-ruling state of emergency ended when Turkey finally lifted its 15-year-old state of emergency in the provinces of Diyarbakir and Sirnak in 2002.[37] The state of emergency had replaced a declaration of martial law, imposed in March 1984 and then lifted in July 1987. The original application of the emergency in 1987 applied to 13 provinces in the south and east of the county as a reaction to violence associated with Kurdish rebels. As in Indonesia, serious allegations of torture, prolonged detention, and physical abuse were leveled at the security forces. According to Article 3/c of Legal Decree Number 430, issued by the Office of the Prime Minister, the state prosecutor can detain suspects for 10 days without informing the subject of the grounds of the arrest. The suspects can also be held incommunicado. Amnesty International has documented numerous cases where Turkish citizens were held in excess of a month. In these cases the state prosecutor would simply wait until the end of the 10 days and then renew the detention on other grounds. (Many of the detainees were never informed of the charges against them. For those who were informed the constant bringing of new charges against them made the detention feel indefinite.) Enrullah Karagöz was held for 40 days, and claimed he was beaten on a daily basis. When he was released he was still not informed of the basis for his imprisonment.[38] Amnesty International has recorded thousands of similar cases.

In some regions, a state of emergency is not even declared; rather the executive simply claims the power to deal with some crisis. Without such a declaration, however, there is no suggestion of a limit on this executive privilege. Very quickly these powers become permanent. In the case of Chechnya, numerous states of emergency have been declared since the collapse of the Soviet Union, the first being issued in November 1991. Just prior to the first Russian intervention in 1994, President Yeltsin declared a state of emergency for both Chechnya and neighboring Ingushetia. Similarly, just prior to the second Russian intervention in December 1999, three states of emergency were declared: June 21, 1998; December 16, 1998; and October 2, 1999. However, since the invasion, no state of emergency has been declared. President Putin claims that it is not necessary for such a declaration, and the Constitutional Court agreed with him. In 1995, the court ruled that it is not necessary for the executive to declare a state of emergency before directing state security services to respond to domestic disturbances. The court stated that the power to quell violence and the means to do so are well established by the constitution in ordinary presidential powers.[39] This is quite an interesting ruling; the ability to claim extraordinary powers is established in the constitution by ordinary means. In Chechnya, since 2000, there has been a de facto state of emergency, where security services regularly detain people without charge, search premises without warrants, monitor communications, and regularly use extreme violence against people the security services deem to be potential threats. There have been numerous claims that the security forces kidnap for ransom, traffic in narcotics, and make many Chechen men "disappeared." The Russian human rights organization Memorial states that between 3,000 and 5,000 Chechens have "disappeared" since December 1999.[40] Official Russian government statistics acknowledge nearly 2,000 disappearances through legal documents. Although there have been 1,814 criminal investigations into the "disappearances," not one has resulted in a conviction.[41] When U.N. Commissioner for Human Rights Mary Robinson called Russia to account for human rights abuses, pointing out that no state of emergency had been declared, Justice Minster Yuri Chaika replied that it was all part of the fight against terrorism.[42]

There is also an undeclared, de facto state of emergency in Jammu and Kashmir in India. Similar to the ruling by the Constitutional Court in Russia, the Indian Supreme Court held in 1997 that the condition of a state of emergency and the exercise of extraordinary powers by the executive was both legal and constitutional. Although no state of emergency was declared, state security services regularly engage in "preventive detention," and exercise extraordinary police powers to arrest, detain, and even shoot those suspected of posing a threat to national security. There are other measures as well that grant special powers to the executive and its security apparatus. The Jammu and Kashmir Public Safety Act (PSA) of 1978 allows for the detention for up to 24 months without indictment or trial of those suspected of posing a threat to the region. Another ordinance, the National Security Act (NSA) of 1980, augments the PSA and applies to all of India, allowing for people anywhere in the country to be detained without trial for 12 months. In 1997, 500 people outside of Jammu and Kashmir were detained under the NSA, and inside the state of Jammu and Kashmir some 2,070 persons were detained without charge—at least 1,300 under the provisions of the PSA.[43] The Armed Forces Special Powers Act of 1958, which still applies to the states Jammu and Kashmir, Nagaland, Manipur, Assar, and Tripura, allows for the arrest of those on suspicion, does not require detainees to be informed of the grounds for their detention, permits security forces to fire on people if necessary, and provides legal immunity to any security personnel or those associated with providing security.[44] Thus, it is possible to suggest that Jammu and Kashmir has been under a state of emergency since the late 1970s. For the past 22 years the state of Manipur has been recognized as a "Disturbed Area" where a similar de facto state of emergency is in place.

In all of these cases can be found a threat to the practice of democracy as the state of exception is a suspension of the previous juridical order. The executive stands outside of the normally valid juridical order, and yet this is not anarchy or chaos. It is something different. Order remains but the executive subtracts itself from any consideration of law.[45] In this way, the state of exception is an "anomic space" in that what is at stake is a force of law without law. Giorgio Agamben suggests that this idea could best be communicated as "force of ~~law~~." The struck-through "law" suggests both its presence and it absence. Agamben suggests that this is not dissimilar to the Roman practice of *iustitium* or "standstill."[46] This suspension of law, or when the law stands still, is a legal space unto itself; yet it is a legal space in which the law is not in effect. An *iustitium* would be declared by the Roman Senate upon news of a threat to disintegrate the Republic. The military could take whatever steps were necessary to defend the Republic and ensure that the juridical order could be restored. This is similar to a commissarial dictatorship when power is seized by a political element that has the aim of defending or restoring the existing constitution. It is possible to suggest that the three Turkish military coups d'etat were to "defend" the secular order (1960, 1971, and 1980), just as General Pervez Musharraf claims that his seizure of the Pakistani government in October 1999 was to defend it against impending collapse. The state of exception does not go as far, although it is a suspension of the rule of law nevertheless. As the executive stands outside of the normal juridical order, the executive still belongs to it, for it is the power of the executive to decide whether or how much of the constitution is to be suspended or when or if it is to be restored.[47] The state of exception is not a dictatorship, but it is a dangerous flirtation with the suspension of the principles of liberal democracy. In places like Nigeria and Iraq, where the focus of the government has been on establishing a liberal democratic order, the imposition of a state of emergency can have significant deleterious effects on the progress of democratic development.

In May 2004, Nigerian President Olusegun Obasanjo declared a state of emergency in the Plateau State after violent clashes between Muslims and Christians. The state had recently seen violence previously when hundreds of people were killed in sectarian attacks in September and October 2001. During the 2001 violence, allegations were made against the government that rather than quelling the unrest, security forces participated in it. The most egregious abuses of state power came in the form of 22 extrajudicial executions at the Jos city prison.[48] After the 2004 state of emergency, which lasted six months, the Plateau State government sued the Nigerian federal government, claiming that the federal government over-stretched its authority when it fired the entirety of the state administration and replaced it with agents of the President's Office and the Ministry of Defense. In January 2006, the Nigerian Supreme Court ruled that the president had such authority under the 1999 constitution, and that the deposed administrators of the state government had no legal standing to challenge the president.[49] After the many years of brutal military dictatorships, the recognition of the significant power in the office of the president was sobering to many in Plateau State and throughout Nigeria.[50]

Likewise, in Iraq, the development of democracy is at times at odds with the necessities of the security concerns. Following a 30-day state of emergency declared immediately after the U.S. invasion in March 2003, three more states of exception were declared, placing Iraq continuously under extraordinary circumstances from November 7, 2004, until June 13, 2005. Throughout that time, the security forces under the direct command of the Prime Minister were authorized to declare curfews wherever and whenever they saw fit. They were authorized to carry out arrests and detentions without warrants or informing detainees of the grounds for their arrest. Detainees could be held incommunicado and property could be seized without compensation during police and military operations. In Iraq, as well as in Afghanistan and the United States, another important power is being exercised under the state of exception: the executive's ability to determine citizenship privilege and prisoner status without judicial hearings.

HOSTIS IUDICATIO AND ILLEGAL ENEMY COMBATANTS

Andrew Norris posits that Giorgio Agamben stands political philosophy on its head when he writes in *Homo Sacer* that the "original political relation is to ban."[51] Rather than seeing community built on the politics of belonging, Agamben suggests that it is a politics of exclusion; the very process of establishing "belonging" is through the elimination of categories of people who are to be excluded from the polis. Once that process of exclusion has ended community remains. "The decision as to what constitutes the life that is thereby taken outside of the polis is a sovereign decision."[52] This is the original form of politics: a cut in life. It is both a biopolitic and disciplinary power. It is the sovereign power to articulate the distinction between "nature and culture, zoe and bios."[53] Norris summarizes the power this way:

> [A]ttending to the etymology of the word "decide" one can understand this sovereign decision as a cut in life, one that separates

real life from merely existent life, political and human life from the life of the non-human. As this cutting defines the political, the production of the inhuman—which is correlative with the production of the human—is not an activity that politics might dispense with, say in favour of the assertion of human rights.[54]

From this Agamben suggests that the Nazi death camps were not an aberration, but rather the most base of human politics. The power decision to determine who is entitled to a full life and who is entitled to a bare life, *nuda vita,* is also to decide who is human and who is not. The act of segregating people into camps, whether they are death camps or concentration camps, refugee camps, detention centers, prisons, or interrogation facilities, is likewise about deciding who is damned to a bare life. The torture of the bare life is the exclusion from the polis. Bare life is not a biological life or some kind of natural life, it is a life exposed to death. It is the political act of denying another's humanity.

Agamben describes this bare life as akin to *Homo Sacer,* a Roman legal category that defined someone as neither human nor dead, but facing death. *Homo Sacer* was neither slave nor object, but something outside—outside of the polis, outside of human life, and outside of Roman property laws. Agamben updates this category by suggesting how those prisoners in the Nazi camps who were not fit for work yet were still alive were similarly cast outside. What is most surprising in Agamben's account of the Nazi camps is that everyone came to understand this category, and even other inmates would turn their backs and exclude those on the edge of the barest life. No longer within the community of prisoners, the walking dead suffered doubly; as their bodies wasted, they could not enjoy the human belonging of community. The connection to this volume is that the designation of *Homo Sacer,* the ability to exclude, to deny access to the polis is a political act. Under the terms of the state of exception it would often appear that suddenly the executive conferred with "full powers" is able to make this most basic of determinations: to decide who will live a bare life exposed to death. As people are detained from Kashmir to Jos, or placed in refugee camps without human dignity from Kandahar to Jenna, a similar condition as the one faced by the undead in the Nazi camps is created over and over again.

The designation "al Qaeda associate," "terror suspect," or "illegal enemy combatant" initiates a whole series of actions that combine to exclude an individual from the polis. Beginning with the loss of the right to an attorney, then access to due process, then to being recognized as a human body within the polis through a writ of *habeas corpus,* the "terror suspect" is extracted from human life. As the "terror suspect" is by law denied specific civil rights constitutionally guaranteed, the "illegal enemy combatant" is denied the recognition of membership in another polis. The covenants and treaties that bind sovereigns together, acknowledging the common human quality across poleis do not apply to "illegal enemy combatant," excluding him from not only the immediate polis but all polis. The "illegal enemy combatant" is a life most minimal, most bare, denied of its access to the human community it must suffer in isolation, in silence, and in ignorance cut off from all meaningful communication.

The "illegal enemy combatant" is tied to another Roman institution of suspending law: the *hostis iudicatio*. Agamben documents how in the extraordinary circumstance when a Roman citizen actually threatened the stability or security of the Republic through treason or conspiracy "he could be declared *hostis*, 'public enemy,' by the Senate."[55] Like the "illegal enemy combatant" denied the status of a prisoner of war and the human rights guaranteed by the signatories of the Geneva Conventions, the *hostis iudicatus* was distinct from the *hostis alienigena,* or "foreign enemy," who was protected by the "laws of the people," *ius gentium.*[56] In this, the status of the hostis iudicatus was bare indeed. He was deprived of legal status. He could be deprived of his belongings or property, and he could be put to death at anytime.[57] With such an act, what is suspended "is not simply the juridical order, but the *ius civis,* the very status of Roman citizen."[58]

The French state of exception issued in November 2005 contains a similar provision. The 1955 law provides for the deportation of legal immigrants.[59] Jacques Chirac's Interior Minister, Nicolas Sarkozy, vowed to expel all foreigners who were convicted of participating in the November 2005 riots, even if they were not in France illegally. He raised the possibility of deporting the children of immigrants, again even if in France legally, to their parents' home country. This suggested that French citizens might be denied their civil status. Sarkozy has been a loud supporter of a 2004 law that permitted authorities to expel foreigners who incite "discrimination, hate or violence against a specific person or group of persons." France is not the only European country moving toward deportations and exclusions as a means of responding to security threats. A 2005 law in Germany allows authorities at the state level to expel legal foreign residents who "endorse or promote terrorist acts" or incite hatred against sections of the population.[60] Italy also passed a series of antiterrorism laws making deportations easier. In August 2005, the British government broadened the grounds for deportation to those persons who "justify or glorify" terrorism.[61] In the United States, one of the more controversial proposals in the Domestic

Security Enhancement Act or PATRIOT II not passed in 2003, but being debated in early 2006 in conjunction with making permanent the sunset provisions of the PATRIOT Act I, was granting the executive the power to revoke citizenship. Nat Hentoff of the *Village Voice* wrote that under Section 501 of the Domestic Security Enhancement Act, an American citizen can be stripped of citizenship if he or she "becomes a member of, or provides material support to, a group that the United States has designated as a 'terrorist organization,' if that group is engaged in hostilities against the United States." Previously, citizenship was only lost if an American declared a clear intent to abandon it. Hentoff reported that in the DSEA "the intent to relinquish nationality need not be manifested in words, but can be *inferred* from conduct."[62] Agents of the executive within the Justice Department would do the inferring. Additionally, as in France and the United Kingdom, legal alien residents could be deported without criminal charges or the presentation of evidence if the Justice Department determined an individual to be a threat to national security.

However, the U.S. judiciary did determine that deprived of the privileges of the Geneva Conventions, "illegal enemy combatants" must be allowed to contest their detention in U.S. courts.[63] This was especially true for two U.S. citizens whom the executive had deemed to be "illegal enemy combatants" and therefore it was asserted that they were not entitled to protections under the constitution. The Supreme Court ruled in 2004 that they too had the right of redress in the U.S. court system, and that the executive could not by decree deny them of their rights under the U.S. constitution.[64]

Two of the most common tools to combat terrorism and insurgencies, the deportation or detention of suspected provocateurs and the declaration of a state of emergency, appear largely to have negative effects on conflicts. This is not to say that states of emergency are not declared in the face of real crises; they are. Many people have suffered greatly in regionalized sectarian violence. States respond in the most expedient fashion. However, a consequence of this expediency is often that the executive seizes additional powers. Additionally, the reaction by the state, particularly military responses, may in fact further alienate a population already under duress. There does appear to be a relationship between the types of targets selected by insurgent or rebel organizations and the amount of power the executive tries to claim for itself in the process of reacting. In response to attacks on civilian targets, states appear to be far more active and aggressive in claiming extra powers. Attacks on military or governmental targets, such as police stations or public offices, appear to elicit more passive attempts to expand executive power.[65]

TARGETS AND RESPONSES

Just as not all political violence is directed at the same targets, not all political violence is the same either. Differentiating between the targets and the aims of organized collective political violence gives rise to different state responses. Rather than treating "terrorism" as a single political movement, this volume has offered case-by-case analysis of what are often seen to be the "flashpoints in the war on terrorism." This detailed analysis has revealed a number of similarities: political Islam is prominently featured in many of these conflicts, but not as a motivator for violence. Rather than demonstrating a "clash of civilizations" or the incompatibility of Islam and Christianity (or Judaism, or Hinduism, or Buddhism, or Nigerian indigenous religions), religion is a *marker of identity*. That violence arises is more a function of a state failure than a social or civilization failure.

In most of the cases presented here, "terrorist" violence is associated with political organizations that are either challenging the state in a nationalist or separatist fashion, or resisting an authoritarian or heavy-handed application of the state interests, including programs of forced assimilation. In none of the cases are the leading organizations associated with political violence agitating for an "internationalist" Islamic empire. There are organizations that promote this idea, and some of them are parties to the various conflicts and provide monies to other political organizations involved in violence. Yet, as John Mueller put it, even al Qaeda is a bounded problem, whose numbers and "terrorist adjuncts are finite and probably manageable."[66] Having the intent (or fantasy) of creating an Islamic Empire from Morocco to Indonesia is not the same as having the capability and opportunity to do so. The most prominent feature common to all of the cases is the rise of violence as a response to a state failure.

As Samina Raja writes of Kashmir, the biggest problem in the region is the state's failure to develop infrastructure. This failure has many wide-reaching repercussions. While terrorism may not be bred in conditions of poverty, it is born of frustration. Life in areas lacking infrastructure can be difficult and trying. Without technical infrastructure, the economy cannot be developed. The worst consequence in such regions is not only a rise of poverty, but also the resulting chronic underemployment. A region without technical infrastructure is stuck in a perpetual depression. No economic sector can grow because no sector takes root; in addition the population becomes economically dependent on the state. This tension between dependence on the state for things economic and feeling estranged from the state in things political creates tensions in such regions. The chronic lack of electrical power in Kashmir, or the lack of an industrial base in southeastern Anatolia, gives rise to a sense of being ignored by the state. The population turns to other organizations to fill the role of the state. The Free Aceh Movement provides protection in Indonesia. In the Gaza Strip, Hamas, like Hezbollah in southern Lebanon, provides social services, medical care, elderly care, and education. While these organizations have a violent component, their support and persistence is based on filling a role the state normally fulfills.

One of the biggest state failures in all of the regions presented in this volume is a lack of educational infrastructure. Without government schools communities turn to alternatives, often sectarian or religious schools with ulterior motives. This is a significant nodal point for international nihilistic Islamic fundamentalism. Often supported through Saudi financial initiatives to promote Wahhabism, these schools become attractive loci for radical agitation. Many veterans of the wars in Afghanistan, who cannot return home to countries like Egypt or Syria, travel through the Near East or South Asia looking for a place to rest and to become part of the community. These radical religious schools become a good place to roost. The lack of educational support is seen as proof of an indifferent if not hostile state. Moreover, while this volume specifically examined cases in which political Islam might be a factor, state failures in educational infrastructure creates tensions in other regions and conflicts as well, such as in Chiapas, Colombia, and Nepal.

Terrorism does not come out of poverty, nor are terrorists the unemployed. Yet support for change through any means comes from disappointed expectations and conditions of chronic underemployment. The leaders of the organizations that step into the void left by failing states are often well educated and quite frustrated. They are denied both the space for self-expression and the means for self-realization. Organizations of resistance like the Muslim Brotherhood in Egypt actively recruit on university campuses, especially among the technically skilled engineers who have little possibility of landing an appropriate job. In India, terrorism occurs most frequently in the country's most prosperous province, the Punjab, and in its most egalitarian, Kashmir, where the poverty rate is less than 4 percent of the population compared to 26 percent for the rest of the country.[67] To be sure, Osama bin Laden and his deputy Ayman al-Zawahiri seek to tap into this frustration and ignite a larger clash of civilizations. But as Bruce Hoffman notes, the current al Qaeda exists more as an ideology than as an enterprise, which was largely destroyed after 9/11 by counterterrorism gains in Afghanistan and Pakistan.[68]

Terrorism is not directly connected to Islam, but many Muslims might support its use. This is similar to American militia movements supporting Timothy McVeigh's 1995 terrorist strike against the federal government or Irish-Americans supporting the IRA's plight to "free" Northern Ireland from British rule. In an astonishing survey of 6,000 Muslims in 14 countries published in *Studies in Conflict and Terrorism*, researchers found that women were more likely to support terrorist tactics and that 47 percent of 62 year olds and 57 percent of 18 year olds were similarly inclined to "support terrorism."[69] The biggest danger from such a survey is the mistaken interpretation from readers (not from the authors) that terrorism is one thing, associated with one cultural project. Outside of Iraq, India continues to endure the most terrorist incidences each year, and while the majority of those are in conjunction with the conflict in Kashmir, radical Marxist-Leninists carry out many of these attacks. Likewise, most of the political violence in South America is connected to leftist movements or indigenous-rights movements. In Europe, political violence is committed in the name of all kinds of political movements including rightist-nationalists, leftist-internationalists, and eco-terrorism.[70] In Japan, more than 10 years ago, one of the biggest recognized terrorist threats came from Aum Shinrikyo, the apocalyptic religious group that launched the sarin gas attack on the Tokyo subway system in March 1995. All of these political elements are associated with organized collective violence, but none would be addressed by policy that focused counterterrorism efforts on Islamic movements. Even on the United States State Department's "foreign terrorist organization designation table," 20 of the 40 terrorist organizations identified are associated with leftist politics.[71] In 2002, when only 36 organizations were listed in the table, the ratio was the same: half of the organizations were connected with leftist-secular politics, not religious.

DANGERS OF WAR IMAGERY

John Mueller warned that the use of war imagery in "combating terrorism" may raise unreasonable expectations.[72] Wars end. They also have objectives and usually identified purposes guiding the belligerents. The rhetorical attempt to suggest that "the terrorists" are a single entity, who will be "defeated," makes it difficult to engage in the type of differentiation and setting conflicts into context as done here in this volume. Stephen Walt pointed out that during the Cold War, the United States fell into a similar pattern of rhetorical conflation. By viewing all leftist, socialist, or Marxist regimes as "indistinguishable parts of a communist 'monolith,'" U.S. foreign policymakers and -executors were unable to deal with each regime on its own terms and in its own context.[73] This lack of nuance often led to "self-fulfilling spirals of hostility" between the United States and these other regimes.[74] Depicting all struggles that include an element of political Islam as part of a "global jihad" can be very dangerous too. It is easy to imagine how the labeling of a group as "terrorist," thereby precluding the possibility of negotiation or intercession on the part of third parties, might drive political actors toward an extremism they might not otherwise approach. In addition, such rhetoric may obscure the goals of the political groups in conflict. The repetition of the rhetoric of "global jihad" prevents policy actors from hearing real grievances and seeing available avenues of conflict amelioration. Walt's warning of the potential of creating a self-fulfilling policy prophecy is an important one that should be heeded.

Much of this is a result of structures of the rhetoric of war in which the enemy is generally highly depersonalized in order to make his elimination more palatable. This act of violent debasement exacerbates the type of alienation associated with the state failures that gave rise to "terrorist" political organizations in the first place. Rather than attempting to identify with the estranged or alienated social group, the discourse of war suggests tension and the necessity to remain separate, often even after victory. Former U.S. military commander General Tony Zinni suggests, "When we [the United States] want to engage in conflicts like Iraq and Vietnam, we must have a cause. We must have somebody to attack us. We must have bad guys we can demonize. Our leaders cooked up the Gulf of Tonkin incident to justify our war in Vietnam. Our leaders cooked up Saddam Hussein's secret weapons of mass destruction and collaboration schemes with Al Qaeda to justify our war in Iraq. We had to cook up the rationale. We had to follow the model."[75]

The employment of war rhetoric may make the use of a state of exception more palatable in the near term; it may also help to justify enormous costs associated with the military in both men and material. For example, the U.S. Defense Department's *National Military Strategic Plan for the War on Terrorism* states that the way to defeat terrorism "is to continue to lead an international effort to deny violent extremists the networks and components they need to operate and survive. Once we deny them what they need to survive, we will have won."[76] However, a declaration of war only distorts the public's ability to see that terrorism is a political technique of the weak that will not go away. It is far more beneficial to engage the political elements in areas marred by terrorism, even if those groups may be associated with terrorism. This is particularly true since the organization responsible for the 9/11 attacks is largely defeated and relegated to a symbolic role hoping to inspire the national-ist struggles detailed in this volume. By incorporating, not excluding, these political organizations it may be possible to co-opt them into the larger political culture, thereby not only reducing political violence, but also building a more vibrant and varied political society.

Even as many questions are being asked as to whether Hamas can be incorporated into the political process after its early 2006 Palestinian parliamentary electoral victory, it must be remembered that a number of terrorist organizations laid down their weapons once they were able to join the political process. Al-Fatah and the Palestinian Liberation Organization ceased calling for the destruction of Israel once the Oslo Peace Accords were being realized. It may well be possible that the same will happen with Hamas. The Muslim Brotherhood, which has largely resisted violence, is now a responsible party within Egyptian politics. The FMLN[77] has become an important and stable political party in El Salvador after fighting a 12-year-long guerrilla campaign during that country's civil war. Similarly the Sandinistas remain an impor-tant political movement and party in Nicaragua, even after their elec-toral defeat in 1990. The African National Congress practiced terrorist tactics for nearly 30 years from the early 1960s until the organization was legalized in 1990. The ANC today is regarded as political move-ment defined by social justice. Although it has taken some time since Sinn Fein first accepted the 1998 Good Friday Peace Accords, the Irish Republic Army apologized in 2002 for harming civilians in its attacks and in 2005 renounced violence as a means to achieving its political ends: a fully independent Ireland. This laying down of weapons has been a long time in coming for Western Europe's oldest active terrorist organization, yet it has come nevertheless. All of these transformations were facilitated by the inclusion of these heretofore declared terrorist organizations into the political process. These conflicts were amelio-rated not by "defeating the terrorists" but by including "them."

If the Department of Defense's Global War on Terrorism Strategy is to be taken seriously in its plan to create a global environment inhospi-table to violent extremists, then it is necessary to engage those segments of the polity that experience estrangement and alienation. Regional autonomy, local self-rule, representation in larger national bodies, and the means for self-expression can be far more useful institutional tools than the state of exception or the declaration of *hostis iudicatio*. Each site of terrorist activity must be dealt with on its own terms. Through more democracy, not less; through free speech, not coded speech; and through transparency and honesty, not opacity and secrecy will these conflicts be ameliorated and the flashpoints in the global war on terrorism be extinguished.

NOTES

1. The jail break and other events of Aubrac's life are depicted in the 1997 Claude Berri film *Lucie Aubrac*. Having been caught and tortured and his wife having been revealed to also be a resistance commando, Raymond and Lucie Aubrac were smuggled to London in 1944. After D-Day and the liberation of the south of France, DeGualle appointed Aubrac Commissioner for the Republic in Marseilles (1944–1945). Later in life Aubrac worked for the United Nations' World Food Program in Rome. Aubrac is also well known for co-founding the underground resistance newspaper *Libération* with Emmanuel d'Astier.
2. Aubrac is a hero in French culture. Out on the street, especially in Paris, people come up to Aubrac in cafes to thank him for his commitment. Not just older people come up to him, but even young people realize the magnitude of his and Lucie's sacrifices for the French Resistance movement.
3. Michael Wievioka, "Terrorism in the Context of Academic Research" in *Terrorism in Context*, Martha Crenshaw, ed. (University of Pennsylvania Press, 1995).
4. *Moscow News*, "Chechen Warlord Basayev admits to being a terrorist: promises more attacks" 29, 07, 2005 14:48 GMT.
5. 22 USC 2656f(d) states "terrorism is premeditated, *political motivated violence* perpetrated against noncombatant targets by subnational groups or clandestine agents, usually intended to influence an audience." Emphasis is ours.
6. Ibid.
7. Martha Crenshaw, Preface in *Terrorism in Context*, Crenshaw (University of Pennsylvania Press, 1995), p. xvi.
8. Robert Pape, "The Strategic Logic of Suicide Terrorism," *American Political Science Review* 97, no. 3: (October 2003), pp. 343–361.
9. Pape, p. 344.
10. Ibid., p. xii.
11. Martha Crenshaw, "Thoughts on Relating Terrorism to Historical Context," in *Terrorism in Context* (University of Pennsylvania Press, 1995).
12. Ibid.
13. See Amnesty International *Chile Briefing: A decade of New Evidence* (London, Amnesty International Publications, 1988) AMR:22/13/88 and Amnesty International *Argentina: The Attack of the Third Infantry Regiment Barracks at La Tablada—Investigations into Allegations of Torture, "Disappearances" and Extrajudicial Executions*, New York, Amnesty International Publications, 1990) AMR: 13/01/90.
14. Paul Globe, RFE/RL *Newsline*, "Authorities seek to convert Beslan's Muslims," RFE/RL September 7, 2005.
15. See Law of Freedom of Conscience and Religious Organization, Lev Krichevsky, "Russian House passes religion bill restricting 'non-traditional' faiths," *Jewish Telegraphic Agency*, 26 June 1997.
16. *The Economist*, "Russia and Islam: Chaos in the Caucasus," 9 October, 1999 Vol. 353 Issue 8140, p. 23.
17. Giorgio Agamben, *The State of Exception* (University of Chicago Press, 2005), p.7.
18. Clinton Rosstier, *Constitutional Dictatorship: Crisis Government in the Modern Democracies*, (Harcourt Brace, 1948), p. 5, quoted in Giorgio Agamben, *The State of Exception* (University of Chicago Press, 2005), p.8.

19. Walter Benjamin, 1942, Über deb Begriff de Geschichte, in *Gesammelte Schriften*, pp. 697/257 quoted in Giorgio Agamben, *The State of Exception* (University of Chicago Press, 2005), p. 6.

20. Agamben, *op cit.*, p. 6.

21. Herbert Tingsten *Les Pleins pouvoirs. L'expansion des pouvoirs gouvernementaux pendant et après la Grande Guerre* (Paris: Stock, 1934), p.333, quoted in Giorgio Agamben, *The State of Exception* (University of Chicago Press, 2005), p. 7.

22. C.f. Walter Benjamin, 1942, Über deb Begriff de Geschichte, in *Gesammelte Schriften*, pp. 313–314, quoted in Giorgio Agamben, *The State of Exception* (University of Chicago Press, 2005), p. 9.

23. On March 16, 1978, Aldo Moro, the then Italian Prime Minister, was kidnapped by the ultra-leftist terrorist organization the Red Brigades. Although some speculate that Moro had been the target of the Red Brigades for some time, it would appear that he was abducted to forestall his attempts at founding a "historic compromise" between the ruling Christian Democratic Party and the Communist Party of Italy. In the end Valerio Morucci and Adriana Faranda, both members of the Red Brigades, were tried and found guilt of Moro's murder. However, it is also speculated the carabinieri, although aware of Moro's location, decided not to rescue the Prime Minister for fear that he might be killed in the raid. He was found dead nonetheless, his body bullet-ridden in the trunk of a Renault, on May 9, 1978. See Thomas Sheehan, "Italy: Behind the Ski Mask," *New York Review of Books*, Vol. 26, Number 13, August 16, 1979.

24. Agamben, *op. cit.* p. 15.

25. Nat Hentoff of the *Village Voice* reported that "David Keene of the Conservative Union, remembering how Ashcroft so swiftly pushed the PATRIOT Act through Congress, said, 'I don't know that 5 percent of the people who voted for that bill ever read it.'" Nat Hentoff "Conservatives Rise for the Bill of Rights!: 'Everyone in This Room Is a Suspect'" *Village Voice*, April 25, 2003.

26. H.R. 3162. Title I, Section 106 (1) (C).

27. Nat Hentoff, op. cit.

28. December 13, 2003, was also the same day it was reported that Saddam Hussein had been captured in Iraq. Very few news organizations picked up the Saturday billing signing. Previously, the Senate passed provision of the DSEA with a voice vote, thereby making voter accountability nearly impossible.

29. David Martin "With a Whisper, Not a Bang," *San Antonio Current News*, December 24, 2003.

30. Quoted in Martin "With a Whisper, Not a Bang," *San Antonio Current News*, December 24, 2003.

31. *Khaleej Times On-line*, February 1, 2006. Online. Available HTTP: <www.khaljeetimes.com>.

32. State Paper of the Republic of Indonesia, Number 139, 1959. See also U.S. State Department Indonesia Brief. Online. Available HTTP: <www.state.gov/r/pa/ei/bgn/2748.htm>.

33. Presidential Decree Number 28/2003. *Jakarta Post*. Online. Available HTTP: <www.jakartapost.com>; *Agence France Press* 18 May 2005.

34. *Amnesty International*, AMI ASA/21/027/2000.

35. *Pacific New Service*, July 28, 2003; *Reuters*, January 23, 2006.

36. International Freedom of Expression Exchange, http://www.ifex.org.

37. BBC, 30 November 2002, 15:55 GMT.

38. *Amnesty International*, AMI EUR/44/010/2002, 1 February 2002.

39. Sergei Kovalev, *Novye Izvestia*, August 27, 2003; WPS Monitoring Agency http://www.wps.ru/e_index.

40. "Chechnya's Disappeared," *The Washington Post*, April 4, 2005.
41. Ibid.
42. BBC News, April 4, 2000, 16:53 GMT, "Chechen Visit Mixed Success."
43. *Imphal Free Press*, Manipur, March 9, 2002. Online. Available HTTP: <www.manipuronline.com>.
44. Ibid.
45. Carl Schmitt, *Die Diktatur* (Dunker & Humbolt, 1921), p. 137, quoted in Giorgio Agamben, *The State of Exception* (University of Chicago Press, 2005), p.32.
46. Agamben, op cit., p.41.
47. Ibid, p. 35.
48. Human Rights Watch, May 11, 2004. Online. Available HTTP: <http://hrw.org/english/docs/2004/05/11/nigeri8568.htm>.
49. *Lagos Vanguard*, January 21, 2006. Online. Available HTTP: <http://www.allafrica.com>.
50. Ibid.
51. Andrew Norris, "The exemplary exception—Philosophical and political decisions in Giorgio Agamben's Homo Sacer," *Radical Philosophy*, Issue 119, May/June 2003.
52. Ibid.
53. Giorgio Agamben , *Homo Sacer: Sovereign Power and Bare Life* (Stanford University Press, 1998), p. 16.
54. Norris, *op cit.*
55. Giorgio Agamben, *The State of Exception* (University of Chicago Press, 2005), p. 80.
56. Ibid., p. 80.
57. Ibid., p. 80.
58. Ibid., p. 80.
59. Loi No. 55-385 du Avril 1955; Decree No. 2005-1386.
60. Ben Ward, "Expulsion Doesn't Help," *International Herald Tribune*, December 2, 2005. Online. Available HTTP: <www.iht.com/articles/2005/12/02/opinion/edward.php>.
61. Ibid.
62. Nat Hentoff, "Ashcroft Out of Control," *Village Voice,* February 28, 2003.
63. Carol Leonnig, "Judge Rules Detainee Tribunals Illegal," *The Washington Post*, February 1, 2005.
64. *The Washington Post*, June 28, 2004.
65. Jeffrey Murer, "La terreur des opprimés—Un examen comparatiste des réponses au terrorisme" in *Topique: Revue Freudienne*, 2003, Number 83, pp. 13–22 (Translated into French by Thamy Ayouch).
66. John Mueller, "Harbinger or Aberration?" *National Interest*, Fall 2002, pp. 45–50.
67. Christine Fair, Husain Haqqani, "Think Again: Islamist Terrorism," *Foreign Policy*, January 2006. Online. Available HTTP: <www.foreignpolicy.com/story/cms.php?story_id=3359>.
68. Bruce Hoffman, "Does Our Counterterrorism Strategy Match the Threat?" Testimony presented before the House International Relations Committee, Subcommittee on International Terrorism and Nonproliferation. September 29, 2005.
69. Ibid.
70. In an interesting collision of perspectives, Pim Fortuyn, a charismatic populist in the Netherlands, who was infamous for attacking Islam, saying it was a backwards religion and that the Netherlands was full so no more immigrants should be welcomed, was assassinated on May 6, 2002, by a radical animal rights-terrorist, Volkert van der Graff. Van der Graff said he was angered by Fortuyn's statement that there "was no time to worry about the environment."

71. Office for the Coordinator of Counterterrorism, U.S. State Department, "Foreign Terrorist Organization Designation Table" Fact Sheet. Online. Available HTTP: <www.state.gov/s/ct/rls/fs/2004/40945.htm>.

72. Mueller, *op cit.*

73. Steven Walt, "American Primacy and its Pitfalls" *Naval War College Review* 55, no. 2: (Spring 2002), p. 23.

74. Ibid.

75. Tony Zinni and Tony Koltz, *The Battle for Peace: A Frontline Vision of America's Power and Purpose* (New York: Palgrave Macmillan, 2006), p. 89.

76. Chairman of the Joint Chiefs of Staff, *National Military Strategic Plan for the War on Terrorism* (Washington, DC: Department of Defense, 2006), p. 5.

77. Farabundo Martí National Liberation Front

CONTRIBUTORS

Arabinda Acharya is manager of Strategic Projects at the International Centre for Political Violence and Terrorism Research in the Institute of Defence and Strategic Studies, Nanyang Technological University, in Singapore. He is also the research coordinator for the Centre for Peace and Development Studies in India. His area of research includes conflict, political violence, and human security. His writings have appeared in *Asian Defence and Diplomacy, Georgetown Journal of International Affairs, Harvard Asia Quarterly, Pacific Affairs,* and *Contemporary Southeast Asia.* His latest book is *Conflict and Terrorism in Southern Thailand.*

Rohaiza Ahmad Asi is a research analyst at the International Centre for Political Violence and Terrorism Research, Institute of Defence and Strategic Studies, in Singapore. She specializes in conflict and terrorism in Indonesia with a specific interest in Darul Islam and Jemaah Islamiyah. Her writings have appeared in the *Straits Times.*

Charles Edel is currently a Ph.D. candidate in American History at Yale University, where he studies American foreign policy, politics, and grand strategy. Previously, he worked as a research associate for U.S. Foreign Policy at the Council on Foreign Relations. He speaks regularly about international relations, American history, and the law. His writings have appeared in the *Los Angeles Times* and the *Cambridge Review of International Affairs.*

Stephen A. Emerson is an associate professor of National Security Affairs at the U.S. Naval War College in Newport, Rhode Island. He has served in a teaching capacity in both American and African educational institutions and has lived and traveled widely throughout most of the African continent. The author of numerous governmental and academic articles and studies on African politics, U.S.-Africa policy, and political development, Dr. Emerson's areas of professional interest include southern African area studies, conflict and political instability, and American foreign and security policy in the developing world. He holds a Ph.D. in political science/comparative politics, an M.A. in international relations, and a B.A. in political science, all from the University of Florida.

Christopher J. Fettweis is an assistant professor of National Security Affairs at the U.S. Naval War College. Since receiving his Ph.D. he has taught classes in U.S. foreign policy and international security at Tulane University, the Naval Academy, Ohio State, and George Washington University. His work has appeared in *Parameters, Comparative Strategy*, the *Journal of Genocide Research*, and *International Studies Review*. In addition, he has done extensive research on the minority groups of Central Asia and the Caucasus for the Minorities at Risk project at the University of Maryland.

Susan Fink Yoshihara is executive vice president of the Catholic Family and Human Rights Institute (C-FAM) in New York. She was a professor of National Security Affairs at the Naval War College from 2003-2006. A retired U.S. Navy helicopter pilot and Gulf War veteran, she graduated from the U.S. Naval Academy, is a frequent public speaker on military and security issues, and has written previously about humanitarian intervention and U.S. foreign policy in Kosovo. She holds a Ph.D. from the Fletcher School of Law and Diplomacy, Tufts University.

Dru C. Gladney is a professor of Asian Studies and Anthropology at the University of Hawaii–Manoa. He received his Ph.D. in social anthropology from the University of Washington–Seattle, and has been a Fulbright Research Scholar twice to China and Turkey. He has conducted long-term field research in Western China, Central Asia, and Turkey. Dr. Gladney has authored more than 50 academic articles and chapters, as well as the following books: *Muslim Chinese: Ethnic Nationalism in the People's Republic, Ethnic Identity in China: The Making of a Muslim Minority Nationality*, and editor for *Making Majorities: Constituting the Nation in Japan, China, Korea, Malaysia, Fiji, Turkey, and the U.S.* His most recent book is *Dislocating China: Muslims, Minorities, and Other Subaltern Subjects*.

Rohan Gunaratna is head of the International Centre for Political Violence & Terrorism Research, Institute of Defence and Strategic Studies in Singapore; a senior fellow, Combating Terrorism Centre at the United States Military Academy at West Point; and an honorary fellow at the International Policy Institute for Counter Terrorism in Israel. He received a master's in international peace studies from the University of Notre Dame and a doctorate in international relations from the University of St. Andrews. He serves on the editorial boards of *Conflict Studies and Terrorism* and *Terrorism and Political Violence*. He is the author of 10 books, including *Inside Al Qaeda: Global Network of Terror*. In 2004, he visited Southern Thailand at the invitation of the Government of Thailand and briefed the Thai National Security Council on the escalating threat. His most recent book is *Conflict and Terrorism in Southern Thailand*.

Michael F. Morris is a colonel in the U.S. Air Force and teaches on the faculty of the National Security Decision Making Department at the United States Naval War College in Newport, Rhode Island, where he also serves as the co-director of the college's Africa Studies Group. He has served as a squadron and deputy group commander in fighter wings in the United States and Europe, and has also served on the staffs of the U.S. Air Force Chief of Staff, the Air Force's Directorate of Legislative Liaison, and the Defense subcommittee of the U.S. Senate Committee on Appropriations. Col. Morris holds master's degrees from the University of Montana and the U.S. Naval War College.

Jeffrey Stevenson Murer is an assistant professor of political science at Swarthmore College in Swarthmore, Pennsylvania. He received his Ph.D. from the University of Illinois at Chicago, for which he was awarded the Annual Graduate Dissertation Prize in 2000. His research focuses on the connections between social and economic transitions and political violence in Central and Eastern Europe. He has been a guest lecturer and researcher at Central European University in Budapest and the Center for Research and Study of Psychopathology in Toulouse, France. He also holds an associate research fellowship at the University of Paris. He has collaborated greatly with colleagues at the Volgograd Academy for State and International Affairs, where he has been a lecturer and guest scholar, exploring issues of state development, ethnic violence and terrorism in Southern Russia and the Caucasus. In 2003 he was an OSCE election observer in the Republic of Georgia and witnessed the origins of the "Rose Revolution." He is the author of numerous articles and book chapters published in the United States, France, and Russia.

Samina Raja is an assistant professor of urban and regional planning at the State University of New York at Buffalo. She received her Ph.D. in urban and regional planning from the University of Wisconsin–Madison. Dr. Raja's research primarily focuses on issues of public finance in urban and regional planning. In the international arena, her research focuses on the nexus between development trajectories and the emergence of conflict. Her primary geographic area of interest is the region of Kashmir in South Asia.

Derek S. Reveron is an associate professor of National Security Affairs at the Naval War College in Newport, Rhode Island. He received an M.A. in political science and a Ph.D. in public policy analysis from the University of Illinois at Chicago. He specializes in democratization, post-conflict reconstruction, and intelligence. He is the author of *Promoting Democracy in the Post-Soviet Region* (2002), the editor of *America's Viceroys: the Military and U.S. Foreign Policy* (2004), and numerous book chapters and articles that have appeared in *Orbis, Defense and Security Analysis, International Journal of Intelligence and Counterintelligence, Low Intensity Conflict & Law Enforcement,* and the *National Review Online.* Additionally, he sits on the editorial board for the *Defense Intelligence Journal.* Before joining the Naval War College faculty, Dr. Reveron taught political science at the Joint Military Intelligence College, National Defense University, and the U.S. Naval Academy.

James S. Robbins is a professor of international relations at the National Defense University in Washington, D.C. His research interests include terrorism and national security strategy, political theory, and military history. He is also senior fellow in National Security Affairs at the American Foreign Policy Council. He is a widely published author in the national security field, and is a contributing editor for *National Review Online.* His work has also appeared in the *Wall Street Journal* and the *Washington Times.* He is a frequent commentator on international television and radio, including the BBC, Voice of America, FNC, MSNBC, CNBC, and CNN/FN. Dr. Robbins received his Ph.D. in international relations from the Fletcher School of Diplomacy. He is the author of *Last in Their Class: Custer, Pickett, and the Goats of West Point* (Encounter Books, 2006).

Kerrie Urosevich holds a Conflict Resolution Certificate from the Spark Matsunaga Institute for Peace and is a Ph.D. candidate in political science at the University of Hawaii–Manoa. She works as a conflict resolution practitioner; facilitated United Nations University conferences, Hawaii State environmental, education, and public health strategic planning sessions; and designs organizational conflict resolution systems. She holds a master's degree in international policy studies from the Monterey Institute of International Studies and bachelor of arts degrees in psychology and Japanese studies from Gustavus Adolphus College.

Stephen Van Evera teaches international relations at MIT, where he is professor of political science. He received his B.A. in government from Harvard and his Ph.D. in political science from the University of California at Berkeley. Dr. Van Evera works in several areas of international relations: the causes and prevention of war, U.S. foreign policy, U.S. security policy, U.S. intervention in the Third World, international relations of the Middle East, and international relations theory. He has published books on the causes of war and on social science methodology, and articles on American foreign policy, American defense policy, nationalism and the causes of war, and the origins of World War I. From 1984–1987 he was managing editor of the journal *International Security*.

Toshi Yoshihara is a visiting professor in the Department of Strategy at the U.S. Air War College in Montgomery, Alabama, and a senior research fellow at the Institute for Foreign Policy Analysis (IFPA) in Cambridge, Massachusetts. His research areas include U.S. alliances in the Asia-Pacific region, China's military modernization, security dynamics on the Korean Peninsula, Japan's defense policy, and China-Taiwan relations. He is the co-author of two monographs entitled *Alliance Diversification and the Future of the U.S.-Korean Security Relationship* (2004) and *The U.S.-Japan Alliance: Preparing for Korean Reconciliation and Beyond* (2003). He has published articles in *Survival, The Washington Quarterly, Comparative Strategy, The Naval War College Review, Issues and Studies, Orbis, Defense and Security Analysis*, and *World Affairs*. Dr. Yoshihara holds a Ph.D. in international relations from the Fletcher School of Law and Diplomacy, Tufts University, and an M.A. in international relations from the School of Advanced International Studies, Johns Hopkins University.

INDEX

9/11 attacks
  and Putin's involvement in Caucasus,
    88–89
  U.S.-Philippine security cooperation
    since, 211–212
  U.S. shift in emphasis to Iraq after, 29
2002 National Security Strategy, xvi
2003 Quartet Roadmap, 16, 17

A

Abboud, General Ibrahim, 272
Abdullah, Muhammed Ahmed bin Al-
    Asyyid, 270
Abdullah Plan, 14
Abdullahi, Khalifa, 271
Abdurixit, Abdulahat, 227
Abkhazia, xxvii, 93
Abu Ghraib prison, xiv, 38
Abu Sayyaf, 215
  greed motivations, xxx
  links to al Qaeda, 206, 207–208
  origins of, 205–206
  possible resurgence of, 216
Aceh, xxix
  demands for self-determination in,
    162–164
  weak integration into Netherlands
    East Indies, 160
Africa
  conflicts in, xxx–xxxi
  Intergovernmental Authority on
    Development (IGAD), 276
  Nigeria, 286–302
  Sudan, 266–283
  trans-Saharan arc, 248–263

African National Congress (ANC),
    incorporation into legitimate
    political processes, 326
Akayev, Askar, 127
Al Arabiya, 10
al-Bashir, General Umar Hassan
    Ahmed, 274
  rapprochement with West and U.S.,
    275
al-Faruq, Omar, 167
  links to pesantren religious school,
    172
  ties to al Qaeda and religious
    boarding school in Indonesia, 165
Al Jazeera, 10
al-Mahdi, Sadiq, 274
al Qaeda
  advantages of local insurgencies to,
    xv
  antidemocratic position in Iraq, 35
  danger of over-interpreting claims
    by, xii–xiii
  failure to take root in Kosovo, 70
  infiltration into trans-Saharan arc,
    252
  insurgency initiatives in Iraq, 35–36
  Israel-Palestine conflict as boon to, 3
  lack of evidence for Thai links to,
    145–146
  links to Islamic Movement of
    Uzbekistan, 124
  links to MILF, 208–210
  links to Omar al-Faruq in Indonesia,
    165
  links to Philippine Abu Sayyaf,
    207–208

links to Sudan, 277–278
links to trans-Saharan arc, 257
Nigeria as strategically attractive
    target for, 287
role in founding Ansar al-Islam, 54
role in Kashmir insurgencies, 192
strategy of exploiting internecine
    divisions in Iraq, 36
suggestion of ties to Ansar al-Islam,
    56
Syrian assistance against, 12–13
tenuous links to Xinjiang, 234
threats to Israeli security, 14
training camps in Philippines, 209
al-Salam Faraj, Muhammad Abd, xi
Al Sunna Wal Jamma, 294
al-Takriti tribes, 33
al-Turabi, Hassan, 273
    continued activity in Sudan, 281
    links to al Qaeda, 277
al Zarqaqi, Abu Musab, 35
al-Zawahiri, Ayman, xiv, 12
    Sudanese links to, 278
Albanian nationalism
    as buffer against radical political
        Islam, xxvii
    and consequences of high birth rates
        in Kosovo, 78
    in Kosovo, 66–67
    opposition to Wahhabi Islam, 72
    secular nature of, 71
Albu Nasir tribe, 33
Algerian civil war, influence on
        terrorism in trans-Saharan arc,
        256–257, 262
Amnesty International, reports of
        Xinjiang executions, 226–227
Anfal Operation, 49
Anglo-Egyptian Agreement of 1899, 271
Anglo-Siamese Treaty of 1909, 139
Ansar al-Islam, 48, 53, 55
    demands for independent Islamic
        state in Iraq, 50
    founding by al Qaeda, 54
    membership increases since U.S.
        invasion, 54
Anti-Americanism
    among Kurdish terrorist groups,
        54–55
    based on U.S. policy in Israel-
        Palestine conflict, 10–12

by Islamist groups in Indonesia, 163
nonsynonymous with terrorism, vii
quiescence in Central Asia, 120
in southern Thailand, 146, 150–151
and U.S. benefits of supporting
    Kurdish autonomy, 59
and U.S. military support in trans-
    Saharan arc, 258–260
Anti-Christian atrocities, 174
Aquino, Corazon, 204
Arab satellite TV, 10
Arafat, Yasser
    death of, 9
    recognition of state of Israel by, 8
Armenia, xx
Arms sales, to Iraq in dual containment
    era, 25
Asia. See also Central Asia
    Indonesia, 158–174
    Kashmir, 178–195
    Philippines, 200–219
    Thailand, 136–153
    Xinjiang, 224–241
Aubrac, Raymond, 305
Authoritarian rule
    and dangers of states of exception,
        309–312
    as incentive to religious
        fundamentalist dissent, 131
    in Iraq, 23
    political Islam as idiom of resistance
        against, xiii
    in Sudan, 272–274, 282
    in trans-Saharan arc, 249, 251
    U.S. support and anti-Americanism,
        129, 130
    vs. fundamentalist Islam in Central
        Asia, 125
Ayalon-Nusseibeh/People's Voice
    initiative, 14
Azerbaijan, xx

B

Baathist party, 32, 33, 34
Baku-Tblisi-Geyhan pipeline, 119
Balance of power, and dual containment
    strategy in Iraq, 25
Balfour Declaration, 6
Bali bombings, 172
    2005 renewal of, 168–169

Hambali links to, 145
Jemaah Islamiah links to, 168, 171
Balkans, historic diversity, 66
Barak, Ehud, 8
Barkey, Henri, 43
Basayev, Shamil, 95–97, 98
  involvement in Beslan School raid,
    101
Beslan School Number 1 raid, 101–103
bin Laden, Khalifa, 208
bin Laden, Osama, xi, xiv, 12, 287
  call for supporters to go to Sudan,
    279
  contacts with Abu Sayyaf, 206
  expulsion from Sudan, 278
  influence on Abdullah Sungkar, 169
  influence on Dokubo-Asari of
    Nigeria, 295
  links to Islamic Movement of
    Uzbekistan, 124
  opposition to U.S. presence in
    Muslim holy lands, 27
  purported Iraqi ties to, 29
  Putin's blame for Chechnya events,
    88
  and rise of al-Turabi in Sudan, 277
  sanctuary in trans-Saharan arc,
    257
  support from Sudan, 274
Blowback phenomenon, 38
Bosnia-Herzegovina, xviii, xxi
Buddhists
  coerced conversions by, 140
  predominance in Thailand, 139
  targeting by Muslim insurgents in
    Thailand, 137
Bush, George W., xii, 287
  plans for coercion of Hamas, 17

C

Caliphate
  distancing of Chechen rebels from
    calls for, 106
  Islamic Party of Liberation advocacy
    of, 125–127
  political Islam strategies for
    establishing transnational, 24
  unlikelihood of establishment in
    Iraq, 38
Catherine the Great, 90

Caucasus
  alliance with Nazis, 92
  Beslan School Number 1 raid,
    101–103
  differentiated Islams in, 104–107
  early Russian colonization, 89–91
  first Chechen war, 94–97
  historical context, 89–97
  independence claims after Soviet
    collapse, 93–94
  Khrushchev restoration of national
    autonomy to, 93
  links to global war on terrorism,
    103–107
  links to international terrorism,
    97–103
  map, 86
  nature of flashpoint, 87–88
  post-Czarist and Bolshevik
    independence movements, 91–93
  progress and prospects, 107–109
  and Putin's connection to 9/11, 88–89
  and rebel acts in Russia, 99–101
Central Asia, xxviii. *See also* Fergana
    Valley
  autocratic leadership *vs.* Islamic
    fundamentalism in, 120–122
  secular autocracies in, 119
Chechnya, xv
  extension of executive power in,
    315–316
  first Chechen war, 94–97
  historical struggle of Mansur, 90
  as key theater for Russian
    contribution to war on terrorism,
    xxvii, 87
  liberal Sufism in, 105
  Shamil rebellion, 90–91
Chevron-Texaco West Africa gas
    pipeline project, 288
  security threats to, 296
China
  difficulties of integrating a religious
    minority into Marxist-capitalist
    system, 238–239
  need to address Uyghur rights and
    environmental issues, 241
  New Criminal Law and anti-ethnic
    feelings, 230
  partnership with U.S. and Russia
    against IMU, 130

proximity to Central Asia, 118
Uyghur conflicts in, xxx
Xinjiang conflicts, 225–226
Chinese-Muslim relations, in Xinjiang,
238–241
Chirac, President Jacques, state of
emergency declarations, 310–311
Christian-Muslim conflict
in Indonesia, xxix
in Kosovo, 65, 66
in Nigeria, 289, 291, 293–294
over resources in Nigeria, 290
in Philippines, 201, 204–205
and state of emergency in Nigeria,
317–318
in Sudan, 267, 269
in trans-Saharan arc, 253
U.S. failure to improve in
Philippines, 203
Christianity, explosive growth in
Nigeria, 290
Citizen-based diplomacy, in Kurdish
question, 57
Citizenship revocation, 321
Clash of civilizations theory, xvii–xxiv
as driving force in war on terrorism,
xxiii
Clinton, Bill, role in Israel-Palestine
peace process, 8
Cold War
centrality of Iraq to U.S. policy
since, 23
parallels to U.S. war on terrorism,
324–325
Colonialism
and roots of Philippine insurgency,
202–204
as source of conflict, xvi
Conflict
among similar *vs.* different peoples,
xxi
economic and political bases for, xiv
falsely framing in religious terms, xiii
global diminishment of, vii
material considerations of, xxiv
processes of internationalizing, xxiv
recommendations for resolution in
Kurdistan, 57–58
regionalization in trans-Saharan
arc, 253

Conflict resolution, 305–307
and cases of state of exception,
312–318
and dangers of war imagery,
324–327
hampered by states of exception,
309–312
and *hostis iudicatio*
pronouncements, 318–321
and illegal enemy combatant labels,
318–321
and politics of terrorism, 307–309
targets and responses, 322–324
Covert searches, 311
Covert surveillance, 311–312
Croatia, xviii
historical enemies of, xxi
Crusades, Christian oppression of
European Jewry in, 4–5
Cultural difference
as buffer against radical ideas, 80
as central issue in Sudan, 269
as dominating source of conflict,
xviii
fluidity of, xxii
in Kosovo conflict, 80
myth of, xxiii
role in international conflicts, xii
Culture talk, xxii
Cyber-separatism, 227

D

Darfur, xxxi
Darul Islam (DI), 168
Dayaks, 161, 164–166
Democracy
al Qaeda position on, 36
cautionary expectations in Iraq, 37
compatibility with Islam, 173
fragility in Philippines, 218
and incorporation of terrorists into
legitimate political processes,
326–327
initiatives in Iraq, 32–36
Iraq as test bed for spread in Near
East, 23
Kurdish promise of, 50
liquidation through states of
exception, 310

progress in Middle East toward, viii
and risk of Islamic fundamentalist
rise to power, 129–130
and strategic role of Kurds in Near
East, 46
Sunni Arabs' ambivalence in Iraq, 34
support for Kurdish initiatives in
Syria and Iran, 45
as tool in Thaification, 148
Western need to promote in pivotal
states, xvi
Deng Xiaoping, liberalization of
religious restrictions, 227–228
Deobandism, 123, 131
in Central Asia, 122
Department of Defense, Unified
Command Plan, 297–298
Deportation
negative effects on conflicts, 321
as response to security threats,
320–321
Detention, negative effects on conflicts,
321
Difference, accommodation as key to
peace, xvi
Disappearance
in Chechnya, 316
in South American terrorism, 308
Dokubo-Asari, Muhahid, 295
Domestic policies, importance on
internal conflicts, xix
Domestic Security Enhancement Act,
311
deportation provisions, 321
Drug trafficking, Kosovo links to, 70
Dual containment, in U.S.-Iraq policy,
25–26
Dudayev, Dzhokhar, 94

E

East Timor, 160
East Turkestan, 225, 226, 227, 232.
See also Xinjiang Uyghur
Autonomous Region
Internet calls for independence,
234–235
East Turkestan Islamic Movement
(ETIM), 232, 235–236
recognition as international terrorist
organization, 225, 237

Economic dislocations, as source of
conflict, xv
Economic stabilization, as determining
factor in Kosovo future, 80
Educational opportunities
accessibility problems in Kashmir,
187
as source of conflict, xv
state failure in, 323
Egypt
oppressive rule of Sudan, 270
restoration of sovereignty over
Sudan, 271
End of history hypothesis, xvii
Enemy depersonalization, in rhetoric of
war, 325
Energy security, in Nigeria, 288–289
Ethnic cleansing
as issue in Sudan conflicts, 269
by Serbs in Kosovo, 68
Ethnic separatism, in Caucasus, 108
Ethnopolitics, xvi
Europe
Caucasus, 86–109
current conflicts in, xxvii–xxviii
Kosovo, 65–80
Executive power
undue extensions in response to
terrorism, 309–312
and USA PATRIOT Act, 311

F

Fallujah, 37
Fatah party, 9
FBI National Security Letters, 312
Fergana Valley
hazards of open practice of Islam in,
123
Islamic Movement of Uzbekistan
(IMU) in, 123–125
Islamic Party of Liberation (HT) in,
125–127
linkages to global war on terrorism,
129–131
linkages to terrorism, 123–129
map, 116
nature of flashpoint, 117–122
progress and prospects, 131
regional leaders as sources of Islamic
unrest, 120–122

turmoil in 2005, 127–129
and U.S. interests in Central Asia, 118–120
Flashpoints
Aceh, 162–164
Caucasus, 87–88
Fergana Valley, 117–122
identifying, xvi–xvii
Indonesia, 159–160
Iraq, 23–24
Israel-Palestine conflict, 3
Kalimantan, 164–166
Kashmir, 180–182
Kosovo, 65–80
Kurdistan, 44–50
Maluku, 166–167
Nigeria, 287–293
Philippines, 201–202
Sudan, 267–268
Thailand, 137–138
trans-Saharan arc, 250–253
in war on terrorism, xi
Xinjiang, 225–227
Food for Oil Program, benefits to Iraqi Kurds, 51
Foreign insurgents
in Iraq, 35–36
in Kosovo, 78–79
Foreign investment, reasons for failure in Kosovo, 77
Foreign policy. *See* U.S. foreign policy
France
2005 riots in, xv
state of exception declaration, 310–311, 320
Free Aceh Movement (GAM), xxix, 162–164, 323. *See also* Aceh
Thai insurgents' links to, 145
Freedom House, 2005 report, viii
French Resistance, 305
Fukuyama, Francis, xvii

G

Geneva Accord, 14
Global jihad, vii, viii
dangers of rhetoric of, 325
dispelling myth of, xiv
role of Chechnya in, 88

Great Britain
betrayal of agreement with Thai Muslims, 141
historical support for Zionism, 5–6
reconquest of Sudan, 271
Greater Albania, KLA ambitions in Kosovo, 68
Green menace, viii
myth of, xiv
Guantanamo Bay, xiv
Gulf of Guinea (GOG), maritime security issues, 298

H

Hamas
control of Palestinian parliament, 9
goal of Israel's destruction, 9
incorporation into legitimate political process, 326
Iraqi ties to, 28
opposition to pro-compromise Palestinian majority, 13
role for U.S. foreign policy, 16
tenuous links to Xinjiang, 234
Hambali, 145
Hisba, 294
Hizb ut-Tahrir al-Islami (HT). *See* Islamic Party of Liberation (HT)
Hizbul Mujahideen, 192
Holocaust, 5
Homo Sacer, 318–319
Hostis iudicatio, 318–321
Hoxha, ties to Hezbollah in Kosovo, 73
Human rights
abuses in Chechnya and Dagestan, 99
ambivalent U.S. policy towards abuses of Kurdish, 56
concerns in Xinjiang Uyghur Autonomous Region, 231–232
and conflict-resolution recommendations for Kurdistan, 57
in Saddam Hussein's Iraq, 27, 29, 32
violations in Xinjiang Uyghur Autonomous Region, 233
Human Rights Watch, 99–100, 107, 126
Human trafficking, in Kosovo, 70, 76
Huntington, Samuel, xviii
Hussein, Saddam
Kurdish opposition to, 44

Kurdish role in overthrowing, 46
militarization of Iraq, 26
power consolidation after Iranian
revolution, 24
and strong man myth, xix
tribal and ethnic politics of, 33

I

Identity politics, 306
religion as marker of identity, 322
U.S. minimization of importance
of, xiii
Igbo people, 289
Ijaw people, 293
Illegal enemy combatants, 318–321
Imperialism, legacy as source of conflict,
xvi
India
accession of Kashmir to, 185
prevalence of terrorist incidents in,
xxviii, 324
resistance by Kashmiris, 194
role of nuclear capacity in Kashmir
conflict, 180
sources of religious conflict in, xix
U.S. economic ties *vs.* Kashmir
problem, 192
India-Administered Jammu and
Kashmir (IAJK), 179. *See also*
Kashmir
Indonesia
Aceh self-determination movement,
162–164
Balikpapan terrorist activities,
165–166
communal conflicts in, 160
conflicts between Christians and
Muslims in, xxix
Dayaks *vs.* Madurese conflicts, 161
ethnic diversity in, 159
Hidyatullah pesantren school, 165,
172
historical context, 160–167
inter-religious rivalry in Maluku,
166–167
Islamist militant groups in, 163
Kalimantan competition over
resources, 164–166
Kentucky Fried Chicken bombing,
171

Laskar Jihad/Laskar Mujahideen,
167
linkages to global war on terrorism,
172–173
linkages to terrorism, 168–172
map, 158
Marriott hotel bombing, 168, 171
martial law and states of exception,
313
McDonald's bombings, 171
nature of flashpoint, 159–160
peace accord between GAM and
government, 164
prevalence of terrorist incidents in,
xxviii
progress and prospects, 173–174
school burnings in, 163
targeting of corporations and civil
servants in, 163
as world's most populous Muslim
state, 159
Infrastructure
chronic failure of electrical power in
Kashmir, 323
state failure of, 322–323
Instability
role of pivotal states in causing, xvi
as source of future global threats, xiii
Insurgency, in postwar Iraq, 32–36
Intelligence, importance of developing
in Thailand, 151
Intergovernmental Authority on
Development (IGAD), 276
Internal repression, as source of conflict,
xiii
International Emergency Powers Act,
311
Internationalization strategy
by al Qaeda in Iraq, 36
in trans-Saharan arc, 252
Internet, calls for Xinjiang rights/
independence, 227, 234–235,
241
Iran
attempts to extend influence over
postwar Iraq, 37
influence on Moros in Philippines,
207
influence on Thai extremists/
separatists, 141
Kurdish assimilation in, 52–53

Kurdish presence in, 52–53
similarities to Central Asian regimes, 131
support to Ansar al-Islam, 54
support to Philippine MNLF, 204
U.S. support for Kurdistan Democratic Party in, 47
Iran-Iraq War, 24–26
Iranian revolution, 24
Iraq, 23
  Baathist party, 32, 33, 34
  battle for Fallujah, 37
  centrality in U.S. national security policy, 23
  Coalition strategy in, 36–37
  concerns over permanent U.S. occupation, 33
  democracy vs. states of emergency, 318
  democratization and insurgency in, 32–36
  dual containment era, 24–26
  economic sanctions against, 28
  effects on global war on terrorism on conflict, xxvi
  ethnic conflict in, 32–33
  foreign insurgents in, 35–36
  historical context of U.S. relations, 24–37
  influence of outside non-state actors in, 32
  Interim Governing Council, 33
  Joint Resolution 114, 30
  Kurdish semi-autonomy in, 49–50, 51–52
  Kuwait invasion era, 26–29
  map, 22
  nature of flashpoint, 23–24
  no-fly zone and Kurdish autonomy, 44
  Oil for Food Program, 28
  Operation Desert Fox, 28
  Operation Desert Storm, 26
  Operation Earnest Will, 25
  Operation Iraqi Freedom, 31
  Operation Prime Chance, 25
  opposition to surveillance of weapons programs, 27–28
  PeaceWatch initiatives in, 46–47
  percentage of global oil reserves in, 23
  purported ties to Osama bin Laden, 29
  as real-world laboratory for urban combat, 38
  regime change as U.S. policy, 29–32
  role in Arab/Muslim popular hostility toward U.S., 12
  Sunni Arab insurgents in, 33–35
  terrorist aftermath of 2003 war with U.S., 24
  ties to Hamas and Palestinian Islamic Jihad, 28
  Transitional Administrative Law (TAL) and Kurdish autonomy, 49–50
  U.N. Coalition strategy, 36–37
Iraq conflict, progress and prospects, 37–39
Islam
  assimilation of Hinduism in Thailand, 139
  association with terrorism in Russia, 102
  Deobandism in Central Asia, 122
  differentiation in Chechnya and Caucasus region, 104–107
  early inroads into Caucasus, 89
  in Kosovo, 71–73
  liberal trends of Shafyism and Khanafism, 105
  Muridism, 105
  non-Arab face of, xxii
  overemphasis on, xxii
  potential crises in Kosovo, 69
  potential to become organizing principle of Thai resistance, 148
  as replacement for ethnonationalism in Thailand, 150
  repression by Serbian government in Kosovo, 65
  role in Northern Caucasus conflicts, 103
  role of religious educational institutions in insurgency, 142–144
  sectarian divisions within trans-Saharan arc, 253–254
  significance in sub-Saharan Africa and India, xviii
  in southern Thailand, 139–140, 144
  Sufism, 105, 122, 190, 192

syncretic practices in Nigeria, 289
violence among secular practitioners
    in Kosovo, 78
vs. autocratic leadership in Central
    Asia, 120–122
Islamic Army Group (GIA), 257
Islamic Jihad
    Iraqi ties to, 28
    Sudanese ties to, 278
Islamic Movement of Uzbekistan (IMU),
    123–125
Islamic movements, lumping together by
    U.S. policymakers, xiv
Islamic Party of Liberation (HT),
    125–127
Islamic resistance, differentiated nature
    of, xiv–xv
Islamic Traditionalism, xiv–xv
Israel-Palestine conflict
    2003 Quartet Roadmap, 16, 17
    1967 war, 7–8
    1948 war and, 6–7
    Abdullah Plan, 14
    Ayalon-Nusseibeh initiative, 14
    as boon to al Qaeda, xxv
    Clinton peace plan, 14
    end of attack threats from East, 14
    four major peace plan elements,
        14–15
    general agreement on peace terms, 13
    Geneva Accord, 14
    historical context, 4–9
    and history of Zionist movement,
        5–6
    importance to popular Arab opinion
        of U.S., 10–12
    Israeli concerns over maintenance of
        Jewish state identity, 14
    Israeli declaration of statehood, 6
    links to global war on terrorism,
        12–15
    links to international terrorism,
        10–15
    map of, 2
    modern origins in Christian
        oppression of European Jewry,
        4–5
    nature of, 3
    post-1948 conflicts, 7–9
    progress and prospects, 15–17
    and states of emergency, 314–315
    Taba peace talks, 8–9
    U.S. pressure for total Israeli
        withdrawal, 16
    violent expulsion of Palestinians, 7
    Western Christian moral
        responsibility for, 7

J

Janjalani, Abdurajak, 206, 207, 216
    meeting with al Qaeda operatives,
        207
    role in Abu Sayyaf, 205–206
Jemaah Islamiyah (JI), xxix, 145
    activities in Indonesia, 165, 168
    formalized command structure *vs.*
        decentralization, 170
    roots in Darul Islam anticolonialism,
        169
    ties to Philippine MILF, 208
Jerusalem, proposals for multistate
    control, 15
Jews
    rebellions against Roman rule, 4–5
    repeated Christian oppression of, 4–5
    revolt against British rule of
        Palestine, 6
    and secular origins of Zionism, 5

K

Kalimantan, 162, 164–166
    communal violence in, 161
Karimov, Islam, 119
    career path, 120–121
    closing of borders with Kyrgyzstan,
        128
    Islamic fundamentalist opposition
        to, 125
    and U.S. pressure to reform, 120, 131
Kashmir, xv, 179–180
    All-Jammu Kashmir National
        Conference, 183
    ambiguous special status within
        India, 186–188
    chronic state failure in, 323
    as contested territory, 179
    continuity of insurgence in, 183
    de facto state of emergency in, 316
    division between India and Pakistan,
        179, 184

educational access problems, 182, 187
ethnic resistance and conflict in,
190–192
failed development as root of conflict
in, 180, 181–182, 186–190
historical context, 182–190
independence-seeking groups in,
191–192
intractability of conflict in, 180, 181
issues of development and economics
in, xxix
lack of political freedoms in, 189
legacy of Dogra Maharajas, 182–186
linkages to global war on terrorism,
192–195
map, 178
nature of flashpoint, 180–182
need for international consortium,
193
partial control by China, 179
physical infrastructure problems as
source of conflict, 187–189
role of al Qaeda in, 192
role of Sheikh Abdullah, 183, 186
stagnating employment
opportunities, 188, 190
Sufism in, 190, 192
threats to ethnic identity, 190–192
Kashmiryat, as identity of resistance,
191
Kongra-Gel, xxvi
Koshman, Nikolai, 100
Kosovo, xviii, xxvii
Albanian nationalism in, 66–67
annexation by Serbia, 67
consequences of demographic trends,
78
consequences of failure to resolve
final status, 75–77
consequences of slow Serbian
repatriation, 74–75
criminal shadow economy in, 77
de factor Albanian independence
with UN administration, 69
decline in political freedoms, 77
disadvantages of international
presence, 75–77
economic stability as determining
factor for future, 80
emerging vulnerabilities in, 77–78
ethnic division and corruption in, 65

historical context, 66–69
historical patterns of inequality, 67
importance of clan identity in, 71
importance of sovereignty, 79
importance of supporting moderates
in, 79–80
lessons for U.S. war on terrorism,
78–80
linkages to terrorism, 69–74
map, 64
nature of flashpoint, 65–66
nature of Islam in, 71–73
negative consequences of
permissiveness, 77–78
poor human development and
economic progress in, 77
potential backlash against EU
policies, 78
progress and prospect, 74–78
Serbian religious nationalism in,
73–74
sluggish Serb repatriation in, 77
as springboard for Islamic terrorists,
72–73
struggle for liberation and terrorism,
67–69
ties to Hezbollah, 73
unemployment in, 75
Kosovo Liberation Army (KLA), 66. See
also Kosovo Protection Corps
(KPC)
increase in popularity with Serb
violence, 68
Kosovo Protection Corps (KPC), 68, 69
Kurdish Alliance, 52
Kurdish United Front, 52–53
Kurdistan, xx, xxvi, 43–44
advancement of U.S. policies through
terrorist groups in, 55–57
calls for independent, 45
conflict-resolution recommendations,
57–58
and conundrum of U.S. alliance with
Turkey, 47–49
historical context, 50–53
linkages to terrorism, 53–57
map, 42
movement for autonomy in Iraq, 37,
49–50
multinational boundaries, 51–53
nature of flashpoint, 44–50

opportunities to advance democracy
through, 59
oppression by Sunnis in Iraq, 33
peshmerga fighters, 46
progress and prospects, 57–58
Kurdistan Democratic Party (KDP),
46, 52
U.S. support for in Iran, 47
Kurdistan Worker's Party (PKK), 43
as designated terrorist organization,
53–55
Kurds
culture and language as uniting
forces for, xx
demands for legal, resource, fiscal
autonomy in Iraq, 49–50
in Iran, 52–53
in Iraq, 51–52
as nation without a state, 44
as pawns for U.S. policy
advancement, 46–47
purported terrorist organizations
among, 53–55
relative lack of power in Turkey,
51
in Turkey, 51
U.S. dilemma of supporting
multinationally, 45
Kuwait, Iraq invasion of, 26–29
Kyrgyzstan, 2005 riots in, 127

L

Language, and Caucasus rebellions, 89
Laskar Jihad, 167, 174
Laskar Mujahideen, 167
Leftist politics, in Kurdish conflicts,
xxvi
Lewis, Bernard, xvii

M

Madurese, 161, 164–166
Malay ethnic identity, in southern
Thailand, 140, 141, 144
Maluku, 162, 166–167, 313
Maps
Caucasus, 86
Fergana Valley, 116
Indonesia, 158
Iraq, 22

Israel-Palestine, 2
Kashmir, 178
Kosovo, 64
Kurdistan, 42
Nigeria, 286
Philippines, 200
Sudan, 266
Thailand, 136
trans-Saharan arc, 248
Xinjiang, 224
Martial law. *See* States of exception
Maskhadov, Aslan, 97, 99, 103
Material politics, connection to terrorist
acts, xxix
Mazen, Abu, 9
Militarization, in trans-Saharan arc,
259–260, 261
Milosevic, Slobodan, 67
Mindanao, xxix–xxx, 201
historical context, 200
U.S. military operations in, 211
Moderates, importance of supporting in
Kosovo, 79–80
Modernization, role in international
conflicts, xii
Moro insurgency, 203–204
Moro Islamic Liberation Front (MILF),
xxx
al Qaeda connections, 208–210
differences from Abu Sayyaf, 209
distancing from Abu Sayyaf, 209
Moro National Liberation Front
(MNLF), xxx
distancing from Abu Sayyaf, 209
origins of, 204
splintered unity, 205
Mubarak, President Hosni, 277
Muhammed, Khalid Sheikh, 207
Mujahedin, 38
Multinational companies
in Balikpapan, 166
GAM violence against, 163

N

Namangani, Juma, 124
Nasser, Gamal Abdel, 8
National Counterterrorism Center
(NCTC), xxvii
National homeland, as goal of suicide
terrorism, 306

National identity
heightening after outbreak of
conflicts, xxi
in Kurdish conflicts, xxvi
National Intelligence Council, xii
National liberation
in Caucasus, 106
as source of conflict, xiii
vs. religious fundamentalism, 104
NATO, importance to al Qaeda defeat,
12
Natural resources
intense competition in trans-Saharan
arc, 254
as issue in Kurdish conflicts, 57
Kurdish demands for control over, 49
and Kurdish resistance in Turkey, 51
Mindanao issues, 202
role in international conflicts, xii, xvi
struggles in Indonesia over, 161
Nazi era
alliance with Caucasus states, 92
death camps as political act of
denying humanity, 319
French Resistance as terrorists in,
305
Hitler's extensions of power through
state of exception, 309
Near East
Israel-Palestine conflict, 3–17
popular association with terrorism,
xxv
proximity to Central Asia, 118
U.S. as second most feared country
in, xxiv
Nexus, 30
Nigeria
as attractive target for al Qaeda, 287
Christian Igbo in Southwest, 289
economic dislocation and political
disempowerment, 293
economic stagnation and political
corruption in, 291–293
effects of states of emergency on
democracy, 317
election concerns, 301–302
energy security issues, 288–289
ethnolinguistic self-determination
objectives, 300
growing internal instability in, xxxi
high unemployment rates in, 291

history of military leadership, 290
influx of Saudi and Pakistani
funding, 294
interfaith marriages in, 295
lack of U.S. presence in north, 295
linkages to global war on terrorism,
296–299
linkages to terrorism, 293–296
as major U.S. strategic ally, 287
map, 286
as most populous country in Africa,
289
nature of flashpoint, 287–293
need for governmental and economic
reforms, 301
patronage system of politics in, 291
plight of Ijaw people, 293
political corruption in, 292
primacy of ethnicity *vs.* religion in
shaping identity, 289
pro-Americanism in Southwest
region, 295
progress and prospects, 299
sources of conflict in, xix
sources of religious tension, 289–291
strategic importance to U.S., 300
support of U.S. efforts against
terrorism, 297
Trans-Sahara Counter Terrorism
Initiative (TSCTI) in, 298
unemployment and low GNP, 292
unrest in Niger Delta region, 288,
295–296
Nimeiri, Colonel Jaffar, 272–273
No-fly zone, 50
and Kurdish autonomy in Iraq, 44,
47, 48
and prevention of Kurdish refugee
influx into Turkey, 47–48
Nuclear capacity, role in Kashmir
conflicts, 180

O

Obasanjo, General Olusegun, 290,
296–297
state of emergency declaration,
317–318
Ocalan, Abdullah, 53, 54
Oil reserves
Baku-Tblisi-Geyhan pipeline, 119

in Central Asia, 118
Chevron-Texaco West Africa gas
    pipeline project, 288
competition for revenues in Niger
    Delta, 296
discovery in Sudan, 267, 268,
    269–270, 275
and energy security issues in Nigeria,
    287, 288–289, 296
and Kurdish political initiatives in
    Iraq, 52
and Kurdish resistance in Turkey,
    51
in Kurdistan, 45
and piracy in Nigeria, 298
standing of Iraq in global, 23
in trans-Saharan arc, 254
Operation Desert Storm, 26
Operation Earnest Will, 26
Operation Flintlock, 258
Operation Iraqi Freedom, 31
Operation Prime Chance, 25
Orthodox Christians
    Kosovo as sacred place to, 73
    and Kosovo struggle, 66
Oslo Accords, 8

P

Pahlavi, Shah Mohammad Reza, 25
Pakistan
    Hizbul Mujahideen and, 192
    initiatives to seek union with
        Kashmir, 190
    religious education in wake of failed
        state education, 313–314
    role of nuclear capacity in Kashmir
        conflict, 180
    as seam state, xvi
    standstill agreement with Kashmir,
        184–185
    suspension of law, 317
Palestine. *See also* Israel-Palestine
    conflict
    self-determination movement in, xv
Palestinian intifada, 7, 9, 10
    role in Arab predisposition to Israel-
        Palestine peace, 13–14
Palestinian Liberation Organization,
    incorporation into legitimate
    political processes, 326

Palestinian refugees
    abnegation of right of return, 15
    demands to return or be
        compensated, 7
    historical origins, 7
    Israeli compensation to, 15
Pan Sahel Initiative (PSI), 258
Panyarachum, Anand, 137
Patriotic Union of Kurdistan (PUK), 46
Pattani insurgency, 137
    origins in British WWII promises,
        141
Pattani sultanate, 138
PeaceWatch initiatives, 46–47
People's Defense Force (HPG), xxvi
Peter the Great, 90
Philippines
    Abu Sayyaf al-Qaeda connection,
        207–208
    airline jet bombing of 1994, 208
    Autonomous Regions in Muslim
        Mindanao (ARMM), 204
    Balikatan 02-1 military exercises, 211
    benefits and risks of U.S.
        cooperation, 212–215
    colonial roots of discontent, 202–203
    corruption in development projects,
        217–218
    counterterrorism activities, 216–219
    dependence on oil and remittances
        from Middle East, 206
    designation as major non-NATO U.S.
        ally, 212
    disconnect between U.S. reviews of
        counterterrorism and reality, 216
    dynamics of rebellion, 205–207
    effects of Marco's martial law decree,
        204
    failure to advance equitable
        socioeconomic recovery, 217
    forced migrations along Christian-
        Muslim lines, 201, 203
    government discriminatory policies,
        203
    government-sanctioned Christian
        relocations, 201
    historical context, 200–207
    linkages to global war on terrorism,
        210–215
    linkages to terrorism, 207–210
    map, 200

MILF–al Qaeda connection, 208–210
Mindanao conflict, xxix–xxx
nature of flashpoint, 201–202
progress and prospects, 215–219
relative success of counterterrorist
    vs. counterterrorism policies,
    215–217
resistance to labeling MILF as
    terrorist entity, 214
rise of postcolonial Moro insurgency,
    203–204
role of nongovernmental
    organizations (NGOs), 218–219
shift from insurgency to politics,
    204–205
states of exception in, 314
strategic position as sole Catholic
    nation in Southeast Asia, 201
terrorist incidents in, xxviii
U.S.-Philippines security cooperation
    since 9/11, 211–212
U.S. use as logistical hub in China-
    Taiwan conflict, 214
weakness of civil society, 218–219
as Western-oriented country in Asia,
    201
withdrawal of U.S. forces in 1992, 211
Philistines, 4
Piracy, in Gulf of Guinea, 298
Pivotal states, xvi–xvii
PKK. See Kurdistan Worker's Party
    (PKK)
Pluralism, promotion as solution to
    violent movements, xvi
Political conflicts. See Conflict; Conflict
    resolution
Political Islam
    Albanian identity as buffer against,
        xxvii
    among separatist groups in Kashmir,
        179
    in Central Asia, 123
    Central Asian secular autocrats vs.,
        119
    four types of, xiii
    groups in Indonesia, 163
    groups in southern Thailand, 141
    MILF goals in Philippines, 205
    nonequivalence with al Qaeda, 104
    in Northern Nigeria, 290, 294

and opposition to U.S. support of
    ruling regimes, xxiv
in Philippines, 204–205
as reaction to forms of political
    domination, xv, xxiv
reasons for renewal in Central Asia,
    129
role in specific conflicts, xxiv
and separatist groups in Kashmir,
    192
as sole avenue for popular outrage
    against oppression, 131
and state education failure, 323
in Sudan, 270–272
tendencies in Iraq, 37–38
threats in Iraq, 23–24
U.S. concerns in Northern Nigeria,
    293–294
Political liberalization, political Islam as
    idiom of resistance against, xiii
Political science, debate on end of war
    vs. renewed instability, vii
Politics of inclusion/exclusion, 326–327
Politics of terrorism, 307–309
Populist Islam, in trans-Saharan arc,
    253–254
Post-Cold War period, tendency toward
    breakdown into smaller states,
    xxii
Post-Soviet Region, 63
    Caucasus, 86–109
    current conflicts in, xxvii–xxviii
    ethnopolitics in, xvi
    Fergana Valley, 116–131
Powell, Colin, suggestion of Ansar al-
    Islam ties to al Qaeda, 56
Protestantism, religious pluralism
    within, xix
Putin, Vladimir, and Caucasus
    connection to 9/11 attacks, 88–89

R

Race, as conflict issue in Sudan, 269
Radical groups. See also Political Islam;
    individual group names
    advancement of U.S. policies in
        Kurdistan through, 55–57
    Al Sunna Wal Jamma, 294
    Hisba, 294

incorporation into legitimate
political processes, 326–327
motivating forces other than religion,
xxii
Mujahedin, 38
return in Sudan, 281
vs. Islamic syncretism in Nigeria, 289
Religion
as central defining characteristic of
civilization, xix
conflicts in Nigeria, 289–291
as marker of identity, 322
noncentrality in Sudanese conflicts,
269
as source of conflict in Maluku,
Indonesia, 166–167
Religious educational institutions, 140
importance of modernization in
Thailand, 152
revival in Xinjiang during Deng era,
227
role in Indonesia, 172
role in Thai insurgency, 142–143
in wake of insufficient state
educational resources, 313–314,
323
Resource competition. *See also* Natural
resources
in Niger Delta, 296
in Nigeria, 288–289, 289, 290, 291
over oil revenues in Nigeria, 292
as source of conflicts, xxiv
in Sudan, 269
and violence in Indonesia, 160
Response to violence, 322–324
Rhetoric of war, enemy
depersonalization in, 325
Rogue states, 30
Roman Empire
Homo Sacer category, 319
hostis/public enemy concept, 320
standstill/suspension of law in, 317
Russia
banning of HT terrorist group by,
126
Chechen terrorist acts in, 99–101
collaboration with U.S. in war on
terrorism, 88–89
early colonization of Caucasus, 89–91
Federation Treaty of 1992, 94

mutual defense pact with Uzbekistan,
129
partnership with China and U.S.
against IMU, 130
proximity to Central Asia, 118

S

Salamat, Hashim, 205
Sandinistas, incorporation into
legitimate political processes, 326
Saudi Joint Relief Committee for Kosovo
(SJRCK), 72
Scapegoat terrorism, 226
Seam states, xvi
Secularization
political Islam as idiom of resistance
against, xiii
and strategic role of Kurds in Near
East, 46
vs. fundamentalism in Uzbekistan,
121
Self-determination movements
in Palestine, xv
U.S. ambivalent support of Kurdish,
55–57
Serbs
demands for Orthodox Christian
minorities in Kosovo, 65
desire to cast conflict in religious
terms, xxvii
discrimination against ethnic
Albanians, 67
historical lack of conflicts with
Croats, xxi
religious nationalism in Kosovo,
73–74
slow repatriation in Kosovo, 74–75,
77
threat of slow repatriation in Kosovo,
74–75
Shanghai Cooperation Organization,
129
Sharon, Ariel
Arab disapproval of policies, 11
role in Israel-Palestine peace talks, 9
withdrawal from Gaza strip, 9
Shatt al Arab waterway, 25
Sheikh Abdullah, 183, 186
Six archetypal civilizations, xviii
South Africa, as seam state, xvi

South Asia, as most active site of
    terrorist incidents, xxviii
South Ossetia, xx, xxvii
Southern Philippines Council for Peace
    and Development (SPCPD), 217
Sovereignty, in Kosovo, 79
Soviet Union
    breakup as source of conflicts, xx
    Central Asian changes after collapse,
        120–122
    collapse and Caucasus independence
        claims, 93–94
Spain, legacy of colonialism in
    Philippines, 202–203
Spanish Inquisition, 5
Specially Designated Terrorist Groups
    (SDTGs), 55
Sri Lanka, states of emergency in,
    314–315
Stalin, Josef
    Caucasus repatriation efforts, 92
    plans for Jewish massacre, 5
State failure
    in education, 323
    in infrastructure development,
        322–323
State violence, 308–309
States of exception, 309–312
    cases, 312–318
    in Chechnya, 315–316
    in Indonesia, 313–314
    in Kashmir, 316
    palatability with war rhetoric, 325
    in Philippines, 314
    in Thailand, 312–313
Strong man myth, xix
Sudan
    1956 independence, 271
    al Qaeda in, 277–278
    alliance with U.S. in war on
        terrorism, 277
    animist religions in, 271
    Arab imperialism fears in, 272
    British hegemony over, 271
    conflict-instability-terrorism nexus
        in, 279–280
    Darfur conflict and possible loss of
        U.S. assistance, 280–281
    effects of chronic domestic instability
        on international community, 267
    endemic conflict, 267

    establishment of radical
        fundamentalist Islamic regime,
        274
    as fertile soil for religious extremism,
        279
    formation of Sudanese Socialist
        Union, 273
    historical context, 268–276
    history of repressive military
        regimes, 272
    institutionalized political instability
        in, 272–274
    involvement in Mubarak
        assassination attempt, 277
    legacy of slavery, colonialism, and
        Anglo-Egyptian rule, 275
    linkages to global war on terrorism,
        278–281
    linkages to terrorism, 276–278
    links between instability and
        terrorism, xxxi
    map, 266
    and myth of religious conflict, xix
    National Islamic Front (NIF), 273
    National United Party (NUP), 271
    nature of flashpoint, 267–268
    need to nurture political pluralism,
        282
    need to reduce military influence,
        282
    political autonomy issues, 270
    political Islam and nationalism in,
        270–272
    progress and prospects, 281–282
    reconciliation with U.S. after al-
        Turabi expulsion, 278
    sanctuary for bin Laden in, 257
    separatist movements in, 270
    sources of conflict in, xix
    southern autonomy/insurgency issue,
        271, 275–276
    strategic regional importance, 268
    stumbling blocks to closer U.S.
        cooperation, 280–281
    ties to Egyptian Islamic Jihad group,
        278
    weak central government, 270
Suharto, General Haji, xxix
    forced relocation programs, 161,
        164–165

repression of challenges to territorial
integrity, 162
unrest following fall of regime, 159
Suicide bombings
by black widows in Caucasus, 108
by Chechnyan rebels in Russia, 100
strategic logic of, 306
Sungkar, Abdullah, 169
Sunni Arab insurgents, in Iraq, 33–35
Suspension of law, 317. *See also* States of
exception
Syria
Kurdish politics in, 53
role in U.S. policy in Israel-Palestine
conflict, 12–13

T

Taba peace talks, 8–9
Tajikistan, xxviii, 117, 120
Taliban
Deobandism religious practices of,
122
links to Central Asian Islamic
fundamentalists, 119
presence of Uyghur activists among,
230
Tanker war, 25
Targets of violence, 322–324
Telephone monitoring, 311
Territorial disputes, as source of conflict,
xiii
Terrorism
in aftermath of 2003 Iraq war, 24
Caucasus links to international,
97–103
in Central Asia, 123–129
as component of Nexus states, 30
connection with leftist secular
politics *vs.* religion, 324
danger in state responses to, 309–312
dangers of label, 308
as focal point in U.S. policy on Iraq,
29
historical development in Kosovo,
67–69
in Indonesia, 168–172
internationalization in trans-Saharan
arc, 252
Iraq conflict as potent recruiting
tool, 38

as justification for social exclusion,
319–320
material *vs.* links in Kosovo, 70
in Nigeria, 293–296
opposing goals of Kurdish groups,
53–55
origins in frustration at state failure,
322–323
as political act, 306
as political label, 307
politics of, 307–308
popular association of Near East
with, xxv
potential in trans-Sahara region,
xxx–xxxi
role of Algerian extremists, 262
South American forms, 308
as tactic in political context, 305, 307
U.S. focus in trans-Saharan arc,
258–260
vs. freedom fighters, 305
Terrorist attacks, vii
Thaci, Hashim, 70
Thaification, 139, 147
Thailand
forcible religious conversions in,
xxviii
formal annexation of Pattani, 138
government response to separatists,
148–150
historical context, 138–144
importance of empowering/co-
opting moderate Muslims, 152
importance of toleration in, 153
indoctrination of southern Muslims,
147–148
Islam in, 139–140
linkages to global war on terrorism,
150–151
linkages to terrorism, 144–150
map, 136
Muslim separatism in, 138
nature of flashpoint, 137–138
non-Pan-Islamic aims of separatists,
146
oppressive educational reform in, 140
origins of Southern insurgency,
140–142
perceived injustice to minorities in,
143–144
progress and prospects, 151–152

role of religious educational
institutions in, 142–143
states of exception in, 312–313
teachers as targets for assassination
in, 142
terrorist incidents in, xxviii
Yala bombings, 137
Theocracy
as goal of al Qaeda in Iraq, 35
tendencies in Iraq, 38
Tito, Josip Broz, xix
Trans-Sahara Counter Terrorism
Initiative (TSCTI), 298
Trans-Saharan arc, 249–250
challenges of growing militarization,
259–260
changing nature of conflicts in,
261–262
clash between tradition and
modernity in, 252
corruption in, 249
domestic and international terrorism
in, 252
fundamentalist proselytization in,
256
geographic scope, 250
historical context, 253–256
importance to U.S. security,
xxx–xxxi
increased intensity of conflicts in,
260
increased internationalization of
conflicts in, 260
influence of Algerian civil war on
terrorism in, 256–257
insecure national frontiers in,
251–252
international debt burden, 251
legacy of French colonialism in,
250
lily pad operating bases in, 258
linkages to global war on terrorism,
258–259
linkages to terrorism, 256–257
map, 248
meeting of Arab and African
cultures in, 252
national power vs. local autonomy
in, 255
nature of flashpoint, 250–253
need for regional cooperation, 262

political power struggles, 253, 255
progress and prospects, 259–262
reducing domestic and international
conflict in, 252–253
religious differences, 253
resource competition in, 254
separatism in, 255–256
as terrorist breeding grounds,
256
tradition of military coups and
authoritarian rule in, 249, 251
uncontrolled population movements
in, 249, 252
ungoverned areas in, 251–252
U.S. military fortification of,
258–259, 261–262
weak central governments in, 249,
251
Treaty of Lausanne, 45, 58
Treaty of Sèvres, 45
Tulip Revolution, 127
Turkey
assignment of Kurds in Treaty of
Lausanne, 45, 48
conundrum of U.S. alliance and
Kurdish policy in, 45, 47–49
Kurdish nationalism and identity in,
xxvi
no-fly zone and prevention of
Kurdish refugees into, 47
opposition to U.S. support of
independent Kurdish state, 48
role of natural resource competition
in Kurdish resistance, 51
state of emergency declarations,
314–315

U

Ukraine, xx
UN Monitoring, Verification, and
Inspection Commission
(UNMOVIC), 28
UN-sponsored truth commissions, in
Kurdish areas, 57
Unemployment, as source of conflict, xv
United Nations
dark side of continued presence in
Kosovo, 75–77
and human trafficking scandal in
Kosovo, 76, 77

Iraq-related Security Council
resolutions, 26–29
role in 1948 Israel-Palestine war, 6
Unrepresented Nations and People's
Organization (UNPO), 227
Urban terrorism, in Thailand, 150
U.S. foreign policy
and ambiguity of local-global
terrorism in Philippines, 210
ambivalence toward Kurds in Turkey
vs. Iraq, 44, 45, 55–56, 59
and anti-Americanism in Central
Asia, 129
averting Kosovar Albanian violence
vs. creating ethnically intolerant
Muslim state, 79
balance-of-power designs in
Southeast Asia, 213
capacity building of vulnerable
states, 213
in Central Asia, 117, 118–120
centrality of Iraq to, 23, 29
colonial domination of Philippines,
203
commitment to territorial integrity
in China, 236
comparison of Tibet and Xinjiang,
237
concerns over state collapse in
Sudan, 280
controversies in Thailand, 144
counterterrorism initiatives in
Africa, xxxi
critique of current, xiii
cultivation of KLA in Kosovo, 68
dangers of supporting militarization
in trans-Saharan arc, 258–259
designation of Mindanao as military
operations base, 211
and development in Kashmir,
192–195
dual containment in Iraq, 24–26
effects on Arab attitudes, xxiv
energy as driver in West Africa, 288
as fuel for international terrorism,
xiv
importance of Israel-Palestine
conflict to Arab popular opinion
of, 10–12
importance of low profile in
Thailand, 151

and Israeli belligerence, xxv
need for investment in Kashmir, 194
Nigeria as African anchor state in,
297, 300
non-NATO ally status for Thailand,
150
opportunities in wake of Indonesian
tsunami, 173
parallels between Cold War and War
on Terrorism, 324–325
proactive approach to trans-Saharan
arc, 250
recommendations for resolution of
Israel-Palestine conflict, 15–17
reduction in military and economic
aid to Philippines, 212
regime change in Iraq, 29–32
stumbling blocks to closer
cooperation with Sudan, 280–281
Sudan as critical player in war on
terrorism, 268, 277, 279
support of Chinese position on
separatist violence, 236
support of Kosovar Albanian
insurgency, 70
support of repressive regimes, xxiv
theater security cooperation
activities in Nigeria, 298
in trans-Saharan arc, 258–259, 261
Turkish alliance vs. Kurds, 47–49
use of Kurds as pawns, 44, 46–47
in Uzbekistan, 119, 129
waffling on Kurdish question, 56–57
U.S. National Military Strategic Plan for
the War on Terrorism, xii, xiii
U.S. national security
Israel-Palestine conflict as major
threat to, 3, 16
requirement for al Qaeda defeat and
Palestinian-Israeli peace, 17
USA PATRIOT Act, dangers of
permanent extensions of, 311
USAID, initiatives in Nigeria, 299
Uyghurs. See also Xinjiang Uyghur
Autonomous Region
decreased educational opportunities,
240
poor relations with neighboring
Muslim groups, 239–240
presence of activists among Taliban,
230

secular nationalism among, 231
support for Deng-style reforms, 228
tension over Han migration, xxx, 240
terrorism among expatriates, 233
Uzbekistan
    as lightning rod of fundamentalism
        in Central Asia, 121
    U.S. relations in antiterrorist struggle
        with, 119

V

Violence
    importance of contextual
        motivations, 305–306
    as response to state failure, 322

W

Wahhabi Islam, 106, 123, 131
    and Abu Sayyaf organization, 206
    in Central Asia, 122
    conflicts with local practices in
        Kosovo, 72
    inroads into Caucasus, 98
    roundups of devotees in Xinjiang
        Uyghur Autonomous Region, 231
    vs. liberal Islamic practices in
        Caucasus, 105
War imagery, dangers of, 324–327
War on terrorism
    Caucasus links to, 103–107
    Central Asian links to, 129–131
    critique of U.S. policy on, xiii
    dominance of clash of civilizations
        hypothesis in, xxiii
    effects of Iraq conflict on, xxvi
    Indonesia links to, 172–173
    Israel-Palestine conflict links to,
        12–15
    Kosovo lessons for U.S., 78–80
    Thai links to, 144, 150–151
    U.S. equation with war on militant
        Islam, viii
    U.S.-Russian collaboration, 88–89
Warrantless surveillance, 312
Weapons of mass destruction (WMDs),
    29, 30
    controversy leading to 2003 Iraq war,
        27–28

groundless rumors of Iraqi
    rebuilding, 31
strategic prevention in Iraq, 24
Welfare state, restructuring as source of
    conflict, xv
West Africa, 49. See also Trans-Saharan
    arc
West Bank
    historical roots, 4
    Palestinian state control of, 15
West Papua, 160
West Timor, 162
Western capitalism, as form of alien
    colonization, xv
Western Christian societies
    historical oppression of Jewry, 4–5
    responsibility for Israel-Palestine
        conflict, 7
Western societies
    national distinctions in, xix–xx
    support for Albanian Muslims, 71
World Conflict Report, xvi
World War I, state of siege declarations
    during, 310

X

Xinjiang Uyghur Autonomous Region,
    xxx
    ambiguity of nature of unrest,
        226–227
    Amnesty International reports of
        executions, 226–227
    disappointment in autonomy after
        Soviet disintegration, 228
    dubious responsibility for Beijing
        unrest, 229
    environmental degradation and
        nuclear testing in, 231, 240
    historical context, 227–230
    Internet campaigns for, 227
    linkages to global war on terrorism,
        236–238
    linkages to terrorism, 230–236
    map, 224
    nature of flashpoint, 225–227
    nonviolent opposition in, 234–236
    past discrimination and religious
        restrictions, 227–228
    progress and prospects, 238–241
    roundups of Sufis or Wahhabis, 231

scapegoat terrorism toward, 226
tenuous ties to al Qaeda, 232–233

Y

Yala bombings, 137
Yeltsin, Boris, 87, 94
Yoruba people, 289
Yugoslavia
    encouragement of Albanian
      nationalism in Kosovo, 66

ethnopolitics in, xvi
Yugoslav *vs.* ethnic identity,
    xx–xxi

Z

Zavgayev, Doku, 96
Zinni, General Tony, xii, xiii, 47–48
Zionist movement, 5–6
Zones of turmoil, xvi